Ada de Swart

3 - 12 - 93

the jazz scene

the Jazz scene

Eric Hobsbawm

Pantheon Books   New York

Library of Congress Cataloging-in-Publication Data

Hobsbawm, E. J. (Eric J.), 1917–
   The jazz scene/Eric Hobsbawm.
     p.   cm.
   Includes bibliographical references and index.
   ISBN 0-679-40633-6
   1. Jazz—History and criticism.   I. Title.
ML3506.H6   1993   91–52657
781.65'09—dc20

Book design by Chris Welch
Manufactured in the United States of America
First American Revised Edition

Contents

Acknowledgements

I am not an expert as experts go in the world of jazz, which has many, and I could not have written this book without picking many people's brains. My debt to several important books and publications will be evident. I have, so far as possible, acknowledged it in footnotes, but should like to add a word of appreciation for the now defunct magazine *Jazz Music* (edited by Max Jones and Albert McCarthy), which cheered us up during the war. My debts to people are too numerous for proper acknowledgement. I would only like to mention two to whom I owe a great deal: Denis Preston, who first introduced me to jazz in 1933 and has continued to stimulate and inform me through the years since; Charles Fox, to whom I owe much of my later education in jazz. Both have read through some chapters in manuscript, but neither they nor anyone else except the author are responsible for the views and mistakes of this book. I am also grateful to the editor and staff of the *Melody Maker,* and to the secretary and staff of the National Jazz Federation for giving me access to their respective files and records and for providing

me with information, and to the *New Statesman,* which has given
me the opportunity for keeping in much closer contact with the
people of jazz than I would otherwise have done. For the rest,
the numerous musicians, critics and journalists, businessmen,
fans, and others whom I have at one time or another consulted
must forgive me if I give them only collective and anonymous
thanks.

E.J.H.
1959

I have taken the opportunity to revise and bring this book up to
date for the present edition. I also wish to acknowledge a few
more debts. While I cannot thank all those who guided me
through the jungle of the American jazz scene, I would like to
say how much I owe to Ralph Gleason of the *San Francisco
Chronicle* for his critical comments on the book and for much
else; to John Steiner and Studs Terkel in Chicago; to Bill Randle
in Cleveland; and in New York, to John Hammond, Nat Hentoff, Whitney Balliett and Martha Glaser. In spite of their efforts,
my errors remain my own.

E.J.H.
1961

I have used the following abbreviations:

tpt	- trumpet	Tb	- trombone
clt	- clarinet	sax	- saxophone
gtr	- guitar	Ss	- soprano sax
bjo	- banjo	As	- alto sax
dms	- drums	Ts	- tenor sax
bs	- bass	Bar s	- baritone sax
acc.	- accompanied by	v	- vocal by
arr.	- arranged by	pno	- piano

Certain technical terms are also widely used, and in case I have done so here and there without previously explaining them, I list a few of the most important:

arrangement: a jazz theme with specific orchestration
ballad: a pop song not otherwise defined
beat: the fundamental rhythm of a jazz performance

combo: any (small) jazz orchestra

gig: temporary live job for musicians, e.g. a one-night engagement in a dance-hall; under certain conditions, any job

horn: wind instrument, sometimes any instrument

jamming: improvising; *jam session:* occasion when players improvise together

lyric: the words of any song

pop, pop music: popular entertainment music as typified by the 'song-hit'

rhythm section: normally composed of dms, bs, gtr, pno

section: coherent group of instruments in a band, e.g. the brass, reeds, rhythm

session: unit of time for recording (e.g. 'on the next session six sides were cut'); more generally, any unit of time in which musicians play several pieces

set: set of pieces played by musicians followed by a rest, or the end of the session

side, track: side of an old 78 rpm record, track of an LP record

sideman: a jazz player who is not a bandleader

sitting in: players who drop into a club and take part in the music (generally unpaid) sit in with the band, or 'have a blow'

A Note on the Old Money

*F*or the benefit of those too young to remember the olden days, before 1971 the pound sterling (£) consisted of 20 shillings (s), each of 12 pennies (d)—hence £.s.d.—the pennies being in turn divided into 4 farthings. There were coins of a farthing, a halfpenny, a penny, threepence, sixpence, a shilling, a florin (2 shillings), and half-a-crown (2/6), and bank notes from 10s upwards. (There was also a purely notional unit of £1/1/0 called guinea, which was a polite upmarket excuse for charging an extra 5 per cent on goods and services worth £1.) The shilling and florin coins were transformed into the present 5p and 10p coins. The decimalized penny was initially equal to 2.4d. Consequently, a single record of 1958 cost, in modern currency, 30p, an LP £1.50. For comparison at about the same time a gallon of petrol averaged 4s 11½d (25p), the annual road tax £12/10/0 (£12.50) and comprehensive car insurance in London £34/0/0.

Discovering jazz, as the Czech writer and jazz-buff Josef Skvorecky has said, is, for most people, rather like first love—on the whole it is more lasting—and it usually happens at much the same time. In the case of the present writer it happened at the age of sixteen, in the year Adolf Hitler took power in Germany. My family had just returned to England after a few years in the movie business in Berlin, and a losing struggle against the slump. My old man brought back a copy of Carl Laemmle's biography by John Drinkwater, a forgotten but on this occasion evidently well-paid minor English literary figure, personally signed by Uncle Carl—and practically no money. Until we could find a suitably cheap apartment, we stayed with relatives in Sydenham, a Victorian white-collar suburb in Southeast London.

My aunt Cissie, living in undefined detachment from Uncle Lou, who was permanently absent pursuing business across the Atlantic, taught school. Her married daughter, also living in the same house, was trying to teach dancing and elocution to the daughters of aspiring mothers in the neighborhood. Her husband was not making a living and was therefore uncommunicative. The one member of our host-family who seemed to be a human being in the full sense of the word was a young man of my own age, my cousin Denis Preston. We had known of one another before, because our families—this is the way of families —had told us to write letters to each other. There had been a half-hearted correspondence between London and Berlin, from which both sides concluded that the other guy was a drip. When we actually met, we were agreeably surprised to find that the other guy was OK. I undoubtedly tried to convert him to communism to which I had been converted while living through the rise of Hitler. He converted me to jazz.

How he had come to jazz I don't know, but in retrospect it is not surprising. He conformed exactly to the type of the 1930s British jazz fan which is sketched in the chapter on the 'jazz public': the intelligent, self-educated young man from the lower middle classes, preferably a little bohemian. (My cousin had dropped out of high school and was studying to be a viola player.) Jazz, of course, meant exclusively the few 78 rpm records the British companies released every month which had to be sorted out from the larger mass of contemptible dance-band noises to which they were attached. Still, there was by then a small British public for jazz and even a reliable guide to what was good, Spike Hughes in the *Melody Maker,* my cousin's bible. My cousin bought these, played them until the grooves groaned and, when money was short (it usually was) made a part-exchange deal with the local record shop. At any time he was likely to have perhaps twenty of these heavy black discs, in brown paper or cardboard covers—sleeves were a generation away.

These were the records we played in a sparsely furnished attic, on the heavy hand-cranked box which in those prehistoric days was not even yet called a record-player but a gramophone. In between records and intensive discussions about how great they were, we restored our strength with potato crisps and spoonfuls of heavily sugared canned milk, the kind that was firmly labelled 'unfit for babies'. We preferred to have these sessions at night. When the days were too long, we drew the curtains.

In retrospect, the jazz we came to through these British releases of the early 'thirties, was as good an introduction to the music as any that was available. The first jazz records I remember were the Fletcher Henderson band's ('Sugar Foot Stomp', 'House of David Blues'), Don Redman's ('Chant of the Weeds'), the Mills Blue Rhythm Band, Bix and Tram, of course, the Mills Brothers—I wonder how that ancient vocal group stands up to rehearing—and the accepted geniuses, Armstrong and Ellington. The Armstrongs we heard were not yet the *Potato Head Blues* Hot Fives and Hot Sevens, but how could we complain when the Armstrong-Hines combinations, *St James Infirmary, Knockin' a Jug* and *West End Blues* were already available? And, fortunately, the great man had not yet been tied up in the strait-jacket of New Orleans archaeology. Though we sighed over the commercial corruption of true art in records like *Confessin'* and *Song of the Islands,* we were lucky to be introduced to a great artist at the very peak of his form. As for Ellington, could anyone hearing *Black and Tan Fantasy* and *Creole Love Call* not be captured for life?

Then Ellington came in person. He was, by this time, a composer taken seriously by the hipper sections of the British musical establishment. He was also a greatly appreciated figure in the younger aristocratic and even royal circles, which probably pleased him at least as much. Two suburban teenagers, who belonged to neither of these groups, could only express their devotion in a suburban way. We made the pilgrimage to the Streatham Astoria in South London, a ballroom where the band was booked for what was then called a 'breakfast dance', midnight to morning. (Of course we knew the great man's record *Breakfast Dance* forwards and backwards.) I assume our elders had pity on us, because the tickets were far beyond our normal financial reach.

There we sat, from midnight till dawn, nursing the glass of beer which was all we could afford, the image of the band burning itself on our brains forever. Maybe, after almost sixty years, I can no longer without prompting recite the entire per- sonnel of Ellington 1933, including Ivy Anderson whose *Stormy Weather* was the hit of the season (as with the other women singers of the band, except Adelaide Hall of the unforgettable *Creole Love Call* we could live without them), but to this day I can see Hodges, impassive as what in those politically unin- formed days we used to call a Red Indian, stepping forward to wind his sounds round our hearts. We walked home four miles in the dawn—the money had run out—and I was hooked for good.

For the next twenty-odd years, like most British jazz fans, I subsisted on records—on the old, heavy, three-minute shellac 78s, because a dispute between the two musicians' unions kept American musicians out of Britain. (We were convinced that only Americans, preferably black, were worth listening to.) In this stored and unreal form the music was available, at least to the network of aficionados, sufficiently small for everyone to know somebody who supplemented the excellent selection of commercial releases by importing discs directly from the United States. It was an artificial situation, though it gave the core group of British fans a considerable influence over the development of the music in Britain. Since they virtually controlled what they heard, they were the taste-makers. To take the most obvious example: The first kind of live native jazz that developed on any scale, from the later years of the war onwards, was that typical phenomenon of collectors and fans, the Dixieland revival. How- ever, whereas Lu Watters and Bob Wilber were peripheral to the U.S. jazz scene, the British revival bands were absolutely central to it. These bands, largely recruited from amateurs, in turn took over from the original aficionados a passion for the country and city blues, some of which had come to Britain via the American communist and radical repertoire of the black folk-protégés (Leadbelly, Brownie McGhee, Sonny Terry, Josh White et al.), and some via the small but passionate groups whose collectors' hearts had always been in Clarksdale rather than New Orleans. As I point out in the 1989 Introduction, a lot of British rock music's ability to capture the world was due to the fact that the average white British 18-year-old was much more likely to have heard Muddy Waters than the average white U.S. teenager.

The downside of this state of affairs was that the British jazz authorities (like most of those who had developed their taste in the 1930s, notably the French) were taken aback by bebop and to be honest, most of them disliked it intensely. It came, not out of the milieu of enthusiastic and, in general, musically illiterate appreciators, but of young professional big-band musicians. (The young British band musicians were much more receptive to bebop, but theirs was a very small scene.) It was a revolution, and European jazz fans didn't need one or want one. They wanted 'authenticity'. Moreover, the wartime recording ban in the U.S.A. broke that continuity of record releases that got even unadventurous fans used to thinking the spectacular transformations of jazz between, say, 1926 and 1941 (few arts have changed more rapidly) not as a series of revolutions in the *avant-garde* manner, but as just growth. After all, the Pope of the Church of Jazz Tradition, Hugues Panassié himself, who denounced the 'modernists' as agents of Satan, had found neither Lester Young nor Charlie Christian unacceptable. The bop revolution caught Europe unprepared, although in suitable countries (notably France and Scandinavia), a new generation of intellectual champions of the *avant-garde* soon appeared. They were rewarded by the expatriate U.S. bop players who settled there in the desert years.

During all these years I had been no more than a fringe observer of the jazz scene. I was no expert. I was neither a collector nor the sort of guy whose name collectors knew, and I neither wanted to write about jazz nor did anyone ask me to. Not even in any of those tiny, short-lived, fact-filled, and denunciatory jazz magazines in which the experts poured out their information and squared up to each other on such issues as black vs. white or the acceptability of swing bands, like entrants for a local amateur bantamweight contest. Through my cousin (who eventually went into the recording business), I knew these people and learned from them, for every jazz expert was and is a passionate educator. But though I also educated others, I was no specialist.

From the jazz point of view I had only one peculiarity which made me noticeable: I was (by the 1950s) a professional historian.

Why this should have struck both jazz and non-jazz people as so bizarre, I still find difficult to understand. Academics who were passionate jazz lovers were a minority but not at all unknown, even in my own generation, the university graduates of the 1930s. It is true that the sounds preferred in the groves of academe were closer to Beethoven than to Basie, and that the new generations of students had not yet begun to flood into universities by the hundreds of thousands, at least in Europe. (When they did, they brought rock with them rather than jazz.) It is also true that most of the substantial but growing academic jazz underground kept their unofficial musical tastes to themselves or shared them only with sympathisers, like dissident sexual or gastronomic inclinations. And yet, profoundly as the cultural atmosphere has changed since the 1950s, a historian who also writes about jazz is still considered in many quarters as freaky, in some way, though attractively so. To have written about professional soccer, or to have been a successful race-horse tipster, or a well-known compiler of chess problems, or a passionate gambler—I am citing real cases—has not become part of the image of the academics who pursue these extra-curricular activities—but to have written a book about jazz has, at least in my case. What's so odd about the combination of jazz and history? Perhaps readers can explain what the author cannot.

So I got into jazz writing because editors and publishers enjoyed the idea of a professor reporting (in those days pseudonymously) on such unacademic music. Conversely, the idea of being reported by a *bona-fide* Ph.D. for *The New Statesman,* which was at that time the ranking guardian of British high culture, tickled people in the British, and later the American, jazz scene. The middle fifties were an ideal time to start writing about jazz. For the first time Brits could regularly hear first-rate American artists live, and shortly after, not without some complications from those who guarded America against red subversion, I began to visit the U.S.A. Meanwhile both musicians and serious jazz-buffs were abandoning the pointless battles between

Rampart Street and 52nd Street: all except the comic novelist Kingsley Amis and the poet Philip Larkin, who continued to see bebop as treason. Larkin even wrote an uncharacteristically sentimental poem about Bechet, full of French Quarter clichés.

I wrote that column for about ten years until remarriage and small children produced a major clash between the nocturnal timetable of a jazz writer and the daytime life of a family man. Eighteen of these columns from 1955–65 are reprinted for the first time in this edition. When jazz started to revive in the 1980s I began to write about it again, in a different and more reflective manner, stimulated by the good luck of living and working within walking distance of *Bradley's* and the *Vanguard* in New York for part of the year. The Introduction to the 1989 British reprint of *The Jazz Scene,* which the present edition reproduces, tried to bridge the gap that separated the jazz of 1960 from that of 1990. Meanwhile Robert Silvers of *The New York Review of Books* gave me the chance to meditate again on why jazz is not only a marvellous noise but a central concern for anyone concerned with twentieth-century society and the twentieth-century arts. These five studies of the jazz revival of the 1930s and the 1980s, and of particular jazz artists in their social context—Ellington, Basie, Bechet—are essentially about the interaction at one particular moment of American history, between the makers of jazz, the self-contained democracy of professional working musicians, the 'community of night people with folk roots,' and the fans who recognized that they were witnessing the birth of art. These pieces are, I hope, logical extensions of the original *Jazz Scene.*

So, one way or another, this book is one person's reaction to sixty years' experience of jazz. (Sixty years? You must be joking. I wish I were). Where, after all those decades, during which the writer has survived most of those he wrote about and too many of those to whom he owes his jazz education, does jazz stand at the end of the century?

The jazz revival I surveyed in *The New York Review* in 1987 has lasted on both sides of the Atlantic, though hit by the Depression of the early 1990s. In November 1991, *Hot House,* the 'Jazz Nightlife Guide' distributed in the New York area, listed forty-one clubs and halls playing the music in Manhattan that month, plus another thirteen in New Jersey. The number of these venues was still rising, but rather slowly. And yet, there was something strange about this revival, even though that strangeness made it more familiar to such ancient jazz-lovers as the present author. The jazz of the early 1990s looked back.

Suppose we look at the *Downbeat Critics Poll* of 1991, which lists as its 'Jazz Artists of the Year' Wynton Marsalis, Benny Carter, Sonny Rollins, Jackie McLean, Dizzy Gillespie, Cecil Taylor, Henry Threadgill, and David Murray. Five of these eight were household names in 1961, two came up in the hard years of jazz exile and are now middle-aged, and only Wynton Marsalis (a second-generation jazz-man) belongs to the 1980s. The *Readers Poll* (December 1990) is not noticeably future-oriented, though it gives more space to middle-aged talents who paid their dues in the dark years (Jack de Johnette, Marcus Roberts, Phil Woods, Pat Metheny).

Suppose we look at what they play. The basis of what is played today is essentially what was played in the 'forties and 'fifties. Every one is a bopper. It is not that nothing has been happening in jazz since then, but rather that the innovations of the past thirty years, from free jazz to fusion, have been silently marginalized. Even the most enthusiastic obituaries of Miles Davis, the key figure in the development of jazz since the early 1950s, grow noticeably more ambiguous about his last twenty years and prefer to keep quiet about his last ten. This suits senior citizens who have no trouble remembering the marvels of the first Quintet, of *Miles Ahead* and *Kind of Blue,* but surely the generation gap should not look quite so narrow? 'Tradition' is the key word now, a term once heard more often among jazz fans deploring the end of Dixieland and their youth, than among musicians. And yet, here is a twenty-five-year-old sax player ('out of Parker and Adderley') as recently reported:

> Bird is the main influence because he covers so many eras and styles in his playing. He stood for the tradition and I figured if I studied enough Bird I'd get hold of it.

Did Bird think of himself that way when he was twenty-five?

Indeed, the *mode retro* goes back along way beyond the original boppers. There has been a return to the standard ballads, even if they are now played with *avant-garde* flourishes by men returned to the mainstream from the more inaccessible frontiers, like Archie Shepp, the terror of the 1960s. There are even signs of the black rediscovery of the original New Orleans tradition, which I predicted in *The Jazz Scene,* admittedly from Wynton Marsalis, who is both from New Orleans and a man in favour of traditions. There has been, above all, an extraordinary return to the blues. Last year's reissue of Robert Johnson is said to have sold 500,000 copies. Benson and Hedges sponsors a Blues Festival in New York. Blues bars are opening right and left in Chicago, to the deserved benefit of old men who could do with a buck or two, and, as I write, they are being imported into a new New York club advertising nothing but Chicago blues.

All this is both comforting and familiar to old-stagers, though it is impossible today to feel, as we did in the later 1950s and in the years from 1936 to 1942, that we are living through a golden age of jazz again. There is just a lot of jazz to listen to, and no shortage (at least in the New York area) of piano-players who are both adventurous and accessible. But it is also a danger sign. Jazz cannot survive like baroque music, as a form of pastiche or archaeology for the cultured public, even among blacks. But this is precisely the danger that threatens it. Black kids do not sing the blues today. They are performed, at best, by elderly artists for elderly neighborhood audiences and, at worst (as in many of the new Chicago blues rooms), in *white* neighborhoods, by the same grey-heads, for white students. Black kids do not dream of playing horns (except, paradoxically, among young Caribbeans in Britain, who have no indigenous jazz tradition), but of being in great rap groups; a form of art which, in my opinion, is musically uninteresting and literary doggerel. In fact, it is the opposite of the great and profound art of the blues. There are good reasons for this—what is one sax compared to the ghetto-blaster?—but it cuts off the roots of jazz. The flourishing black media and art scene—what might be called the Spike Lee belt—is impregnated with jazz and so, obviously, are musicians black or white. But jazz has always lived not by the hipness of the public (which has, with the rarest exceptions, always been a minority public), but by what Cornel West calls 'the network of apprenticeship', the 'transmission of skills and sensibilities to new practitioners'. The cords of this network are fraying. Some of them have snapped.

Is jazz then being transformed beyond redemption into another version of classical music: an accepted cultural treasure, consisting of a repertoire of mostly dead styles, performed live by artists—some of them young—for a financially comfortable middle-aged and middle-class public, black and white, and the Japanese tourist? Will it be, once again, accessible to its potential mass constituency basically through radio and recordings, as it was to my European generation half a century ago? To listen to most jazz stations today is to be back in the esoteric world of those who have the true faith, where three days devoted *exclusively* to, say, recordings of Clifford Brown are seen as three days well spent.

Is jazz becoming terminally fossilized? It is not impossible. If this should be the fate of jazz, it will not be much consolation that Clint Eastwood has buried Bird in a celluloid mausoleum and that every hairdresser and cosmetics store plays tapes of Billie Holiday. However, jazz has shown extraordinary powers of survival and self-renewal inside a society not designed for it and which does not deserve it. It is too early to think that its potential is exhausted. Besides, what is wrong with just listening and letting the future take care of itself?

E. J. Hobsbawm
London 1992

This book was first published almost thirty years ago, under the pseudonym Francis Newton (based on Frankie Newton, the trumpeter), which was then intended to keep the author's writings as an historian apart from his writings as a jazz journalist. The attempt did not succeed, so it is now republished under my own name. To reprint a work of 1959–61 may seem like reprinting an old telephone directory. Three decades are a large enough chunk of the life of a human being, but they are a much larger fraction of the history of so rapidly evolving, so constantly changing a music as jazz. However, *The Jazz Scene* may be a reminder of the days when Armstrong and Ellington were still alive, when it was possible to listen within a few days or weeks to the living Bechet and Basie, to Ella Fitzgerald, the dying Billie Holiday and the glorious Mahalia Jackson, to Gillespie, Miles Davis, Coleman Hawkins and Lester Young, to Mingus, Monk, Pee Wee Russell, Jack Teagarden, Hodges and Webster. It was a golden age for jazz, and we knew it. What is more, the years between 1955 and 1961 were one of the rare periods when the old and the new coexisted in jazz and both prospered.

The sounds of New Orleans were alive, played both by old men now dead and young white disciples. So, but only just, were the big bands: in fact the great Ellington was just entering on a new lease of life with the Newport Festival of 1956. Bebop had reentered the mainstream of jazz, out of which its revolutionaries had emerged and against which they had rebelled. Dizzy Gillespie could already be seen, not simply as an innovator but as Armstrong's successor to the crown of jazz trumpeters. And a new generation of rebels had already come together in what looked like a new *avant-garde*, organizing, in 1960, an antifestival to the Newport Jazz Festival which, in the 1950s, had come to be the major ecumenical attempt to bring the best in jazz together. While the older battles between the traditionalists and modernists faded into the historical background, Ornette Coleman, Archie Shepp, Eric Dolphy, Don Cherry and others were now joined, in the ill-defined area of 'free jazz', by established *avant-garde* stars like John Coltrane, Charles Mingus or Cecil Taylor. In fact, most of the developments of the 1960s and 1970s were already being anticipated in 1960, when the author, on his first visit to the U.S.A., found the nights too short to listen to everything that could be heard in New York from the Half Note and the Five Spot in the Village to Small's Paradise and the Apollo in Harlem, and further west in Chicago and San Francisco.

But is it enough merely to recall a golden age? And if not, what else can justify reprinting a book which plainly can't tell readers much about the state of jazz in the late 1980s, and does not intend to. But then, even in 1960 it was not the object of *The Jazz Scene* to provide a survey of the scene at that time. It tried to do two things. First and foremost I set out to see jazz, which is one of the most significant phenomena of twentieth-century world culture, in historical perspective. I set out to trace its social roots and history, to analyse its economic structure, the body of its musicians, the nature of its public, and the reasons for its extraordinary appeal, both in the U.S.A. and elsewhere.

This was one of the first books to investigate jazz in this manner. I hope a good deal of what it says retains its interest, and much of its argument can still stand, even if certain chapters—for instance the study of the jazz business in the later 1950s, which was based on first-hand documentation—is now only of historical interest and the pop music it discusses is dead. In any case, *The Jazz Scene* is a contribution to the history of jazz, and especially of the jazz public, in Britain, a subject which is still not adequately known.

In the second place, the book set out to provide a general introduction to jazz for the generation of fans and sympathizers which had discovered it in the 1950s, and for the educated and 'cultured' readers in general, who were just then becoming aware that they ought to know something about it. For it was in the middle 1950s that the guardians of established culture for the first time felt that they had to inform their public about jazz, which is why the *Observer* commissioned a jazz column from a fashionable novelist, and (inspired by this) I talked myself into becoming jazz correspondent for Kingsley Martin's *New Statesman*.

Jazz has always been a minority interest, like classical music, but unlike classical music the taste for it has not been stable. Interest in it has grown by spurts and, conversely, there have been times when it was in the doldrums. The later 1930s and the 1950s were a period when it expanded quite strikingly, the years of the 1929 slump (in the U.S.A. at least) when even Harlem preferred soft lights and sweet music to Ellington and Armstrong. The periods when interest in jazz has grown or revived have also, for reasons obvious to publishers, been the times when new generations of fans wanted to know more about it.

But we are once again in a period when interest in jazz is reviving quite dramatically in both Britain and the U.S.A. For, shortly after *The Jazz Scene* appeared, the golden age of the 1950s came to a sudden end, leaving jazz to retreat into rancorous and poverty-stricken isolation for some twenty years. What made this generation of loneliness so melancholy and paradoxical was that the music that almost killed jazz was derived from the same roots that had generated jazz: rock-and-roll was and is very obviously the offspring of American blues. The young, without whom jazz cannot exist—hardly any jazz fan has ever been converted after the age of twenty—abandoned it, and with spectacular suddenness. Three years after 1960, when the golden age was at its peak, in the year of the Beatles' triumph across the world, jazz had been virtually knocked out of the ring. 'Bird Lives' could still be seen painted on lonely walls, but the celebrated New York jazz venue named after him, Birdland, had ceased to exist. To revisit New York in 1963 was a depressing experience for the jazz-lover who had last experienced it in 1960.

This did not mean that jazz disappeared, only that both its musicians and its public grew older, and were not reinforced by the young. Of course outside the U.S.A. and Britain, which were the main centres and sources of rock, the youthful public for jazz, though probably socially and intellectually select and upmarket, remained substantial and commercially far from negligible. More than one American jazz-player found it convenient for this reason to emigrate to Europe in those decades. In France, Italy and Germany, Brazil and Japan, Scandinavia and—commercially less relevant—the USSR and Eastern Europe, jazz remained viable. In the U.S.A. and Britain its public was confined to middle-aged men and women who had been young in the 1920s, 1930s or, at best, in the 1950s. As an established English saxophone player put it in 1976: 'I don't think I could make a living totally in this country. I don't think anyone could. . . . There aren't enough people, there isn't enough money. . . . The band has been to Germany more times in the last couple of years than it's done gigs in this country.'*

Such was the reality of jazz in the 1960s and much of the 1970s, at any rate in the Anglo-Saxon world. There was no market for it. According to the *Billboard International Music Industry Directory* of 1972 a mere 1.3 per cent of records and tapes sold in the U.S.A. represented jazz, as against 6.1 per cent of classical music and 75 per cent rock and similar music. Jazz clubs went on closing, jazz recitals declined, *avant-garde* musicians played for each other in private apartments, and the growing recognition

* J. Skidmore in *Jazz Now* (London 1976), p. 76.

of jazz as something which belonged to official American culture, while providing a welcome subsidy to uncommercial musicians through schools, colleges and other institutions, reinforced the youthful conviction that jazz now belonged to the world of the adults. Unlike rock, it was not *their own music*. Only a certain exhaustion of the musical impulse behind rock, which first became obvious in the later 1970s began to leave room for a revival of interest in jazz, as distinct from rock. (Some jazz musicians had, of course, devised a 'fusion' of jazz and rock, to the horror of purists especially from the *avant-garde,* and it was probably through this merger that jazz retained a certain public presence in the years of isolation: through Miles Davis, Chick Corea, Herbie Hancock, the British guitarist John McLoughlin and the Austrian-American combination of Joe Zawinul and Wayne Shorter in 'Weather Report.')

Why should rock have almost killed jazz for twenty years? Both derived from the music of black Americans, and it was through jazz musicians and jazz fans that the black blues first came to the attention of the public outside the Southern states and the Northern ghettoes. Since they were among the few whites who were familiar with the artists and repertoire of 'race record' catalogues (diplomatically renamed 'rhythm-and-blues' in the late 1940s), white jazz- and blues-lovers were instrumental in launching rock. Ahmet Ertegun, who founded Atlantic Records, which became a leading rock label, was one of two brothers who had long formed part of the tiny international community of jazz-record collectors and experts. John Hammond, whose crucial role in the development of jazz in the 1930s is recorded in *The Jazz Scene,* also developed the careers of Bob Dylan, Aretha Franklin and, later, Bruce Springsteen. Where would British rock have been without the influence of the handful of local blues-enthusiasts like the late Alexis Korner, who inspired the Rolling Stones, or the ('trad') jazz enthusiasts who imported American country and city blues singers like Muddy Waters and made them familiar in Lancashire and Lanark long before more than a handful of Americans outside some black ghettoes even knew of their existence?

Initially there seemed to be no hostility or incompatibility between jazz and rock, even though attentive readers of *The Jazz Scene* will register the note of gentle contempt with which critics and, above all, the musical professionals of jazz, then treated the early triumphs of rock-and-roll, whose public seemed unable to distinguish between a Bill Haley ('Rock Around the Clock') and a Chuck Berry. A crucial distinction between jazz and rock was that rock was never a minority music. Rhythm-and-blues, as it developed after the Second World War, was the folk music of urban blacks in the 1940s, when one and a quarter millions of blacks left the South for the Northern and Western ghettoes. They constituted a new market, which was then supplied chiefly by independent record labels like Chess Records, founded in Chicago in 1949 by two Polish immigrants connected with the club circuit, and specializing in the so-called 'Chicago Blues' style (Muddy Waters, Howlin' Wolf, Sonny Boy Williamson) and recording, among others, Chuck Berry, who was probably—with Elvis Presley—the major influence on 1950s rock-and-roll. White adolescents began to buy black r&b records in the early 1950s, having discovered this music on local and specialized radio stations which multiplied during those years, as the mass of adults transferred its attentions to television. At first sight they seemed to be the habitual tiny and untypical minority which can still be seen on the fringes of black entertainment, like the white visitors to Chicago ghetto blues clubs. Yet as soon as the music industry became aware of this potential white youth market, it became evident that rock was the opposite of a minority taste. It was the music of an entire age-group.

Almost certainly that was the result of the 'economic miracle' of the 1950s, which not only created a Western world of full employment, but also, probably for the first time, gave the mass of adolescents adequately paid jobs and therefore money in the pocket, or an unprecedented share of middle-class parents' prosperity. It was this children's and adolescents' market that transformed the music industry. From 1955, when rock-and-roll was born, to 1959 American record sales rose by 36 per cent every year. After a brief pause, the British invasion of 1963, led by the Beatles, initiated an even more spectacular surge: U.S. record sales, which had grown from $277 million in 1955 to $600 million in 1959, had passed $2,000 million by 1973 (now including tapes). Seventy-five to 80 per cent of these sales represented rock music and similar sounds. The commercial fortunes of the record industry had never before depended so overwhelmingly on a single musical genre addressed to a single narrow age-band. The correlation of record sales with economic development and income was utterly obvious. In 1973 the highest per-capita expenditure on records occurred in the U.S.A., followed (in rank order) by Sweden, West Germany, the Netherlands and Britain. All these countries spent between $7 and $10. In the same year Italians, Spaniards and Mexicans spent between $1 and $1.4 per head, and Brazilians $0.66.

Almost immediately rock music thus became the all-purpose medium for expressing the desires, instincts, feelings and aspirations of the age-set between puberty and the moments when adults settle down in some conventional social niche, family or career: the voice and idiom of a self-conscious 'youth' and 'youth culture' in modern industrial societies. It could express anything and everything within this age-range, but while rock clearly developed regional, national, class or politico-ideological variants, its basic idiom, like the equally demotic-populist costume associated with youth (notably jeans) crossed national, class and ideological barriers. As in the lives of its age-groups, in rock music the public and the private, feeling and conviction, love, rebellion and art, acting as doing and as stage-behaviour, were not distinguishable from each other. Older observers, for instance, used to keeping revolution and music apart in principle and to judging each by its own criteria, were apt to be perplexed by the apocalyptic rhetoric which could surround rock at the peak of the global youth rebellion, when *Rolling Stone* wrote, apropos of a 1969 rock concert:

An army of peaceful guerrillas established a city larger than Rochester, New York, and showed itself immediately ready to turn back on the already ravaged city and [its] inoperable life-styles, imminently prepared to move onto the mist-covered field and into the cool, still woods. And they will do it again, the threat of youthful dissidence in Paris and Prague and Fort Lauderdale and Berkeley and Chicago and London criss-crossing ever more closely until the map of the world we live in is viable for and visible to all of those that are part of it and all those buried under it.★

Woodstock was obviously a marvellous experience for the participants, but even then its political significance and the strictly musical interest of a lot of its performers were not as obvious as all that.

A universal cultural idiom cannot be judged by the same criteria as a special kind of art-music, and there was and is no point in judging rock by the standards of good jazz. However, rock deprived jazz of most of its potential new listeners, because the young people who flocked to rock found in it, in a simplified and perhaps coarsened version, much, if not everything, that had attracted their elders to jazz: rhythm, an immediately identifiable voice or 'sound', real (or faked) spontaneity and vitality, and a way of directly transferring human emotions into music. Moreover, they discovered all this in a music which was related to jazz. Why would they need jazz? With rare exceptions, the young who would have been converted to jazz now had an alternative.

What made that alternative increasingly attractive, and helped to reduce the space for an embattled and isolated jazz still further, was its own transformation. As the bebop revolutionaries rejoined the mainstream of jazz in the second half of the 1950s, the new *avant-garde* of 'free jazz', moving towards atonality and breaking down everything that had hitherto given jazz a structure—including the beat round which it was organized—widened the gap between the music and its public, including the jazz public. And it was not surprising that the *avant-garde* reacted to the desertion of the public by taking an even more extreme and

★ Cited in S. Chapple and R. Garofalo, *Rock'n'Roll Is Here to Pay* (Chicago 1977), p. 144.

embattled stance. At the start of the new revolution it was perfectly easy to recognize in, say, Ornette Coleman's saxophone the blues feeling of his native Texas, and the tradition of the great horn-players of the past was obvious in Coltrane. Yet those were not the things the innovators wanted the public to notice about them.

But the situation of the new *avant-garde* in the dark decades was paradoxical. The loosening of the traditional framework of jazz, its increasing shifts towards something like *avant-garde* classical music developed from a jazz base, opened it to all manner of non-jazz influences, European, African, Islamic, Latin American and especially Indian. In the 1960s it went through a variety of exoticisms. In other words, it became less American than it had been, and far more cosmopolitan than before. Perhaps because the American jazz public became relatively less important in jazz, perhaps for other reasons, after 1962 free jazz became the first style of jazz whose history cannot be written without taking account of important developments in Europe and, one might add, of European musicians.

At the same time—and equally paradoxically—the new *avant-garde* which broke with jazz tradition was unusually anxious to stress its links with the tradition, even when they had previously taken very little notice of it: as when Coltrane (1926–67) in 1961 took up the soprano-saxophone, hitherto virtually monopolized by the recently deceased Sidney Bechet, and was followed by numerous young *avant-garde* horn-players. Bechet had been little more than a musically irrelevant name to most musicians of Coltrane's generation. This reassertion of tradition was political rather than musical. For—the third aspect of the paradox—the 1960s jazz *avant-garde* was consciously and politically *black,* as no previous generation of black jazzmen had been, though *The Jazz Scene* already noted the links between jazz experimentation and black consciousness. As Whitney Balliett put it in the 1970s: 'Free jazz is actually the blackest jazz there is'.★ Black and politically

★ Whitney Balliett, *New York Notes: A Journal of Jazz in the Seventies* (New York 1977), p. 147.

radical. Thus *Charlie Haden: Liberation Music Orchestra* (1969) contained four Spanish Civil War songs, a number inspired by the riots at the 1968 Chicago Democratic Convention, a commemoration of Che Guevara and a version of 'We Shall Overcome'. Archie Shepp (tenor and soprano sax), one of the major figures of the *avant-garde,* created a musical commemoration of Malcolm X and an *Attica Blues* inspired by the well-known black prison riot. Political consciousness continued to link the *avant-garde* to the mass of the American black people and its musical traditions, and therefore provided a possible way back to the mainstream of jazz. However, in the short run it must have made the isolation of that *avant-garde* from an uncomprehending black public particularly frustrating.

A rejection of success (except on those uncompromising terms proposed by this artist) is characteristic of *avant-gardes,* and in jazz, which has always lived by the paying customer, concessions to the box office seemed particularly dangerous to the player who wanted the status of 'artist'. How could they compromise with rock? ('There is a certain political position involved in the choice of those who seldom refer to the more readily assimilated rock-rhythms'.)* And yet, for three reasons, rock had to influence jazz.

The first is that American (and British) jazz musicians born since the 1940s grew up in an atmosphere drenched in rock, or its ghetto equivalent, and therefore could hardly avoid assimilating some of it. The second is that rock, an art of amateurs and the musically or even the alphabetically illiterate required—and because of its limitless wealth could call upon—the technical and musical competence of jazz professionals, and jazz musicians could hardly be blamed for wanting to cut themselves thin slices of so huge and sweet a cake. But third, and most important, rock was musically innovative. As so often in the history of the arts, major artistic revolutions come not from self-described revolutionaries but from those employing innovation for commer-

---

* Valerie Wilmer, *As Serious As Your Life: The Story of the New Jazz* (London 1977; second edn, 1987), p. 27.

cial purposes. As the early movies were more effectively revolutionary than cubism, so the rock entrepreneurs have changed the musical scene more profoundly than classical or free jazz *avant-gardes*.

The major innovation of rock was technological. It secured the mass breakthrough of electronic music. Pedants may point out that in jazz there were pioneers of electrified instruments (Charlie Christian revolutionized the guitar that way and Billie Holiday transformed the use of the human voice by marrying it to the personal microphone) and that revolutionary ways of generating sound, such as synthesizers, were pioneered for classical *avant-garde* music concerts. However, it is undeniable that rock was the first music that systematically substituted electrified instruments for acoustic ones and systematically used electronic technology not for special effects but for the normal repertoire accepted by a mass public. It was the first music to turn the technicians of sound and recording studios into equal partners in the creation of a musical performance, chiefly because the incompetence of the actual rock performers was often such that no adequate records or even performances could have achieved otherwise. It is evident that such innovations could not but interest musicians of genuine originality and talent.

The second rock innovation concerns the concept of the 'group'. The rock group not only developed an original instrumentation behind the voice or voices (basically, percussion and various kinds of electric guitars, the bass guitar taking the place of the bass), but consisted essentially of a collective rather than a small group of virtuosos who expected to demonstrate their skills.★ Of course the members of very few rock groups, unlike those of jazz combos, had any individual skills to demonstrate. Moreover, the 'group' was ideally characterized by an unmistakable 'sound', an auditory trade-mark by means of which it, or rather its studio technicians, attempted to establish its individual-

---

★ It also, incidentally, gave a virtual monopoly to singing groups, hitherto somewhat exceptional in jazz and blues, and—in spite of the overwhelming superiority of women in vocal blues, gospel-song and jazz—to (young) men.

ity. And, unlike the old 'big band' of jazz, the rock group was small. It produced its 'big sound' (which does not necessarily mean a large volume of sound, though rock preferred ultra-strong amplification) with a minimal number of people. This helped to bring small jazz groups back to something had had commonly been lost sight of in the days of the bebop succession of solos, namely the possibility of collective improvisation and small-group *texture.* Sophisticated rock arrangements like the Beatles' *Sergeant Pepper,* not unreasonably described as 'symphonic rock', could not but give intelligent jazz musicians ideas.

The third interesting element in rock was its insistent and pulsating rhythm. While initially it was plainly much cruder than jazz rhythm, the combination of various rhythm instruments which made up the rock group—for all its keyboards, guitars and percussion would normally have belonged to the rhythm section of a jazz band—produced its own potential complexities, which jazz players could transform into multilayered and shifting ostinatos, and rhythmic counterpoints.

And yet, while, as we have seen, some of the most talented jazz musicians developed a jazz-rock 'fusion' in the 1970s—Miles Davis's *Bitches Brew* of 1969 set the pace—the merged style did not permanently shape the future of jazz, nor did the injection of jazz elements provide a permanent life-giving blood transfusion for rock. What seems to have happened is a growing musical exhaustion of rock in the course of the 1970s which may or may not be connected with the retreat of the great wave of youth rebellion which reached its peak in the late sixties and early seventies. Somehow, insensibly, the space for jazz seemed to become a little less cramped. One began to observe that intelligent or fashionable fifth- or sixth-formers once again began to treat parents of their friends who possessed Miles Davis records with a certain interest.

By the late seventies and early eighties there were undeniable signs of a modest revival, even though by then much of the classical repertoire of jazz had been frozen into permanent immobility by the death of so many of its great and formative figures, ancient and modern: the jazz life has not favoured longevity. For by 1980 even some of the formative 'new music' stars had disappeared: e.g. John Coltrane, Albert Ayler, Eric Dolphy. Much of the jazz which the new fans learned to love was thus incapable of further change and development, because it was a music of the dead, a situation which was to provide scope for a curious form of resurrectionism, by which live musicians reproduced the sounds of the past; as when a team under the direction of Bob Wilber reconstituted the music and sound of the early Ellington band for the film *Cotton Club*. Moreover, initially a very high proportion of the live jazz the new fans could hear came from musicians ranging from the rather middle-aged to the very ancient. Thus at the time I wrote a similar introduction for an Italian reprint of *The Jazz Scene* which appeared in 1982, jazz-lovers in London had the choice of listening to a variety of veterans: to Harry 'Sweets' Edison, Joe Newman, Buddy Tate and Frank Foster, who had been enrolled in the Basie band of long ago; to Nate Pierce, known since the days of Woody Herman; Shelly Manne and Art Pepper, familiar from the 'cool' days of the 1950s, Al Grey, who went back to the swing bands of the thirties, Trummy Young of 1912 vintage, who had spent long years with Louis Armstrong, and other members of the older generation. Indeed, among the important players performing that week perhaps only the pianist McCoy Tyner (born 1938), known for his work with Coltrane in the 1960s, would not have been immediately familiar to most jazz-lovers in 1960.

The jazz revival has continued since then. It has, inevitably, benefited the diminishing band of survivors, some of whom, returning from exile in Europe or in the anonymity of television, film and recording studios, have reconstituted groups dissolved long since, at least for occasional engagements and tours, such as the Modern Jazz Quartet, the Art Farmer–Benny Golson Jazztet. It has been a particular blessing for the survivors of the first jazz revolution, for it is bebop that has emerged or re-emerged as the central style of 1980s jazz and the basic model for youthful musicians. Conversely, the new revival has left out the old, the first 'return to tradition' of those who wanted to recapture the music of New Orleans, and the twenties. 'Trad', 'Dixieland' or what-ever it may be called, the longest-lasting of jazz styles, the one which, based on the happy nostalgia of white middle-class and increasingly middle-aged amateurs best resisted the cavalry charge of rock, but also the one which, it has been said, created nothing of musical value,* has not felt the new wind in its sails.

The players who have probably benefited most from it are the gifted musicians who soldiered on through the dark days of the *avant-garde* in the 1960s and 1970s and who are tempted back into the jazz mainstream by the reappearance of a living jazz public. Such players were not young by the standards of the days when an Armstrong won a world reputation in his twen-ties, a Charlie Parker was dead at thirty-five, and nobody was surprised that the jazz guitar was revolutionized by a player (Charlie Christian) who was scarcely out of his teens. Thus the members of the influential World Saxophone Quartet, which made its reputation in the 1980s (Hamiett Bluiett, Julius Hemp-hill, Oliver Lake, David Murray) were born, respectively, in 1938, 1940, 1942 and 1955—that is to say all except one were, at the time of writing (1988), in their late forties. Where we find new American jazz stars with a reputation while in their twen-ties, they are, very likely, second-generation players like the brothers Marsalis (Wynton, classical and jazz trumpet, was born in 1960), Branford, a saxophonist, in 1961).† Genuinely youthful first-generation musicians of major achievement are still scarce in the U.S.A.—or at least they have not yet emerged—although in Britain the jazz revival has inspired a substantial number of the young, especially in the (black) West Indian community, which has produced players of brilliance and originality such as the saxophonist Courtney Pine.

* *The New Grove: Gospel, Blues and Jazz* (London 1987), p. 292. This is a little unfair—the New Orleans revival recovered important artists who would otherwise have dropped out of sight, like Sidney Bechet, and produced some enchanting music with their help—but it is not grossly unfair.

† Their father, Ellis Marsalis, a New Orleans pianist and passionate sup-porter of Ornette Coleman and the *avant-garde,* made a commercial living in order to bring up his family. In New Orleans, music is still often a family trade, as it was in the days of the Bachs.

The shape and development of the present jazz revival cannot yet be seen in perspective, and if they could, a few introductory pages to a book republished after almost three decades are not the place to make the attempt. Even the size and scale of the revival are not yet clear. However, its existence is undeniable. The resuscitation of *The Jazz Scene* is a small and marginal symptom of it. Moreover, one or two things about it, which distinguish it from its predecessors, are already discernible.

It occurs at a time when jazz has had time to establish itself as a recognized part of twentieth-century culture, including musical culture, as was not yet the case in the 1950s. It would today no longer be necessary to assume complete ignorance about it on the part of the sort of people for whom 'Francis Newton' wrote in *The New Statesman,* and whose ideal type was defined for him by its great editor Kingsley Martin as 'a civil servant in his forties', i.e. an educated person of the professional classes in early middle age. Conversely, jazz musicians are no longer, to any extent, musical illiterates of untutored natural talents. Most of them are today musically educated, sometimes—as in the case of Wynton Marsalis from the jazz end of the scale, the pianist Friedrich Gulda from the classical end—equally well known in jazz and classical-music circles. It is no longer necessary to make the case for jazz.

Second, in the course of its twenty-year exile jazz probably moved both economically and intellectually upmarket as its public grew older, i.e. away from the simple foot-tapping or dancing entertainment and towards a more self-conscious, and certainly a more expensive, experience. An evening for two at Ronnie Scott's in London is not designed for the impecunious, and neither is taking in a set in Greenwich Village. Indeed, the now fashionable Manhattan combination of restaurant dinner to live jazz accompaniment underlines the shift away from the demotic milieu. It seems equally probable that the new white jazz public contains a large middle class and intellectual component, as witness the multiplication of serious books about jazz, a very high proportion of which in the U.S.A. are published by university presses. This, as well as the emergence from the underground of the population of academic jazz-buffs (among them the present author), has had a beneficial effect on our knowledge of the jazz phenomenon.

Third, I have already suggested that live jazz by now be a little over-shadowed by the corpus of its own dead 'classics', the substantial body of the great records of the golden ages, and notably the 1940s and 1950s, so that current creative musicians are more inspired by the past than their predecessors were. This, it has been suggested (and not only by disappointed supporters of the *avant-garde*) may be the first era of neo-traditionalism among the original talents; for the earlier 'New Orleans' tradi-tionalism was a movement of fans rather than players, even though some fans became players.★

Nevertheless, a jazz revival means the recruitment to jazz of a new generation of the young, including the impecunious and the unestablished, and certainly those not content with things as they are. In Britain jazz venues are cheap and multiplying. It is un-likely that the music the young play or listen to can or will remain confined within the limits of what is culturally and insti-tutionally recognized, or what can be bought with a middle-class income, or even of what Charlie Parker and the Miles Davis Quintet played. Jazz is unofficial, unestablished and unpredict-able, or it is nothing. The only thing that can be safely said about it is that it has survived the most difficult years of its extraordi-nary career. New relays of men and women will once again hear its marvellous sounds for the first time in their lives, and fall in love with it as we did; generally at the age of first love, as we did. They will not know that, fifty years later, through it one can relive the miraculous revelations of youth, and if they knew, they would not care. But it is true.

The book is republished as it appeared in 1961. I have updated nothing but the Guide to Further Reading, for the list of records

★ 'Currently also jazz risks limiting itself to a period of classicism—begin-ning with Charlie Parker . . . and ending with Ornette Coleman boarding a plane for New York in 1959. During those two decades bebop became syn-onymous with jazz, and, like many of his generation, Marsalis owes strongest allegiance to this era'. Francis Davis, *In the Moment: Jazz in the 1980s* (New York 1986), p. 30.

then recommended (see Chapter 2) are themselves a historical record of what was available to the British jazz-lover at the start of the 1960s. *The Jazz Scene* was translated into French, Italian and Japanese shortly after its original publication, and into Czech in the early 1970s (thanks to the devotion to jazz of Lubomir Dorůžka, an aficionado since 1943). It was reprinted in the U.S.A. in 1975 and has been republished, with new introductions in Italian (1982) and, newly translated by Mr Takis Tsiros, in Greek (1988).

Of those who helped me while I prepared *The Jazz Scene* three friends are now dead: Denis Preston, John Hammond Jr and Ralph Gleason. I would like to dedicate this edition to the memory of all three, but especially of Ralph Gleason and Jeanie Gleason, who is still alive: in memory of days and nights in San Francisco, Oakland, Berkeley and London. As they used to sing: a good man is hard to find. He was one of the best.

EJH

This book is about one of the most remarkable cultural phenomena of our century. It is not merely about a certain type of music, but about an extraordinary conquest and a remarkable aspect of the society in which we live. The world of jazz consists not only of the noises which emerge from particular combinations of instruments played in a characteristic way. It consists also of the musicians who play them, black and white, American and non-American. The fact that British working-class boys in Newcastle play it is at least as interesting as and rather more surprising than the fact that it progressed through the frontier saloons of the Mississippi valley.

It consists of the places in which they play, the business and technical structure which is built round the sounds, the associations they call up. It consists of the people who listen to it, write about it, and read about it. You who read this page, I who have written it, are not the least unexpected and surprising parts of the world of jazz. What business have we, after all, with what was not so long ago a local idiom of blacks and poor whites in the Southern states of the U.S.A.? It also consists of that vast section of modern popular entertainment and commercial music which has been profoundly transformed by the influence of jazz. In fact, this book is not simply about jazz as a self-contained phenomenon, the hobby and the passion of what is by now a rather large public of enthusiasts, but about jazz as a part of modern life. If it is moving, it is because men and women are moving: you and I. If it is a little lunatic and out of control, it is because the society in which we live is so. At all events, leaving aside the value-judgements, jazz in society is what this book is about. For this reason I have not confined myself to writing about the history and stylistic development of jazz (the subjects dealt with in Parts 1 and 2) but have also included sections on Jazz as a Business and Jazz and People—the Jazz Musician and the Jazz Public—and Jazz and the other Arts.

At the moment I write this, in the spring of 1958, there is probably no major city in the world in which someone is not playing a record of Louis Armstrong or Charlie Parker, or of players influenced by these artists, or improvising on the theme of the *St Louis Blues,* or *Indiana,* or *How High the Moon.* W. C. Handy, who first turned the blues into a written form, has died and been laid in his grave to the accompaniment of a hundred or two hundred thousand fellow-citizens of Harlem and a wall of verbiage by (white) politicians and journalists as solid, if not as relevant, as the wall of blue sound which emerges from Miss Carrie Smith and the Back Home Choir of Newark, New Jersey (formerly Savannah, Georgia), singing *I Want Jesus to Walk with Me.* Louis Armstrong has been invited to the Edinburgh Festival. The Demochristian Party in the Italian election campaign is hiring Dixieland bands to cheer up its meetings because its rival, the Communist Party, proved in the last local elections that they pulled in the crowds. (The late Boss Crump, whose election campaign in 1909 produced the *Memphis Blues,* had the same idea.) An 'international band', composed of players from virtually all European countries between Portugal in the West, Czechoslovakia and Poland in the East, is to play at an American Jazz Festival. Jazz bands and skiffle groups accompany the march of the opponents of the nuclear arms race to Aldermaston. A Mr Jack Kerouac has published a novel designed to symbolize the fate of the 'beat generation': it is symbolized largely in terms of 'cool' jazz. A fashionable novelist and literary figure reviews jazz for the most intellectual of the London Sunday papers. Before me there lies a pile of records brought back by a friend from Johannesburg: in Sophiatown and the rest of the South African ghettoes the 'jive bands' play what is patently jazz, derived from American records of the 1930s. The *Birmingham Mail*'s 'Jazz Panorama' column reports on the latest jazz clubs to be opened among and by the juveniles of the British Midlands, and records the fact that the most popular jazz records in the second city of England at present are by Duke Ellington, Oscar Peterson, and Miles Davis.

And yet, when men and women now barely middle-aged were born, none of this existed. This very word 'jazz' entered print and printable meaning a little over forty years ago—say around 1915. Even if we trace the music back beyond its present label, the lifetime of an elderly, but not a very old, man spans its entire history. In the early 1900s even Southern blacks from outside the Mississippi Delta heard it with surprise. When the Original Dixieland Jass Band came to Reisenweber's in New York in 1917, the management had to put up notices pointing out that this music was intended for dancing. Since then jazz has conquered and evolved in a wholly extraordinary fashion.

It is hard to find a parallel for its unique history. Other local musical idioms have had the power to proselytize: the Hungarian, Spanish, Latin-American. Our age and culture is one that needs periodic blood-transfusions to rejuvenate tired and exhausted or thin-blooded middle-class art, or popular art whose vitality is drained by systematic commercial debasement and over-exploitation. Since the aristocrats and the middle class first began to borrow the waltz from the 'lower orders' and the polka from the peasantry of an exotic and revolutionary nation, since the romantic intellectuals first discovered the thrill of the Andalusian Carmens and Don Josés (they have been significantly transposed into a jazz setting in the film *Carmen Jones*), Western

xliii

civilization has been a push-over for exoticism of all kinds. And yet, the triumph of jazz is greater, more universal and all-embracing than that of previous comparable idioms. It has become, in more or less diluted form, *the* basic language of modern dance and popular music in urban and industrial civilization, in most places where it has been allowed to penetrate.

It has done more. Most exotic idioms have created for themselves a body of enthusiasts who appreciate them not only as the bringers of some new musical tinge or sensation, but as arts to be studied, discussed, and generally 'taken seriously'. Most of these bodies of 'aficionados' have remained small self-contained groups without wider influence, and consist mainly of people with a first-hand knowledge of their subject. We know of the existence of these communities dedicated to the attractions of the gypsies, bullfighting, flamenco, Rumanian folk-music, or West African dancing, but only as we know of the existence of the small groups who have fallen in love with Ethiopian culture or with the Basques. They are of no general importance. But the community of jazz-lovers is not only larger, more influential, but also more international, and of more significance on the cultural scene. After all, how many serious or frivolous daily papers, intellectual weeklies, periodicals devoted to the arts (outside the countries directly concerned) print regular columns of flamenco criticism or discussions of Indian dancing? The social history of the twentieth-century arts will contain only a footnote or two about Scottish Highland music or gypsy lore, but it will have to deal at some length with the vogue for jazz.

Moreover, jazz itself has changed with startling rapidity. Folk-music and similar idioms are not, of course, as unchanging as romantics like to believe. There is a great difference between the first flamenco songs of the 1860s and the flamenco of today, unless it deliberately (and often unsuccessfully) strives for archaism. But this difference is as nothing compared with the gap which separates the New Orleans street music of the early 1900s from, say, the series of miniature flügelhorn concertos of Miles Davis and Gil Evans in 1958. Jazz, in fact, has developed not only into the basic idiom of popular music, but also towards something like an elaborate and sophisticated art music, seeking both to merge with, and to rival, the established art music of the Western world. Compared to the musical idioms which might at first sight appear to belong to the same order, it is not only vastly more successful but more unstable and far more ambitious.

How are we to get this remarkable phenomenon into some sort of perspective? It is not really the business of this book to construct general theories, or a sociology of jazz. (If it were, there would be enough awful examples to scare at least this author back into caution.) My main object is to survey the world of jazz for the benefit of the intelligent layman, who knows nothing about it, and perhaps also for that of the expert who has hitherto overlooked some of its non-technical corners. Nevertheless, it is impossible to look at jazz with any sort of curiosity without trying to find out, however crudely, how it fits into the general framework of twentieth-century civilization. Ever since the beginnings of jazz, observers have speculated about this. Their speculations are often totally valueless, except as an indication of their own prejudices and desires (though these also belong to the world of jazz, in so far as they deal with it). If before sketching the sort of approach I have found useful I quote an awful example of such earlier speculation, it is simply to warn the reader that my own ideas may turn out to be quite as silly in time as these.

Thus it used to be customary in the 1920s in intellectual circles to talk of jazz as 'the music of the future', the one whose rhythm and clang reproduced the quintessential sound and movement of the machine age, the robots' melody. Admittedly such statements were normally made by people who had rarely been inside a twentieth-century factory or heard any jazz which we would today recognize as such. Nevertheless this does not excuse their almost total irrelevance.

For in the first place, as we shall see, the very essence of jazz is that it is *not* standardized or mass-produced music (though jazz-influenced popular music is), and in the second place jazz has very little connexion with modern industry. The only machine which jazz has ever tried to imitate in sound is the railway train which is, throughout American folk-music of the past century, a universal and most important symbol of the multiple kind welcomed by the literary analysts, but *never* a symbol of mechanization. On the contrary, as scores of railway blues demonstrate, it is a symbol of movement which brings personal freedom:

> *Gonna catch myself a train fifteen coaches long,*
> *When you look for me, I'll be gone.*

It is a symbol of the flux of life, and therefore of fate:

> *Two-nineteen took my babe away,*
> *Two-seventeen will bring her back some day.*

It is a symbol of tragedy and death, as in the numerous songs about railroad disasters and the suicide blues:

> *Gonna lay my head on that old railroad line*
> *And let the two-fifteen pacify my min'.*

Of yearning and grief: 'How I hate to hear that freight train go boo-hoo'; of the labour in building it, as in the great ballad of John Henry; of male power in the running of it; of sex, as in Bessie Smith's *Casey Jones*.★ Indeed, the most usual use of mechanical metaphors in jazz—e.g. telephones and cars—is for sexual symbolism: 'Got Ford movements in my hips'. The railroad is a symbol of man's journey to paradise or perdition, as in numerous black sermons ('The Gospel Train'). Jazz players, especially blues pianists, have reproduced the sound and sensation of this, the only product of the industrial revolution to have been fully absorbed into poetry and music, with uncanny power, as

---

★ 'Riding', 'rocking', and 'rolling' are words applied both to the railroad and to coitus. In the prison and labour-camp songs the railroad is also the vehicle which brings the prisoner's girl to him.

in Meade Lux Lewis's *Honky Tonk Train Blues* or Red Nelson–Clarence Lofton's *Streamline Train*. But if this reflects any phase of industrialization, it is not the mass production of the twentieth century but the unmechanized society of the late nineteenth. There is nothing in 'railroad jazz' which could not have been created in the 1890s.

All this is a warning against wild and comprehensive generalizations based on insufficient knowledge. And yet one might as well generalize, and I propose to do so. Readers who feel unhappy about such general discussions may perhaps skip the remainder of this introduction and go straight on to the more down-to-earth sections of this book.

The history of the arts is not one history, but, in every country, at least two: that of the arts as practised or enjoyed by the wealthy, leisured, or educated minority, and that of the arts as practised or enjoyed by the mass of the common people. Beethoven's last quartets, for instance, belong almost entirely to the first; it is reasonably certain that even in Vienna very few members of the average football crowd would accept even free tickets to hear them. On the other hand, in Britain certain kinds of music-hall comic belong almost entirely to the second. I daresay a number of, say, university lecturers have at one time or another seen Lucan and McShane, or Frank Randle, but almost certainly without pleasure; nor would they normally think of putting them into a history of the twentieth-century arts, assuming they were to write one. There are, fortunately, overlaps. Education or national and social pride turn minority artists into universal ones. Democracy, modern mass media, or national pride make the minority public aware of the common tradition, and there are art forms which, even without these aids, are sufficiently powerful to press inexorably into new territory: jazz is one of them. But it is still true, outside countries whose major cultural tradition is the popular one (and even sometimes within them), that when the books are written, 'culture' or 'the arts' means minority culture and the minority arts. Arnold Bennett, Thomas Hardy, G. K. Chesterton are in the *Oxford History of England,* but not Marie Lloyd, or the Cup Final as an institution. Sterndale

Bennett and the London Philharmonic Society are in, but not the Northern brass band movement and the choral societies singing their *Messiah*. If it comes to that, even the Americans, who have much less excuse for neglecting their popular tradition, spend a great deal more time on analysing the adequate but by no means sensational classical composers they have produced than they do on their folk-music and jazz, which are far more original and influential contributions to world culture.

Little need be said about the place of jazz in minority culture, the 'official arts'. As we shall see, until recently it has had only a marginal place among them, partly because the official arts were ignorant of it, partly because they resented it as a sort of populist revolt against their superior status and claims, or as an aggression by philistinism against culture. It is both these things, though it is also a great deal else. In so far as jazz has been absorbed by official culture, it is as a form of exoticism, like African sculpture or Spanish dancing, one of the 'noble savage' types of exoticism by means of which middle- and upper-class intellectuals try to compensate for the moral deficiencies of their life, especially today when they have lost the nineteenth-century confidence in the superiority of that life. This is no criticism of jazz. A blues singer from North Carolina, a trumpeter from old New Orleans, a professional showman-musician, the veteran of decades of bread-and-butter touring and dance-hall playing, are not responsible for the fact that European or American intellectuals (including, I suppose, the writer of these observations) read the answer to their frustrations into their music.

They would be well advised to listen to the voice of Mr Rex Stewart, the trumpeter: 'And that stuff about us not being sincere! Listen, when a band walks into a studio to do a session the boys don't sit down to get sincere. They just play. That's all there is to it'. Or of Mr Harry Carney, the saxophonist: 'The critics take it too serious. They keep writing theories about it and talking about its history and the jungle and tom-toms and white man's influence. You got to take it easy. You play jazz for the kicks in it, not to make up history'.

Well, it is not as simple as all that. In any case, the intellectual jazz-lover cannot 'take it easy'. If he could he would probably not feel the need for jazz except perhaps as a good rhythmic music for dancing.

Where jazz plays its really important part and has its real life is in the common tradition of culture.

This lies in analytical darkness, lit only by a few vague and sometimes misleading generalizations. I suppose the best known of them (which also reflects the incurable romanticism of most people who deal with the subject) runs something like this. Popular culture today, in industrial and urbanized countries, is a matter of commercialized, standardized, and mass-produced entertainment, disseminated by mass media like the Press, TV, the cinema, and the rest, and producing cultural impoverishment and passivity: a people of watchers and listeners who take in packaged and predigested stuff. Some time the past—just when depends on the point of view of the observer—popular culture was lively, vigorous, and largely self-made, as in rural folk-song, folk-dance, and similar activities. There is much rough truth in this. The trouble is that such generalizations leave out everything which might help us to understand the world of jazz, and a great deal about the problems of popular culture besides.

In the first place they leave out the question, What really happened to the flourishing old, pre-industrial popular culture? Some of it undoubtedly died out with industrialization, like most rural English folk-song, or survived merely in remote corners of the countryside to await the tape-recorders of the itinerant folk-song enthusiasts. But other kinds of popular culture were more adaptable, and succeeded in flourishing quite vigorously in an urbanized or industrialized society, at least until the rise of mass-produced and standardized entertainment: for instance, English music-hall song and comedy acts. Yet others were resistant and powerful enough to survive even the environment of mechanized entertainment, or even in part to dominate it. Jazz is the chief among these. If I had to sum up the evolution of jazz in a single sentence, I should say: It is what happens when a folk-music does not go under, but maintains itself in the environment of modern urban and industrial civilization. For jazz in its origins

xlix

is folk-music of very much the type studied by the collectors and experts: both rural and urban. And some of the fundamental characteristics of folk-music have been maintained in it throughout its history; for instance, the importance of word-of-mouth tradition in passing it on, the importance of improvisation and slight variation from one performance to the next, and other matters. Much of it has changed out of all recognition; but that, after all, is what we should expect to happen to a music which does not die but continues to evolve in a dynamic and tempestuous world.

In the second place, the generalizations about popular culture leave out the question of how the mass-production entertainment industry which unquestionably takes over from pre-industrial forms of culture, gets at the standardized entertainment it purveys, how it standardizes it, and how that standardized entertainment conquers the public. For Tin Pan Alley no more *invents* its tunes and fashions in a sort of commercial laboratory than the canning industry invented food: it discovers what it most profitably processed and then processes it. This is particularly important to remember, for unlike other modern industries, which sometimes create genuinely new demands—for instance for aeroplanes—the entertainment industry caters for demands which have remained substantially unchanged through the ages. Nowhere is the contrast greater than between the technically revolutionary methods by which entertainment and the arts are today brought to the people—TV, juke-boxes, films, and the rest—and the conservatism of the actual matter brought to them. A medieval fairground showman would be lost in a television studio, but perfectly at home with most of television entertainment.

Now the original raw material of mass entertainment is chiefly an adapted form of earlier entertainment, and even to this day the industry continues to revive itself from time to time by drawing on this source, and finds some of its most fruitful activities in the oldest and most perennial, the least 'industrialized' forms of popular creation. Consider the 'Western', which has maintained a steady, perhaps even an increasing, popularity

1

throughout a period of dizzying technical revolutions. At bottom the 'Western' is a system of myths, morality, and adventure tales of the kind which can be found in any society. This particular set happens to have been devised by the most vigorous and lively tradition of popular culture in the modern Western world to fit the needs of that world. It has merely been taken over, tricked out, modified from time to time, and mass-produced by the entertainment industry. Other 'pre-industrial' popular arts and themes have been taken over in a much more distorted and diluted form. Jazz is among these, though it has also been strong enough to maintain a separate life of its own. There are sound reasons why the idiom which has become fundamental to Western popular music should be drawn from an American source, and within it, from an Afro-American mixture, though some of them are still obscure. But when we consider the vast, tepid lake of modern, more or less jazz-coloured pop music, we must remember not only the commercial processing which makes it so insipid, but the cold and authentic springs from which it has drawn, and sometimes still draws, its water.

We must remember this, because the phenomenon of popular culture, even today, cannot be understood at all unless we constantly remember how contradictory it is. When people switch on their television they expect to be 'taken out of themselves', but at the same time they expect to be 'brought back to themselves'. The same people in Victorian music halls clapped the songs about impossibly dressed toffs twirling canes and moustaches (*Champagne Charlie*) and those about mothers-in-law, rent, and pawn-brokers. The same people in yesterday's cinemas applauded the never-never land of supernaturally beautiful, rich, and trouble-free divinities and Charlie Chaplin's accusations of the helpless poor against the powerful rich. Popular art is myth and dreamland, but also protest, because the common people always have something to protest about. The tabloid papers, which have time and again discovered that the profitable formula is a combination of cheesecake and radicalism, know what they are about.

At the same time the demand to be 'taken out of' and

'brought back to' oneself is both an acceptance and a rejection of the entertainment industry. For in the nature of its technical and economic structure that industry tends, if left to itself, to develop one side of this demand more than the other. In this sense the prophets who have for a century predicted that commercialism would turn the masses into a collection of blank faces waiting to be spoon-fed, into TV morons, are not wholly mistaken. The industry produces ready-made articles for sale to audiences; and the most convenient audiences are those who come in regularly and quietly and sit back in darkness to enjoy the spectacle open-mouthed: the vastest audiences, those who sit at home, alone or in small groups, looking at the paper or switching on the radio or TV. If the industry has not succeeded in turning the public into an aggregation of morons it is because the public does not *only* want to sit back as a statistical population to enjoy the show. It *also* wants to make its own entertainment; to participate in it actively, and above all socially. There are British working men who go to football matches in sleet and frost rather than see them, better and more conveniently, on the telly, because the active partisanship, the roar of the crowd which makes the team play better, is as much part of their enjoyment as the mere sight of the players. There are far more citizens who would not enjoy their television unless they could also talk about it, argue the merits of each programme, or perhaps simply gossip, a tendency as natural as that of most people to take their drinks together rather than in solitude. Among young people this desire for making and actively participating in social entertainment is naturally much stronger. It was the young who abandoned cinemas and television screens in Britain in the 1950s for jazz clubs and skiffle groups.★ The demand of popular culture is both 'com-

★ It is possible that the increasing spread of middle-class or lower-middle-class standards among the working class may really create cultural moronism; for the practice of sitting back and soaking in individual cultural impressions as an end in itself is much more characteristic of the middle classes than of any other. What is culturally harmless, or even beneficial when done with Rembrandt, becomes pretty gloomy when done with a *Daily Sketch* portrait study of the Royal family.

mercial' and anti-commercial, though of course it belongs to the scheme of things that as soon as an anti-commercial demand is large enough it automatically (under conditions of capitalism) becomes commercial and is supplied, to the best of the industry's ability, until it in turn is diluted into pap.

The appeal of jazz has always been due to its capacity to supply the things commercial pop music ironed out of its product. It has made its way as a music which people made and participated in actively and socially, and not one for passive acceptance; as a hard and realistic art and not sentimental maundering; as a noncommercial music, and above all as a music of protest (including the protest against the exclusiveness of minority culture). It has been astonishingly and universally successful. But it has made its way by two routes. One route has led through the ordinary, commercial, popular entertainment industry, within which jazz lived, and still lives, and which has constantly borrowed from it those things it could not give the public unaided, until it enfeebled its borrowings. Jazz has made much of its way as part of the pop world, as a special flavour in an increasingly jazz-influenced pop music. But jazz has also made its way independently, as a separate art, appreciated by special groups of people quite separately from, and generally in flat opposition to, commercial pop music. However, pop music has never quite let jazz out of the reach of its tentacles—and so long as it remains part of the popular tradition in the arts it is difficult to see how it can. For, as I have tried to argue, the popular entertainment industry is merely a processing and adaptation (almost always a debasement) of that tradition.

Jazz has been kept in this odd and complicated family relationship with popular music for another reason or, if you like, by another facet of its 'populism'. Throughout most of its history it has been largely ostracized or ignored by the official minority arts. It has not 'belonged'. No eyebrows have normally been raised in the circles where it would be fatal not to have heard of Wozzeck or Petrushka when a citizen thought that Art Tatum was a boxer or Charlie Parker somebody's old school chum. More than this: among very many educated and cultured persons now barely into middle age, and especially among musical ones, jazz has been actively disliked and despised, partly perhaps because the world of jazz was, and is, to some extent a rebellion against the values of minority culture. Nowadays jazz has come to be much more widely accepted. Too much so, perhaps, for its own good, for it is quite possible that jazz will flourish as poorly in the atmosphere of conservatoires and chamber-music recitals as Marie Lloyd would have done in country-house drawing-rooms. But there is no doubt that the long relegation of jazz to a world below that of the official arts has had its effect. For one thing, it has caused jazz to have much less influence on the other arts, and to be much less seriously studied and analysed than one would have expected.

I think it needs such study and analysis, though this book does not pretend to do more than survey the world of jazz, to get it into some kind of perspective, to introduce readers to its different regions. It is a completely and utterly fascinating world, even to the man or woman who has no intention of analysing it, or who does not particularly like the noise which ceaselessly emerges from it: the noise of music, the noise of the tapping of fans' feet, the noise of businessmen talking one another into deals. But it is twice as fascinating if we consider it not simply as a film show of human behaviour, often in Technicolor, but as one of the keys to the problem that concerns us all.

The old New Orleans banjo player Johnny St Cyr once told an interviewer:

> You see, the average working man is very musical. Playing music for him is just relaxing. He gets as much kick out of playing as other folks get out of dancing. The more enthusiastic his audience is, why, the more spirit the working man's got to play. And with your natural feelings that way, you never make the same thing twice. Every time you play a tune, new ideas come to mind and you slip that one in.

If we need an illustration of the sort of art, and the sort of relation between art and the people, of which William Morris dreamed ('an art made by the people for the people as a joy for the maker and the user') we might do worse than this. It is a good deal. It is demonstrably far from the reality of the arts in our Western urban and industrial society, and the chances are that every decade, by industrializing and standardizing the production of mass entertainment, shifts it farther away. How are we to restore the arts to their proper place in life, and to bring out the creative capacities in all of us? I do not claim that jazz holds the answer. Indeed, much of it has gone down one or other of the blind alleys which bedevil the arts in our world: either into commercialized pop music, or into esoteric art music. But the history of jazz, that remarkable noise from the Mississippi Delta which has, without benefit of patronage or advertising campaigns, conquered an astonishing range of geographical and social territory, can supply some of the material for an answer. We can see how one genuine and exceptionally vigorous and resistant popular art actually works and changes in the modern world, and what its achievements and limitations are. We can then draw conclusions. It is not the business of this book to draw them. I have written an introduction to jazz, not a programme for the arts. But it might be as well to point out that if readers are so inclined, they can get more than information and entertainment from the world of jazz.

*T*his interlude may be safely skipped by the informed reader. It is addressed to readers who, while interested in the subject, know nothing whatever about jazz, are unable to recognize a jazz record when they hear one, and do not care to consult friends or relatives on the subject. It is also addressed to readers who have put the question 'What is jazz?' to aficionados and who have been met (as is extremely likely) by noise and confusion. It contains a fairly cursory description, or rather 'recognition-model', of jazz, and a brief list of some of the chief artists and some of the characteristic records in this music.

There can be no firm or adequate definition of jazz, except in the most general or non-musical terms, which are of no help in recognizing it when we hear it. As we have seen, jazz is neither self-contained nor unchanging. No frontier line, but a vast border zone, divides it from ordinary popular music, much of which is in varying degrees tinged by it and mixed up with it. No fixed frontier divides it from the older types of folk-music out of which it has emerged. Until the last war the frontier between it and orthodox art music was much sharper, but even that has been made hazier by raids across it from either side. As we have also seen, jazz has in its short history changed to a remarkable degree, and there is no guarantee at all that it will stop changing. Just as a definition of jazz which described it adequately in 1927 had to be modified and widened to describe the jazz of 1937, and again to describe that of 1957, so it is extremely probable that any incautious description today will in turn grow out-of-date. Jazz lovers and jazz critics, inhabitants of an argumentative and exclusive universe, have tried to find arbitrary definitions which will safely separate 'jazz' from 'pop music', or whatever they consider the 'true jazz' from its degenerations. It cannot be done; not because it is impossible to make and establish such conventional definitions—the orthodox arts are doing it all the time—but because jazz, being a modern popular art, has hitherto lacked the authorities and institutions which can make such definitions stick. Army musical schools, singing masters, and ballet academies may impose a 'correct' way of playing cornets, singing coloratura, or moving one's feet, which can be broken only by deliberate technical revolution or secession. Tradition, in custom-bound pre-industrial societies, can impose an equally 'correct' repertoire for the player, dancer, or singer. But jazz is in the position of the famous Hollywood producer who, when told he could not put a rendering of Mozart playing the *Blue Danube Waltz* into a film biography of that composer, said: 'Who's going to stop me?' Nobody. *There* is a difference between jazz in the strict sense and commercial pop music. There may well be a point in the evolution of jazz where it might be better to stop calling it by that name. But it is in its nature a music without precise boundary lines.

Nevertheless, as a rough guide it may be said that jazz, as it has developed up to the present, is music which contains the following five characteristics; jazz-coloured pop music contains some of the first three or four but not the last, or the last only in considerable dilution:

1. Jazz has certain musical peculiarities, which arise mainly from the use of scales not usually employed in European art music, but derived from West Africa; or from the mixing of European and African scales; or from the combination of African scales with European harmonies. The best-known expression of these peculiarities is the combination of the 'blue' scale—the ordinary major scale with the third and seventh approximately flattened—which is used for melody, and the common major scale, used for harmony. (The flattened notes are the so-called 'blue notes'.)

2. Jazz leans heavily, and probably fundamentally, on another African element, rhythm. Not indeed in the African forms, which are normally much more complex than most jazz. However, the element of constant rhythmic variation, which is quite vital to jazz, is certainly not derived from the European tradition. Rhythmically jazz consists of two elements: a steady and unchanging 'beat'—normally two or four to a bar, at least approximately—which may be stated or implied, and a wide range of variations round it. These may consist of various kinds of syncopation (the placing of an accent on a normally unaccented beat or the omission of an accent from a normally strong one), or of a much subtler ranging round the beat, placing the accent just before or after it, or of other devices such as 'attack' and intensity. The interplay of the various jazz instruments, each of which has rhythmic as well as melodic functions, complicates the matter further. Rhythm is essential to jazz: it is the organizing element in the music. It is, however, extremely difficult to analyse, and some of its phenomena, such as that vaguely called 'swing', have so far resisted analysis altogether. They can merely be recognized. It is for instance difficult to see why good drummers, while maintaining a rock-steady beat, can and do give the sensation of continuous acceleration, or 'driving'.

3. Jazz employs peculiar instrumental and vocal colours. These derive in part from the use of instruments uncommon in art music, for though jazz has no specific instrumentation, it happens that the jazz orchestra has evolved out of the military orchestra, and therefore normally uses string instruments very little and brass and woodwind for purposes unusual in symphony orchestras. It also uses exotic instruments from time to time, e.g. vibraphones, bongo-drums, and maracas.* However, in the main the colour of jazz comes from a peculiar and unconventional technique of playing all instruments, which developed because many of the pioneer jazz musicians were entirely self-taught. They therefore escaped the long-established conventions of European art music as to the 'correct' way of using instruments or trained voices. This standard European convention has aimed at the production of a pure, clear, accurate instrumental tone and of a voice as nearly as possible like a special kind of instrument. The simplest way of explaining the jazz tone is to say that it automatically and spontaneously took the opposite road. Its voice is the ordinary untrained voice, and its instruments, so far as possible, are played as though they were such voices. (It is even reported that the great cornetist King Oliver, when on bad terms with his bandsmen, refused to talk to them and 'talked' to them only by means of his cornet, or that 'eighty-five per cent of what Lester Young says on the sax you can understand'.[1] There is no such thing in jazz as an illegitimate tone: vibrato is just as legitimate as pure tone, 'dirty' ones as clean ones. Some players, influenced by orthodox music, have from time to time—notably in cool jazz—experimented with orthodox instrumental tones, but so far as jazz is concerned this is merely another proof that any sound which comes out of the instrument is a legitimate sound. Jazz players are also great experimenters who try to explore the utmost technical resources of their instruments, for instance, by trying to play a trumpet with the flexibility of woodwind, or a trombone in the normal register of the trumpet. Such pieces of often excessive craftsman's bravura produce their own unorthodox tone-colours. But at bottom jazz has used instruments as voices for most of its history. Since the voices on which the instruments based themselves, and what they had to say or felt, belonged to a particular

---

* Particular jazz styles and periods have very characteristic instrumentations, and some instruments lend themselves better to jazz playing than others. But there is no reason why someone should not play jazz on any instrument, and someone generally has done so; even on the organ and the flute.

people living in specific conditions, the colours of jazz all tend to belong to a particular and recognizable spectrum. For instance, it is rather likely that, if brass and reed instruments had been developed in an analogous way by Bengalis or Chinese rather than by Southern Negroes, their sounds, though equally unorthodox by conventional European standards, would be very different. The pitch and inflexion, the general pattern of expression, are obviously not the same in Dacca or Canton as in Vicksburg.

4. Jazz has developed certain specific musical forms and a specific repertoire. Neither are of very great importance. The two main forms used by jazz are the *blues,* and the *ballad,* the typical popular song adapted from ordinary commercial music. The blues, an extraordinarily powerful and fruitful foundation of jazz, is normally in music a unit of twelve bars and in words a rhyming couplet of iambic pentameters (the blank verse line) with the first line repeated. The pop ballad varies, but is often of a standardized thirty-two bar type. Both, in simple or complex forms, serve as the basis of musical variation. The repertoire consists of so-called 'standards'—themes which, for one reason or another, lend themselves to profitable jazz playing. They may be drawn from any source, the traditional blues and the current popular song being the most important. 'Standards' tend to vary from one style or school of jazz to another, though some have proved suitable for all. The listener who hears a band announce the title of one of these—either a blues, say, or one of the evanescent pop songs of the past which have been given permanent life as jazz standards—can be pretty certain that the band at least intends to play jazz. (It does not follow that it will.) Once he knows his way around he will probably also know by the title what type of jazz the band intends to play: there was a time when *Margie* or *Avalon* would almost certainly produce a 'Dixieland' number; *Christopher Columbus* a number in the style of the thirties; *How High the Moon* or a Cole Porter number, 'modern' jazz. By now a body of more elaborate jazz compositions or arrangements is also in existence.

5. Jazz is a players' music. Everything in it is subordinated to the individualities of the players, or derives from a musical situation when the player was supreme. A musician or impresario who wishes to get together a jazz band looks round not merely for so many trumpets, trombones, reeds, etc., but like a producer casting a play, or a selector of a goods sports team, for a Buck Clayton on trumpet, a Henry Coker on trombone, a Sonny Rollins on tenor sax. Until recently the composer, the key figure in Western art music, was, with rare exceptions, a wholly secondary figure in jazz. His place was taken, if at all, by the modestly and correctly named 'arranger'. The conductor remains totally unimportant, at least in his orthodox role. The traditional jazz composition is merely a simple theme for orchestration and variation. A piece of jazz is not reproduced, or even recreated, but—ideally at least—created and enjoyed by its players every time it is played. Hence—once again ideally—no two performances of the same piece by the same band should be exactly alike, and if two performances of the same piece by different bands sound identical, even in the same arrangement, then one of them is deliberately imitating the other. Every jazz player is a soloist, and just as the operatic listener ought to be able to recognize the voice of Flagstad or Schwarzkopf after a bar or two of an aria, so the jazz listener ought to be able to identify Armstrong, or Hodges, or Miles Davis—or, if he is very expert, some scores or hundreds of lesser recorded players —after a few notes.

It is therefore natural that individual and collective improvisation plays an immense part in jazz. A good deal of nonsense is naturally talked about this. Jazz musicians play a limited repertoire far too often, and the possibilities of improvisation on a given theme are in practice too limited for their performance not to become standardized to some extent. Literate musicians find scored music too convenient not to use it. Just so it is quite certain that even such improvised performances as those of the old *commedia dell'arte* in time settled down into routines, collections of standardized gestures, expressions, and business which actors would string together, quite possibly recording them in a rough sort of notation. To talk as though the only legitimate jazz was the one which was never heard before is silly romanticism. (Anyway, what is wrong with a player who, having hit on a good idea and elaborated it in a series of performances, decides to stick to what he now regards as an adequate solo?) Jazz is not simply improvised or unwritten music. But it must, in the last analysis, be based on the individuality of particular musicians, and very likely on their actual improvisations, and it ought to leave room for improvisation.

Nor is this difficult, for even with great technical efforts jazz cannot at present be adequately noted down on paper, and if it could, would almost certainly be far too complex for players to sight-read, and perhaps even to learn from the score. A piece of jazz, unless recorded, copied by ear, and checked against the record (which in jazz takes the place of the score) time and again, cannot be reproduced by anyone else even in approximately identical form. The effort to do so has sometimes been made, for instance by devoted 'traditionalists' attempting to reproduce with complete fidelity the sound of some cherished band of the past. But for most jazz purposes—and especially for the routine of ordinary bread-and-butter performance—the effort is too great to be worth the time and trouble. Most jazz scores, if they exist at all, are therefore rather simple and rough approximations, which leave at least the detail of tone, rhythm, inflexion, and the like to the jazz instincts of the players.★

I do not propose to discuss the attempts to define jazz in narrower terms which have often been made; for instance, the one which holds that its essence is 'collective improvisation' and that anything which lacks this characteristic is 'not jazz'. Such definitions are normally manifestoes of what jazz ought to be, not descriptions of what it actually is. Nor is there any need to describe jazz-influenced popular music. It is extremely unlikely

★ To a much slighter extent this is true of any music. But in European art music this difficulty is minimized by its rhythmic simplicity and by the fact that the orchestral instruments are trained to produce a much more standardized sound.

that any man or woman in the Western world has escaped the constant bombardment by barrages of such music from theatres and cinemas, records, dance bands, radio, and television. Much of this music, though disavowed by the strict jazz-lovers, claims to be jazz—generally by adopting one of numerous trade names such as 'jazz', 'hot', 'swing', 'jive', 'cool', 'ragtime', 'blues', 'bop', 'syncopation', 'rhythm', 'dixieland', and the rest, not counting the names of dances. (Such trade names change rapidly with fashion: a dance band wishing to advertise its connexions with jazz would, in the early 1920s have said it played 'jazz' or 'syncopation', in the late twenties 'hot' or 'dirty', in the thirties 'swing' and so on.) Just as there has always been a public which actively dislikes the idea of jazz, so there has always been one, including the jazz-lovers but much more numerous, which is strongly attracted by the idea of jazz. Since pop music exists by selling itself on the market to buyers, the jazz trade-mark has been a distinct selling point from time to time.

At the risk of offending purists, it must be said that such hybrid and diluted jazz has a perfect right to the name. Though the jazz-lover may have fits at the idea, the reporter can no more deny the right of the late Paul Whiteman to call himself a jazz musician, the late Al Jolson a jazz singer, or the least and most cretinous rock-and-roller to claim jazz citizenship than the literary critic can deny the right of the average businessman to claim that he writes English. The world of jazz as a cultural phenomenon of our times includes anything that calls itself jazz, or borrows enough from the jazz idiom to be significantly affected by it. However, just as the critic who writes about English literature will not spend his time on business letters or Christmas-card doggerel, so the jazz-lover need not trouble much about the technicalities of pop music, except in so far as it has influenced the sort of jazz which is, rightly, the subject of critical enjoyment and appreciation.

A few brief notes may help to guide the reader into the world of this more valuable kind of jazz. The subject is discussed at greater length in Chapters 6–8. Here I merely wish to help the beginner find his or her bearings by listing some characteristic records which jazz lovers of one kind or another find powerful, moving, enjoyable, or interesting. It is not a list of the 'best' jazz records, for no such list could be drawn up with any hope of agreement. However, it contains examples of the work of most jazz artists of agreed stature, and a wide enough range from which the listener can conclude what jazz sounds like, and whether he or she likes it. The references are to British record catalogues, where available. Readers should be warned that the unpredictable behavior of record companies will make it certain that several of the records they want will be out of print, or will have changed their labels and numbers by the time they need them. This also applies to the following list:

A. *Black Folk-Music and the Blues*

1. *Murderers' Home* (Nixa NJL 11). Worksongs, blues, etc., recorded in a Mississippi labour camp in 1947. One of the fundamental records for the student of jazz or of black and any other folk-music. 12″.
2. *The Country Blues* (Folkways RF 1). The best anthology of the male blues singer. 12″.
3. *The Saga of Leadbelly* (Melodisc, four records). Black folk-singer whose style and repertoire have been extremely influential even beyond the jazz public.
4. *Gospel Singing at Newport* (Columbia 33 CX 10112). Good examples of contemporary black gospel song groups. 12″.
5. *Harlem Congregation* (London-Ducretet-Thomson TKL 93119). Tape-recordings of actual modern urban church services. 12″.
6. *Mahalia Jackson* (Vogue LDE 005). The finest gospel singer of the present day and one of the great artists of our time. 10″.
7. *The Bessie Smith Story* (Philips, four records). An adequate selection of the work of the queen of classic blues singers, often with extremely fine accompaniment. All 12″.
8. *Piano Jazz*, vol 1 (Vogue-Coral LVA 9069). A selection of urban honky-tonk and blues piano. 12″.

B. *Early Jazz*

9. *Ragtime Piano Roll,* vol 1 (London AL 3515). Old pianola rolls by the leading composer-players of this earliest jazz style. 10″.

10. *King Oliver's Creole Jazz Band* (London AL 3504). The classic New Orleans Orchestra as recorded in 1923. 10″.

11. *The King of New Orleans Jazz* (RCA, RD 27113). Jelly-Roll Morton. The most sophisticated development of orchestral jazz in the New Orleans tradition. 12″.

12. *The Louis Armstrong Story* (Philips, four records so far). The chief works by the unquestioned genius of early jazz. 12″.

13. *Mezzrow-Ladnier Quintet* (HMV, DLP 1110). Among the first, and still the most original and effective records 'reviving' New Orleans jazz after its eclipse in the 1930s. 10″.

14. *Mezzrow-Bechet Quintet, Really the Blues* (Vogue LAE 12017). Modern music in the New Orleans idiom.

15. *Chicago Style Jazz* (Philips BBL 7061). Jazz as played by the young white players in the Middle West. 12″.

16. *The Bix Beiderbecke Story* 2 and 3 (Fontana TFE 17060, 17061). The greatest of the early white jazzmen, generally accompanied by inferior players. 7″.

C. *Middle Period Jazz*

17. *Duke Ellington and His Famous Orchestra* I (Vogue-Coral LRA 10027). 10″.

18. *In a Mellotone* (RCA, RD 27134). 12″.

19. *Historically Speaking* (Peralophone PMC 1116). Three stages (1927–31, 1940–2, 1956) in the evolution of the most significant jazz composer and the finest jazz orchestra. 12″.

20. *Spike Hughes and His Negro Orchestra* (Decca LK 4137). A black band of remarkable players in top form (Hawkins, Carter, Wells, Catlett, Berry, Allen) performs the works of a British composer-critic. 12″.

21. *Dickie Wells in Paris* (HMV, CLP 1054). A 1937 record

of a first-rate trombonist with excellent accompaniment, including Django Reinhardt, the gypsy jazz guitarist. 12″.

22. *Art Tatum* (Columbia 33CX 10115). The most impressive piano virtuoso of the middle period. 12″.

23. *Benny Goodman Quartet* (HMV, DLPC 6). Excellent small-group jazz of the thirties, with Lionel Hampton (vibes), Teddy Wilson (pno). 10″.

24. *Lester Young Memorial Album,* 1 and 2 (Fontana TFL 5064, 5065). A major soloist and innovator against the background of the finest swing band. 12″.

25. *The Real Fats Waller* (Camden CDN 131). The most charming of pianists in characteristic performances. 12″.

26. *Spirituals to Swing,* 1 (Top Rank 35/064). A cross-section of jazz in 1938–9, a golden year. 12″.

27. *Billie Holiday* (Commodore 30008). The finest recording by the most superb and tragic of jazz singers. 12″.

28. *Charlie Christian* (Philips BBL 7172). A revolutionary guitarist and a first-rate group play jazz on the borders between middle period and modern. 12″.

29. *Lionel Hampton, Jivin' the Vibes* (Camden CDN 129). The most extrovert and talented of rhythmicists in casual small-group jazz of golden quality. 12″.

30. *James Rushing, If This Ain't the Blues* (Vanguard PPL 11008). Jazz of the perennial kind, played and sung by musicians in the Kansas City tradition. 12″.

31. *Vic Dickenson Septet,* 1 (Vanguard PPT 12000). Easy, relaxed, jam-session music by players in the middle-period idiom. 10″.

D. *Modern Jazz*

32. *The Immortal Charlie Parker* (London, five records). 1944–48 works by the genius of modern jazz and other musical revolutionaries.

33. *Charlie Parker–Dizzie Gillespie Quintet* (Columbia 33C 9026). The leading modernists in 1952. 10″.

34. *Thelonious Monk, Brilliant Corners* (London LTZ-U

15097). A wayward and notable pianist-composer produces small-group ballads and blues in the modern idiom.

35. *SPJ Jazz* (Esquire 32-049). Bud Powell, the leading modern pianist, with Sonny Stitt, an excellent saxophonist. 12″.

36. *Miles Davis: Milestones* (Fontana TFL 5035). Characteristic and superb performances by the leading artist of the 1950s and excellent accompanists (Coltrane, Adderley, Red Garland, Philly Joe Jones Chambers). 12″.

37. *Sonny Rollins Plus Four* (Esquire 32-025). A first-class modern drummer, trumpet, and tenor. 12″.

38. *West Coast Jazz* (Vogue LAE 12038). Examples of the 'cool' white school in 1955 (Mulligan, Baker, Sims, Konitz, *et al*.). 12″.

39. *Modern Jazz Quartet: One Never Knows* (London LTZ-K 15140). Cool jazz chamber music, beautifully played and directed by the sophisticated musical intelligence of John Lewis. 12″.

40. *Ornette Coleman, Tomorrow Is the Question* (Vogue LAC 12228). The revolutionary of 1959–60. 12″.

One further record must be recommended. It is *What Is Jazz?*, an illustrated lecture by Leonard Bernstein, pianist, composer, and conductor of the New York Philharmonic Orchestra (Philips BBL 7149). It is the clearest and wittiest brief musical introduction to jazz for the layman published so far.

part one
History

o n e

Prehistory

Jazz emerged as a recognizable music around 1900. At least that date seems as good as any; a few years one way or the other hardly matter. Before that lies its pre-history, with which this chapter deals: the period when the various social and musical components of the future jazz emerged and fused. After that comes the double story of the evolution of jazz and of its unique and triumphant expansion.

THE COMPONENTS

There is not much disagreement among the experts about the African components of jazz. Most of the slaves imported into the Southern states of the U.S.A. were West Africans, the French (in whose Louisiana territory jazz first emerged) having a special preference for slaves from Dahomey. Little of the social organization of the West African blacks survived in the slave

3

society, except certain religious cults, notably the Haitian and Louisianan *vodun* ('voodoo') with its ritual music, and this, as Marshall Stearns points out, survived better under Catholic than under Protestant slave owners, for the Catholics did not greatly worry about their slaves' souls and tolerated a barely Christianized paganism among them. Hence Africanism survived in a purer form in the French zone of the U.S.A. In the Protestant zones, African cults went underground, or were transmuted into shouting revival music with far greater European admixtures. Among the musical Africanisms which the slaves brought with them were rhythmic complexity, certain non-classical musical scales—some of them, like the ordinary pentatonic, familiar in non-classical European music*—and certain musical patterns. The most characteristic of these are the 'call-and-response' patterns which dominate the blues, and indeed most of jazz, and are preserved in their most archaic form (as one might expect) in the music of primitive black gospel congregations, with its echo of 'shouting dances'. Certain types of functional songs were no doubt also brought over by the slaves: 'field-hollers' and work-songs in general, satirical songs and the like. Such characteristic African musical practices as vocal and rhythmical polyphony, and the ubiquitous improvisation also belong to the slaves' musical heritage. The only instruments they brought with them from Africa were rhythmic or rhythmic-melodic ones, and voices; but the characteristic timbres and inflexions of the African voice have coloured every jazz instrument since.

It may be well to point out, as clearly as possible, that none of these musical elements need be connected with race, in the biological sense of the word. There is no proof that the black sense of rhythm is 'inborn': it is learned like anything else. The herding together of blacks as slaves and their subsequent social segregation are quite enough to account for the great and persistent strength of the original Africanisms. Nor do these make jazz

---

* There is some argument about the characteristic 'blue' tonality of American black music, which does not seem at all general in pure West African music. It has been explained as an 'Africanization' of European scales.

4

into an 'African music'. One has only to listen to West African music of any sort to see the difference, and as a matter of fact, modern West Africans have been rather slower to take to jazz than South Africans or young Englishmen who have no traditional link with it. They prefer, if anything, the Caribbean forms of Afro-American music.

Reasonably pure African music survived in America, partly in ritual music, pagan and more or less christianized, and in such things as work-songs and hollers. In Louisiana it was to some extent officially encouraged as a safety-valve for the slaves, perhaps much as tribal dancing is encouraged by the South African authorities among their serfs. The officially sponsored voodoo drum-dances on Congo Square in New Orleans did not die out until the middle 1880s. (They seem to have been started after the Napoleonic Wars.) However, black music rapidly began to fuse with white components, and the evolution of jazz is the result of the fusion.

Jazz arose at the point where three different European cultural traditions intersected: the Spanish, the French, and the Anglo-Saxon. Each on its own had produced a characteristic Afro-European musical fusion: Latin-American and Caribbean music, Caribbean-French music (as in Martinique), and various forms of Afro–Anglo-Saxon music, of which the spiritual gospel song, and country blues are, for our purposes, the most important. (On the North American continent we can probably neglect the Indian component.) The Mississippi Delta, with its Protestant Anglo-Saxon hinterland, its arms opening on the Spanish-Caribbean, and its native French culture, combined all these as no other region did.

Afro-Spanish influence affected jazz only as a 'Spanish tinge', to quote the pioneer New Orleans musician Ferdinand 'Jelly-Roll' Morton: an admixture of certain rhythms such as the tangana, or the habañera which, as W. C. Handy already noted, roused a particularly vivid response among continental blacks.★

★ Handy wrote a 'tangana' passage into his famous *St Louis Blues,* where it may still be heard.

The deliberate adoption of Afro–Cuban rhythms in modern jazz, which included the importation of Afro–Cuban ritual drummers such as Chano Pozo, does not belong to the prehistory of jazz. It is fair to say that Afro–Latin-American music, which is probably the only modern musical idiom which can rival jazz in its capacity to conquer other cultures, went its own way, and only overlapped at the edges with jazz.

The French musical tradition is far more important, particularly as it was fully assimilated by the peculiar class of freed slaves which grew up in New Orleans: the *gens de couleur* or Creoles. They were normally former black mistresses of French settlers and their descendants. The Creoles in turn brought it among the lower-caste blacks in the 1880s, when the progress of segregation deprived them of their privileged position. The instrumentation of early New Orleans jazz, which is essentially that of the military band, the instrumental technique, particularly obvious in that French speciality, the woodwind, the repertoire of marches, quadrilles, waltzes, and the like—all are unmistakably French, as indeed are the dialect and the names of many of the early (Creole) New Orleans musicians: Bechet, Dominique, St Cyr, Bigard, Picou, Piron, and the rest. It has been pointed out, incidentally,[1] that Martinique, where similar conditions obtained, has developed a musical blending which is remarkably similar to that of New Orleans Creole music.★

Equally important, probably, is the French—or perhaps more exactly the Mediterranean or Catholic—social tradition of New Orleans: the profusion of public festivals, carnivals, fraternities (which merged easily with the strong African *penchant* for secret societies), and parades, in which New Orleans jazz grew up. The jazz band, after all, is the most characteristic product of jazz, and only an area with a very large and constant demand for bands was likely to produce it.

The Anglo-Saxon components are in many respects the most

★ But Mobile, Ala., though virtually a twin to New Orleans, did not develop such a blending. Why it did not is one of the many problems of jazz history which await solution.

6

fundamental. They consist of the English language, the religion and religious music of the colonists and, in a smaller way, their secular folk-songs and folk-music. After the emergence of jazz a fourth component became, alas, of growing importance: commercial popular music, which is itself a mixture of all sorts of elements, including, even before the triumph of the diluted jazz idiom, some coloured ones.

The English language provided the words of black speech and song, and in it black Americans have created, with the jazz idiom, the finest body of English folk-poetry since the Scots ballads: the work-song, gospel song, and secular blues. The secular music of the colonists—perhaps mostly the Scots-Irish poor whites of the South—provided a mass of songs many of which, taken up and modified by the black travelling minstrels, entered the jazz repertoire. *Careless Love,* the Kentucky mountain ballad, or *St James' Infirmary,* whose derivation from an early English original A. L. Lloyd has traced, are examples. After 1800 religion —more especially the 'great awakening' which swept the Southern and frontier poor, black and white, into a frenzied, egalitarian, democratic Protestant sectarianism—provided the musical framework. The harmonies of the blues, as distinct from semi-African melodies and rhythms, are those of Moody and Sankey's type of hymn. But perhaps more important than the juicy harmonium chords, which were thus later to be strangely adapted to jazz, was the fact that the 'great awakening' achieved the first systematic blending of European and African music in the U.S.A. outside New Orleans. Moreover, since this was not the imposition of organization and orthodoxy from above, but a largely spontaneous mass conversion from below, the two were equally blended, the African component not being subordinated to the European. More: it did not even subordinate European folk-music to European art-music. Culturally the 'great awakening' was the counterpart to the American War of Independence; or perhaps more precisely, to the rise of Jacksonian frontier democracy. It ensured that religious music, white and black, should remain a people's music, just as the defeat of Hamilton's by Jefferson's ideals ensured that American secular music

7

should remain a people's music. From our point of view the important thing about this was that even black music thus won its right to independent development.

For the crucial factor in the development of jazz, as of all American popular music, the factor which more than any other accounts for the unique American phenomenon of a vigorous and resistant folk-music in a rapidly expanding capitalist society, is that it was never swamped by the cultural standards of the upper classes. English musical working-class culture in the nineteenth century consisted of a patently dying rural and pre-industrial folk-music,* a musically extremely shoddy music-hall song, and the twin pillars of organized working-class music, the classic oratorio and the brass band. But however admirable the *Messiah* or the test pieces at the brass-band festivals, they are working-class conquests of orthodox culture, not independent folk-music. American popular and folk-music in the nineteenth century retained the initiative, and its persistent supremacy over Britain, even in the field of commercial pop music, derives largely from this.†

THE EVOLUTION OF BLACK FOLK MUSIC

Once the initial blending of the components had taken place, black folk-music began to evolve fairly rapidly. The details of this evolution before the 1890s are largely obscure, since it was not systematically observed.

The sung blues, the heart of jazz, may have emerged in its

* The efforts of devoted folk-music lovers like A. L. Lloyd, Ewan McColl, and Alan Lomax have not succeeded in seriously shaking the traditional view that English folk-song went into a permanent decline from the 1840s on.

† After all, even in the period when American political and economic power was not yet as great as ours, the traffic in song hits was mostly one way, as witness Stephen Foster's songs, *Nellie Dean, Tararaboomdeay, Waiting for the Robert E. Lee,* and the rest.

most primitive forms even before the Civil War, though almost certainly not yet in the standard twelve-bar form, and quite certainly as yet without using European or any other harmony. Possibly, as Wilder Hobson suggests, it—

> may originally have consisted merely in the singing, over a steady, percussive rhythm, of lines of variable length, the length being determined by what phrase the singer had in mind, with equally variable pauses (the accompanying rhythm continuing) determined by how long it took the singer to think up another phrase.

Possibly it emerged out of field-hollers or work-songs, or secularized pieces of gospel music. After black emancipation its evolution was greatly speeded up, if only because of the emergence of professional black beggar-minstrels, often blind, who roamed the road, some of whom have fortunately been recorded in our century. However it appears not to have acquired its name before the early twentieth century.[2] The important point about the blues is that it marks not merely a musical, but a social evolution: the emergence of a particular form of *individual* song commenting on everyday life. No doubt the banjo, an African instrument which could be adapted for melody, was used to accompany it. The blues turned into an instrumental form on the pianos of barrooms, barrel-houses, honky-tonks, and brothels of the South, most probably in those of navvies' and other labourers' camps, perhaps in the South-West. It has been traced back to the 1880s.

The first women who sang it publicly were almost certainly prostitutes like Mamie Desdoumes of New Orleans—'a hustlin' woman. A blues-singing poor gal. Used to play pretty passable piano around them dance-halls on Perdido Street', as Bunk Johnson recalls.[3] But that was probably not before 1900 or so.

The first *spirituals* go back much earlier—before 1800 certainly. The various stages of their evolution from the primitive ring-shout to modern forms need not detain us, and the evolution of the special branch of the concert spiritual need not concern us, for this most Europeanized form of American black music has evolved far away from jazz. Spirituals and gospel songs at all stages of evolution continue to be sung or chanted, and all of them have continued to provide an inexhaustible reservoir for jazz in general and for particular jazz pieces. Thus the blues *How Long, How Long* is said to derive from a spiritual, *St James' Infirmary* echoes *Keep Your Hand on the Plough, Hold On,* and the last chorus of the *St Louis Blues,* according to its composer, owes much to the eloquence of Brother Lazarus Gardner, presiding Elder of the African Methodist Episcopal Church of Florence, Ala. We need merely note that the separation of blacks into wholly black churches—mostly by secession from mixed churches in which they occupied a lower rank—began on a significant scale in 1816, when the African Methodist Episcopal Zion Church became an independent sect, but became a mass movement in the Civil War period. Perhaps from our point of view the crucial decade in this development, which naturally intensified the black character of spiritual music, was the segregation of the black Baptists, between 1865 and the 1880s, for this denomination and the twentieth-century (and therefore segregated) 'shouting' sects like the Pentecostal Holiness Churches, Churches of God in Christ, and the like, have made the most powerful single religio-musical contribution to jazz.

Meanwhile a second phase of the blending of African and European music took place. This time—and forever after—it was not religious song, but commercial popular entertainment, which stirred the mixture. Blacks naturally entered the profession of entertaining whites early, partly because they were good at it, partly because it was their best chance of leaving the worst forms of slavery or labouring, partly because slave-owners would naturally recruit their musicians, like their house servants, from among the slaves. A good many blacks thus learned white music, and no doubt in performing it imbued it with some of their traditions. In turn, white composers like Stephen Foster introduced some characteristic Southern black touches into white song, and in the North a flourishing industry of imitation black entertainers developed, black-faced and banjo-strumming. One may hope that Hitler is kept restless in his grave by the thought that it was pioneered by a German, Gottlieb Graupner who sang *The Gay Negro Boy* to banjo accompaniment in the opera *Oronooko* at the Federal Theatre, Boston, in 1799. Most of the minstrels, who became the rage from 1830 to the beginning of our century—they still live a shadowy existence on remote British seaside piers—were whites, but elements of black music penetrated through them into American popular music. In fact it was the most important channel through which black influences first passed into pop music. But it also served as a training ground for black musicians in European-style popular music, and later as an employer of early jazz and ragtime players. Minstrelsy was a channel which could be navigated both ways.

By the 1890s this mixture was about to reach boiling-point. In and around St Louis, where West-Midwest and South meet, the first identifiable style of jazz emerged: *ragtime*. This was almost exclusively a style of solo pianists, trained in European music and often with high musical ambitions: Scott Joplin, its most noted composer-player, composed a still-born ragtime opera in 1915, and James P. Johnson, the glory of Harlem's ragtime pianists, created equally unsuccessful symphonies, choral works, and concertos. The black tradition was dominant, because ragtime was syncopated rhythm; limited, because it was nothing else. By 1900 Tin Pan Alley had taken it over. Thus the perennial pattern of an original jazz style, almost immediately absorbed and vulgarized by pop music, was established from the start. Perhaps a little later the second independent jazz style appears: the *classical blues,* sung by professional women entertainers on the music-hall stage. The 'mother of the blues', 'Ma Rainey' (Gertrude Pridgett), a trouper's daughter, soon to be married to William Rainey of the 'Rabbit Foot Minstrels', seems to have begun singing the stage blues around 1902. The last decades of the century were also, as we have seen, the formative period in the development of the blues piano. Meanwhile there is a little evidence that in Southern cities like Atlanta, Mobile, and Charleston, the elements of an Afro-American band music were also emerging.[4] None of these were yet within range of Tin Pan Alley.

It is therefore obvious that jazz was not simply 'born in New Orleans'. In one way or another the mixture between European and African elements was crystallizing into musical shape in many parts of America. Nevertheless, New Orleans can defend its title as the cradle of jazz against all comers, for there, and there alone, did the jazz band emerge as a mass phenomenon. How massive is indicated by the startling fact that this city of, say, 89,000 black inhabitants—the size of Cambridge—in 1910 contained at least *thirty* bands whose reputation has survived. The priority of New Orleans cannot be disputed. No other jazz players who have since become more widely known were born as early as the 1870s, like Bunk Johnson (tpt), Alphonse Picou (clt), or Manuel Perez (tpt), not to mention the legendary Buddy Bolden, who led the first historically attested jazz band around 1900.

Why did jazz emerge at the end of the nineteenth century? Why did it emerge above all in New Orleans?

The second half of the nineteenth century was a revolutionary period in the popular arts everywhere, though this has been overlooked by those orthodox observers of the arts who are snobs. Thus in Britain the music hall separated from its parent, the pub, in the 1840s and 50s.[5] By general agreement it reached its peak in the 1880s and 90s, which also saw the startlingly rapid rise of the other phenomenon of working-class culture, professional football. In France the period after the Commune produced the working-class *chansonnier,* and after 1884 his culturally more ambitious bohemian derivation, the Montmartre cabaret: the great Aristide Bruant produced his famous collection of lumpen-proletarian art 'Dans La Rue' in 1889.[6] In Spain an evolution strikingly similar to that in America produced the *cante hondo,* the Andalusian *flamenco,* which, like the blues it so much resembles, appeared as a professionally transformed folk-song in the 'musical cafés' of Cadiz and Seville, Málaga and Cartagena, from the 1860s to 1900s.*

* Thanks to the respect of progressive Spanish poets and folklorists for their common people, its early history is much better known than that of the blues.

All these phenomena have two things in common: they arose out of the professional entertainment of the 'labouring poor', and they arose in big cities. They are, in fact, the product of urbanization; commercially, because it became worthwhile at a certain point to invest a fair amount of money in such entertainment, culturally, because the town poor (including the recently settled immigrants from the country or abroad) needed a special kind of entertainment. An analogous development for the middle classes occurred at the same period: the rise of musical comedy or operetta, but this had very little bearing on the evolution of the working-class arts. Now such working-class entertainment was of two types: either it might grow out of the professional entertainments which had always been provided in pre-industrial times, especially in permanent great metropolitan towns, as in the variety theatre, which combined, and still combines, aspects of the circus, the freak show, the sporting event, song-and-dance, and the rest. The New Orleans jazz band was clearly a development of such a metropolitan tradition of entertainment, in this case the public musical parade. (It is significant that it owes little to official dance music, as witness the virtual absence of stringed instruments.) Or else such entertainment might be a straight development of rural or urban amateur folk-song, as in the case of the flamenco and the blues. It is obvious that all country blacks knew the blues; equally so that a commercial demand for public performance of it could only arise when 'those blues, cotton-picking Negroes, what they called in the old days yard and field Negroes' became a box office force. This process is not recorded for the blues, but for the flamenco it is remembered by the old minstrel Fernando el de Triana, who claims to have been the first to carry the original miners' fandangos of Alosno into the wider world:

'Demofilo'—the great folklorist and father of poets, Antonio Machado Alvarez —published the first sketch of its evolution and collection of its verses in the 1880s. His pseudonym 'friend of the people' indicates the spirit in which Spanish intellectuals approach their subject.

All the world knows that for the past forty years pretty nearly all retail shops in Spain were run by sons of this famous mountain pueblo . . . There was no capital city in Spain without its group of Alosneros, who, in their leisure hours, kept only their own company. As they were always great lovers of song, they frequented the singing cafés, and since I was in those days the idol of the Alosneros, and travelled all over the place, singing professionally in the cafés, I always came across them in all parts of Spain.[7]

The emancipation of the slaves and the northern migration produced a black proletariat technically free to choose its own entertainment. A glance at the figures of black urban population in 1900—87,000 in Washington, D.C., 78,000 in New Orleans, 61,000 in New York and Philadelphia, 79,000 in Baltimore, 30–50,000 in several other cities *—shows that they already provided a modest public. But then, the entrepreneurs who catered for them were also modest like those who ran the tent shows and the Savannah joints in which, by 1903, 'a low form of vaudeville is carried on'.[8] However, by 1910–14 the first ambitious theatres for an exclusively black audience were being built —e.g. the New Palace in New York, the Booker T. Washington in St Louis, the Pekin and the State in Chicago.[9] What is equally to the point, the striking increase in the demand for entertainment among the white poor in the rapidly growing cities accelerated the development of music among black entertainers. But among these cities New Orleans occupied a special position as the unique metropolis of the South. With 216,000 inhabitants in 1880—a population almost doubled since 1850— it is very much larger than its rivals in the Deep South.

This rapidly swelling metropolis, export port, and capital of the plantation country of the Mississippi Delta has odd parallels with the very similarly placed port cities in which the Andalusian flamenco began its career: Seville and Cadiz. Two things helped to precipitate jazz as we know it there: the breakdown of the old

* Chicago, St Louis, Memphis, Atlanta.

traditional slave culture and the fall of the free 'creoles of colour'. The 1880s are the crucial period for both: the Congo Square dances were abandoned and systematic racial discrimination came. The end of formalized African entertainment left the way free for a much less inhibited mixture of European and African idioms in the street parades and other brass band music which flourished like poppies in a cornfield after the Civil War.

The fall of the Creoles brought European musical know-how into the new popular idiom, but above all, it secured the musical supremacy of the low-caste, black, 'uptown', blues blacks. There are plenty of Creoles in New Orleans jazz, but (except perhaps for the clarinets) they had to learn to play dirty and improvise like the uptown boys. As the disgusted old Creole Paul Dominguez told Alan Lomax, 'A fiddler is *not* a violinist, but a violinist can be a fiddler. If I wanted to make a living I had to be rowdy like the other group. I had to jazz it or rag it or any other damn thing. . . . Bolden did that.'[10] Bolden and Bunk Johnson and Johnny Dodds and Louis Armstrong and Mutt Carey and Jim Robinson and other descendants of slaves from the Anglo-Saxon hot-gospelling Protestant upcountry.

Out of this mixture New Orleans jazz—perhaps still much like ragtime European marches—appeared, like a black Venus out of the foam. And we may still hear it, in its primitive form, in the famous funeral marches reconstructed by Jelly-Roll Morton and Louis Armstrong for the gramophone, and in the classic description of old Bunk Johnson:

On the way to the cemetery with an Odd Fellow or a Mason —they always buried with music, you see—we would always use slow, slow numbers, such as *Nearer My God to Thee, Flee as a Bird to the Mountains, Come Thee Disconsolate.* We would use most any 4/4, played very slow. They walked very slow behind the body.

After we would get to the cemetery, and after the particular person were put away, the band would come on to the front, out of the graveyard. Then the lodge would come out . . . and they called roll, fall in line, and then we'd march away from the cemetery by the snare-drum only, until we got about a block or two blocks away from the cemetery. Then we'd go right on into ragtime—what people call today swing—ragtime. We would play *Didn't He Ramble, When the Saints Go Marching In,* that good old piece *Ain't Gonna Study War No More,* and several others we would have, and we'd play them just for that effect.[11]

And meanwhile, in the honky-tonks, there were the hustlin' girls and 'those blues players that didn't know nothing but the blues', like the *Game Kid,* who played them all night long in the good-time houses, for a couple of dollars' worth of drinks:

> *I could sit right here and think a thousand miles away*
> *Yes, I could sit right here and think a thousand miles away.*
> *Got the blues so bad, I cannot remember the day.*

t w o

Expansion

*J*azz was born. But the unique thing about it is not its existence
—there have been plenty of specialized local musical idioms—
but its extraordinary expansion, which has practically no cultural
parallel for speed and scope except the early expansion of Mohammedanism. This is what we must therefore consider next. It
falls, broadly, into phases: *c.* 1900–17 when jazz became the
musical idiom of black popular music all over America while
some of its gimmicks (e.g. syncopation and ragtime) became a
permanent component of Tin Pan Alley; 1917–29 when 'strict'
jazz expanded very little, but evolved quite rapidly, and when a
highly diluted infusion of jazz became the dominant idiom of
Western urban dance music and pop songs; 1929–41 when
'strict' jazz began its conquest of European minority audiences
and *avant-garde* players, and a much less diluted form of jazz
('swing') permanently entered pop music. The real international
triumph of jazz, the penetration of yet 'purer' jazz idioms into
pop music—New Orleans jazz, *avant-garde* modern jazz, and the
country and gospel blues—have come since 1941.

The traditional picture of the diffusion of jazz is as simple as it is mythical: it stayed in New Orleans until the American Navy closed down the red light quarter in 1917, after which the musicians, some already with experience on the river-boats, migrated up the Mississippi to Chicago, and thence all over America, notably to New York. This picture not only lacks much relation to the facts, but also makes it totally impossible to understand how jazz developed as it actually did. For it implies that other musicians learned their jazz relatively late, and that they learned it in terms of New Orleans music. But this is demonstrably not so. Though New Orleans musicians were highly appreciated and very influential, New Orleans jazz as a *style* had virtually no lineal descendants, except among a group of young white jazz fans from the Middle West who anticipated later fashions among the jazz public. Plenty of jazz who played in black bands by the early 1920s, but it was not in New Orleans style jazz, except when played by groups actually hailing from that city. Plenty of black bands were started in that period, but they contained surprisingly few players from the Delta, or even the Mississippi river-line, and very few indeed from Chicago. In fact, jazz emerged after the First World War as a highly varied music, played by musicians all over the country, the New Orleans style being only one among many, though still the most fully formed. Purists may of course argue that what the rest played was 'not real jazz', but this type of argument need not detain us.

The truth is that New Orleans players began to tour the hinterland and the rest of the country almost immediately, even getting as far as Europe, though nobody took much notice of them there before 1919. It would be tedious to list such of their movements as have been traced. We need only recall that in 1907 Jelly-Roll Morton reports how he went to Chicago, then to Houston, Texas, then to California, then back to New Orleans via Texas and Oklahoma, getting a new girl in each place and winning a lot of money at pool. Touring was part of the economy of entertainers anyway, and New Orleans, a major reservoir of musicians even before the rise of jazz, must have been frequently tapped. W. C. Handy recalls how his road company (Mahara's Minstrels) took over two New Orleans clarinetists between 1900 and 1903, when black players took over that instrument, hitherto to preserve of whites: obviously bandmasters would think of New Orleans.[1] The Delta musicians themselves soon discovered the possibilities of engagements further afield.

No doubt they stimulated musicians wherever they went; nothing advances jazz more than a mixing of players. No doubt they influenced ambitious boys, who in turn taught others within the radius of their music. But, as we have seen, all black America was ready to burst out into one form or another of the jazz idiom anyway. Nor was the New Orleans influence the only one. The ragtime pianists, the blues singers in their tent shows, were already on the scene. In the East, for instance, a local piano style, based on ragtime and Appalachian gospel shouts, was almost contemporary with the New Orleans players. Walter Gould ('One Leg Shadow') born in Philadelphia in 1875, piano player and obscure salesman of lottery tickets, or Eubie Blake (born 1883) claim to recall men who 'ragged' quadrilles and schottisches even before their birth: Old Man Sam Moore, 'No Legs' Casey, Bud Minor, 'Old Man Metronome' French.[2] New Orleans was no pioneer to these North-Easterners, who were in any case out of its normal line of influence. How little the simple 'New Orleans' myth reflects reality may be illustrated by the example of Paul Howard, born 1895 in Steubenville, Ohio, of free black ancestry, whose musical career started in church. Gospel music stood at one of his sides, military music at the other; he acquired a saxophone from an ex-soldier before 1910, becoming the first black saxophonist in Los Angeles, where he migrated in 1911. There, it is true, he discovered New Orleans jazz with Keppard's New Orleans orchestra which played a two-week vaudeville season in 1915, and had some difficulty as a trained 'reading' musician in adapting himself to collective improvisation. But how far from New Orleans jazz were contemporary local bands like the Black-and-Tan Band which he joined, a cake-walking, ragtime brass band, originally from Texas, which reshuffled itself into a 'jazz band' as soon as the word had a saleable value in 1918?[3] At most New Orleans accelerated whatever tendencies towards jazz existed locally.

By 1920, therefore, jazz was already a national idiom with

different dialects. That is why the subsequent movements of jazz musicians reflect not only the traditional touring routes of vaudeville artists and minstrel shows, but, with some precision, the routes of migration of ordinary blacks. For this mass migration, rather than the temporary purity drive in New Orleans, pushed even the New Orleans musicians northwards. (The best friends of the city will not claim that it has ever lacked a considerable and publicly tolerated night life for more than a few months on end.) From about 1916 the blacks who had hitherto been remarkably immobile flooded north in extraordinary numbers. The combined black population of New York, Chicago, Philadelphia, and Detroit almost doubled between 1910 and 1920, and more than doubled between 1920 and 1930. In absolute figures, it rose from 226,000 in 1910 to 902,000 in 1930. In 1910 there had been only three cities with black populations of 90,000 or more; in 1920 there were six, in 1930 eleven including three with black populations of over 200,000. The black population of Chicago almost trebled, that of Harlem almost doubled between 1910 and 1920, and both more than doubled again in the next ten years. To take a single year, in 1922–3 nearly half a million blacks migrated from the Southern states.[4]

Evidently jazz spread with the migrants. Just as ordinary blacks from Florida, Alabama, Georgia, etc., were likely to move along Eastern routes towards Washington, Baltimore, Philadelphia, and New York, so did the musicians from these areas: Duke Ellington's orchestra (1926) contained no New Orleans man and only one player from St Louis, but it did contain men from Massachusetts, New York, New Jersey, Virginia, South Carolina, Washington D.C., and Indiana. This was natural, for it was a Washington–New York band.[5] Just as migrants from the Delta were likely to move up-river, so did the New Orleans and Memphis musicians. The black quarters of St Louis were likely to attract migrants (and musicians) from the middle Mississippi valley, those of Kansas City from the Oklahoma–Texas hinterland. There is, in fact, no great mystery about the geographical diffusion of jazz musicians.

There is, however, a mystery about the notable musical

centres which were established as the result of this mass migration. For some of the major black ghettoes proved far more receptive to jazz than others, or rather, produced more musicians and independent musical activity than others. Obviously New York and Chicago led the field in the North, though Chicago, oddly enough, produced surprisingly few black orchestral jazz players of standing for a city so legendary for its jazz.* The much smaller border metropolis of Louisville, Kentucky, compares favourably with it.† Perhaps the youth of Chicago's black belt, or the competition of the famous out-of-town players who all passed through the city, accounts for this scarcity. Then there is the odd fact that the more industrial the city to which blacks migrated the less fertile apparently its jazz. Detroit, Cleveland, and for that matter Chicago itself, are instances. Few black ghettoes grew more rapidly than Detroit, which had under 6,000 coloured inhabitants in 1910 and 120,000 in 1930. Few were more purely industrial. Yet thought the city contained a great deal of jazz, being the headquarters of both leading white and black bands (McKinney's Cotton-Pickers and Jean Goldkette's Orchestra), it is extremely hard to think of a prominent jazz player of the premodern period who actually hails from there. In the modern period, however, Detroit became one of the most important breeding-grounds of young musicians. Perhaps the relatively well-paid industrial jobs took away boys who would otherwise have been driven into entertainment. On the other hand, there is Pittsburgh, a typically industrial city, which has been extraordinarily fertile in producing original jazz musicians.‡

* Out of the seventy-six black musicians listed as 'giants of jazz' in Feather's *Encyclopedia* only three were born or raised in Chicago (one of them a performer on a minor instrument, the violin), as compared to nine in New York.

† Among musical sons of Louisville the best-known are J. Harrison (trombone), Al Casey (guitar), Lionel Hampton (rhythm)—who was, however, educated in Chicago—and Meade Lux Lewis (piano.)

‡ To mention only some born before 1914, when the Pittsburgh ghetto must have been very small—it is still not among the ten largest black communities—Earl Hines (piano), Mary Lou Williams (piano and arranger), Roy Eldridge (trumpet), Billy Eckstine (singer), Kenny Clark (drums). Younger

But then, Pittsburgh seems always to have been an exceptionally thriving centre of night-life and entertainment for the Pennsylvania industrial belt and—perhaps because of local segregation —of black consciousness.

It is perhaps less surprising that cities on the fringe of the South should have been good nurseries for jazz, though a little puzzling why some of the older centres of the Deep South— Atlanta, Charleston—have not been strikingly productive; or for that matter why, in the North, Philadelphia, which ran Harlem close in numbers until 1920, has made infinitely feebler contributions to jazz. But why is it that among the Southern border cities—Washington D.C. and Baltimore, St Louis and Louisville, Oklahoma City and Dallas—Kansas City, Mo., with barely more than 30,000 black inhabitants in 1920 and not yet 100,000 in 1940, should have become so abnormally important in the evolution of jazz? Because it was a great centre of communication? Perhaps. As Iain Lang has said, the list of Kansas City's railroads is more than a catalogue, it is almost an incantation: [6]

> Chicago Great Western, Union Pacific, Missouri Pacific, Frisco System, Chicago Burlington and Quincy, Atchison Topeka and Santa Fe, Chicago Milwaukee and Saint Paul, Chicago and Alton, Wabash, Kansas City Southern, Chicago Rock Island and Pacific, Missouri Kansas and Texas, Leavenworth Kansas and Western, Kansas City Mexico and Orient, St Louis Kansas City and Colorado, Quincy Omaha and Kansas City, St Joseph and Grand Island.

Because it never suffered from the Depression, as some say? Perhaps. Certainly, being run by the most corrupt political machine in the U.S.A., it remained as wide open as the Kansas cattle towns in the great days of the West, and a much bigger employer of musicians than most cities. Actually, its jazz history

---

Pittsburghians include Billy Strayhorn (arranger), Erroll Garner (piano), Ray Brown (bass).

goes back to the 1890s, when it was one of the pioneer centres of ragtime.

The truth is that, though we may guess at the answers to some of these questions, we do not know. A great deal more will have to be discovered about the sociology of black immigrant communities, a great deal more information will have to be collated about their entertainments, a good deal more careful biographical analysis of players and their careers will have to be done, before such fascinating historical puzzles can be solved. In the meantime we can note them only in passing.

This huge increase in the black public produced the phenomenon which has given us our basic documentation of jazz: the 'race record'.[7] From 1920 on, gramophone companies found it worth while to issue records purely for the black market, and from 1923 several companies systematically built up such 'race-catalogues'. The most famous of them is that of the OKeh company (1923–35) which included, among much rare folk-material, most of Louis Armstrong's early small-group work.* Thanks to the extraordinary growth of this market between 1923 and 1927 almost every artist who had ever been heard by anyone connected with show business had a chance of at least one or two recording sessions. Some of those recorded on race series—especially the most primitive singers and pianists—remain to this day little more than names, perpetuated on two or three historically invaluable discs: Bessie Tucker, Montana Taylor, 'Speckled Red', Romeo Nelson, Dobby Bragg, Henry Brown. Black orchestral jazz did not long remain confined to the 'race series', but such series have continued (re-baptized 'rhythm and blues' in deference to black susceptibilities) to this day. The recent rock-and-roll vogue rests almost entirely on the pillaging of such catalogues by Tin Pan Alley.

Authentic undiluted jazz made no great impact on the general

* The man chiefly responsible for this catalogue in the early stages was Clarence Williams (born 1893), a coloured composer, leader, and pianist, second only to W. C. Handy as a popularizer of jazz, who had been in music publishing since 1913.

white public, though the northern tour and the records of the (white) Original Dixieland Jass Band in 1917 caused a temporary sensation, and conveniently serve to mark the beginning of the 'jazz age'. Both the date and the label are misleading, for the 'jazz age' had begun—though not under that precise trade-mark—some years earlier and it was not so much an age of jazz as of the mass conversion of ordinary pop and dance music to some idea vaguely involving syncopation, rhythm, instrumental novelty effects such as barnyard imitations, and the like. This new idiom was undoubtedly influenced by jazz, but it is safe to say that ninety-seven per cent of what the average white North American and European heard under that label between 1917 and 1935 had as little to do with jazz as the costume of drum-majorettes has with battledress.

The triumph of this hybrid jazz is so important a phenomenon that we must look at it more closely. In the first instance it was almost certainly due to the triumph of ballroom dancing and especially—among the younger twentieth-century generation—of a fairly fast type of dance. The typical nineteenth-century pop music number, on which the fortunes of Tin Pan Alley then rested, was designed for singing solo or in chorus, and indeed was rather hard to dance to, as may be tested by trying to do so to Stephen Foster or the classical pub and barber-shop repertoire, say *Nellie Dean*. But from about 1910 on, publishers seem to have observed that no song was likely to become a smash-hit unless it was also danceable. Within a decade practically all songs would automatically be supplied with a dance orchestration in strict time, however little suited to them. (The pop term 'ballad' for any song which cannot be otherwise classified echoes the sound of these Victorian warblings.)[8] Ragtime and jazz rhythms, which can be used to adapt practically any tune for dancing, were naturally invaluable. The history of ordinary popular dancing is, as usual, rather obscure and we do not know exactly how and why the vogue for ballroom dancing grew, though we can trace it in its more commercial and publicized aspects: the first 'dance marathon' put on by Sid Graumann (of Graumann's Chinese Theatre in Hollywood) in 1910, the vogue for *'thé dansants'* on the eve of the First World War, which made the fortunes of the famous dancing team of Irene and Vernon Castle, the small American neighbourhood dance halls grossing 2,500 dollars a week on a dime admission, the penny dances in parks organized by the Cincinnati city fathers in 1914, and the rest.[9] (British dance halls came later: the Hammersmith Palais in 1919, characteristically with the Original Dixieland Band as resident orchestra.) Fortunately it is the fact of the dancing vogue rather than its explanation which concerns us here. I daresay it was closely connected with the loosening of Victorian conventions of social behaviour, and especially with the emancipation of women.

At all events, the dancing fashion was also a search for newer, faster, and less conventional dance rhythms and dance sounds which edged aside even the very resistant dances of the late nineteenth century—above all the waltz—with more exciting rhythmical Africanisms, North or South American.

From 1900 the invention of new rhythmic dances became a minor industry. The crop of 1910–15, Turkey Trot, Bunny Hug, etc., produced the most lasting formula, the Foxtrot. It is safe to say that without the foxtrot and its cousins (the Shimmy, originally a Barbary Coast indecency, was particularly popular in Europe in the 1920s) the triumph of hybrid jazz in pop music would have been unthinkable, just as the advance of Latin-American rhythms rested firmly on the adoption of the tango, also on the eve of the First World War. Subsequent innovations —the Black Bottom, Charleston, Lindy Hop, Big Apple, Truckin' and the rest—mostly borrowed from those abundant sources of new dances the Western and Mid-Western cabarets, and later the big Harlem dance halls—have been mainly temporary crazes.

The dancing vogue automatically brought an infiltration of Afro-American idioms into pop music: even the Castles had a black band, and a craze for drumming and drum solos, such as has periodically seized the more moronic part of the public, was already running its course in 1914–16. From 1912 or so the blues entered popular music. W. C. Handy published some of his finest pieces between then and 1916 *(Memphis Blues, St Louis Blues, Yellow Dog Blues, Beale Street Blues)*, and 1916 saw a battle between pop music publishers over the priority of their respective blues.★ From about the same time the term 'jazz' (or jass, jaz) came to be used as a generic label for the new dance music, since few knew that it had hitherto been an African slang word for sexual intercourse.[10] It was adopted rapidly and almost universally, no doubt because by 1916–17 the need for such a label was obvious. There was not only the Original Dixieland Jass Band, which was a jazz band, but a host of competing 'inventors of the jazz dance', and of Tin Pan Alley numbers of the genus 'everybody's doing the X now': *Cleopatra Had a Jazz Band, Everybody's Crazy 'bout That Doggone Blues, Mr Jazz Himself,* by Irving Berlin, who was quicker off the mark with jazz than with ragtime; all from 1917. Former minstrel and quasi-military bands like Wilbur Sweatman's, Isham Jones's, and Paul Whiteman's drove their bandwagons in the new style, and those who could not, added a saxophone to their string trios and called themselves jazz bands anyway. Towards the end of 1917 'jazz bands' were already being formed in Britain.[11]

This mixture was not without its repercussions on authentic jazz. It was from the pop bands that the saxophone came. New Orleans players hardly knew or used it. 'Straight' minstrel bands had borrowed it from the military long since, as when Mahara's Minstrels 'picked up a quartet of saxophones in Chicago' who 'contributed wonderfully to the religioso' when W. C. Handy played *The Holy City* as a cornet solo.[12] This mawkishness, which became the trade-mark of 'sweet' pop music in the 1920s, was about their limit then. Saxes entered jazz because they were popular with the audiences: King Oliver was prevailed upon to try a couple in the early 1920s because another band was attracting the customers with these instruments.[13] Again, the pop song of the immediate post-war period provided a high proportion of the standards for the jazz repertoire of the twenties, especially

★ This contest is immortal because of the expert testimony of one Professor White, a blues writer called in by the court to explain what it was. 'Blues are blues', explained the professor. 'That's what blues are. See?'

among white bands, and stimulated the publication of a good many straight jazz and blues numbers. The characteristic repertoire of 'Dixieland' jazz was to consist largely of such numbers: *Indiana* (1917), *After You've Gone, Ja-da* (1918), *Someday Sweetheart, The World Is Waiting for the Sunrise, I've Found a New Baby, I Wish I Could Shimmy Like My Sister Kate, Royal Garden Blues, Ain't Gonna Give Nobody None of My Jelly Roll* (1919), *Margie, Avalon, Japanese Sandman, Ida* (1920).[14]

The interesting thing about this vogue is that from the beginning it was seen not simply as just another, and perhaps abnormally deplorable, fashion in pop music, but as a symbol, a movement—at any rate something important. Moralists, of course, declared war on it immediately, as usual with a splendid inability to make up their minds whether they objected to it because of its association with low life or the lower classes. The New Orleans *Times-Picayune*'s outburst is well known (20 June 1918):

Why is the jass music and, therefore, the jass band? As well ask why is the dime novel or the grease-dripping doughnut. All are manifestations of a low streak in man's tastes that has not yet come out in civilization's wash. Indeed, one might go further and say that jass music is the indecent story syncopated and counterpointed. Like the improper anecdote, also, in its youth, it was listened to blushing behind closed doors and drawn curtains, but, like all vice, it grew bolder until it dared decent surroundings and there was tolerated because of its oddity . . . It gives a sensual delight more intense than the Viennese waltz or the refined sentiment and respectful emotion of an eighteenth-century minuet. In the matter of jass, New Orleans is particularly interested, since it has been widely suggested that this particular form of musical vice had its birth in this city. . . . We do not recognize the honour of parenthood, but with such a story in circulation, it behoves us to be the last to accept the atrocity in polite society?

'Unspeakable jazz must go!' cried the *Ladies' Home Journal* in 1921. Rabbi Stephen T. Wise, with the natural talent of clergymen for this type of statement, held that 'when America regains

27

its soul, jazz will go—not before—that is to say it will be relegated to the dark and scarlet haunts whence it came and whither, unwept, it will return after America's soul is reborn'.[15] The revulsion of conservative musical classicists was equally astonishing. Readers may find juicy examples in the files of the *Musical Times*.

On the other hand, the cultural *avant-garde* hailed it with equal enthusiasm and almost equal ignorance as the music of the machine age, the music of the future, the revitalizing force of the primitive jungle and so on, normally on the strength of hearing bands like Mr Jack Hylton's, which the author remembers as the accepted last word in jazz in Central European secondary schools, 1928–33. A characteristic, if late, example of this woolly rhapsodizing may be found in an article on 'The Heart of Jazz', by a certain J.-H. Levesque (*Le Jazz Hot,* No. 23, 1938), which quotes Bergson, Stravinsky, Valéry, Minkowski, Blaise Cendrars, Roupnel, Thomas Aquinas, Apollinaire, and Lecomte de Nouy, and argues that jazz is the intensity of life as shown in other fields 'where life is manifested powerfully and freely'. Napoleon, Georges Carpentier, Theodore Roosevelt, Chaplin and cartoon films, Cochet the tennis player, Henry Ford, Rimbaud, Cendrars, Casanova, Picabia, Marcel Duchamp, Nuvolari and Malcolm Campbell the racing drivers are given as examples. There is, oddly, no reference to Cocteau, Picasso, or Freud. As a matter of fact, *avant-garde* musicians who actually heard some authentic jazz, such as Ernest Ansermet and Darius Milhaud, commented on it with considerable acumen and open-mindedness, though some of them were reluctant to tear themselves away from the beauties of 'this music which is as mechanized and as precise as a machine' (Darius Milhaud)[16] to consider unmechanized jazz, and though their borrowings from it were superficial.

Within hybrid jazz itself there were also strivings and ambitions rarely found among the modest craftsmen of Tin Pan Alley. In a vague sense, not wholly determined by the advertising value of classiness, they felt it to be 'serious' in a way in which the idiom of, say, *Ireland Must Be Heaven, for My Mother*

Came from There, or *There's a Broken Heart for Every Light on Broadway* was not. Paul Whiteman's famous Aeolian Hall concert of 1924, designed to establish the academic credentials of 'symphonic jazz', may deserve all the musical sneers of the really serious cats—but they rarely object to it because it tried to bring jazz to the concert platform. (Incidentally, Gershwin's *Rhapsody in Blue,* which had its first performance then, is a very reputable piece of jazz-influenced light music.) Jazz has had a hankering for recognition as something more than dance music ever since it emerged from the Deep South, and with reason.

Hybrid jazz spread with uncanny rapidity round the world, aided by the gramophone, the upper-class fashion for Anglo-Saxonisms and Americanisms (e.g. 'le five-o'clock', the tea-dance), and the prestige and horrible fascination of the U.S.A. in the heyday of Henry Ford, Wall Street, Lindbergh, and Prohibition. At the tailend of the twenties, however, we observe the tiny beginnings of an expansion of the thoroughbred jazz among small obscure and untypical communities in Europe, and to a much lesser extent, in America.* The imported gramophone records of white New York musicians, and later of the great black players, were almost entirely responsible—in Europe at least—for the creation of these small groups of devotees.

It is fortunate that by the time the Depression swept across the U.S.A. a few hundreds—they could hardly yet be counted in thousands—of European jazz fans were ready. No doubt jazz historians have exaggerated the catastrophic effect of the slump on their music, though it is evident that bad times must decimate any industry which depends on the spending of spare money, except in so far as it relies on the rich who are never short of cash. Jazz did not die in America between 1929 and the start of the 'swing' craze in 1935. The new big black jazz bands, playing for dances, survived, though sometimes a little shakily. They were capable of competing with the cinema. Ellington, Lunceford, McKinney's Cotton Pickers, Benny Moten, Earl Hines, Fletcher Henderson, Cab Calloway, Luis Russell, Andy Kirk,

---

* See Chapter 10.

and others saw the Depression through, aided by the flourishing big clubs of gangster (and therefore 'wide-open') cities like Chicago and K.C., and by the major Harlem ballrooms. Indeed, for the big bands these were the formative years of their style. But innumerable marginal musicians and singers, men of traditional or inadaptable styles who had been carried by the modest prosperity of the black market, innumerable men who had preferred the casual high-stepping life of small combos in small clubs and gigs, found themselves on the streets.[17] And for the record industry the slump was an unbelievable catastrophe: between 1927 and 1934 its sales dropped by 94 per cent.

The small European market could at least ensure that some records were made of certain kinds of jazz for which the American demand had virtually folded up. The most notable examples are those made by the great jazz Maecenas, John Hammond Jr, for the English Gramophone Company from 1933 on. Europe could also provide temporary jobs for American musicians, though political and union action cut down the scope for foreign touring in the 1930s.* Armstrong toured here—1932 and 1933–5, Fats Waller spent much of the thirties on this side of the Atlantic, Benny Carter was in Europe from 1935 to 1938, Coleman Hawkins from 1934 to 1939, Sidney Bechet toured frequently from 1928 to 1938, while several musicians expatriated themselves for long periods—the trumpeter Bill Coleman in Paris from 1933, the pianist Teddy Weatherford in China (joined in temporary exile by Buck Clayton 1934–6), the clarinetist Rudy Jackson in India and Ceylon. Their presence naturally helped to increase the number of European jazz-lovers.

European combinations trying to play 'authentic', or 'hot' jazz also began in the late 1920s. Fred Elizalde's group in 1927 is the British pioneer. These were mostly small groups playing in odd nightclubs, or pick-up bands for recordings into which the al-

---

* Fascism in Germany and Italy, disputes between the British and American musicians' unions (1935–56), and the increasing cultural isolation of the U.S.S.R., where American jazz bands had toured in the 1920s, closed large areas of Europe to them. However, in Britain solo acts could still perform.

ready existing fifth column of jazz fans sometimes managed to talk the gramophone executives. Why, after all, should they not risk the £45 which covered all the salaries and expenses of Spike Hughes' pioneer British for a session?[18] From the early thirties on, the 'hot' public was large enough to found clubs and therefore modest audiences. The first Norwegian jazz club dates back to 1928, a now highly prosperous music publisher found it worthwhile to organize 'hot record recitals' in London in 1930, and by 1935 Denmark, which claimed to be 'the world's hottest country', had jazz lectures in its schools and three jazz concerts a year organized by the leading serious newspaper.[19] The most ambitious musical enterprise of these sects, and also the most original enterprise of European jazz up to the present, was the famous Quintet of the Hot Club of France (1934–9) whose star was the remarkable gypsy guitarist Django Reinhardt (1910–53). A number of mixed European-American recording sessions were also organized mainly in Holland and France, which became increasingly the European headquarters of jazz, thanks to the loudly and well-blown intellectual trumpets of its jazz writers and collectors.

If the Depression had almost exiled authentic jazz from America, that country was triumphantly reconquered in the middle 1930s. In 1935–40 pop music once again capitulated to jazz (now called 'swing'), as it had done in 1914–20. Moreover, the jazz it capitulated to was a great deal more like the real thing than it had been in the days when anxious band leaders put some saxes behind their stands, some syncopation in their arrangements, and played the *Blue Danube* as the *Blue Danube Blues*. In fact pop music adopted, almost *in toto,* the instrumental techniques and arrangements elaborated by the black players, and especially the black big bands, in the 1920s. This was all the easier, since these innovations in authentic jazz had themselves been the result of pop music influence, not to say the natural desire of black entertainers to jump on the white pop musicians' gravy train. At all events, the difference in *genre* between Benny Goodman's 'hot' band, which became the queen of the musical battlefield, and the ordinary 'sweet' band—itself infiltrated by hybrid jazz—was a

31

great deal smaller in 1935 than such differences had been in 1917, when patrons at Reisenwebers in New York had actually to be instructed that the Original Dixieland Jass Band's sound was intended for dancing.

Why 'swing' conquered in the middle 1930s is therefore not quite so difficult a question as why jazz conquered pop music in 1914–20. It could in any case not have done so much earlier: the instrumental and orchestral innovations, and indeed the very rhythmical 'swing' from which the vogue took its name, were hardly elaborated before the second half of the twenties, and the Depression intervened after that. 'Swing' made its appeal by a combination of increasingly insistent rhythm and considerable noise. A series of brazen walls of sound advancing inexorably on the listener like Pacific breakers, a driving drum-pulse occasionally breaking out into volleys of virtuoso sharpshooting: such was its basic formula. Its appeal was almost exclusively to adolescents. The modern phase of pop music, in which the crucial section of the public stretches from the age of twenty-one backwards as far as pocket-money will allow, begins with the middle 1930s. At any rate youth—especially white college youth—made the fashion. Glen Gray Knoblaugh's Casa Loma Orchestra (anticipating the later Glenn Miller Band), which catered largely to college audiences in the early thirties, is said to have been the first white band with a deliberate jazz policy, and the pioneer of 'swing'. It was probably not quite the first. Benny Goodman's Band (formed in 1934), sold to business by an ex-college-boy executive, had little success until it hit the teenage and college public in California in the middle of 1935. The 'swing' public was a dancing public, but with a difference, for the athletic, acrobatic dances it evolved ('jiving', 'jitterbugging') were simple releases of physical energy by rhythm rather than excuses for anticipating sexual caresses. It is extremely difficult to be very sexual when one is throwing one's limbs about and whirling partners at arms' length, especially in the aisles of concert halls and theatres. (This also anticipated later developments.) Indeed, 'swing' was no longer primarily a dancing music, but quite as much a music for 'active listening'—tapping the feet, agitating the torso, but listening. The crowed of fans surrounding the bandstand, which have become characteristic of jazz occasions since, began in this period. This tendency to listen rather than to dance was not confined to 'swing': the leading 'sweet' band, Guy Lombardo's Royal Canadians, claimed to owe its success largely to the discovery that its vast radio public rarely bothered to dance to it.[20] Perhaps the triumph of broadcasting accounts for this rediscovery of pop music as something which can be passively taken in. Consequently the characteristic product of the 'swing era' was the touring big band giving concert or variety performances as well as playing for dances: a formula which has lasted. However, since bands of this type and standard were virtually confined to the U.S.A., 'swing' made its foreign conquests—perhaps with the partial exception of Britain—mainly by means of the gramophone record. Its public abroad was therefore more restricted than that for the hybrid jazz of the 1920s and seems to have been largely a rather expanded version of the public for authentic jazz.

Meanwhile developments were taking place which were to make authentic jazz itself into an international mass movement, and eventually to commercialize it. These were the so-called 'Revival' movements, which produced their first important results in 1938–9 and their massive consequences, almost simultaneously in America and Europe, in the last years of the war and the first post-war years. They were quite unique phenomena, for they arose neither out of the internal logic of jazz development—i.e. the tendencies evolved by the players themselves— nor out of the logic of commercialism. They were almost wholly the products of intellectual doctrinaires who aimed, in the first place, at the rediscovery of the forgotten and 'pure' sources of jazz and the folk-music behind it. In America Roosevelt's New Deal gave them a powerful political impetus. An era which proudly claimed to go back to the grass-roots of American politics among the poor, the disinherited, the Radicals, revolutionaries, and Populists, found it only natural to go back also the grass-roots of American culture, and to rediscover the astonishing wealth of the American popular idiom. Nor was this mere archaeology. After all, organizers in Southern Illinois, Tennessee, and Alabama encouraged their militants with trade union blues, trade union hill-billy songs and trade union spirituals, for the simple reason that these were still a living, cultural language. Minstrel fiddlers and guitarists like the great Leadbelly (who was discovered and recorded for the Library of Congress at this period) made up union songs as naturally as gospel songs, and in the same manner:

> *Have you belonged to dis union;*
> *Do you belong to dis union;*
> *We are union people.*
> *Yes, lord, we went to dat office*
> *And sho' have signed.*
> *Got our name on de record*
> *An we sho' done joined.*

The period from 1930 to 1941 therefore saw intellectuals 'going to the people', collecting, recording, and singing their music with passionate satisfaction. American folk-songs, old and new, became part of the atmosphere of the American left; no party in Greenwich Village or the Hollywood scriptwriters' belt became complete without someone who could sing *John Henry* to a guitar. Most of the material thus collected was 'pre-jazz'; but among the forgotten music thus resuscitated was early jazz also. The Lomaxes of the Library of Congress produced the most impressive single document of New Orleans jazz in 1938, when they opened their recording shops to a dapper elderly 'Creole Benvenuto Cellini' with gold rings and a diamond set in gold in his front incisor, who wished to defend his claim to be the only inventor of jazz: Ferdinand 'Jelly-Roll' Morton. In doing so they helped to create a classic.

A parallel movement was gaining force among the specialized jazz-lovers and collectors, whose ranks, of course, overlapped a good deal with those of the musical or political New Dealers, friends of the Spanish Republic, Communists, and others, in Britain as in the U.S.A. Here it took the form chiefly of a protest against the increasingly 'commercial' tendencies of jazz in the swing era. Now that even good authentic jazz was in the headlines, the nostalgia for the old days, when only those in the know could find and appreciate it, became irresistible. From about 1938 collectors and critics began systematically to organize the recording of forgotten jazz and blues artists, but especially of attempts by the original players to recapture the quintessential jazz, which was that of New Orleans. Out of the many signposts in these years two deserve our special attention: the recording, by the French critic Hugues Panassié, of a splendid group of 'New Orleans' discs with Sidney Bechet, Tommy Ladnier, Mezz Mezzrow, and one or two others (1938), and the publication in 1939 of an erudite and nostalgic volume, *Jazzmen,* the first major fruit of years of devoted historical scholarship.[21] In the international world of jazz-lovers every one of these records and publications, imported at first in single copies from America, created a sensation. In America itself the archaeologists went farther, and, by the middle of the war—1943 is the crucial year—had reached the point of actually restoring retired old New Orleans players to activity, buying them dentures and trumpets in the process, and launching them on a receptive public of young whites. California was the centre of this movement.

Even before the first grey-haired player tested his new denture on his new horn, young white players—for reasons to be discussed later the young black ones were quite immune to revivalism—had begun the painstaking reconstruction of the original New Orleans style. Lu Watters and the Yerba Buena Band, who opened around San Francisco at the tail-end of 1939, strongly supported by the Stanford and Berkeley students,[22] were the pioneers of this movement, which is probably—and paradoxically—the most characteristically 'white' style in the history of jazz.* The slowness with which records were issued in Europe

* Bing Crosby's brother Bob had launched a semi-commercial Dixieland band in 1937, and in 1939 an old Chicagoan, Muggsy Spanier, launched the short-lived and wholly enchanting career of his Ragtime band, while in New York an even more typical Chicagoan, Eddie Condon, made a hit with the

(not to mention the impossibility of issuing American jazz in Nazi-occupied territories) postponed the emergence of the young revivalists outside America. However, by 1943 Australia had some (the Graeme Bell group), by 1944 the star of New Orleans rose over the Red Barn pub in the unlikely Bethlehem of Bexley Heath, Kent (George Webb and his Dixielanders), while after liberation revival bands emerged, with fanatical purism in Paris (Claude Luter), with a little more freedom in Holland, where their foundations had been laid as far back as 1939 (Dutch Swing College), and elsewhere. The characteristic small cellar jazz band with its trumpeter trying to play like Louis Armstrong and its clarinet like Johnny Dodds, became part of the West and Central European scene.

For political or rather quasi-moral reasons it was kept out of Eastern Europe. Why the Soviet authorities took against jazz, about which they knew virtually nothing, is obscure. The prejudice against it long ante-dated the Cold War, though it was confined entirely to the Russians, western Communists and left-wingers being among the most enthusiastic champions of the music.[23] I dare say it was regarded as 'decadent' because it did not fit into the pattern of puritan social respectability which the Soviet authorities south to inculcate. Nor did it. The most enthusiastic champions of jazz, and those most convinced of its moral harmlessness or positive value will not claim that it has a historical or natural affinity with puritanism. At all events the Russians kept it out, with the result that East Europeans had to get their jazz from the broadcasts of the AFN network and Radio Free Europe, or from western visitors to youth festivals. However, it is significant that when the restrictions of the later Stalin period were lifted in 1955–6 what emerged in Poland, East Germany, and Czechoslovakia was—the Dixieland revival.

Meanwhile jazz had made an even more important conquest: Africa itself. The astonishingly rapid urbanization of black Africa since 1940 produced the need for an urban popular music, which

---

old-fashioned unplanned jazz of his youth. But these were men from the old generations, not youngsters.

—for obvious reasons—the orthodox pop industry was slow to satisfy. In West Africa the music which thus emerged was chiefly based on local idioms, crossed with Caribbean influences, and a dash of New Orleans, but not very much. In South Africa, on the other hand, specially in Johannesburg, the urbanized black population took to American jazz, mainly derived, by the sound of it, from the big bands of the swing era. Probably South Africa is today the most flourishing centre of creative jazz outside America.

By the middle 1950s, therefore, jazz had become a world idiom. It met with the greatest resistance in countries whose musical tradition was wholly non-European or non-African, e.g. in the Moslem world, and Asia (except for Japan, always open to Western influences), and in countries with particularly vigorous popular musical traditions, such as the Iberian and Iberian-American ones. Indeed, from these it actually encountered opposition. The Andalusian flamenco, in the life-time of jazz, has shown considerable powers of propagation within the Hispanic areas, though outside them it has had no popular influence. Latin-American music, on the other hand, has disputed Western popular music with jazz, its attack spearheaded by the tangos, rhumbas, and sambas, while it has, since the 1940s, actually encroached upon jazz itself with the fashion for mixed Cuban-jazz music. Caribbean music has made modest progress in America, Britain, Scandinavia, and West Africa, mainly through the miserable doggerel of the calypso, but perhaps (except for West Africa) only as a novelty. Flourishing traditions of light and popular music elsewhere have also imposed some limitations on jazz, though they have not prevented it establishing bridge-heads: the Italian *canzone,* the French *chanson* and accordion-type music, and various other older idioms have resisted it. Of course, except among particular age-groups or social groups, jazz, however diluted, has nowhere ever had a musical monopoly. Even in the U.S.A. other forms have maintained themselves, and everywhere such older kinds of dance as the waltz persist, though in a more modest position than before. Again, except in the most urbanized Anglo-Saxon areas, jazz has been far slower to penetrate the countryside than the town, the small town than the big city. But there can be no doubt that it is today a world idiom, not only in the hybrid form of jazz-tinged dance-music, but in a much more thoroughbred version. Nor that, but for political factors, it would be even more widespread.

How much of this is due to the prestige and propaganda of the U.S.A. and to the dominant position of the American entertainment industry is a matter for debate. Probably not very much, except perhaps for the original spread of hybrid jazz. The main international agency for the dissemination of the American way of life, Hollywood, has paid very little attention to jazz, since this was and remains a minority taste in America. The American pop music industry has been much less capable of international penetration outside the Anglo-Saxon radius than jazz alone: until almost the present, Tin Pan Alley has not substantially disturbed the national pattern of the French, German, Italian, Spanish, etc., song-hits. In fact, jazz—especially authentic jazz in its various forms—has made its way under its own considerable power. Only when it had done so did the American Government recognize it as an agent of propaganda for the 'American way of life' in the Cold War, and use it to penetrate the East–West barrier, flooding the air with daily jazz broadcasts and sending prominent musicians abroad as 'cultural ambassadors'. Since 1947 the expansion of jazz has therefore almost certainly owed something to official sponsorship. However, jazz had travelled a long way without it, and would undoubtedly have continued to do so in any country in which jazz records were freely available.

The most recent phase of the expansion of jazz is perhaps too early to assess: it is the entry of the almost undiluted rhythm and blues into pop music, as in the rock-and-roll or the British skiffle crazes. This is the product of the middle 1950s. In many ways it is probably the most formidable of the many advances jazz has so far made, for there can be no doubt that rhythm and blues have not only swamped ordinary pop music in America and Britain, at least in terms of the sales chart, but that their power to penetrate the juke-boxes of the world is far, far greater than that of any previous product of America's Tin Pan Alley. It is an awe-inspiring experience to see substantially the same selection of shockers on the automatic gramophones of little Italian towns as in Manchester, and no doubt Wichita, and to reflect that complete freedom of cultural competition would almost certainly put them on those of Moscow and Shanghai. Perhaps this is because this latest fashion has reduced the music appeal to its simplest elements: a relentless, elementary beat, and a shouting voice. In America the phenomenon was a creation of the pop industry, analogous to the jazz injections of 1914–20 and 1935–40. In Britain, however, it had much more interesting origins, in a wholly spontaneous and uncommercial popular movement of amateur music-making with guitars and improvised rhythm instruments, with a repertoire of American folk-songs. These 'skiffle groups' which flourished for a few months until killed by commercialization were the direct children of the New Orleans revival, and indeed originally consisted of singers and guitarists from revival bands who entertained the audience with blues and Leadbelly-type songs while the rest of the boys had a drink. The public for skiffle and rock-and-roll was wholly adolescent or sub-adolescent; indeed the habitual rock-and-roll fan, unless mentally rather retarded, tended to be between ten and fifteen years of age. Probably the universal appeal of the fashion was due to this infantilism. Though it had begun to recede slightly by 1960, the rhythm-and-blues element remained powerful in pop music addressed to juveniles, who had been discovered to constitute the major market for Tin Pan Alley in the prosperous fifties.

three
Transformation

*F*orty years after the publication of the *St Louis Blues* (1914) jazz had become, in one form or another, an international musical language. A publicity-conscious American impresario could advertise a plan to recruit an 'international' orchestra including players from thirteen European countries, and he might as readily have recruited them from the other continents. However, international jazz remained almost entirely a second-hand version of the American music. The history of the evolution and transformation of jazz, as distinct from the history of its propagation, remains an American subject. Its musical details will be discussed in Chapters 4–6. This chapter merely tries to get the whole business into perspective. This is very much worth doing, for the internal development of jazz has been quite as rapid and startling as its expansion, and even more surprising. The evolution of Western classical music, which is rather rapid and revolutionary by the standards of past history, is measured in centuries. Jazz has passed through equally profound and revolutionary transformations—though on a much more modest scale

—in decades. The road from the New Orleans funeral procession to Mr Charles Mingus's 'jazz experiments' is at least as long as that from Monteverdi to Alban Berg.

We may conveniently divide the history of jazz into four main phases: (1) the 'prehistoric' from *c.* 1900 to 1917; (2) the 'ancient' from *c.* 1917 to *c.* 1929; (3) 'middle period' from *c.* 1929 to the early 1940s; and (4) 'modern' from then on; or, in terms of the commercial labels attached to each, 'ragtime', 'jazz', 'swing', and 'bop' or 'cool'.* The historian of the future may detect some subsequent turning-points—for instance the rise of jazz to quasi-art-music status and the irruption of the blues into pop music—but it is wisest to leave these discoveries to those who will be able to see the 1950s in perspective. 'Prehistoric' and 'ancient' jazz might also be conveniently considered together.

¶ 'Ancient' jazz (e.g. in the 'New Orleans', 'Dixieland', 'Chicago', and 'New York' styles) is a music of small improvising bands with rudimentary arrangements, of blues singers and pianists. 'Middle period' jazz is essentially a music of larger commercial bands and the virtuosi they bred; a much more 'composed' and 'arranged' as well as a more technically demanding music. The 'modern' period has fled back into improvisation, and the small group, whether in the form of a deliberate return to 'ancient' jazz (the 'revival' movements) or a deliberate leap forward into a revolutionary *avant-garde* music ('bop'), some of which has increasingly turned into a hybrid between jazz and classical music ('cool'). In the course of this it has dropped a good deal of improvisation for ambitious, sophisticated, if not always successful genres of jazz composition. Socially, ancient jazz was a music for Southerners or first-generation black migrants to the North, which was also adopted or listened to by minorities of whites. 'Middle period' jazz was a music for blacks acclimatized to big city life, and for a mass American white public of youngsters. 'Modern' jazz was and is *avant-garde* music

* I do not propose to argue with the experts who would prefer to date or sub-divide these periods a little differently or who wish to call them by different names.

for musicians and a coterie public of white intellectuals and bohemians, though its public has grown, as its original revolutionary sounds became familiar and accepted, much as have the Matisses and Picassos of our century in painting. Revivalist jazz is not a music for black audiences at all, but for white youths and intellectuals. In Europe, but not in America, it has increasingly become a standard type of dance-music for adolescents.

Beneath these fashions, however, one kind of music has continued comparatively unchanged: the quintessential sound of the urban and rural blacks, the blues. Speeded up in the cities, it has provided the 'jumping', shouting noise which is the heartbeat of the black ghetto, whether it emerges from dance halls, bar rooms, or churches. At bottom the public of (unintellectual) city blacks, which is the fundamental audience for jazz, has remained faithful to this rather than to any particular phase of jazz, at any rate since the 1920s. This is why the middle period jazz of rocking and swinging bands like Chick Webb's and Lionel Hampton's, or of 'jumping' saxophone players like Earl Bostic, has perhaps come nearest to permanent popularity in the black quarters than any other. Perhaps this is also why rock-and-roll, which is remotely based on the 'jump' blues, made greater inroads on the black public than previous fashions in commercial music. The blues, urban and immigrant, has remained the constant background to jazz evolution.

This outline, crude to the point of caricature, is not intended to provide the reader with an account of jazz evolution. It is merely supposed to give some rough orientation, like the maps on airline time-tables, which are not to be judged as accurate geographical representations. But even such diagrams must draw attention to important traffic junctions. In the history of jazz there are two. The first marks its change from an old-fashioned folk-music to a hybrid between folk and commercial music, and the growing isolation of the jazz musician from his old public. On the whole the evolution of jazz up to 1941 can be chiefly accounted for in such terms. The second marks a much more deliberate musical break: the revolution which produced 'bop' and 'cool' jazz, but also—neither modernists nor traditionalists will thank me for this observation—the deliberate return to archaism of the 'revivalists'. In some respects this was the product of the tendencies which had dominated earlier jazz evolution, but it also reflected what can only be described as an 'ideological' revolt, in which the 'political' elements were incomparably greater. Let us put it another way. Jazz evolution up to the end of the middle period was the product of unselfconscious popular musicians, playing as such musicians have always played, for an unselfconscious public which wanted to be entertained. (The self-conscious small jazz public appreciated but did not determine jazz evolution.) Jazz evolution since 1941 or thereabouts (or, to be more accurate, since 1938–42) has also been the product of self-conscious musicians playing for a self-conscious public; i.e. it has had far greater affinities with modern minority culture. Modern jazz has not been played only for fun, for money, or for technical expertise: it has also been played as a manifesto—whether of revolt against capitalism or commercial culture, or of black equality, or of something else. The line between the two periods is naturally not very clear. Just as there are ancestors of the 'modern' approach before the end of the thirties, so a great deal of jazz has continued to move along the old tracks since; but this does not disturb the broad validity of the generalization. In terms of music, the break between the two periods is very sharp indeed. Jazz evolution until the end of the thirties proceeded in something like a single general direction: each successive 'style' tended to derive from its immediate predecessors, adding to and modifying them. The modern evolution begins with a deliberate about-turn. The 'revivalists' (a movement of the public rather than the musicians) deliberately rejected the existing jazz for a kind of music which had been virtually dead for at least a decade. The 'boppers' (a movement of the musicians rather than the public) deliberately rejected the existing jazz for a music which, by existing standards, would sound dissonant, anarchic, and technically so difficult to play as to be almost beyond the reach of more than a small *avant-garde*. They also rejected (as we shall see in the chapter on the jazz musician) most of the social conventions of the older jazz musicians.

43

The *first* crucial change was in the public for jazz. There is all the difference in the world between music played for a home or an away audience. For the New Orleans man the *Canal Street Blues* was about an identifiable street, the *2:19 Blues* about an identifiable train. For the country minstrel who sings

> *I'm goin' to Houston, Texas, 'Lightning' Hopkins is*
> *the man I want to see,*
> *Oh, Houston, Texas, 'Lightning' Hopkins is the man*
> *I want to see*
> *Well now, if you can't stand my jivin', I'm gonna give*
> *you the third degree*[1]

his blues has a specific purpose: in this instance the challenge of one guitar-picker (Sam 'Lightning' Hopkins) by another (Brownie McGhee). For an outside audience it is just a blues, whose title and text—and hence whose music—mean as little as the records named after phrases of esoteric Harlem slang mean to Blackburn adolescents. Folk-art inevitably loses much of its concreteness as soon as it leaves communities which recognize its detailed allusions and references. As jazz became the general idiom of music for the black city immigrants, it inevitably lost some of its roots.

This loss was temporarily camouflaged by the unlimited demand for nostalgia which uprooted communities produce, and which made home-sickness into an endemic disease of nineteenth- and early twentieth-century Europe. It also made the song recalling the (idealized) past into the most typical product of nineteenth-century Tin Pan Alley, in which Irish mothers and Yiddisher mommas abounded, and home was on the range, where never is heard a discouraging word. Black migrants were fortunately immune from the temptation to idealize either good old Dixie or their childhoods, but the mass migration to the North and into the cities unquestionably multiplied the demand for 'music from down home.' On its most modest levels this produced what has been called the 'urban blues singers' circuits', the bar rooms and 'rent parties'* in Harlem or on the Chicago Black Belt, served by the guitar-pickers and itinerant piano players. At a higher level it produced the mass public for the classic blues singers in the big urban vaudeville theatres, and the demand for New Orleans jazz in cities like Chicago. Commercially it produced the large crop of blues and other jazz pieces named after specific places in the South: St Louis, Beale Street, Perdido Street, Memphis, Dallas, Nashville Woman's Blues, Milenberg Joys, and so on. However, the demand for 'the old music' was strictly limited, if only by the vast contempt of urbanized and Northern blacks for rural and Southern ones. City ways, emancipation, and progress were what they wanted, except perhaps in religion. The rapid decline and fall of the great classic blues singers after 1927 illustrates the tenuousness of their loyalty to the old music. It is no accident that the black public has remained totally immune to the revival of traditional jazz and blues.

The *second* crucial change, which almost followed from the first, was the retreat of traditional music before commercial pop music; or more precisely, the increasing encroachment of pop music on jazz. Once out of its traditional social setting, nothing is less resistant than folk-art, for its artists and public practise it not because they have a strong preference for it, but because it is the only art they know. The new public, contemptuous of its miserable past, wanted new entertainment. The musician wanted to earn money. The established entertainment industry of the modern city provided the money and the standards. Why should the musicians object? Jazz became heavily and progressively infiltrated with 'pop' elements. But it did not become pop music. It remained, in important respects, the dominant partner in the marriage with commercialism, because the jazz musician, while welcoming commercialization also, and inevitably, rejected it as boring and automatic, an activity unfit for the creative

---

* A rent party was technically organized by tenants who could not pay their rent, hired a piano-player, laid in some liquor and pigs' feet, and charged admission to friends and neighbors, hoping to make enough profit out of the affair. The classic description is by Bessie Smith in *Gimme a Pigfoot.*

45

artist: 'Mickey Mouse music', as the hot players called it in the thirties. Much of the evolution of jazz was therefore determined by this mixed attraction and repulsion of the pops.

Both transformed the jazz orchestra. As we have seen, jazz history from the early 1920s on is mostly that of progress towards the large 'swing' band; but the big band with its characteristic instrumentation and 'arrangements' is merely the result of the attempt to make jazz more like successful commercial entertainment. Jazz, however, transformed the big band which, in pop music, is merely a collection of musical zombies who do not greatly mind how they play. The big band of jazz musicians, who play well only when there is a creative spark about, required considerable musical innovation before it would work well. Some of the most important musical developments in jazz can be traced back to this need to adapt the big band to it; notably the constant and progressive improvement and sophistication of rhythm, on which the entire structure of jazz must always rest. The progress from the older beat to the supple 'swing' of the middle-period rhythm sections is an example.

Again, commercialization transformed the jazz repertoire, which—for obvious reasons—rested increasingly on the current pop song, the 'ballad'. The history of jazz since 1917 might well be written as that of its attempts to come to terms with the song-hit. The ballad formed no serious part of the repertoire of New Orleans or the old blues; any pop songs used were assimilated to the traditional marches, stomps, blues, etc., in the manner habitual among folk-artists. Bessie Smith's well-known version of *Alexander's Ragtime Band* is a good example.* At the other extreme, the repertoire of modern jazz is almost exclusively based on the ballad, the fundamental experiments of the boppers being simply transformed song-hits like *How High the Moon,* or *All the Things You Are.* Even when playing the blues, a modern trum-

---

* It has happened that a former pop song, thus assimilated, has eventually —via the later popularity of blues singers—made its way back into the hit parade. This is the case of *Goodnight, Irene,* a song of 1892 vintage, taken into the stock of the folk-minstrel Leadbelly, and rediscovered through him in the 1940s.

peter like Miles Davis thinks automatically in terms of the way in which a ballad is played, rather than in terms of a traditional blues piece.[2] But jazz transformed the ballad out of all recognition. When playing or singing it 'straight', it either deliberately mocked it, as in Fats Waller's satirical piano-songs, or it took it at its word, turning it into a touching or profound and perfectly sincere expression of emotion, as in the songs and trumpet solos of Louis Armstrong and the songs of the great women jazz singers like Billie Holiday and Ella Fitzgerald. When using it as the basis for jazz improvization, it progressively elaborated it, until in modern jazz the actual theme of the song-hit, as originally written, may not even appear at all. In both cases it selected. Each jazz 'style' chose from among the mass of current hits a certain number of 'standards', pieces which practice had shown to be particularly suited for jazz elaboration, and these became the nucleus of its permanent repertoire. Thus, out of the eighty-odd pop tunes published in 1928 and listed in Spaeth's *History of American Popular Music,* only four have become anything like jazz 'standards': *I Can't Give You Anything but Love, Diga-diga-doo* (both written for the black show 'Blackbirds of 1928'), *Sweet Sue,* and *Nagasaki.*

Inevitably, however, commercialized music repelled and bored the jazz player, and the large band imposed awkward impersonal discipline on him. The history of Duke Ellington's band, surely the least low-brow of successful jazz orchestras, is one of progressive disillusion and discontent among the players almost from the moment in which the small, freely blowing group of musicians turned into the organized and 'arranged' band: 'no longer', as its historian says, 'was playing the exultant personal expression it had once been.'[*] If this was the case in fairly uncompromising jazz bands, if was naturally even more so in those which deliberately went out to please the crowds at all costs, not to mention the 'sweet' and 'corny' bands in which many white jazz musicians had to earn their living.

The *third* crucial development in jazz is the consequence of

[*] Barry Ulanov, in *Duke Ellington,* pp. 108–9, describes the sag in the band's morale very clearly.

47

this revulsion. The jazzmen learned to live in two musical worlds: the one in which they earned their living, and the one after hours in which they played to please themselves—the world of the 'jam session'. Except for those who, like many early white jazz players before 1935, worked in purely commercial bands, the two worlds were not as sharply distinct as one might think. The 'jam session' was often regarded merely as the experimental laboratory in which ideas later to be used in public were tried and elaborated. Moreover, all jazz players still dreamed, and continue to dream, of small 'combos' in which they could both play as they please and please the public; or at any rate earn their living and play for a public which does not get in the way too much. The history of jazz is littered with such small groups, on temporary engagements in some club, but always turning into 'jam sessions' as other musicians drop by to 'sit in'; or got together for the recording studio. But the sharp distinction between playing for musicians and playing for the public was established; and so, increasingly, was the distinction between playing 'commercial' and playing for interest:

'Well, Dizzy and Milt Hinton', says Danny Barker the guitarist, 'between those two-and-a-half-hour shows at the Cotton Club . . . would retire to the roof. Dizzy would blow his new ideas in progressions, and he and Hinton would experiment on different ideas and melodic patterns, and they would suggest that I come up and join them. But after that two-and-a-half-hour show, sometimes I'd go up and sometimes I wouldn't. Because what they were doing called for a lot of mental concentration on harmonies. It was very interesting, but I couldn't see going up there and wasting energies on something not commercial.'[3]

Jazz, originally an urban folk-music, therefore simultaneously developed towards commercial pop music, and towards a special kind of music for musicians, i.e. the embryo of art music. The 1920s and 1930s in jazz evolution were dominated by the drift towards commercialism (though, as we have seen, this produced not pop music, but an independent music based increasingly on pop materials). The 1940s and 1950s have been equally dominated by the reaction towards musicians' music—the *avant-garde* semi-art music of the 'boppers' and 'cool' players, much of it designed to be incomprehensible to the non-expert. But, in spite of considerable efforts, it has not so far produced art-music in the orthodox sense either, but an independent music increasingly infiltrated by elements of classical music. Suspended somewhere between its folk-music origins and the pop and art-music towards which it is simultaneously urged, jazz remains hard to classify.

This difficulty—and with it most of the merits of jazz—arises from the fact that, at bottom, it had never ceased to be folk-music. It has merely retired from the wider community of the traditional folk-public and folk-artist into the narrower but real and vivid community of the professional craftsman-musician. Within this community the music has gone on living the same sort of life as in folk-music; fluctuating and shifting, personal, traditional, propagated by word of mouth and apprenticeship, created as it is played, reflecting all facets of the players' lives. Its terms of reference were more restricted. The titles of jazz records from the middle twenties on often reflect esoteric jokes and allusions, sometimes expressed in the Harlem slang of the 'hipster', which is deliberately designed to baffle the outsider. The cryptic titles of Ellington's numbers in the late thirties are good examples: *Hip Chic, Old King Dooji, Portrait of the Lion* (Willie, 'The Lion', Smith, a well-known New York pianist), *Little Posey* (nickname of one of Ellington's trumpeters), *Weely* (nickname of his arranger), *Cotton Tail,* etc. On the other hand, its evolution was vastly speeded up, for the life of the jazz player is, like that of the chess player, who resembles him in his exclusive devotion to his art, nothing but a succession of matches and tournaments, of constant comparisons of achievement, a mixture of cooperation and competition. The 'jam session', in which players get together after hours for their own pleasure, is both collective experiment and contest. Jo Jones the drummer, writing of Kansas City, recreates one aspect of it:

Now those were pretty tough times and yet the guys did take the time to study, and when they had found something new they would bring it to the session and they would pass it round to the other musicians, no matter what instrument they played. So they would try that particular riff or that particular conception at a session and perfect it. The idea of a jam session then wasn't who could play better than somebody else—is was a matter of contributing something and experimentation. Jam sessions were our fun, our outlet.[4]

But Mary Lou Williams the pianist, writing about the same town at the same time, also recreates the other, competitive aspect of the session—the 'cutting', or trying to outplay someone else:

The word went round that Hawkins [the best tenor sax player of the period, EJH] was in the Cherry Blossom, and within about half an hour there were Lester Young, Ben Webster, Herschel Evans, Herman Walder, and one or two unknown tenors piling into the club to blow.

Bean (Hawkins's nickname) didn't know the Kaycee tenor men were so terrific, and he couldn't get himself together, though he played all morning. I happened to be nodding that night, and around 4 a.m. I awoke to hear someone pecking on my screen.

I opened the window on Ben Webster. He was saying 'Get up pussy-cat, we're jammin' and all the pianists are tired out now. Hawkins has got his shirt off and is still blowing. You got to come down.'[5]

The community of jazz players existed—and exists—in every city in which jazz is played, like the old communities of craftsmen; and as the old travelling journeymen would automatically visit the 'house of call' in each town, to meet colleagues and pick up news and jobs, so the new or touring musician in every town from Los Angeles to London and Paris knows where to drop in, how to find those who can tell him who's in town, what music is on, and where a man can sit in with a band. (For jazz is collective music, practised and discussed only in common.) The peculiar atmosphere of these half anchored, half freely floating communities of players, who know the pattern of each others' lives, which is not that of the 'squares' or outsiders, whether musical or non-musical, made jazz. It has to be experienced, if only from the side lines. The outsider will not really grasp it until he has seen an out-of-town, hard-bitten professional, with twenty years of touring behind him, put a good-looking chorus girl whom he has picked up for the night on some remote couch, while he spends two hours listening to and discussing jazz records with a few local musicians and collectors. And not even his own records: simply good and interesting records from which a musician can learn something. Perhaps a description by a player can give a slight impression of this milieu:[6]

On Sunday afternoons, in the early forties, some of the guys would get together at my house . . . we'd have a little session listening to records. We'd listen to a lot of Hawk's records. He was making some in Europe that we'd get. And we'd play things of our own. . . . Then on Sunday nights we'd go to Lewisohn Stadium when the symphonic session was on. 'We're going to church,' we'd say.

Then later that night we'd go to the Savoy to hear Chick Webb. That was a band that really swung. Then after the Savoy we'd go to Puss Johnson's, an after-hours spot, 130th and St Nicholas, I think. Everybody would come in there. All the guys from the bands downtown. I remember one particular session. Ben Webster and Pres (Lester Young) were there and everybody knew about it. . . .

As for that session with Ben and Lester, there never could be a decision. The house was divided. Most of those there were musicians. There were very, very few outsiders except some real jazz fans. They used to sell lots of chicken and whisky at those sessions.

This particular place was especially for Sunday nights, that was the off-night around New York at about that time. It would start about three in the morning and last to about 9 or

10 a.m. It was always bright daylight when we came out. It just blinded you.

Naturally the music played in this community of craftsmen was not folk-music in any traditional sense. But it grew out of the old fold-music, because that was the mould in which the musicians, their techniques, and their entire idiom had been formed, and above all because the artists remained at all times creator-players and never became mere executants. The craft-pride of the players added to this the powerful elements of competition, experimentation, and the constant striving to master increasingly difficult technical problems. (In doing so the players were untrammelled by conventional ideas as to what the capacities of instruments were.) To play a trumpet with the flowing ease of the saxophone, a trombone with the glitter and speed of a trumpet, to make the drums 'play tunes' as well as indicate the rhythm: such achievements would test the expert, and perhaps enable the good player to keep ahead of the copyist. 'We're going to play something that they can't steal because they can't play it' is the refrain which runs through all the discussions of the revolutionary 'boppers'. And as each phase of the musicians' 'private' music became in turn commercially successful—a thing half-welcomed, half-deplored by then—the incentive to push still farther ahead grew.

That is why the latter half of the thirties was so crucial a point in jazz evolution. Until 1935 jazz itself had scarcely been commercial. The broad white public demanded the hybrid jazz-coloured pop music, the 'true' jazz fans were not yet numerous enough to make a market, the blacks were too poor to make a worth-while one. 'Ancient' jazz had dropped out of sight. 'Middle-period' jazz lived a submerged life anyway, flourishing best in the modest black ghettoes like Harlem and Kansas City where nobody minded what was played so long as it 'jumped', and in the joints and night-spots where nobody minded what was played either so long as the musicians went on playing. Now black big-band jazz turned out to be box office, though more for its lesser white practitioners (Goodman, Shaw, Dorsey,

Glenn Miller) than for its genuine stars—the Ellington, Basie, Lunceford, and Chick Webb bands. The specialized jazz-lovers themselves became a commercial public, demanding the impossible, to hear the spontaneous, unplanned jazz of the jam session played to order on the concert platform. Commercialization bit deeper and deeper into the 'private' sector of the jazz world. And so both players and public began the unending search for the genuine unspoiled jazz that would be theirs alone; the former by advancing into the technically revolutionary territory of 'bop', the latter by retreating farther and farther towards the remote fastnesses of the Mississippi Delta. Alas for such hopes! As soon as the commercial value of 'true' jazz was recognized, the pop men fell over themselves to adopt any innovation almost as soon as it was made. Within a few years of the end of the war every commercial big band worth its name played 'bop' arrangements, and the boppers were driven yet farther forward towards the Bartóks and Milhauds who, heaven knows, have never yet produced a hit record, while the 'revivalists' retreated from the Armstrong of 1925 to the Oliver of 1922, from Oliver to Bunk Johnson's Eagle Band of 1913, and thence to the putative sound of Buddy Bolden. But the hot breath of the box-office was on their necks. Not that the professional players regretted it: they merely regretted the inevitable limitations on their inventions, experimenting, and freedom which it imposed: for instance the tyranny of the 'request number' which forced them to repeat *ad nauseam* a limited repertoire of 'standards'.

From 1935 to the present the race has gone on, and the end is not in sight, though the pursuers have slightly changed in character. For whereas in the hey-day of swing they were mainly the uninstructed 'square' audiences, the running has been increasingly made by the growing mass of 'true' jazz-lovers, whose very weight tends to strangle the music they wish to embrace.

It is easy to understand why the jazz of the early 1940s tended to take the form of manifestos against commercialism, or against the public, or against the excessively esoteric activities of the musicians: against one aspect or another of the unhealthy situation into which the music had, inevitably, drifted. However, there is more to the jazz revolution than this. From the point of view of the public—the specialized white jazz public—the 'revival' was the first large-scale revolt within the framework of popular music, against art as mass production. There is historic justice in the fact that the very heart of 'Mickey Mouse' music in its most literal meaning, the Walt Disney Studio, illustrates the revolt of the individual. One of the most characteristic revivalist bands, the 'Firehouse Five Plus Two', overflowing with collective improvisation and the musical simple life, was composed of technicians, writers, and animators of that establishment. (Another aspect of this nostalgia for the age before mass production also found a characteristic early outlet among these Californian intellectuals: the hankering after machines with rough corners. A leading member of the band was also a leading light in the 'Horseless Carriage Club'—the American equivalent of the vintage car craze—and the band was actually named in honour of the 1914 fire engine the band bought and with which it played about.) Nor was this revolt against modern capitalism and its works confined to a few intellectuals. It is fair to claim that the revival became a mass movement among the West-European young on its anti-commercial as much as on its musical appeal. It was self-made music, or at least music made in the image of the amateur. Its bands—in Britain at least—resisted professionalization for the best part of ten years. Moreover, in Britain and Australia, to a very marked extent, they had and maintained links with the political left. World youth festivals, anti-nuclear marches, May Day demonstrations, or other expressions of hostility to the social *status quo* have rarely lacked their quota of imitation New Orleans jazz players, blues and folksingers, or 'skifflers'.★

The modern revolution—'bebop'—which took shape in New York in 1940–2, was a musician's revolt, not a movement

★ Since this is a subject which rouses prickly feelings I might as well point out in so many words that I know nothing of the ideological or political views of American revivalists in general and the Firehouse Five in particular, and am *not* implying that they ever had left-wing sympathies.

of the public. Indeed, it was a revolt directed against the public as well as against the submergence of the player in standardized floods of commercial noise. But it was also a much more profound and ill-defined manifesto in favour of black equality. The inventors of this revolutionary music were without exception young black players at most in their early twenties, mostly still unknown: John Birks ('Dizzy') Gillespie, the trumpeter; Charlie ('Bird') Parker, the saxophonist; Thelonious Monk, the pianist; Kenny Clarke and Art Blakey, drummers; Charlie Christian, guitar (the only one who had made a name for himself); Bud Powell (piano); Milt Jackson (vibraharp); Tadd Dameron (arranger); Max Roach (drums); Kinny Dorham (trumpet), and the rest. The nature of their attitude is described more fully in the next chapter and the chapter on the Jazz Musician. What follows is only a brief general survey sufficient to place the jazz revolution into its general setting.

The musical revolutionism of the early 1940s is inconceivable without the political upheavals of the 1930s, which gave American blacks increased confidence, while at the same time bringing them closer to the apparently insurmountable barriers which stood between them and equality. The bebop revolution was political as much as musical. The savage hostility to 'Uncle Tom' musicians, which for the first time split the community of jazz players into bitterly feuding sections, the passionate insistence on inventing a music so difficult that 'they'—the whites who always cash in on black achievement—will 'not be able to steal it', even the personal peculiarities of the new players, cannot be explained in musical terms alone. They stood for a certain attitude of the black artist and intellectual in his own world and that of the whites, whose slang name, *ofays*—from the pig latin for 'foe'—sufficiently indicates the tension between the races. Theirs would be a music as good as the whites', even in terms of art-music, but based on black foundations. But they also expressed the resentment and insecurity of blacks who had tried the old recipe for equality—emigration to the northern cities—and who found that the farther it took them from the world of Uncle Tom, the farther off did the world look in which there would be neither whites nor blacks but only American citizens. Moreover, they were isolated even within the black world. They had raised themselves by their talents and achievements above the level of the ordinary labourers from whom they had sprung, or they hoped to do so as artists and intellectuals: but they found themselves shut out not only from the white world but even by the black middle class, that puny body of white-collar and professional workers which hid its consciousness of impotence behind the attempt to construct a feeble caricature of white petty-bourgeois respectability.[7] It is small wonder that their social behaviour was anarchic and bohemian, their music a multiple gesture of defiance.

Oddly enough—thanks mainly to the whites, for the black middle class failed to recognize them[8]—the achievements of the jazz revolutionaries were speedily recognized. White commercial men, ever on the watch for the cash value of novelty, turned 'bop' into a slogan. Young white intellectuals and bohemians, recognizing a malaise and unspecified rebelliousness akin to their own, made modern jazz into the music of the 'beat generation', the American equivalent of the Continental existentialists. Musical schools and institutions and universities, softened up by the propaganda of the 1930s, were prepared to recognize an important addition to native American culture even when it came from an unexpected and 'unrespectable' source. The American Government itself, aware of the propagandist value of jazz as a cultural export, has sent Dizzy Gillespie abroad as a cultural ambassador just like—indeed earlier than—Louis Armstrong. From 1949–50 on, modern jazz has been no more an art of outlaws than cubism in the 1930s. Perhaps the shift from the 'bebop' to the 'cool' styles of modern jazz about this period reflects this greater acceptance. It certainly helped to make the 'cool' period since 1949 one in which jazz has made more persistent and massive efforts than ever before to fuse with orthodox art music, though the artistic results of this hybridization were generally mediocre, in terms of the achievements of art-music. It also, paradoxically, helped to turn modern jazz, whose founders were without exception black players of plebeian ori-

56

gin, into a music favoured particularly by a host of young white players, notably in California (hence the name 'West Coast School'). However, in the later fifties 'cool' jazz was in turn replaced by a yet more consciously musico-Nationalist revolt of the black players, who favoured a return to the blues, blew 'hot' (or 'hard' as the phrase went), advertised their connexions with gospel-song, and sometimes chose themes reflecting their hankering for Africanism.

When the chronicler of jazz reaches this point the question 'What next?' automatically raises its head. I do not propose to answer it. Prophecy is not the business of this book, and the prophetic record of jazz critics, though no worse than that of, say, academic economists, is too poor to encourage speculation. The evolution of jazz has constantly snatched the victory of fine achievement out of the disasters of commercialization, and today perhaps out of academic etiolation. It has also left its victims; but that is only natural in an art which is by definition 'impure', i.e. which operates in a musical environment subject to permanent and increasing contamination. Jazz critics have expressed their fear and disquiet at these dangers by the invariable statement that 'jazz is in a state of crisis'. Virtually every critical discussion ends on this note of potential doom, even that of M. Hodeir, the standard-bearer of modernism.[9] And so it is, inevitably. Developing as it does through a series of contradictions, actions, and reactions, jazz must be in constant crisis. It is quite possible that one of these crises will see jazz evolution either finally merging with commercial evolution or with the evolution of American art-music. It is more than probable that whatever jazz is played in future will be unpalatable to many critics on musical or social grounds. However, at present there is no reason to believe that the history of jazz is finished.

Even if it were—i.e. if the evolutionary progress of jazz as we have known it should end—it would not mean the end of the music. So long as men and women still sing the blues in Chicago bar rooms, so long as sax players and trumpeters still like to get together over some whisky and chicken sandwiches to jam for their own pleasure, so long as craftsmen and artists in music resist the pressures to turn them into mere executants of some-one else's product, some jazz will be played. It may be played in styles which have ceased to develop, but that does not make it less genuine. Jazz as an idiom and a way of playing is too well established to disappear from the scene for a long time and the world is large. It may turn out to be as indestructible as the Wild West, which haunts the imagination of the world long after it has ceased to exist in its own country.

part two
Music

four

Blues and Orchestral Jazz

*I*n this chapter and the following I propose to guide the reader in somewhat more detail through the maze of orchestral and instrumental jazz styles. Unlike some other chapters, these inevitably make very little sense unless the reader also has access to gramophone records and a desire to listen to jazz seriously, and readers who have neither are advised to skip much of the next pages. My survey is necessarily very condensed and elementary, but there is a fair amount of more specialized literature available for those who want to go farther.

THE BLUES

The blues is not a style or phase of jazz, but a permanent substratum of all styles; not the whole of jazz, but its heart. No jazz player or band which cannot play it can reach the peaks of jazz achievement, and the moment when the blues ceases to be part of jazz will be the moment when jazz, as we know it, ceases to exist. There is no real disagreement on this point. The most sophisticated and advanced modernists, full of eighteenth-century classical echoes, will, like John Lewis, claim an affinity with the blues, and rightly so. The great and revolutionary Charlie Parker observed on the last day of his tormented life 'that it was a sad thing the way many of the young guys coming up didn't know or had forgotten their foundation—the blues'. 'That's the basis of jazz', he said.[1] Ordinary jazz players merely say, again and again, unasked, apropos of nothing: 'The blues has to be there all the time: it's the way you feel.' It is to jazz what the earth was to Antaeus in the Greek myth. If he lost contact with it, he lost his strength. Whenever in the blank patches of some session a musician calls out 'Hey, Charlie, let's play the blues', this contact is renewed.

So far as jazz is concerned the blues are both a mood and a feeling—not necessarily of sadness and depression, though mostly so—and a musical form or idiom—not necessarily the classic 'twelve-bar blues'. But the blues also exists as a folk-music outside jazz and beside it, with its own evolution which runs alongside that of jazz, though not independent of it. There also it may mean two things: the general idiom of black folk-song and a specific type of secular song. When Marshall Stearns speaks of the 'almost solid wall of blue tonality' in Mahalia Jackson's gospel song, he means the first. When Sonny Terry, the singer and harmonica player, says, 'If only Mahalia would sing the blues she'd be the best of them all' he means the second. However, since the blues is so pervasive and important a part of American black music and jazz, most musicians or jazz-lovers use the word fairly indiscriminately. There is little risk of misunderstanding.

In the most rigorous sense of the word the blues is a strict musical and poetic form. Musically it seems to have stabilized itself best as a theme of twelve bars, though earlier blues may have been shorter and 'composed' blues may be more elaborate, like the *St Louis Blues,* which has two distinct twelve-bar themes and a sixteen-bar one, and the *Beale Street Blues,* which has two of twelve bars and one of eight. Poetically the (twelve-bar) blues consists of something like a blank verse couplet, the first line being repeated twice as in:

> *I looked down the road far as I could see*
> *Well, I looked down the road, far as I could see*
> *Well, a man and my woman, the blues sure had poor me.*[2]

The verse-line and rhythm, as one might expect, are extremely flexible, but the five main accents remain. The poetic aspects of blues couplet will be briefly discussed in Chapter 7.

The blues in its original form is essentially an 'accompanied' song; more precisely an antiphonal song, in the long African tradition of such 'calls and responses'. The voice may make two statements—say of two or two and a half bars length each in a twelve-bar blues—and a response of equal length. These might occupy, for instance, bars 2 and 3, 5 and 6, 9 and 10. The remainder is filled by instrumental 'breaks'. In fact the accompanied blues becomes a duet between voice and instrument(s) which echo and respond to it. When singer and player are in sympathy and are good blues performers, the result can be of heartrending beauty for the lover of such things: as in Bessie Smith's duets with Louis Armstrong *(St Louis Blues, Reckless Blues)*, with Joe Smith, perhaps her most sensitive accompanist *(Weeping Willow Blues)*, or James P. Johnson *(Backwater Blues)*. Solo instrumental blues are derived from vocal ones and preserve, so far as possible, the antiphonal characteristics (e.g. the famous *Five O'Clock Blues* or *How Long*, by Jimmy Yancey). Being often played on the most unvocal instrument, the piano, this may not be obvious, but it remains true that virtually all primitive piano solos 'are the blues, so far as melody, harmony, and length of theme are concerned'.[3]

There is some argument about the characteristic 'blue scale' and its harmony. It is probably best regarded as an adaptation of European scales to African ones, though many primitive blues and the vocal line of many classic ones are almost purely African; for it is easier to sing such things as quarter-tones than to play them on some European instruments. The simplest way to recognize the blues scale is by its use of the 'blue notes', the (approximately) flatted thirds and sevenths in the melody, but not the harmony, which is European. The conflict between the two produces the characteristic effects of the blues. This scale is remarkably deep rooted in American black sound. Sermons in black churches, which tend to pass insensibly from speech to chant, will normally be found to settle down on the basis of two or three notes from the blues scale—say the tonic and the 'blue third' above it.[4] In the vocal blues the theme is repeated, stanzalike *ad lib,* with an infinity of variations. A fine example of this is Bessie Smith's five-verse version of *Careless Love.* This song, which exists in innumerable versions, is not, as it happens, a native blues but an Elizabethan and later Appalachian mountain song turned into a blues by black singers, and into a most marvellous and haunting one:

> *Love, oh love, oh careless love,*
> *You go to my head like wine.*

There is no particular reason why the twelve-bar blues should be slow or sad. However, since the blues is also a mood, most characteristic secular blues are in fact slow or dragging in tempo and 'low down' in feeling. 'Low down' is a quality as difficult to define as 'lyrical,' but it will be recognized by anyone who has ever heard any record by Bessie Smith.

This essentially simple form has an infinity of artistic possibilities. In its vocal form it has produced not only melodies of great beauty—for instance *See See Rider, How Long?, In the Evening,* and *Trouble in Mind*—but an extraordinarily intense and sensitive expression of emotion. The blues is essentially expressionist. Technique is totally subordinated to content, and indeed determined by it. One has merely to listen to the wonderful flexibility of the blues line as sung or played by a fine artist to appreciate the way in which every slight variation in intonation, rhythm, or melody serves to express emotion with the utmost accuracy and power, like the movements of a great dancer. I do not think

64

any form of art has ever been developed which can transform ordinary emotion, as felt by all of us, into artistically valid statements more directly and with less loss of intensity. This is perhaps a major reason why the vocal blues is one of the rare artforms which, like dancing and acting, are perfectly adapted to women, for whom the most natural kind of art is that least separate from body, gesture, and voice. In the blues ordinary women, the sort who are generally inarticulate unless written about, painted, or filmed, have found their voice: if Carmen had spoken herself, she would not have said what Mérimée and Bizet said, but what Bessie Smith sang in *Young Woman's Blues:*

I'm a young woman, and I ain't done running round.
Some people call me a hobo, some people call me a bum
Nobody knows my name, nobody knows what I've done.
I'm as good as any woman in your town:
I ain't no high yaller, I'm a deep yaller brown.
I ain't going to marry, ain't going to settle down
I'm going to drink good moonshine, and run these browns down.
See that long, lonesome road? Don't you know it's got to end.
And I'm a good woman, and I can get plenty men.

As Iain Lang has said of this great and terrifying singer: *'C'est Vénus toute entière à sa proie attachée'.* But how often has Venus spoken, rather than been spoken about? It is therefore not surprising that the best women blues singers utterly outclass the men, good though these often are.

At a more complex level, the blues has proved to be a uniquely suitable foundation for solo or collective improvisation in jazz; that is to say for jazz composition.

The vocal secular blues has passed through several stages of evolution.[5] The 'country blues' seems to have emerged as a recognizable form towards the end of the nineteenth century, perhaps among travelling minstrels. It may be heard, e.g. on the records of Blind Lemon Jefferson, of Galveston, Texas (*c.* 1875 to *c.* 1930). Country blues are still emerging from folk-song: anonymous voices, distinguished only by having a special *timbre* or skill or trick, singing anybody's blues, not yet those of a recognizably unique individual. Recorded chiefly by men, the country blues has continued to be sung, though modified by the migration into the city, by the mixing styles, and lately by the demands of the jazz public. Good examples are on record by Big Bill Broonzy, Leroy Carr, Brownie McGhee, Sonny Terry, and in America by Howlin' Wolf, Lightning Hopkins, and other splendidly named bards, most of whom are more sophisticated, a little more self-conscious, and to be honest, better artist-craftsmen than their predecessors.

The 'classic blues' emerges with Ma Rainey (1885–1939). It is exclusively a woman's art, whose greatest glory is Bessie Smith (1900–37), followed by Ma Rainey herself and, a long way after, various lesser singers among whom Clara Smith, Sippie Wallace, and Bertha Hill may be mentioned. It was virtually dead by 1928. Being the song of professional music-hall stars the 'classic blues' is individualized art in the full sense. Purists, of whom jazz is full, have regretted the loss of the anonymity and impersonal grandeur of the folk-blues, which still echoes in Ma Rainey, but the gain in technique, expressiveness, and individualism more than offset this. It also had far more complex accompaniment from the mature jazz players and bands who served these prima donnas in the 1920s.

There is no need to say much about Bessie Smith,[6] the most impressive artist produced in any branch of jazz, for her numerous records form a sort of self-portrait. If we allow for their technical deficiencies (they were mostly cut between 1923 and 1927) they bring us all of Bessie Smith except that dense radiation of power and femininity with which she hypnotized her live audiences. 'She dominated the stage', says an old guitarist. 'You didn't turn your head when she went on. You just watched Bessie. You didn't read any newspapers in a night club when she went on. She just upset you'. She was a big, handsome, raucous, drunken, and infinitely sad woman: 'she liked to sing her blues slow; she didn't want no fast stuff'. She was that rare thing in jazz, or anywhere else, a major tragic artist, even in her moments of exultation; and nobody could exult more powerfully than Bessie singing 'Got the world in a jug, got the stopper in my hand', or 'I'm as good as any woman in your town.' She was raised in the slums of Nashville, Tennessee, and the travelling tent-shows of the South. She was alone all her life, and sang of the transitoriness of money, friends, liquor, and men with the deep and wary bitterness of somebody who knows that 'You can't trust nobody, you might as well be alone'. Lesser artists, or less percipient artists, have forgotten the penalties of the isolated, community-less life of the slum-bred entertainer in the temporary joys of his 'good times'. Not Bessie, for whom the standard refrain of the blues singer, 'You must reap just what you sow', had a constant and terrible reality. An individual rebel, bitter and undefeated, she died after a motor accident in the South. There has been nobody like her.

From the early 1930s the girls who might earlier have become blues singers, made their way as band vocalists, singing essentially a repertoire of 'ballads' or normal pop songs, in a style and with a technique which kept pace with the evolution of orchestral jazz. Ella Fitzgerald (born 1918) is the finest of the singers of this kind produced by the 1930s, and perhaps, with the older music-hall artist Ethel Waters (born 1900), the most gifted jazz singer on record; Sarah Vaughan (born 1924) is the finest singer produced in the atmosphere of the 'modern' jazz school. The classic blues itself either dropped from sight, or developed in the 1930s into what may not unfairly be called 'cabaret' blues, which differs from the classic music-hall song as, let us say, Gracie Fields's early songs differ from Yvette Guilbert's. Incomparably the finest singer of this more sophisticated and intimate type is the magical 'Lady Day', Billie Holiday (1915–59), who is incidentally the only blues singer to have made a total success out of an art-song, the anti-lynching poem *Strange Fruit*.[7] But among the leading black secular women singers the evolution has been strongly away from the formal blues; so much so that some of them are today incapable of singing a classic blues at all.

The post-classic blues tradition fell back into the hands of the modest 'city blues' singer, who had probably emerged from the country blues shortly after the formation of the classics; let us say in the 1920s. Mostly men, but after 1928 also some women —Bessie Jackson (a pseudonym) and the Yas Yas Girl perhaps deserve mention—they developed the blues mainly as a song of urban low-life. Musically perhaps the main development was the speeding-up of the blues, which increasingly adopted the insistent 'jump' beat, which has since made its fortune in pop music. The best performers in this genre were and are men, often very inadequately known on British records, such as Sonny Boy Williamson, who sang to his mouth-organ, and the Kansas City 'blues shouters' who were the first group of male blues singers to be integrated into orchestral jazz; Joe Turner and James Rushing, the vocalist of Count Basie's band. Here again the evolution has been away from the traditional country blues —partly by the absorption of pop song influences, partly by a crossing with the rhythmic excitement of urban black church music.

Black religious song differs from the secular blues in having remained primarily collective. The gospel choir and the gospel group to this day provide far more black church music than the individual gospel singer. The evolution of this music has not been studied anything like as fully as that of secular jazz or blues, largely because it has until recently been much less fully recorded. Consequently it is at present impossible to summarize it, however sketchily, in any adequate fashion. However, a few general points may be noted.

The first is that religion, a notoriously conservative institution, preserves archaic and sometimes African features in its song much more clearly than all but the most obscure rural work-songs, field-hollers, and other rapidly vanishing precursors of jazz. Secondly, it does so in the modern urban environment. The basis of modern gospel music lies in the swelling big city ghettoes, in which the church—ranging from the bare store-front tabernacle to the highly capitalized temple of the middle class—provides the most important single community centre for the immigrant. Since the thirties, and very markedly in the fifties, this vast and growing market has led to a commercialization of religious music, religion being perhaps the largest single business under black control. The professional or semi-professional gospel group, singing for churches and revival meetings other than its own, the local radio station for blacks with its unbroken programme of revival meetings, gospel song, and rhythm-and-blues, are familiar to any student of the city black today. Thirdly, this commercialization has led to a musical modification of gospel song. My impression—and in the present state of our knowledge one must be tentative—is that it has tended to produce, at one end the increasingly Europeanized large choir, at the other the group exploiting the most obvious tricks for arousing revivalist hysteria, such as heavily accented and endless rhythmic repetition and hot-gospelling call-and-response patterns.

Choral gospel song has probably been little influenced by secular jazz, but its own influence has been profound, notably on the big swing band. Moreover, in the fifties the commercialized gospel technique was universally adopted for secular purposes as rock-and-roll. The immense vogue of church song also helped, towards the end of the fifties, to carry the heritage of the blues back into the mainstream of modern jazz, and among a generation of musicians who had been brought up to despise it as old-fashioned and primitive, and who were almost totally ignorant of the vocal blues, as of most pre-modern jazz.

Some itinerant individual gospel singers similar to the secular blues-men had long existed. One of them, Blind Willie Johnson, gained a short-lived popularity during the slump, when hunger and despair echoed his wild calls to God.[8] But in the main the solo gospel singer seems to have been gradually individualized out of the complex mixture of choral song and private improvisation in the traditional black service, where originally the only fully personal voice was that of the preacher, slipping insensibly from rhythmic prose into chanting. The most prominent of these singers are women, who began to record in quantity only in the 1930s. By far the finest of them is Mahalia Jackson (born 1911), a great artist who combines a superb voice with marvellous emotion, and an unerring sense of the construction of a solo.

Formally the gospel song is often remote from the twelve-bar blues; but the good gospel singers are nevertheless as blue as any secular singer, and the best of them can recreate the extraordinary emotional expressiveness of the classic blues, even though the emotion expressed is joy in salvation, or fervour of faith, rather than secular grief. As a member of the Sanctified Church in Mount Vernon is supposed to have said: 'Mahalia, she add more flowers and feathers than anybody, and they all is exactly right.' That is the blues. But it may well be that the tendency of the gospel song has been towards a much more baroque style than is to be found in the spare classicism of the best secular blues.

The instrumental blues can be best discussed under the headings of jazz orchestral and instrumental styles.

The Styles of Jazz

I have already given a brief list and sketch of the chief 'styles' of jazz in Chapter 3. In the remainder of this chapter and the next I shall try to discuss these styles in greater detail. Like all art-historians, jazz experts are naturally much given to arguing about where one 'style' or 'school' ends and another begins, and the sub-divisions I have used are open to many such arguments, in which neither the reader nor the author need join. The only point to bear in mind is that the appearance of a new style does not mean the disappearance of the old. Today, for instance, all the styles discussed below are played by someone or other, except perhaps 'ragtime' and the 1920s East Coast styles. Some of them have, however, ceased to develop.

'Ragtime'[9] was essentially a pianistic rather than an orchestral style which, being a 'written' music and a way of playing ordinary music—almost any piece can be 'ragged'—gradually grew away from the jazz traditions. Its fundamental musical characteristic is syncopation, on which various other rhythmic devices are superimposed. The form of its compositions is, as Stearns suggests, a sort of rondo deriving from minuets, scherzos, and indeed marches. However, ragtime was adapted for the jazz band in the ancient period, notably by the extraordinarily talented and raffish pianist, arranger, and band leader Ferdinand Jelly-Roll Morton (1885–1941), in whose Red Hot Peppers records of the middle 1920s this adaptation may be heard to perfection. Rags or rag-flavoured numbers also became part of the staple repertoire of New Orleans jazz, or more exactly, of the white Dixieland music derived from it, and can still be heard in any 'traditionalist' jazz band: e.g. *Maple Leaf Rag, Eccentric, That's a Plenty,* or *Muskrat Ramble, Original Dixieland One Step,* and *Ostrich Walk.*

The earliest style of 'ancient' jazz was that of *New Orleans,*[10] whose origins in military band-music are still evident. Its instrumentation normally consisted of cornet (from the mid twenties also trumpet), clarinet, trombone, tuba (later bass), and snares and bass drums. The banjo (later guitar) was added subsequently, as was the piano, which obviously had no place on the carts or in the hands of the perambulating musicians. It was a solo instrument for ragtime or blues. The saxophone never had a place in New Orleans music. The instrumental technique combines the African vocalizing of the uptown blacks with the orthodox French style of the Creole, especially obvious in the woodwind: thus Johnny Dodds plays technically mediocre, but wonderfully blue and vocalized clarinet, while Bigard or Simeon play the liquid 'Creole clarinet'. The repertoire, which even the gloomiest jazz haters admit to be jolly and tuneful, was again largely derived from European dances and marches, with the French influence dominant and a marked 'Spanish tinge' owing to the proximity of the Caribbean. The actual derivations have in many instances been established, e.g. for *Tiger Rag,* which comes from a quadrille. Though New Orleans knew the blues, it seems never to have integrated it as fully into its jazz as the Kansas City players or Duke Ellington did later; perhaps because of the strength of the Creoles and their dominant, and quite 'unblue' musical tradition. The blues in New Orleans was regarded mainly as whorehouse music. Not until after 1914 or so was a link between blues and instrumental jazz firmly forged. As for the country blues, its absorption into the New Orleans tradition is the product or the invention of the intellectual jazz fans of the 1940s. When Leadbelly, the country minstrel, visited the city he hated it, and it ostracized him.[11]

The chief vocal characteristic of New Orleans jazz was a three-part vocal polyphony. The cornet carried the main melody and the band, the clarinet, with its capacity to make itself heard over a mass of noise, filled in its own melody rather more elaborately between the lead notes and answered them, the trombone set up a brass counterpoint to the cornet. The rhythm section laid down a rock-firm beat, normally accenting two of the four beats to the bar, but initially with relatively little syncopation or rhythmic subtlety. The melodic and rhythmic complexity of the music emerged from the interplay of all the instruments, which normally improvised collectively, with not much scope for long individual instrumental breaks or solos. Later this tended to develop into a three-part musical form: an opening section, in which the instruments, led by the cornet, played together, a middle section, in which the individual players could show their paces in solos or duets, and a final section in which everybody once again went to town: one of the most exhilarating sounds in jazz. The former style is illustrated by the (rather late) first recordings of black New Orleans jazz in the early 1920s from King Oliver's band, the latter by many of the ravishing records of Louis Armstrong's Hot Five.*

The black New Orleans style was adopted by white bands from the city, but though these played it less movingly, they added little to it (Dixieland style). In the 1920s, under the influence of the changed social and musical environment of the North, the style evolved towards greater instrumental and rhythmical finesse, and greater individualism. This evolution may be profitably traced in the records of Louis Armstrong who, according to the purists of the style, had ceased to play it by 1928. The only interesting experiments in composed and

---

* Experts on New Orleans music will observe that this rough sketch greatly over-simplifies a long musical evolution, even within primitive New Orleans jazz, but this is not the place for greater detail.

rehearsed New Orleans ragtime jazz also occurred in this period, under Jelly-Roll Morton.[12] On the whole, however, the style as a style was unadaptable. Its only offshoot was the Mid-Western white Chicago Style, developed by young players who deliberately copied the New Orleans musicians.

The Chicago style[13] differs from New Orleans in several important ways. It introduces, though only tentatively, the saxophones into New Orleans polyphony, drops the trombone and —another absorption of 'pop music' influences—it adopted the pop song as the basis of the jazz repertoire: most of the classic Chicago records are 'hot' versions of current song-hits, *Liza, Sugar, I've Found a New Baby,* etc. However, the problem of how to use pop tunes as an adequate foundation for jazz was not really solved until later. Chicago jazz is also much more individualized. Chicago *is* the individual players, Bix, Teschemacher, Tough, Spanier, Floyd O'Brien, much more than anything else. That is one reason why, as Berendt has acutely observed, there is no big or small band to represent this style, as King Oliver or the Hot Five represent late New Orleans. (The other is economic.) There are only the individuals, playing together in casually changing combinations. Lastly, though it is difficult to put a finger on this, there is in the best Chicago records a peculiar and distinctive atmosphere, which can best be described as 'not relaxed', or 'ill at ease'. The metaphors which spring to mind for records like the Chicago Rhythm Kings' *I've Found a New Baby* or *There'll Be Some Changes Made* are the literary ones of the Scott Fitzgerald and Hemingway era; what Wilder Hobson calls the 'hardboiled eloquence' of a Chicago blues, like *Home Cookin',* is the Hemingway prose-style translated into jazz. But in the last analysis Chicago was much less a single style, than a place where 'white boy met horn'. Chicago music ranges all the way from performances which are virtually white New Orleans or white blues, to performances which, like those of Bix and Teschemacher, are quite original white developments.

The white 'Eastern' style of the middle and late 1920s is rarely called by this name, but the records made by Eastern-based pick-up bands like Red Nichols and His Five Pennies, Miff Mole and His Little Molers, the Venuti-Lang Blue Four and others, were so influential in their day, and have so consistent a character, that they deserve a separate label. Their origins were in ragtime and Dixieland music rather than in the main New Orleans traditional though they came into contact with this at second hand through Chicago and Western migrants to New York in the late twenties. They were a white school derived from white players, but unquestionably an 'ancient' one, for they flourished in the twenties and as yet made no attempt to play hot jazz in anything except the characteristic small combination. However, several members of the group became leaders of large 'swing' orchestras in the thirties: the Dorseys, Glenn Miller, Benny Goodman, originally a Chicagoan. The white Eastern style is a sort of chamber-music jazz, a line which seems rather suited to white musicians, and of which the Nichols groups, the Blue Four, and the Bix-Trumbauer records are good examples. There is elegance and polish, but almost no blues feeling. Orthodox influences are marked, for instance in the instrumental smoothness. the instrumentation, though originally traditional (as in the original Memphis Five: trumpet, trombone, clarinet, piano, drums), is also eclectically derived from orthodox and light pop music. The violin, the guitar, saxophones, including freak instruments like the bass sax (A. Rollini), are normal. In fact the nearest thing to the Easterners of the twenties is found in the small white 'cool' combinations of the 1950s, though these approach orthodox light music *via* serious classical ambitions from hot jazz, rather than emerging a little way out of it through the influence of hot jazz.

Like the Napoleon, Nichols, Mole, Venuti-Lang combinations which produced a deal of tasteful and pleasant music in their time, the modern groups of this kind enjoy a grossly inflated reputation today (1958). The Easterners are at present equally grossly underrated in jazz circles. Their most interesting achievements were in instrumental technique, and it is significant that the smooth, light, well-bred tones of their instruments have been influential among modern 'cool' players, whose ancestor, the saxophonist Lester Young, claims to have imitated the leading white player Trumbauer.[14] It is arguable that, had they continued to evolve, the Easterners and some of the Chicagoans might have 'been playing music much like bebop',[15] in which case they would occupy an important place in jazz evolution. At all events the claim of white jazz to have to have made really original contributions to the music must still rest mainly on the Eastern and Chicago traditions. In fact, however, both led into temporary blind alleys.

Though 'middle period' jazz belongs to the 1930s, certain developments of the twenties must be considered with it, for it is essentially the adaptation of jazz to the large band. By orthodox standards this is still not very large—fourteen or fifteen players, as against the seven or eight of New Orleans. A typical line-up is that of Duke Ellington's Orchestra in the early thirties: three trumpets, three trombones, four reeds, piano, bass, guitar, drums. This is still the basic pattern of the large band, allowing for variations or the addition of the occasional odd instrument. It will be obvious that the systematic use of the saxes and the enlargement of the band entailed fundamental musical changes, if only because if is impossible to have old-style collective polyphony, improvised or not, with ten melody instruments. As Borneman has pointed out, beyond four melodic lines this becomes unmanageable. In a word, the rise of the large band poses problems of instrumental style and of arrangement and composition.

Since these were not solved in any universal way, it is difficult to fit the big bands into styles and schools. Fletcher Henderson (1898–1952),[16] the pioneer of the big band, began with a black pop group which he turned increasingly toward jazz by importing suitable musicians and drawing on the New Orleans repertoire. The hot quality of his players imposed jazz even on his arrangements which had, to begin with, been modelled on the ordinary 'sweet' bands such as Paul Whiteman's. His talented arranger Don Redman (who later became the brain behind such large black bands as McKinney's Cotton Pickers) evolved what was later to be called the 'swing' formula, which consists, essentially, of scored ensemble passages for all the horns, and alternating the various melodic groups—brass and reeds, trumpets, trombones, and saxes—building up an antiphonal rhythmic background, intermitted, when dramatically desirable, for the solo players. It is, as it were, the translation of the African and gospel-song antiphony into terms of the band sections.* Most of these early arrangements were awkward and sound dated, like a farmer in his first dinner jacket. The quality of the soloists and the swing and vigour of the ensemble passages give what permanent interest they have to bands like McKinney's, Luis Russell's, Claude Hopkins's, or the Blue Rhythm Band. Smaller combinations drawn from the same bands were more successful; for instance the admirable Chocolate Dandies. The practice of making up temporary sub-units from the members of large bands has since become common. Duke Ellington has done so extensively.

Of the early big bands only one achieved more than this, Duke Ellington's from 1926.[17] It has about the same sort of relation to the rest of its competitors as Shakespeare had to the rest of the Elizabethan dramatists—*toutes proportions gardées*—and cannot therefore be fitted into any schools or measured by other musicians' standards. Ellington (born 1899), who is the most important talent produced in jazz so far, triumphantly, and at the first attempt, solved the triple problem of big band jazz: the composition of a jazz repertoire, the problem of jazz orchestration, and (by a judicious selection of players) the problem of the instrumental styles. Admittedly he did so in an extremely individual manner, beyond the reach of others who possessed neither his many talents nor his unique instrument, a permanent large band. Highly sophisticated though all his achievements are, they are almost invariably direct deductions from the fundamental principles of the original, popular, spontaneous, and improvised jazz.

Ellington plays mainly his own compositions (which are nat-

* I owe this point, as indeed much else in this and the next chapter, to Charles Fox.

76

urally the result of collaboration between him and his musicians), but he has also brilliantly adapted the standard forms to his own ends. He has given the blues orchestral form by basing himself on blues harmonies, developing blues melody, and translating its antiphonies into terms of the band. The improvising musician retains his old freedom within a framework of 'composed' jazz, even when deprived of the chance of a straightforward break or cadenza. Both the construction of Ellington's pieces and the lines written, or left free, for his soloists are primarily based on the blues antiphony, so that his compositions often tend towards the duet or the miniature concerto, and the solos of his players more often to the brief 'answering' improvisations of the blues accompanist than to the long choruses of the freely improvising player. As for the pop ballad, he has 'dropped the melodic line, which was generally meaningless, and developed (its) diatonic chromatic harmonies',[18] which, from the point of view of the jazz tradition, were new and interesting. Though Ellington's music looks logically forward from old-fashioned jazz towards some sort of art-music, he has not attempted to introduce any of the intellectual architecture of classical music, as some modern jazz composers have done. His own preoccupation has been with the blending of orchestral colours and the expression of moods, to both of which the old jazz lent itself easily. Among classical musicians he therefore found composers like Debussy, Delius, or Ravel most useful, though they seem to have influenced him indirectly rather than at first hand. Ellington compositions are essentially—if we must use orthodox analogies—romantic rather than classical. If anything, they tend to paint small impressionist pictures which grow into suites *(Creole Rhapsody, Black, Brown and Beige)*.

To be frank, his success as an artist is probably less than as an innovator. (How much of this is due to the immense difficulties of a man building a serious art-music out of, and in, commercial mass entertainment, and virtually starting alone and from scratch, is a matter of debate.) Though no composer or band has maintained a more constantly high level of musical intelligence and achievement, and though his plateaux—1929–33, 1939–41

—are very elevated indeed, few of his records will be as certain of individual immortality as some of the masterpieces of Bessie Smith or Armstrong. Those which are certain of it may owe as much to the planned glory of their solos as to his composing, e.g. the remarkable *Concerto for Cootie,* of which A. Hodeir has given a twenty-one-page analysis. Ellington's music is a process of discovery rather than a series of achievements. It is character-istic of the man that he has, throughout his career, taken up, developed, and improved his earlier composition so that pieces like his pioneer *East Saint Louis Toodle-oo* (1926) or *Black and Tan Fantasy* (1927) exist in a series of versions. His main weaknesses are an occasional tendency to sweetness and lushness—less marked in the informal sessions of the Ellington band's subunits —an early tendency to obvious 'jungle' effects, and indeed, an occasional pretentious vulgarism. However, his place in musical history is quite secure. 'He may be called a kind of Haydn of jazz, reconstructing all the old material of jazz in terms of the new sound demanded by his times, as Haydn brought together elements from folk-song, comic opera, serenade, and street music and infused them into the budding symphony'.[19]

His most lasting gift to orchestral jazz is the discovery that bands can have a distinctive 'sound', i.e. orchestral colour, the palette being mixed by the composer-arranger from the colours of the individual musicians, carefully chosen for the purpose. The Ellington sound is quite unmistakable. It contains a mixture of New Orleans colours—especially the liquid creole clarinet which he alone of all band-leaders has used consistently to the present day—the carefully controlled blue sound of the brass, especially as played with mutes, as a well-mixed reed sound, originally based on the interplay of the baritone sax (another instrument largely confined to his band) and the alto. He has evolved this mixture from the personalities of his musicians, notably Bubber Miley and Cootie Williams, trumpeters; 'Tricky Sam' Nanton, trombone; Barney Bigard, clarinet; Harry Car-ney, baritone sax; and Johnny Hodges, alto sax; but the sound has survived their death or departure. Long after his pioneer work other bands discovered the virtues of a 'sound' as a trade-mark, and it has been widely exploited—as its best in bands like Lunceford's (*floruit* 1934–9) and Basie's (from 1936), at its most commercial in bands like the late Glenn Miller's.

The only other style of jazz which, in a much less conscious way, achieved a similar revolution was that of Kansas City.[20] Here, building not so much on New Orleans jazz and the elements of light metropolitan entertainment music, but on the professional individual jazz musician and the urbanized country blues, the second integration of the blues into the big-band style took place. This process was the very opposite of Ellington's: simplification rather than elaboration. Ensemble playing was reduced from the New Orleans counterpoint to simple repeated phrases, 'a rock-like foundation, allowing men to get a firm grip of the melody, the harmonies, and the rhythmic pattern before launching forth on the paths of their individual solos'. The main themes for these improvisations were pop songs, but above all the twelve-bar blues, whose chords and form everyone knew, and which allowed full freedom for development. The blues thus adapted was made the basis both of fast and of slow numbers—there is nothing in the blues form which imposes sadness—and of ensemble work. There it was normally simplified down to the 'riff', the repeated melodic (blues) phrase played between and behind the solos, which is so characteristic of Kansas City's most successful product, the band of Count Basie.

Since it was evolved by players for their own convenience, this apparent regression to primitivism had three major musical advantages. First, it provided a flexible framework for big-band jazz which could be more widely adopted than the highly individual technique of Ellington, or perhaps even than the Redman formula; and it has been so adopted. Second, and more important, it allowed the big band to absorb directly the most flourishing and vigorous elements of black folk-music, the sung blues and the blues piano. Kansas City style is the only one which has used unspoiled blues singers as band vocalists and integral parts of the orchestra, e.g., James Rushing. Third, and most important, it allowed and even encouraged the utmost technical inventiveness and adventurousness among the players. For this reason

79

Kansas City, more than any other style, became the incubator of the musical revolution in jazz, while at the same time its most radical innovators, like Parker, remained rooted in the blues. The style may be heard at its best in the early records of Count Basie's band: an unmistakable combination of brazen ensembles, solid rhythmic movement, and the solo blues.

The other brands of middle period jazz, bred mainly in Harlem and other large Northern ghettoes, are less easy to reduce to type, unless it be the 'Harlem jump', 'the most constant rhythm developed in jazz',[21] an urbanized, speeded-up beat, fusing the shouting rhythm of the city gospel congregation with the dance rhythm of the city ballroom.[22] Often vulgar and showy, this 'Harlem music' (often played by non-New-Yorkers) tended to commercialism. Its vocalists are ballad—not blues—singers, its musicians play acrobatic tricks, and often build up rhythmic frenzy as a sales device. At its best, as in Chick Webb's (1926–39) and Lionel Hampton's bands (from 1934), it generates irresistible swing, though its technically superb musicians have, unless bandleaders, less individual scope than in Kansas City. However, musicians from these big bands also contributed to the jazz revolution. Except for its rhythm, 'Harlem' cannot be regarded as a 'style', but only as a show case and a meeting place for talented and storming players. The New York tradition of solo (piano) music has followed a rather different line.

The common denominators of all these types of middle period jazz are tremendous technical virtuosity and swing which is an aspect of the same thing. There can be no argument about the increasing technical mastery of the players, though this must not be confused with increasing emotional expressiveness. Jazz, after all, is designed for maximum emotional expressiveness even with defective technical equipment, and though Louis Armstrong almost certainly could never have let off the fireworks of a Shavers or Gillespie on his trumpet, he has never had trouble in holding his own as an artist. Nevertheless, middle period jazz is designed for virtuosi, and largely created by the generation which first got the full technical possibilities out of their instruments. A similar technical sophistication took place in the drums. Ancient jazz (ragtime and New Orleans) had used a beat which still echoed European music, accenting the first and third beats of the bar. Its derivations—Dixieland and Chicago music, etc.—though still 'two-beat' jazz, tended to accent the off-beats. But with swing we enter the period of 'four-beat' jazz, the evenly accented bar, though there is still an instinctive tendency to stress the off-beats. The resulting rhythms, and rhythmical variations, are far subtler, and produce that indefinable swaying and living pulse which is called, for want of a better term, 'swing', but this, though as Hodeir observes essentially a rhythmic phenomenon, is not simply the affair of the rhythm section. In jazz every instrument has rhythmic as well as melodic functions, which is why 'swing' as a general phenomenon was hardly possible until a high average level of expertise had been reached. Novices, with a bit of feeling, can produce a passable imitation of a New Orleans brass band, or even a good Dixieland number; but not one of Lionel Hampton's *Flyin' Home*.

Though nobody predicted it at the time, we can now see that 'modern' jazz developed logically out of the middle period, partly as a prolongation of it, partly as a reaction against it.[23] Here we need be concerned only with the stylistic and musical aspects of this revolution in jazz, which is comparable to the revolutions of the twentieth century, in modern painting and classical music.* The jazz public has always been divided, but before the modernist revolution normally only into 'purists' and 'impurists'; that is into those who wish to preserve jazz from innovation because they believed it to lead to the ultimate horror of 'commercialization', and those who grudgingly recognized that not all innovation turned jazz into pop music. But modernism produced rival purity schools, though in its early stages the defenders of old-style 'pure' jazz purported to regard it as merely another commercial novelty gimmick. But modern jazz was far from aiming at mass appeal. On the contrary, it was the first jazz style which deliberately turned its face away from the ordi-

* Other aspects of this revolution are discussed in Chapters 3, 9, 10.

nary public and created music for initiatives and experts only. The dangers which beset it were not those of degenerating into best-sellerdom.* To this day its public remains considerably smaller than the public for pre-modern jazz.[24] Its temptation has been rather to slide over into something increasingly difficult to distinguish from classical art-music (and normally rather mediocre art-music at that).

The best way to explain its musical genesis is to say that musicians became bored and frustrated with the increasingly standardized and repetitive music of the big bands of the 1930s. (The original 'bop' revolutionaries almost all came from such big bands: Gillespie the trumpeter from Teddy Hill and Cab Calloway, Charlie Parker the alto player from Jay McShann, Kenny Clarke the drummer from a variety of bands, Charlie Christian from Goodman.) In spite of occasional big bop bands such as Gillespie's, Herman's, and Eckstine's, modern jazz is essentially small-band music. Also it was essentially a reaction against entertaining a large or even a small lay public: it was musicians' music. As such it naturally developed the virtuoso tendencies of middle period jazz to hitherto undreamed heights: Parker swung at 360 quarter-notes per minute, a thing hitherto believed impossible.[25] Clarke and his imitators tried to get their drums to play not only rhythm but 'tunes'. Christian played his electric guitar as though it were a wind instrument, J. J. Johnson the trombone as though it were a trumpet. Indeed, whatever were think of their musical value, the sheer technical achievements of the moderns are breathtaking.

Similarly, the revolutionaries assumed a degree of musical sophistication which automatically made jazz into an élite activity. Bop rhythm no longer indicated the beat, except perhaps by a legato agitation of the cymbal, a sort of rhythmic shiver through which the basic pulse might be glimpsed. Musicians were supposed to *assume* the beat, over which rhythmic com-

* Though it has produced a few artists whose marked individuality allows them to outsell many ostensibly more 'popular' performers, notably Miles Davis.

plexities of almost African subtlety were played.* They were expected to assume the melody, for the modernists no longer improvised on the simple theme—normally the pop ballad—but built a new theme out of the harmonies of the old and improvised on that, changing the harmonies slightly while doing so; or even elaborating the process. So far as they were concerned the really competent player ought to hear not merely the final theme and is often remote improvisation, but behind it the unplayed original theme: a duet between the actual music played and the ghost-music from which it was originally derived. (They often did not trouble even to indicate the title of the original theme: a competent musician was supposed to know or reconstruct it.) The whole thing was nearly as great a test of musical expertise as is the following of a Bach mirror fugue without the score. If a musician could do this, well and good. If he or the listener could not, to hell with him. It is small wonder that modern musicians have often shown a marked hankering for the intellectually more demanding constructions of classical music. For them, not Delius and Debussy, but Bach, Schoenberg, and Bartók.

These tendencies toward written architectural music were, however, later developments. The original 'boppers' were essentially improvisers in what we can now recognize as the old jazz tradition, however revolutionized. The jam session in which each artist built his own musical structure out of a series of solo choruses (based at bottom on the characteristic middle period musical device of the short repeated phrase, the riff) was their characteristic home. The musicians approached composition mainly in so far as fully worked-out solos were much prized and often repeated note for note. The bop innovations were hardly at all architectural and orchestral. The innovators revolutionized tonality and harmony but left the typical 'bop' piece architecturally as primitive as any old small-band piece: a theme (now

---

* Insofar as the beat was actually articulated, it might shift from place to place, from instrument to instrument, though it has tended to settle with the bass.

generally stated in unison by the players), followed by variations, and perhaps restated. In some respects 'bop' retreated from the complex orchestral writing which Jelly-Roll Morton, Duke Ellington, Don Redman, Sy Oliver, and other composer-arrangers had brought to jazz, though this retreat was only temporary. The modern school in time developed its own extremely able arrangers who normally carried on, roughly speaking, where Ellington left off: Tadd Dameron, John Lewis, Gil Evans.

The listener hearing the unfamiliar rhythmic complexities, the discordant and apparently disconnected solos, the free and continual key changes, the extraordinary use of the instruments, might well regard 'bop' as not only new but chaotic. But its fundamental structure was quite old-fashioned, as was its fundamental material: the blues or the pop song. Modern jazz has indeed concentrated mainly on the pop ballad, which it has for the first time turned into something like a musically usable form. It did so partly by using it, as we have seen, as a foundation on which a new counter-melody was built, partly by twisting it into adventurous shapes—adorning it with little chromatic figures or broken chords, modulating into surprising and remote keys, transforming its phrases rhythmically. But it also did so by, for the first time in jazz history, systematically breaking down the distinction between ballads and blues. For the blues lies at the heart of modern jazz as of all jazz. We recognize it, even in its transformation, in the greatest of all modern players, the tragic Charlie Parker who, as Finkelstein rightly says, 'is almost wholly a blues performer, as moving in his own way as Johnny Dodds in the old music'.[26]

The early 'bop' music, was played in 1941–9 by its pioneers, and since then by some of the intransigent survivors, was a manifesto of revolt, though we can now see that the revolt moved within the frontiers of traditional craftsmen's jazz. Like so many other and similar artistic revolutions, its first stage was in some respects the most extreme. The mere existence of a new idiom makes it familiar: abstract painters in the 1950s are no longer revolutionaries—at least not against their predecessors—but traditionalists. The public, in turn, becomes accustomed to a

new sound. The Gillespie-Parker-Monk records of 1946–8
which struck non-expert listeners at the time as wholly incomprehensible, are now accepted quite easily, if not always with
enthusiasm. Phrases which ten years ago would have raised the
hair of the ordinary listener, now occur as a matter of course in
orchestras and solos which make no claim to special modernism.
Indeed, the revolutionaries have begun to suffer the last indignity
of their kind. Their carefully elaborated complexities sound simple: just tunes, though tunes of a new kind—background noise
for dreaming, chatting, flirting, even dancing. And modern jazz
has to some extent domesticated itself, meeting the public halfway. Little by little it has reintroduced a less revolutionary type
of melody: the Modern Jazz Quartet, or Miles Davis, the leading
soloist of the latest phrase of jazz, play altogether gentler and
more recognizable tunes, often no more demanding than those
of Ellington. The 'beat', that essential of jazz, is perhaps easier to
recognize today than it was in the adventurous forties. Some of
this is due to regression, but some to a further evolution in jazz
which has been called the 'cool' style of the fifties.

The 'cool' style is the most extreme point as yet reached in
jazz evolution—the point which almost lies on the borders between jazz and ordinary art-music. The very name is a paradox.
The jazz of the past was in its very nature *hot*—sensuous, emotional, physical—and 'dirty'—instrumentally unorthodox because emotionally expressive (the word was used as a synonym
for 'hot' in the 1920s). Even bop, as we have seen, retained this
fundamental emotional heat and musical impurity. With all its
insistence on musical bravura, what the boppers played was
expressionist and not abstract music. Cool jazz aimed at a hitherto irrelevant ideal of musical purity, that is to say in many
respects at the complete reversal of most jazz values. Cool
players tried to make instruments sound like orthodox classical instruments, e.g. with a minimum of vibrato. Classical
instruments, whose main recommendation for jazz was that they
sounded smooth and had snob appeal, were for the first time
used as more than oddities: flutes, oboes, flügelhorns. The main
melodic pillar of jazz, the 'horn' or wind instrument, came under

suspicion: small combinations consisting exclusively of such things as piano, bass, drums (perhaps supplemented with a vibraharp, an oboe-sounding sax, a well-bred clarinet, or even a bowed cello) became common sights. What Hodeir has called a 'wispy' sound became the ideal of many cool men. More than any of their prececessors, the cool players and arrangers also dreamed of an educated composed jazz capable of competing with the classics. Leading 'progressive' players like the pianist Lennie Tristano, the saxophonist Lee Konitz, even took to theorizing, founding academies, and teaching, a thing hitherto unheard of in jazz, where musicians said what they had to say in notes and not words, and learned what they had to learn by apprenticeship, like Renaissance painters. These are the players and composers who claim to be inspired by Johann Sebastian Bach and eighteenth-century classicism—an admirable model, but a very surprising one. Intellectualized and formalized jazz such as this, drained of much of its old-fashioned red blood, naturally appealed particularly strongly to young white players who are much better able to compete with black ones on territory which is, after all, close to the one in which all white musicians have been brought up. Cool jazz therefore attracted an abnormally large number of young white recruits, especially in California, where Los Angeles became the headquarters of a 'West Coast school'.

The cool players did not wish to abandon jazz, though many critics feel that the work of some of them—say of Dave Brubeck in California and the Tristano group in New York—often crosses the border from jazz into jazz-tinged art-music. Nor, in fact, do the best of them eliminate genuine and powerful emotion, though it tends to be eerie, sleepwalking, dreamlike stuff as in the finest player of the school, the trumpeter Miles Davis. They maintain their pride in the jazz tradition, and especially the blues (even when least capable of playing it). They derive directly from previous styles—notably via bop from the middle period —by the usual link of jazz evolution, craft virtuosity. For just because it was so much harder to play hot by means of a 'pure', spare, and sober technique, players had long tried to do so.

86

Benny Carter on sax and clarinet, Teddy Wilson on piano, had long 'underplayed' their attacks, or substituted delicacy for drive. One of the most formative musicians of the thirties, Lester Young, tenor sax in Count Basie's band, had demonstrated that it was possible to produce remarkable jazz while avoiding virtually all the characteristics of the 'hot' sound, mainly by means of a quite extraordinary suppleness, the product of muscular relaxation.[27] Young's 'cool' sound was one of the components of the bop revolution; indeed, he is commonly regarded as its most important single precursor. But whereas the boppers retained hot jazz while also taking over the new cool technique, their successors developed coolness, purity, relaxation into an exclusive system. In doing so they brought jazz to the very verge of its possibilities as jazz.

It would be logical to argue that the future evolution of modern jazz must take it over that border into art-music; or rather over the border into that territory where it disintegrates as jazz, while art-musicians absorb its various fragments into their own music as nineteenth-century nationalist composers absorbed the elements of their peoples' music into the general body of classical music. But this will not necessarily occur. For though modern jazz has tried, more and more systematically, to escape from the musical limitations of the older jazz—or to react against them—its social situation has so far continued to link it to its old and unreconstructed musical kindred. Some jazz may well go permanently over the border, just as one sort of black spiritual has gone permanently into the concert hall. But just as gospel music in the Mount Tabor African Strict Baptist Tabernacle continues a vigorous life quite independent of Miss Marian Anderson's kind of spirituals (though not unaffected by musical developments), so jazz, including much modern jazz, is likely to continue even if some versions of it pass beyond its frontiers. Indeed, the exclusive concentration on coolness led to a stylistic reaction in the later fifties. Modern players who had never stopped 'blowing out', pioneers of the original bop era who had been in eclipse, such as the pianist-composer Thelonious Monk, came into their own. A succession of powerful saxophonists sounding

87

anything but thin and wispy, captured the fancy of the *avant-garde:* Sonny Rollins, John Coltrane, Ornette Coleman, and the more widely popular Cannonball Adderley. The reaction against coolness, the search for heat and emotion, took musicians back to those obvious sources of musical passion, blues and gospel song, and even some way towards the swinging music of the thirties, which was beginning to enjoy more popularity among the advanced than it had for many years. Indeed, while the neo-hot jazz of 1960 (variously named 'funky', 'hard-bop', or 'soul-music') remained solidly modern, and sometimes highly experimental, its very search for heat and roots made it the first 'traditional' style of modern jazz. Its implicit slogans were backward-looking: back to Parker, back to blues and gospel, back even to the central tradition of big-band jazz. The reasons for this reaction were of course ideological as well as musical.

Whether this return to the main tradition of jazz is permanent or not, it is too early to say. It may well be that this latest phase (1960) will once again lead to a counter-movement, and that modern jazz will continue as an interplay between the hot and cool tendencies. But we do not know.

One thing is clear. So long as jazz is jazz it will always be anchored to some sort of stylistic pattern by the need to be a music for dancing. I recall the wise remarks of Mr Gus Johnson, a Kansas City drummer practised in the best of all jazz schools, Count Basie's band. 'They used to say bop was here for all time', he said. 'I didn't see it that way. It was something new: that's good naturally. But you take a line of girls. They have to dance, and if they have to dance they have to hear the beat, like this'— and Mr Johnson tapped it out, rock-firm and swinging, with his fingers. 'Now that beat has got to be there all the time, or else nobody can dance to it.' For the past dozen years or so a great deal of jazz has not been played for dancing, but for listening, often in concert halls and recital rooms. But so long as jazz is not exclusively a recital music; that is, so long as it is not played for an exclusively expert or snob audience, so long as it is played in dance halls, theatres, and clubs as well as in halls, some listeners will also want to dance to it, if only in the aisles. And so long as

the demand for jazz to dance to continues, some jazz of all styles
—old, middle period, or modern—will adapt itself to this demand. It will not be hard either; for jazz is a music made to get
people's limbs moving, whatever other and higher achievements
it also has to its credit.

f i v e

The Instruments

*E*xcept for the piano, the evolution of the jazz instruments is part of that of the jazz orchestral styles. It may be broadly summed up as follows: The clarinet reached its peak of development in New Orleans jazz, and has since then dropped progressively into the background. The brass reached its peak of development in the 'swing' era, and has since then also lost ground. The saxes follow an ascending curve from the early 1920s until the 'bop' period, when they reach their peak, but have remained stationary since. The percussive instruments follow a steadily ascending curve until the cool period, when they become, in some instances, the major carriers of melody as well as of rhythm (e.g. Modern Jazz Quartet: piano, vibes, drums, bass). In spite of repeated attempts, nobody has yet managed to do more with bowed string instruments than use them for occasional effects. If they have a future in jazz, it is still to come. There are signs, as in the use of a cello by Oscar Pettiford or of the bowed bass by various artists, that players are today making efforts to conquer even these highly recalcitrant instruments for jazz. Within this general framework, however, there is infinite variety. Jazz is what individual players make it, and each player has his individual voice. Attempts have been made to trace the evolution and cross-fertilizations of instrumental styles in diagrammatic form,[1] but even the most lucid diagram looks rather like a wiring plan for a complex electrical installation. I do not propose to give a detailed account of these instrumental marches and counter-marches here, but merely to list a few of the major players and influences.

The two clarinet styles of New Orleans—the liquid 'creole' and the dirty 'blues' clarinet—reach their respective peaks early in the triumvirate of Jimmy Noone (1895–1944), Johnny Dodds (1892–1940), and Sidney Bechet (1897–1959), who is better known for his adaptation of the clarinet to the otherwise scarcely used soprano sax. The reserve team of Bigard (born 1906), Nicholas (born 1900), Hall (born 1901), and Simeon (1902–1959) is somewhat less powerful. All these musicians come from New Orleans. Among white players the Chicagoans Teschemacher (1906–32) and 'Pee-Wee' Russell (born 1906) developed the 'dirty' style, while Benny Goodman (born 1909) is technically perhaps the most brilliant player of the instrument, white or black.[2] It is doubtful whether, if all records later than 1930 were destroyed—except for those of Bechet, who was poorly recorded in those days—our picture of the technical and emotional possibilities of this instrument as hitherto used in jazz would be incomplete. Dodd's marvellous playing with Louis Armstrong and with his own New Orleans Wanderers, Simeon's contributions on the Jelly-Roll Morton records, and Bigard's with Morton and Ellington demonstrate the range of the instrument.

The cornet, and from the later 1920s its successor the trumpet, is hereditary king of jazz, though for a time it was in semi-exile under the moderns. There are therefore more brilliant trumpeters than stars of any other instrument in jazz history. However, all discussion of the jazz trumpet must begin and end with Louis Armstrong (born 1900) the greatest jazzman of them all, in whose art New Orleans music culminates and is surpassed.[3] Louis Armstrong is not just a trumpeter: he is the voice of his people speaking on a horn. A natural genius, who intuitively organizes his art with the automatic assurance with which the bodies of lesser men manage their breathing, he has been exceptionally lucky. Born twenty years earlier, he would have been a splendid folk-trumpeter, a leader of a street band, lacking both the technical equipment and the capacity to speak with a fully individual voice. Born fifteen years later, or anywhere but in New Orleans, he would have lacked those firm roots in the folk-music of his city which allow the tree of his genius to grow steadily. For Armstrong is not made to find his way through the eclectic jungle of middle period jazz or the intellectual mazes of the moderns: he is a simple man; in terms of verbal intelligence even an inarticulate one. But he was born just at the time when he could pass logically from the folk-jazz of New Orleans to complete individualism in art, without losing either his bearings or the wonderful, simple, singing quality, the common touch, of a music made for ordinary people. There is nothing more to be said about Armstrong, except that he has the rare gift of complete innocence, which, because it reads the genuine emotions of men into the phoney formulae of pop songs, can make even these moving and totally convincing. Armstrong's evolution out of New Orleans jazz can be followed in his records with King Oliver, in the marvellous Hot Fives and Hot Sevens of 1925–7, and in the astonishing freedom of the Hot Sevens of 1928–30, when he played a music untrammelled by any formal traditions in the company of players who could hold a candle to him: in the *West End Blues* or *Potato Head Blues,* one of which would probably win in a poll for the best single jazz record ever made, in *Tight Like This, Muggles, Mahogany Hall Stomp,* and the rest. After this, though Armstrong's powers improved, he rarely played in ensembles worthy of him, except sometimes after 1940, when he was, however, somewhat confined by the purist tastes of the 'revivalist' public which has been his main support. His solos in the thirties and even in the late fifties are sometimes even better than they were, but the originality and perfection of the records as a whole are less. There is plenty of argument about him, but if one thing is certain in the world of jazz, it is that every critic worth his name would, were he asked to name a single person who personifies jazz, vote for him.

Good trumpeters are so numerous that it is hardly possible to mention more than a few who were in some sense innovators, though perhaps Tommy Ladnier (1900–39), a technically limited player, and Joe Smith (1902–37) ought not to be left out, for the perfection with which they played the classic blues, Frankie Newton (1906–54), and Buck Clayton (born 1911) because this writer is fond of them, and Cootie Williams (born 1908) for Ellington's *Concerto for Cootie*. Bubber Miley (1902–32) pioneered the systematic use of the mute and the 'growl'. Red Allen (born 1908) and the more important Roy Eldridge (born 1911) developed the more brilliant trumpet style of the 'swing' era. Charlie Shavers (born 1917) approaches modernism, which emerges fully fledged in Dizzy Gillespie (born 1917), technically the most brilliant and revolutionary trumpeter of the modern era. Miles Davis (born 1926) is pre-eminently the player who represents the cool style, though the death of Fats Navarro (1923–50) almost certainly deprived us of a modern trumpeter to hold his own with both.[4]

Among white players only one can be named in this company, Leon Bismarck ('Bix') Beiderbecke (1903–31), who is pretty generally admitted to be the finest white jazz musician up to the present.[5] Bix's evolution out of a modified Dixieland style was cut short, but his astonishing combination of melodious sweetness, drive, a spontaneous sophisticated jazz sense and a constant, veiled melancholy even in his most joyous solos, can still move us. The other white players are good journeymen, except perhaps for Bunny Berigan (1909–42), a lesser Bix, Bobby Hackett (born 1915), a lesser swing player, and Max Kaminsky of Chicago (born 1908). Not that in jazz 'journeyman' is a dishonourable title. Men like Muggsy Spanier (born 1906), who has played honest and moving Dixieland cornet, have no cause to regret their careers.

The trombone had barely glimpsed its full instrumental possibilities in New Orleans jazz, though it could, with Charlie 'Big' Green (1900–36), play the blues, and was always essential to the polyphony. Jimmy Harrison (1900–31) in the 1920s virtually made it into a solo instrument in the full sense, much as Armstrong emancipated the trumpet from the limitations of the New Orleans ensemble. Ellington's 'Tricky Sam' Nanton (1904–48) developed its possibilities with the growl mute. Dickie Wells (born 1909), perhaps with Johnson the best trombonist in jazz history, the lesser J. C. Higginbotham (born 1906), and Vic Dickenson (born 1906) adapted the instrument to the swing era and brought it to its highest pitch of achievement. J. J. Johnson (born 1924) is the trombonist of the modern style, though perhaps his chief innovation is the technically dazzling one of playing the instrument with unprecedented speed and brilliance.

Among the whites, who are a little less outclassed in this field, Miff Mole (born 1898) and Tommy Dorsey (1904–56) developed the technical possibilities of the instrument without exploiting them for jazz purposes, while the Dane, Kai Winding (born 1922), among the moderns, should be mentioned. There are few Red Indians in jazz, but those few seem to have a taste for the trombone: Jack Teagarden (born 1905) leads them, the best non-black player of the blues on his instrument, though a little lacking in bite.[6]

The saxophone entered jazz late. The years when journalists identified jazz by its 'wailing saxophones' were precisely those when the few jazz saxophonists had barely emancipated themselves from the New Orleans clarinet tradition. However, from the middle twenties a number of brilliant and sensitive instrumentalists developed a technique for it and made its remarkable flexibility fully available to jazz. In the swing, and especially the early modern period, the saxes really did become the central instrument of jazz, almost displacing the clarinet and pushing even the brass into the background. This is no doubt because they lend themselves to musically justified technical virtuosity: they are the string-section of jazz. The natural styles of trumpet and trombone are sober. These are strong and rigid rather than nimble instruments. The technical fireworks of the modernists have not added anything substantial to their possibilities, but have merely shown that they can be played faster and with a smoother tone, and hit higher notes than before, or that they can be made to sound like other instruments. However, the saxes did have unexploited possibilities. Their sound ranges from the reediest and dirtiest vibrato to a flute-like smoothness, and they combine a flexibility admirably suited to jazz expressiveness with a force and drive which can make them the main propellents of smaller bands. It is perhaps true that their natural style is one of romantic rhapsody or baroque floweriness, such as was developed by the pioneers of the instrument—say Hodges on alto and Hawkins on tenor—or, with a deliberate restriction of the instrument's musical palette, by the great Charlie Parker. The natural classicists among jazz lovers will always hanker for the simple lines of brass. But if any instrument was jazz between 1930 and 1950 it was the sax.

More specifically, the tenor sax, which has become increasingly popular since Coleman Hawkins (born 1904) made it, virtually single-handed, into a solo instrument in the 1920s. Hawkins, whose supremacy was long unchallenged, and who is still as good a tenor player as any, evolved a powerful but soft sound, making full use of the instrument's reedy qualities, and a characteristic style of rhapsodic improvisation. Virtually, all sax players of the earlier generation are his pupils: Chu Berry (1910–41), Herschel Evans (1909–39), Don Byas (born 1912), Ben Webster (born 1909), Lucky Thompson (born 1924), and Illinois Jacquet (born 1921). Meanwhile in Kansas City the other great innovator, Lester Young (1909–59), laid the foundations of the cool style with a smoother, deliberately much less 'beautiful' tone and a tendency to play long melodic lines consisting of relatively few notes. (The white musicians Bud Freeman [born 1906] and Frank Trumbauer [1900–57] had actually pioneered this development.) Young's disciples are numerous: Wardell Gray (1921–55) among blacks, Stan Getz (born 1927), Zoot Sims (born 1925), Al Cohn (born 1925), Gerry Mulligan (born 1927) on baritone among whites.[7] The great Charlie Parker claimed not to have been influenced by either, which leaves those who like to argue derivations free to argue them at length.

The rest of the sax family has a less coherent history. The

soprano, baritone, and bass have never really established themselves. The soprano remains the private voice of Sidney Bechet, one of the glories of New Orleans, the bass a rarely used freak. The baritone was for long the monopoly of Harry Carney (born 1910) of Ellington's band, but became more popular in the cool period among white players like Serge Chaloff (1923–57) and Gerry Mulligan (born 1927), who plays it as though it were a tenor.

The alto was established in jazz by a trinity of notable musicians: Benny Carter (born 1907), Willie Smith (born 1908), and Johnny Hodges (born 1906) of Ellington's band, who would, but for the existence of Charlie Parker, be the unquestioned king of this instrument today as in 1929: a marvel of skill, sensitivity, and flexible, but not weak, melodic beauty. 'Pete' Brown (born 1906) and Earl Bostic (born 1913) developed it into a swing instrument, with a honking, jumping, sometimes tasteless style much appreciated in Harlem. But it was the accident that Charlie Parker (who also played tenor) preferred this lighter and more individually distinctive horn, which made it, from 1941, compete in influence with the tenor. The whites, Lee Konitz (born 1927) and Art Pepper (born 1925), have developed the Parker tradition, though it is characteristic that among the blacks the most typical Parker disciples, like Sonny Stitt (born 1924) and Sonny Rollins (born 1929), reverted to the tenor.[8]

Charlie 'Bird' Parker (1920–55), the one unquestioned genius in 'modern' jazz, is more than an alto player.[9] He was a musical revolutionary, whose ideas dominate virtually everything that has been written in modern jazz since the early forties. He was also a volcanic soul, whose eruptions sent, and send, shivers of awe down the spines of listeners and colleagues. His deliberate revolutionism temporarily obscured his roots in tradition: for what Parker plays is the unadulterated, lowest of low-down blues. He is to jazz in the forties and fifties what Armstrong is to the earlier jazz. But it is typical that this quintessential figure of modern jazz was not only (like Armstrong) a lumpen-proletarian boy—in this instance from Kansas City—but, unlike Armstrong, a twisted, displaced person. A vagabond, a

96

drug-addict, an unhappy, unattached wanderer who died at 35, he is the Rimbaud of modern jazz.

THE RHYTHM INSTRUMENTS

The evolution of the rhythm instruments—again with the exception of the piano, which counts as such in jazz—is first towards subtler rhythmic possibilities, and then towards a sort of fusion between rhythm and melody, such as is wholly new in European music, though there are plenty of African precedents for it. Since rhythm is the heart-beat of jazz, and the essential organizing medium of this music, the importance of these instruments, notably the drums, is obvious. The weakness of all European jazz hitherto has been at bottom the weakness of its rhythm sections. For, while Europe has produced plenty of musicians who can hold their own in any good American band, and plenty more who could do so if they had as much practice as the Americans, it has so far produced only one rhythmicist of stature.* He, characteristically enough, was a gypsy—the guitarist Django Reinhardt (1910–53), and equally characteristically, he is the only European jazzman who has so far found a certain place in the jazz pantheon.

The evolution of rhythm towards a fusion with melody must not be confused with increasing virtuosity, though the two go together; nor with the turn from rhythm to melody. There is a tendency, notably among white players, to separate these things. Thus the Sicilian Eddie Lang (Salvatore Massaro, 1904–33), who developed the solo melodic and harmonic possibilities of the jazz

* Among the non-American jazz players of stature we may mention the Frenchmen Combelle and Lafitte (sax), the Dane Kai Winding (trombone), the Swedes Hasselgard and Wickman (clarinet) and Bengt Hallberg (piano), the Belgian Jaspar (sax), the West Indian Dizzy Reece (trumpet), the Britons Bruce Turner, Don Rendell (sax), George Chisholm (trombone), Kenny Baker (trumpet), and the South African Keipie Moeketsi (clarinet, sax). But there are plenty of others.

guitar very far indeed, did so at the expense of swing. White drummers have often played with solo rhythm at the expense of the rhythm of the whole band, which is the rhythm-maker's primary responsibility, except perhaps in an instrumental break: the drummer Gene Krupa of Chicago (born 1909) has this tendency.

The lesser rhythm instruments, guitar (banjo) and bass, can be considered together. The bass is played pizzicato in jazz. It provides the harmonic basis for instrumental improvisation, but also—and increasingly—the main, unchanging beat of the music. As Berendt observes, the fact that the bass replaced the tuba, which had first been used in this function, 'tells us more about the spirit of jazz than many theoretical arguments: the plucked strings of the bass are rhythmically more precise and clear than the blown notes of the tuba'.[10] At all events, the classic jazz bass Pops Foster (born 1892) in New Orleans, John Kirby (born 1908), and that rock of Kansas rhythm Walter Page (1900–57), developed the instrument increasingly into a steady pillar of the beat. The melodic development of the bass is, until the middle forties, almost wholly the work of Ellington, who persistently attempted to capture the special tone-colour of the instrument for his orchestral palette (with the help of the recording microphone, which could make it audible through the rest of the band). He drew out Wellman Braud (born 1891), but above all, in 1939 he discovered Jimmy Blanton (1921–42), with whom he played duets. Blanton revolutionized the instrument. He 'improvised as though the bass was a horn, phrasing fluently with frequent eight- and sixteen-note runs, using harmonic and melodic ideas which were unheard of on the instrument.'[11] Blanton's successor, Oscar Pettiford (1922–60), was also his disciple, as are all the sophisticated and ambitious modern players, notably Charles Mingus (born 1922), Percy Heath (born 1923), and Ray Brown (born 1926). The banjo (later guitar) had, from the start, two possibilities: to provide rhythmic and harmonic foundations for the band and—a technique developed by the individual blues singers—to respond to the voice in the blues in single notes and clusters. Johnny St Cyr (banjo, born 1890) provided the perfect solution in the first style for New Orleans jazz, Freddie Greene (born 1911) of Basie's band for the swing period. Their self-abnegation and avoidance of solos should not obscure their tremendous merits. The 'single-note' style was first popularized in bands by the blues player Lonnie Johnson (born 1894), and developed by Teddy Bunn (born 1909), and Al Casey (born 1915), who combine the two approaches, and Django Reinhardt. But once again a single musician revolutionized the instrument at the end of the 1930s: Charlie Christian (1919–42), perhaps the greatest single precursor of bop, in whose early experiments he took part.[12] Christian, a dazzling technician, developed the guitar into a primary melody carrier—admittedly at the price of electric amplification—sophisticated its rhythm and, imitating the tenor sax, which he also played, developed a legato way of playing melodies on it. His harmonic innovations went far beyond the field of his instrument.

The piano in orchestral jazz, belongs, with drums, bass, and guitar, to the rhythm section, but is too powerful an instrument to be confined to it. It is also the genuine solo instrument of jazz, i.e. the one whose performances can stand unaccompanied, though it benefits from rhythm accompaniment. Other unaccompanied instrumental and vocal solos have been recorded in jazz, e.g. by trumpet, various saxophones, and guitar (which can function like a lesser piano), but these are abnormalities. The piano solo is the only one to have established a permanent place in jazz. The history of piano jazz is therefore both different from that of the other jazz instruments and more complex.

Two major pianistic styles stand at the beginning of jazz, one extremely sophisticated, one extremely primitive: 'ragtime' and 'blues piano' or 'boogie-woogie'. Ragtime has already been briefly described in the section on the orchestral styles of jazz. Ragtime style and technique were evolved, on the whole, by musically educated and ambitious players, perhaps the only case of its kind, if we except the evolution of the creole clarinet style. It soon died out, but apart from a wide general influence, it left two important lines of descent. The first was the New Orleans brothel-piano style, whose finest recorded master is Jelly-Roll

Morton (1885–1941). The second, much more influential, is the 'Eastern' or 'Harlem' style, which has produced the most vigorous pianistic tradition in jazz. Its chief figures, from the New York circle, are James P. Johnson (born 1891), Willie 'The Lion' Smith (born 1897), and Fats Waller (1904–43), all of whom are ragtime pianists or very close to it, Duke Ellington (born 1899) and Count Basie (born 1904), less eminent as soloists but more important for their orchestral use of the piano, and—remote modernist descendants—Bud Powell (born 1924) and Thelonius Monk (born 1920). Probably we should also count the extraordinarily fertile 'Pittsburgh circle', which has produced such innovating players as the dazzling Earl Hines (born 1905), Mary Lou Williams (born 1910), and among the modernists, Erroll Garner (born 1921), with the 'Eastern school', whose remote origins, the experts tell us, go back to the gospel shouts of the Eastern Appalachians. Stylistically the most brilliant virtuoso of the jazz piano, the late Art Tatum (1910–56), belongs to the New York tradition, standing somewhere between Fats Waller and Bud Powell. However, though he also belongs to the North-East, he was born in Toledo, Ohio.[13] *

All these descendants of ragtime piano are normally characterized by lightness, wit, sophistication, technical virtuosity, and melodiousness. At their best, as in Fats Waller, they produce perhaps the most universally pleasing type of jazz music. These solo piano styles seem to have evolved in two directions. On the one hand, with Earl Hines—one of the most remarkable of a remarkable group of musicians—players attempted the feat of adapting the piano to the vocalizing style of the other instruments (the so-called 'trumpet style'); Hines's partnership with Louis Armstrong in 1928–30 produced some of the most satisfactory and impressive jazz on record. On the other hand, play-

---

* This North-Eastern monopoly of good black jazz pianists is startling. Of the ten pianists listed among the 'giants of jazz' in Feather's *Encyclopedia*, all but three come from this area of the U.S.A.; and the exceptions include the one boogie-woogie pianist in the list, who belongs to a separate category, and Jelly-Roll Morton, who belongs to an earlier historical period.

ers exploited the capacity of the piano for a combination of technical brilliance and original harmonic experiments, which led logically to the modern pianists' styles. At all times the capacity of the piano to combine rhythm, harmony, and melody has been the foundation of jazz piano playing.

Blues piano [14] ('barrel-house', 'honky-tonk', 'boogie-woogie') is as primitive as ragtime was sophisticated, though it shows ragtime influences, probably because many barrel-house pianists taught themselves to play the instrument by copying the movement of the keys on automatic player-pianos performing ragtime piano rolls. It seems to have originated in the lowest saloons and dives of the South and South-West, where piano players shouted the blues and beat it out on battered out-of-tune uprights through the haze of smoke and the noise of levee camp labourers, railroad gangs, roustabouts and the like. Of all instrumental jazz styles this is the most folky and anonymous: even the research of the jazz lovers has failed to turn many of its casually recorded pioneers into more than names, vaguely attached to a location, a blues or two, or a particular pianistic trick ('the chimes', 'the rocks', 'the fives', 'the chains'). There are no masters of the blues piano comparable to the virtuosi of ragtime and its descendants. Many well-known 'boogie-woogie' pianists— Meade Lux Lewis (born 1905), Pete Johnson (born 1904) are limited, while Jimmy Yancey (1898–1951), a most moving player of the blues, is technically downright bad. Some of the forgotten pioneers of the 1920s were probably, within their limitations, better executants, for instance Clarence 'Pinetop' Smith (1904–29), Cripple Clarence Lofton (born c. 1900), and Montana Taylor; so is Albert Ammons (1907–49). As one might expect, blues piano is also by far the most African of jazz piano styles: one might almost say that its tendency is to play the piano as a pure percussion instrument and to concentrate entirely on its rhythmic interest, reducing the melody to endlessly repeated, sometimes very little varied, phrases. Though the blues piano has had considerable influence on the jazz orchestra, notably through the Kansas City tradition, it has not developed much. Like the blues itself, it has remained a substratum of jazz. Until the middle thirties it led a self-contained life in those bar rooms and honky-tonks where it had originated, or in the parlours of Northern immigrant flats, virtually ignored by the main jazz tradition outside Kansas City.

In European art-music drumming is a device to produce incidental effects; in jazz it is the foundation and organizing medium of the entire music, the engine which draws the jazz train along its rails.[15] However, the drum-kit is also a group of instruments in its own right, for, as we have already seen, if every instrument in jazz also has a rhythmic function, every instrument also has a melodic one. Drums are perhaps the hardest of all jazz instruments for the European-trained listener to appreciate and to analyse. It is often difficult enough for him to train himself actually to listen to them, which is why exhibitionist drum solos are more wildly applauded than they normally ought to be: they are the only drumming that undiscriminating fans can recognize as such.

The evolution of the jazz drum begins with a paradox. Though jazz rhythm is, thanks to its Africanism, far more complex, vital, and important than European rhythm, it was also, to begin with—and still largely is—much cruder and simpler than its African ancestors, thanks to its Europeanism. The history of jazz drumming is the story of its increasing emancipation from the marching military band, with which it started in New Orleans. The old New Orleans drummers, among whom Warren 'Baby' Dodds (1898–1959), Zutty Singleton (born 1898), and perhaps Kaiser Marshall (1902–48) are the most eminent, had already turned the heavy march rhythm into a more complex, dancing, jazz rhythm, but their style was still largely determined by its origins. The drums chiefly used are the big bass drum for the main beat, the snare drum for rolls on the weak beats, and the cymbal. Drumming is fairly austere, avoiding solos, except for brief breaks. The accent is on the first and third beat of the four-beat unit, as it is in European music, though the developments of New Orleans music tend to accent the weak beats (two and four).

This development, oddly enough, seems to have come more from the white Dixieland and Chicago players, who also seem to have been the first to develop the exhibitionist, virtuoso aspects of solo drumming (e.g. Gene Krupa of Chicago). For though no instrument shows the inferiority of white players more than the drums—perhaps only Dave Tough (1908–48), the Chicago pioneer, is on a level with the best black drummers —the evolution of black and white drumming seem to have run roughly parallel.

The next great step, and the one most difficult to define or to describe, is the evolution of 'swing' drumming, which produces both a more dynamic, and a subtler, more suspended rhythm, and is the foundation of middle period jazz. To say that 'swing' accents all four beats evenly, while tending instinctively to lean a little towards the off-beats, does not help us much. To say that the main drums are liberated from the duty of carrying the main beat, leaving the whole kit free to play much more subtly with the rhythm, is also true, but inadequate. The evolution of the pedal-operated 'high-hat cymbal' which entered jazz around 1928, is very important in this respect: both Jo Jones (born 1911) on the black side (the magnificent drummer of Count Basie's band in its great days), and Dave Tough on the white, were to make this cymbal the main carrier of the beat, giving the rest of their kit a vastly increased scope. However, the great big-band and swing drummers of the 1930s achieved their astonishing combination of rhythmic tension, relaxation, and subtlety with more old-fashioned methods. The chief among them are Chick Webb (1907–39), Cozy Cole (born 1909), Sidney Catlett (1910– 51), and Lionel Hampton (born 1913) (who also plays virtually every other rhythmic instrument with extraordinary and instinctive mastery). Oddly enough, some of the most successful big jazz bands, notably Duke Ellington's and Jimmy Lunceford's in the 1930s, created considerable swing while relying on far from sensational drummers; but these were orchestras dominated by jazz arrangers of remarkable talent (Ellington and Sy Oliver, born 1910), who could utilize the rhythmic possibilities of all jazz instruments in combination admirably. (Anyway, even a mediocre black American drummer is normally very good indeed by European standards.)

Swing drumming took the drums to the verge of the revolution achieved by modern jazz, which is the drummers' jazz *par excellence*. It is doubtful whether a technically more brilliant group of drummers has ever existed in jazz than that of Kenny Clarke (born 1914), Max Roach (born 1925), Art Blakey (born 1919), Chico Hamilton (born 1921), and the rest of the modernists.[16] The sort of task the 'modern' drummers set themselves can best be explained in the words of their pioneer Clarke:

> I was trying to make the drums more musical instead of just a dead beat. . . . Around this time I began to play things with the band, with the drums as a real participating instrument with its own voice. . . . Joe Garland, who played tenor, bass sax, and baritone . . . used to write things for me. He'd write out a regular trumpet part for me to read. . . . He'd just leave it to my own discretion to play the things out of the part that I thought the most effective. What I mean is, I played rhythm patterns, and they were superimposed over the regular beat.[17]

The tendency to make the bass carry the fundamental beat left the drummer increasingly free for such activities. Thus it allowed him to experiment with complex rhythms of the African or Caribbean type, such as were rarely used in jazz. If the reader cares to try to play, or even to recognize when played, four totally different rhythms simultaneously, on hand- and pedal-operated drums, he may get an idea of the rhythmic complexities involved. Some Cuban drummers, notably Chano Pozo (1920–48), were imported into jazz for this purpose around 1948–50, but American drummers themselves adopted some of this complexity thus, paradoxically, producing the most African of all jazz rhythms out of the most urbanized and sophisticated of jazz styles.

The fundamental rhythm of modern jazz continues the evolution from New Orleans to swing: it marks the four beats quite evenly, superimposing stresses on them as occasion requires. It also tends to substitute a fashion of beating the drum legato, to the sharply separate (staccato) beats of traditional drumming.

The remainder of the jazz instruments can be briefly dismissed, since their use has so far not been systematic. The strings have virtually never been used collectively in jazz, though jazz musicians, either for the sake of the schmaltz, or the highbrow prestige which they mistakenly believe to attach to string sections, have sometimes had them in the background; always with awful results. It will take some powerful revolutionizing to produce a jazz string orchestra. Solo violins have been used quite a lot, on and off, without ever quite making their mark except in a few (generally white) chamber-type combinations like the Venuti-Lang Blue Four of the late 1920s with Joe Venuti (born 1904), and the Quintet of the Hot Club of France, with Stephane Grapelly (born 1910) and Django Reinhardt (guitar). Stuff Smith (born 1909) and Eddie South (born 1904) are generally considered the best jazz violinists. Modern jazz, as one might expect, has tended to experiment with bowed string sounds, both on the bass and lately on the cello.

A number of other instruments have been used from time to time. The vibraphone (a set of electrified tubular bells) has established itself in the place of the earlier xylophone, and to some extent of the guitar, chiefly due to the dazzling talent of a few players who, for unaccountable reasons, like this sugary instrument, notably Lionel Hampton and Milt Jackson (born 1923).[18] The celesta is occasionally used by pianists, normally to add touches of orchestral colour. The organ has been used by some, notably Fats Waller, but even in his hands produces the same sort of impression as a man trying to write with a shaving brush. Nobody has yet succeeded in producing good jazz on the accordion, but several blues singers have played astonishingly rhythmic and expressive stuff on mouth organs and jews' harps. Modernists have, as usual, been tempted by uncommon wind instruments—flugelhorns (Miles Davis) or flutes (Frank Wess, born 1922)—but the bassoon, Bach trumpet, basset horn, and the rest of the instrumental lunatic fringe still await their jazz discoverers.

There remains the human voice. Though it has been used to incomparable purpose in the blues, nothing is more difficult to discuss than its use in jazz proper. Nobody is really prepared to say what makes a good jazz singer, or what he or she sounds like; or more specifically, what distinguishes jazz singing from jazz-tinged popular singing. Critical evaluation is made all the more difficult because the appeal of the best jazz singers is largely non-musical; in the case of the women, sentimental and sexual. This observer is prepared to say that he knows no male jazz singer worthy of note. Admirable as the gravelly and expressive voice of the great Louis Armstrong is, it seems grotesque to compare his vocal achievement with his wonderful instrumental one. As for women, I am prepared to put my money on Ethel Waters, Billie Holiday, Ella Fitzgerald, and Sarah Vaughan as jazz singers of superb attainments, though the last two slide easily into commercial pop singing in which they excel because of their remarkable sense of rhythm, timbre, and the management of the vocal line. Frankly, however, it would be unwise to base the claims of jazz to great artistic achievement on any jazz singer, with the possible exception of the incomparable Billie Holiday at her best. The blues are another matter. But blues singing, though a very profound art, is also a very inadaptable one, and the blues singer tackling anything but his or her speciality often makes a sad spectacle.

s i x
The Musical Achievement

*T*he first thing to do when considering the musical achievement of jazz is to forget that of classical Western music. The two are non-competitive, in spite of the efforts of stubborn adversaries of jazz among the classicists, and of some jazz and classical modernists, to establish that they are not. If we ask: has jazz produced anything like the Beethoven Ninth, or the Bach *B Minor Mass,* or *Don Giovanni,* the answer must be a flat no. Nor is it likely to produce music to compete with the Western classical art tradition, except conceivably in the field of opera. If we judge jazz by the standards of Western art-music, we can say that it has produced a number of beautiful melodies—but no more beautiful ones than Western art, or even light and pop music,★ a particularly successful genre of accompanied *lieder,* in the vocal blues, a

---

★ Let us not be superior about light and pop music. Utterly feeble in every other way, it has at its best, and even at its top-level average produced numerous splendid melodies, as witness Stephen Foster, George Gershwin and others. That some of us prefer other melodies is another matter.

107

few suites of the late romantic type, a great variety of formally uncontrolled, but imaginatively most fertile 'variations on a theme', and a few exercises in such forms as fugues and canons. The achievement is a minor one, in terms of absolute and architectural music.

If we judge jazz playing by the standards of Western art-playing, the balance-sheet is more impressive, for not even the most stubborn classicist will deny that jazz has vastly extended the range and technical possibilities of every instrument it has touched, with the exception of the smaller stringed ones; and few will even deny that, man for man, the finest jazz players are —perhaps with the exception of the pianists—considerably superior to their classical opposite numbers. But we are, after all, here considering jazz not as a pioneer of novel instrumental combinations and colours and new instrumental possibilities, but as a music with self-contained achievements.

It has achievements but not in terms of art-music, the very concepts of which are alien to it. This does not mean that jazz may not influence art-music, or fuse with it. Indeed it has shown a marked tendency to do so of late. But when it does it will no longer be jazz, but jazz-based art-music, just as Bizet's *Carmen,* and even de Falla, are not Spanish popular music, but Spanish or Spanish-tinged art-music. Jazz already has its Bizet: George Gershwin's *Porgy and Bess,* the finest American contribution to opera so far, bears the same sort of relation to jazz as *Carmen* does to Spanish music; indeed, a rather closer relation, since a diluted form of jazz belonged to Gershwin's musical idiom.* It has not yet developed its de Falla, or more exactly, its Bartók or Mussorgsky, but there is no *a priori* musical reason why one day it should not.

The fundamental unit of the orthodox arts is the 'work of art' which, once created, lives its life independently of all but its creator; sometimes, as when critics object to a Yeats or Auden revising their own verses, even of him. If it is a picture, it has

---

* Thus the melody of *Summertime* is a literal, and doubtless unintentional, copy of the well-known spiritual *Sometimes I Feel Like a Motherless Child.*

merely to be preserved; if a book, to be produced. Music and drama have to be performed, but in our academic generation this has increasingly come to mean 'interpreted as nearly as possible in the way intended by its original producer'. Virtually all historic-musical scholarship is no more than an attempt to recapture this original, authoritative authenticity: there are men who regret that we cannot hear our Handel exactly as Handel meant us to because, unfortunately, we no longer castrate boy singers. The 'work of art' which is particularly appreciated we call a masterpiece, a category wholly independent of performance. No one thinks less of Figaro because the Lesser Wigston amateur operatic society murders him.

Now jazz simply does not function this way. Its art is not reproduced, but created, and exists only at the moment of creation. The nearest orthodox parallel is in those arts which have never been quite able to get rid of their popular, not to say vulgar, origins: on the stage. For actors, and indeed for most of us part of the time, drama is what the actors and other stage people make it. A play, however poetic, which is not at the same time a 'vehicle'—i.e. which does not allow actors to act—is dead. A great drama abominably acted is merely potential drama. A Henry Irving, who probably never in his life acted in a good unspoiled play, produced a greater emotional catharsis more often than Mr X who has never acted except in the most authentically produced Shakespeare, because Irving was a greater artist. When it comes to music-hall artists, we admit this freely: a Chaplin or a Marie Lloyd produce great art, even when their subject-matter is, by orthodox standards, minor art or no art at all.

This is the way jazz works—though its supreme contribution to the popular arts is a combination of individualism and collective creation, which has long been forgotten in our orthodox culture. It happens that, thanks to the gramophone, bits and pieces of that continuous process of joint creation which is the life of the jazz musician in employment are separated out as 'works', even as 'masterpieces'. But they are not finished works, even if they are 'composed' or 'arranged'. A Louis Armstrong may say to himself on hearing a play-back of his 1928 *West End Blues:* 'That's a good version, I'll stick to it whenever I play this piece in future at three-minute length', and a Duke Ellington or John Lewis may say of a recording: 'That is about how it ought to sound.' But if we could hear every *West End Blues, Across the Track,* or *Django* ever played, even by Armstrong, the Ellington band, and the Modern Jazz Quartet themselves, we should hear an unending series of re-creations and modifications, a life-long flux. Moreover, the individual piece is not, for the jazz musician or the jazz-lover, the real unit of the art. If there is a natural unit of jazz, it is the 'session'—the evening or night in which one piece after another is played—fast and slow, formal and informal, the whole gamut of emotions. Continuous creation is the essence of this music, and the fact that most of it is fugitive troubles the musician no more than the ballet dancer.

If there is no authenticity and no permanence in the sense of our orthodox arts, neither is there the sharp distinction between the genius and the rest. It is not the object of jazz to produce works, or even performances, which can be classed in a special category of critical excellence, but to enjoy the music, and to make others enjoy it, while creating it. There are, of course, geniuses: Armstrong, Bessie Smith, or Charlie Parker for example. But the essentially collective and practically-minded character of the music means that the value of the music, even of a particular piece, is largely independent of them, so long as there is a sufficiently large body of professional craftsmen of adequate competence and creativity. Nobody can draw up a list of the twenty best recorded instrumental blues. After one or two obvious choices, there are hundreds of records (and in real life, thousands of performances) which would be, in their way, equally good. Good jazz, like a good cook or couturier, is not judged by producing works which, even in memory, stand out as the best ever, but by the capacity to produce constant variety at a high level of excellence. Jazz, in fact, is 'music for use', to use Hindemith's phrase, not museum music or music for ranking by examiners.

None of this means that jazz is minor art in the way in which light and pop music is; merely that it gets its effects as major art in a different, and formally more economical, way from art-music. Stephen Foster's or George Gershwin's songs are pretty and enjoyable, but nobody would expect to get the emotion out of them that we draw from Schubert's *Erlkönig* or *In diesen heil'gen Hallen*. But from Bessie Smith's *Young Woman's Blues* we *can* draw this emotion. Kreisler playing *Caprice Viennois* merely shows off a dazzling technique in a pleasant tune; but Louis Armstrong playing *It's Tight Like This* takes us into the emotional realms of Macbeth's soliloquies. Even Johann Strauss's *Emperor Waltz,* perhaps as high-grade a piece of light classical music as has been composed, merely gives us a great deal of pleasure and satisfaction, but it is well worth swapping it, even as recorded by the Vienna Philharmonic, for *Parker's Mood*. Admittedly the relatively small scale on which jazz operates as art limits its scope: after all, a single speech of *Phèdre* is quite within the compass of jazz whereas the whole tragedy is not. But what there is of jazz at its best is heavy stuff: it is small, but made of uranium.

The pleasures of jazz are therefore first and foremost in the emotion it generates, which cannot be isolated from the actual music. This may be illustrated by the persistent prejudice of everybody connected with the music—players, critics, and fans —in favour of improvisation. There is no special musical merit in improvisation, which is merely spur-of-the-moment composition, and therefore likely to be less good than considered and revised composition.* For the listener it is musically irrelevant that what he hears is improvised or written down. If he did not know he could generally not tell the difference. But improvisation, or at least a margin of it around even the most 'written' jazz compositions, is rightly cherished, because it stands for the

---

* Of course the jazz composer—i.e. every creative player—does consider and revise, but in the process of playing his parts over and over again, and, as it were, working them slowly into their finished form; that is, assuming he does not change his ideas and want to turn an elaborated piece into something else.

constant living re-creation of the music, the excitement and inspiration of the players which is communicated to us. There is very little doubt that the most powerful effects of jazz lie in the intensified communication of human emotion. That is why the primitive sung blues has retained its unchallenged place in it, and why the technically imperfect and primitive discs of New Orleans jazz hold their own, so long as they 'blow out', while the orchestrations and compositions often date. This is true even of modern jazz, in spite of the claims of some of its supporters. What survives in Parker, and has conquered even many of those who were originally most repelled by his innovations, is its 'tortured, searing, blasting beauty, reminiscent of the shouting gospel congregations of the South'.[1] His innovations belong to history, and if there had been nothing more to him than this he would be no more important than W. C. Handy, who first wrote down the blues.

Jazz is thus players' music and music directly expressing emotions, and its technical forms of creation and musical possibilities reflect both facts. For instance, it does not depend on a 'composer'—for we can hardly call the collection of simple themes which make up the general jazz repertoire (the so-called 'standards') compositions. They may be good tunes or bad, folk blues or pop ballads, or some other themes, but their merit is irrelevant. If their harmonies lend themselves to jazz development, they will do. The blues always do, and fortunately they are good music, but the only lasting merit of *All the Things You Are* or *How High the Moon,* which have become 'modern' standards, or *I Can't Give You Anything but Love, Baby* and the other standards of the 1920s is that they are good pegs on which to hang jazz. The original jazz 'composition'—i.e. performance—emerged simply from the interplay of various musicians on a given theme, according to certain rough rules of convenience or tradition. A 'new' composition could come into being in three ways: by playing a different theme, by getting together a different group of players—provided always they knew one another well enough to cooperate smoothly—and by playing the same theme with the same musicians another time, when one or more of the players had different ideas. The result was a mass of varied 'compositions' of the same scope and in the same idiom. It is obvious that accident plays a great part in such musical creation which is, in a sense, like good talk or a good football match, in which anything—the combination of a particular group of people, the presence of one particularly stimulating person, a good audience, or just one of those good moods—can make all the difference. (The old-established tendency for some players to take drink or marihuana, or some other drug, is merely an attempt to eliminate this fortuitousness by artificially establishing the 'good mood' in which the musician creates freely. How far it does so is a matter for debate.)

This accidental factor remains strong, even when jazz composition becomes somewhat more systematic with the 'arrangement'. The most intelligent jazz composers have always recognized that jazz is not composed with notes or instruments but with creative men and women. As M. Hodeir, the best of the classically trained critics has put it, in jazz the 'fusion of individualities' takes 'the place of architecture'. The good jazz composer-arranger either imagines his sound and then looks for particular individual players whose personal voice comes nearest to his ideas, or derives his ideas from the personalities of his actual team. The greatest of the Creole composers, Jelly-Roll Morton, seems to have chosen the first course, a relatively easy matter in so unified a style of playing as that of New Orleans. The young Duke Ellington generally leaned more towards the second: we can actually observe him 'discovering' the 'growl' sound of his brass from Charley Irvis (trombone) and the late Bubber Miley (trumpet), and later building some of his most characteristic orchestral effects on it. In his earlier works the 'composition' is often little more than the assembling and shaping of the ideas spontaneously produced by the players. This is why the successful jazz composer has almost invariably been a band-leader, or at least permanently attached to a band; and why the most elaborate jazz compositions (for instance Ellington's) have rarely been taken up—except as straight imitations—elsewhere. As soon as they are played by other players they change.

Conversely, the composer himself is limited by having to find musicians who have his house style, or else he is obliged to modify his own style. Thus Ellington has been visibly troubled by the loss of Barney Bigard in 1942, for his liquid creole clarinet had become part of his musical palette, and subsequent replacements have not been wholly successful. Of course capable musicians entering a band with a marked house style of its own can very often adapt themselves to it. Jazz composition has only slowly emancipated itself from this dependence on the individual personalities of its players. Perhaps this is a major reason why so far no full-scale jazz composition, e.g. a jazz opera, has emerged. Gershwin, who has brought off the nearest thing to it in *Porgy and Bess,* was used to working in the orthodox tradition, i.e. to writing in terms of notes on paper and not of specific men. Ellington, whose idea of a 'concerto'—and a highly successful one too, as witness the marvellous *Concerto for Cootie*[2]—was to write a piece bringing out the special qualities of each of his soloists, has undoubtedly found the step to impersonal composition hard to make.

If jazz composition is limited technically by the need to compose men rather than notes, it is equally limited by the nature of jazz creation, as we have sketched it above. To put it in a word, it stands or falls by the human emotions it generates, and not by its qualities as 'pure' music. It is, to quote the sagacious M. Hodeir again, 'precisely the kind of music that can be listened to without burying one's forehead in one's hands . . . in jazz "sensorial interests" greatly outweigh "intellectual passion" . . . a sharpened sensuality takes the place of loftiness, and the fusion of individualities takes the place of architecture.' The most intelligent jazz composers have instinctively recognized these limitations. Jelly-Roll Morton gave New Orleans music deliberate shape and elegance, but did not attempt to change it. Duke Ellington is almost exclusively a composer of pieces expressing moods, or re-creating sense-impressions, as the titles of his records indicate: *Mood Indigo, Misty Mornin', Creole Love-Call, A Portrait of Bert Williams, Such Sweet Thunder.* Modern jazz composers have found their most fruitful field in incidental music to

114

films, in which the jazz gift for mood-expression and music-painting is used to great effect, as in Chico Hamilton's music for *Sweet Smell of Success* and John Lewis's for *Sait-on jamais?* And why not? It is a long time, even in the classical arts, since anyone has objected to Hugo Wolf because he illustrates poems in song, or to Bizet, because a concert selection of *Carmen* does not sound so well as a Beethoven Quartet, or to Prokofiev's *Cinderella*, because it is intended to go with a ballet. There is plenty of precedent for serious music which buttresses its own architectural weaknesses by leaning on other arts, and strengthens these in turn. In the composite work of art—the ballet, the opera, the film—there is wide scope for jazz, and indeed this seems the most natural way of further development for a music which emerges from the popular arts, whose more elaborate achievements have always been in the nature of 'mixed' entertainments —'variety' at the lowest level, the composite pantomine-allegory-ballet-opera at its highest.

Jazz certainly possesses a 'natural' bent towards 'pure' music, but even this must not be confused with the tendencies of art-music. It emerges from the ordinary player's pride in his technical expertise, which makes good players vie with one another to play increasingly 'difficult' things. Modern jazz is largely the product of such technical experimenting. Technical, but not architectural. Left to themselves, jazz players or composers formed in jazz will experiment with everything except musical forms. If they play fugues or canons it is because they are trying to imitate classical music. Anyone anxious to tell the difference between a 'pure' jazz composition and a jazz composition borrowing from classical music should compare, say, *Brilliant Corners* by Thelonious Monk with, say, John Lewis's *Concorde*. In the first we will find experiments in tempo, and in the combined sound of saxophones, such as vibrato explosions in unison. In the second we shall find an orthodox, relatively simple, fugue. Not that architecture is lacking in such 'pure' jazz compositions; but, as might be expected in a players' music, it is the architecture of the instrumental solo.

This is not a criticism of the increasingly numerous attempts to marry jazz and classical music. In the first place, there is no law against it. In the second place it is a perfectly reasonable thing, both for classical composers and for jazz musicians with ambition for more complex things, to break through the technical limitations of jazz. After all, it may be plausibly held that a genuine American classical music will emerge only when American composers have assimilated the idiom of their native folk-music (i.e. of jazz) as Spanish, Hungarian, Russian, Czech, Finnish, and English composers have in their own time assimilated theirs. In the third place, it is no doubt a good thing for the self-respect of jazz musicians (especially of black ones) that their music should prove its ability to satisfy even the intellectually more ambitious listener. I merely wish to establish the important distinction between the sort of jazz which evolves toward more elaborate and 'legitimate' music in its own way, and the sort which results from the crossing of jazz and 'straight' music: the distinction between Jelly-Roll Morton's *Deep Creek Blues* and Paul Whiteman's 'symphonic jazz' in the 1920s, or between Thelonious Monk and Dave Brubeck in the 1950s. So far, of these two types of jazz, the first has produced better and more fruitful results than the second, though it is quite conceivable that this might one day cease to be the case.

What then, are the musical achievements of jazz? Its major, perhaps its only real achievement, is that it exists: a music which has rescued the qualities of folk-music in a world which is designed to extirpate them; and which has so far maintained them against the dual blandishments of pop music and art-music. Taken in isolation, no recorded version of the blues *How Long* is a great work of art, in the serious sense, though many of them are extremely moving, and though the tune is beautiful and the poetry good.

> *How long, long, has that evening train been gone*
> *How long, how long, baby how long?*

> *I've got a girl who lives upon the hill*
> *If she don't love me, I know who will*
> *How long, how long, how long?*

If I could holler like a mountain jack
Go up on the mountain and call my baby back,
How long, how long, how long.

The important and artistically valid thing is that this theme should produce works as different as Count Basie's orchestral-cum-vocal version, the late Jimmy Yancey's beautiful piano solo, or Joe Turner's shouting blues,[3] and that it should remain alive, and capable of stimulating every group of players who touch it to produce their own music: some good, some mediocre, some poor, but, given a certain competence and feeling, all of it genuinely touching the genuine music. Whatever other and higher merits it has or may acquire, its chief merit is that of proving that genuine music, even in the twentieth century, can avoid both the blind-alleys of commercial pop music, which establishes its *rapport* with the public at the expense of art, and *avant-garde* art-music, which develops its art at the expense of cutting itself off from all but a chosen public of experts.

It has produced a great deal more, as M. Hodeir has demonstrated for the rare readers who possess both a good knowledge of jazz and of orthodox music, in his excellent book. (Note especially the chapters on The Romantic Imagination of Dickie Wells, Concerto for Cootie, Charlie Parker and The Problem of Improvisation.) There are artists of superb calibre and overpowering genius, works of permanent value, which may be played with equal or greater enjoyment thirty years after their original performance, and a crop of technical innovations of which orthodox music has so far made practically no use, perhaps because of the deficiencies of both its composers and its players. However, the very attempt to express the achievements of jazz in terms of art-music must, as I have already suggested, distort the nature of that achievement.

Admittedly, all this is small-scale work. Jazz is little music and not big music, in the same sense as lyrics are little poetry and epics big poetry; pottery little art and cathedrals big art. Limitation of scope and relative smallness of scale do not make an art less good or true or beautiful. They do, however, put certain artistic achievements out of its reach: a sports car is not a worse vehicle than an aeroplane, but one designed for different purposes. Jazz has many merits, and a large number of people have derived from it consistent and intense and self-respecting pleasure, and have been profoundly, and justifiably, moved by it. But there are things which jazz cannot do (as conversely, there are things which modern classical music cannot do), and no purpose is served by pretending otherwise, except to butter up the self-esteem of people who are too lazy or ignorant to understand the more complex forms of art. Jazz, like Keats's definition of poetry, is 'simple, sensuous, and passionate', though, unlike Keats's definition, it can also be technically highly sophisticated and demanding, while the apparent simplicity of its emotions often conceals very great complexity. Of course, so do apparently simple emotions in real life. But there are other things in life and the arts than these, and jazz does not supply them.

Nevertheless, its place in the musical not to mention the general cultural history of our century is already assured. It has demonstrated the vitality, and the possibilities of evolution, of a people's music; and if ever a way is to be found out of the impasse into which the orthodox arts have penetrated in our age, it may well be found by studying the nature of jazz, its creators, and its public. (This no more implies that the orthodox arts are to be saved by imitating jazz than the study of the aerodynamics of birds means that planes have to be constructed to look like seagulls.) It has been increasingly unavoidable. However little orthodox musicians have done with it, they have not escaped its presence. And it has been pretty certainly the most important musical achievement of the United States of America to date; and quite certainly the only one to win international acceptance. No orthodox American composer is a genuinely international figure, as the great classical composers were in their day; all are provincial figures blown up by local pride, and perhaps enjoying a limited appreciation or a *succès d'estime* among the musically better-informed international public. But Louis Armstrong, Bessie Smith, Charlie Parker are accepted without question all over the world, wherever there is a public for jazz, and indeed wherever American culture is discussed; and so is jazz itself.

118

seven

Jazz and the Other Arts

Though it has been almost impossible to grow up in the Western world since 1920 without hearing something influenced by jazz, until recently it has been rather difficult to hear much jazz in the strict sense of the word. After all, perhaps the most famous of all jazz records, Louis Armstrong's *West End Blues* which has been continuously in print since 1928, sold not much more than 20,000 copies in its first twenty years in Britain, which is modest, even by the standard of some pretty highbrow arts. Moreover, as we have seen, the jazz public has been, for historical and social reasons, rather sharply distinct from the rest of the public for the orthodox arts, even when it did not itself keep aloof from them. It is therefore not surprising that until recently jazz has had very little echo indeed among the rest of the creative arts.

The list of works influenced by, or inspired by, or 'about' jazz is therefore very unimpressive. It is obviously longest in music, though every compiler (and there have been several) is forced to fall back on the same names and works, mostly from the 1920s: Debussy's *Golliwog's Cakewalk,* Ravel's *L'Enfant et les sortilèges,*

119

and piano concertos, Milhaud's *La Création du monde*, Stravinsky's *Histoire du soldat*, *Ragtime pour onze instruments*, and *Piano Rag Music*, all of which echo the post–1918 preoccupation of the French *avant-garde* with this type of exoticism, Krenek's *Jonny spielt auf* and Weill's music for Brecht, which reflects that of the German *avant-garde* with low life, Constant Lambert's *Rio Grande*, and the like.[1] Only in America, and there mainly on the verges of popular and light music, can we detect a more persistent jazz influence, notably in the musicals (Gershwin's *Porgy and Bess*, Marc Blitzstein's *The Cradle Will Rock*, Leonard Bernstein). Frankly, the record is modest. The history of modern classical music can still be written virtually without reference to jazz. Of the major contemporary composers—say Schoenberg, Berg, Webern, Stravinsky, Bartók, Prokofiev, perhaps Shostakovitch, Vaughan Williams, Sibelius, and Hindemith—only one has shown any signs of jazz influence; and as Hodeir rightly points out, his flirting with jazz was unimportant: 'Stravinsky made history when he wrote *Le Sacre du printemps;* he placed himself on the margin of history when he wrote *Ragtime*.[2]

The list of literary works with a bearing on jazz is even less impressive, and, before the 1930s, quite negligible, if we except a few things by the irrepressible Cocteau. A few of the poets on the verges of (British) neo-romanticism and surrealism have written mediocre poems inspired by jazz players, and with titles like *An Elegy for Herschel Evans* ('The band will continue its music, as life its laughter: the world will be gay or sad with age or season: and the marvellous sounds of jazz will thrill or bless . . .'), or *A Measure for Cootie* ('we play the way it comes to us, we play elegies for the past, blues for the present . . . a trumpeter as you, a poet as I'), or *Piano—a Surrealist Prose Poem* ('Piano shouting the lice of New York and the scabs of New Orleans the yellows and the browns and the blacks but above all the blues').* Auden experimented a little with the blues, in one case—the *Refugee Blues*—not at all unsuccessfully. There is by

---

* In fairness to the poets concerned I shall not embarrass them by quoting their names at this late date.

now a crop of generally mediocre novels about jazz and jazz players, and of late a certain amount of what may be called 'jazz-steeped' writing, e.g. by the San Francisco 'beat generation'—Jack Kerouac *et al.*—who combine a passion for jazz with one for Zen Buddhism. The sociological interest of this stuff is real, the literary merit so far uncertain. The best piece of writing inspired by jazz is probably still one of the earliest—and one written, significantly enough, by a poet whose mode of life was highly unliterary even by American standards: Vachel Lindsay's *The Daniel Jazz.*

Among black writers jazz has naturally been more influential, though even among them only a few, notably Langston Hughes, have been seriously and consistently influenced by the blues. Much of Hughes's writing is plain blues, such as might be composed and sung by any guitar-picker:

> *Sun's a settin', this what I'm gonna sing.*
> *Sun's a settin', this is what I'm gonna sing:*
> *I feels de blues a-comin', wonder what de blues'll bring.*

Or the *Gal's Cry for a Dying Lover:*

> *Heard de owl a-hootin', knowed somebody's 'bout to die.*
> *Heard the owl a-hootin', knowed somebody's 'bout to die.*
> *Put ma head un'neath de kiver, started to moan an' cry.*

> *Hound dawg's barkin', means he's gonna leave this world.*
> *Hound dawg's barkin', means he's gonna leave this world.*
> *O, Lawd have mercy on a po' black girl.*

> *Black an' ugly, but he sho' do treat me kind.*
> *I'm black an' ugly, but he sho' do treat me kind.*
> *High-in-heaben Jesus, please don't take this man o' mine.*[3]

Hughes is pretty consistently aware of jazz and the blues as components of black American life; but even among writers of his people this awareness was not always habitual.

This paucity and poverty of jazz literature is all the more extraordinary since, as we have seen, the world of jazz is, at the very least, fantastically good "copy' for any writer with an interest in human beings. Moreover, jazz itself has produced at least two types of literature of value: the poetry of the blues, and the talked autobiography; not to mention the literary experimentalism of 'jive talk'. It is little short of incomprehensible that an environment which has turned out stuff like the following passage almost by routine should not have tempted the poets and prose writers more:

> But when you write about me, please don't say I'm a jazz musician. Don't say I'm a musician or a guitar player—just write Big Bill was a well-known blues singer and player and has recorded 260 blues songs from 1925 up till 1952; he was a happy man when he was drunk and playing with women; he was liked by all the blues singers, some would get a little jealous sometimes but Bill would buy a bottle of whisky and they all would start laughing and playing again, Big Bill would get drunk and slip off from the party and go home to sleep. . . .[4]

The balance-sheet in painting and sculpture is even more meagre, unless we include the flourishing but recent trade of decorating the sleeves of long-playing records. Fortunately for the arts (and not only for those concerned with jazz), popular records rely largely on the eye-catching appeal of their covers, and these are therefore much more interesting and enterprising than the miserable designs on so many classical LPs. Fortunately for jazz, a large body of commercial artists have always been among its most loyal and passionate supporters. The sleeves of jazz LPs therefore maintain a pretty high standard. Admittedly most of them get their effects by montage (mostly of photos), layout, and type design. Comparatively few are painted or drawn. Admittedly also jazz illustration of this kind has produced its crop of clichés, the shirt-sleeved black piano player at his upright being the most common. But the 'applied art' of jazz is a flourishing affair none the less. It is the 'pure art' which has always languished. Jazz has tempted one or two abstractionists (several artists have attempted to re-create its sensations in abstract films), but hardly any representationalists. Perhaps this is because the iconography of jazz is a triumph for photography: how much else, one may ask, need be said when the camera already says so much about these concentrated, grave faces and shut eyes behind the instrumental mouthpieces?

For almost the only art which has taken jazz seriously and on its own terms is that of photography. The crop of jazz films, or of films with some relation to jazz, is small enough; for over most of its history the subject did not appeal to the indeterminate mass public by which the film industry lives. Nevertheless it is not negligible. There is *Jammin' the Blues* by Granz and Gjon Mili; or *Momma Don't Allow* by Karel Reisz, one of the few films which also deals with the jazz public. There is *Jazz on a Summer's Day,* a documentary about a Newport Jazz Festival, and bits and pieces smuggled into commercial films, doubtless by devoted jazz-lovers connected with their making. The actual commercial films on jazz subjects, mostly of the usual Hollywood 'famous show-biz lives' type, multiplied towards the end of the fifties, but remained totally vacuous. But above all, since the early fifties in Hollywood, since the late fifties in American television and the European cinema, there has been the fashion for giving films, often about crime, sex, and lost generations, serious and uncompromising jazz scores, mostly very modernist ones. Musically the French have been most successful in arranging such liaisons, notably with sound-tracks by Miles Davis and the Modern Jazz Quartet. The most ambitious American attempt, an Ellington score for a mammoth murder story, will not be counted among the master's most successful works. However, for obvious reasons, the combination of jazz with the James Dean, Marlon Brando, TV-Private-Eye kind of film in the U.S.A. is much more of a marriage, much less of a passing affair, than in most European films, for jazz in America is a common language and not merely, as in France, a form of upper class slang.

Perhaps the closest combination of jazz with other media has occurred in television commercials and cartoon films. Probably this is the only genre of modern art which is as fully impregnated by the influence of jazz as is ordinary life in our times. Nevertheless, compared to previous epochs, the later fifties marked a very striking *rapprochement* between jazz and the only other original mass arts of the twentieth century, those of the moving camera.

There remains the ballet, an art which one would expect to be sensitive to jazz, which is, after all, essentially music combined with movement. However, the classical ballet (even as loosened up by Diaghilev and others) rests on a stylized vocabulary of movement which is extraordinarily difficult to combine with the very different vocabulary of black American dancing. Even *Petrushka,* danced by Harlem dancers, would look as odd as Mozart's clarinet quintet would sound if played by Sidney Bechet with his normal intonation; a Harlem *Petrushka* would be quite a good experiment nevertheless. Semi-heterodox ballet companies, such as the French Champs Elysées have allowed themselves to be influenced by jazz, with indifferent success, but in the main jazz has affected ballet most—and most fruitfully— where it is least of an orthodox art: in the dancing in American cabarets, vaudevilles, musical shows, and films. (We need not specially mention the occasional companies which specialize in exoticism or black folk-lore, such as Katherine Dunham's Company.) Jazz has patently transformed what we may call the democratic as against the aristocratic or classical ballet. More precisely, like modern ballroom dancing, modern American musical-show dancing is inconceivable without jazz influence.

Taking it all in all, the influence of jazz has been surprisingly small. If we consider only the 'outsiders', those creative artists who have not grown up within the world of jazz, whether as players or fans, or in some other close connexion with it, it becomes negligible. Other kinds of exotic music have produced far more. The cultural field is littered with literary and musical works inspired, however remotely, by the Spanish equivalent of the jazz scene, from Gautier and Mérimée onwards. Its visual props—the shawls, combs, castanets, and *vaquero* costume which are the Andalusian equivalents to the zoot suit, the characteristic gestures and movements of flamenco dancing—are familiar to every civil service clerk with cultural ambitions, from Cardiff to Vladivostok, through pictures, ballets, operas, and the rest. Not so jazz which, with all its remarkable power to expand and proselytize, has rarely succeeded in capturing its public unless, like the Jesuits, it caught its subjects young. I know men and women of high intelligence, great musical sensitiveness and expertise, and almost painful eagerness to discover what others see in jazz, who are quite unable to see the difference in quality between two jazz pieces, while their contemporaries, who heard their first Fletcher Hendersons and Armstrongs at the age of fifteen, have no difficulty in doing so. Possibly a prior training in the orthodox arts is an active disqualification; for though innumerable people have widened an original love of jazz to include classical music, the opposite evolution has been much rarer.

The non-musical achievements of jazz among the arts are therefore largely in the hands of the 'insiders'—the musicians and singers, and the public which has grown up with jazz. Since a great many people have grown up with it, its cultural infertility is still rather surprising, especially in literature. After all, though the films have so far produced no literary masterpieces, they have provoked a remarkable crop of technical and analytical writing, a significant body of poetry—at least about Charlie Chaplin—ranging from Hart Crane and Umberto Saba through Rafael Alberti to Aragon and Mayakovsky, and a large block of semi-sociological, semi-satirical fiction mainly, it must be admitted, expressing the self-laceration of script-writers. However, the world of jazz is not comparable to that of the films. Like the world of the stage, the circus, the classical musician, it is far more self-contained, not to say esoteric: a craftsmen's and critics' world. It is self-contained also, inasmuch as for most of its earlier history players and public got their cultural satisfactions almost exclusively within it, and had much of their remaining energies pre-empted by the desire to crusade for its recognition. Between the pure 'jazz fan' whose chief object (whatever his profession) was to advertise the cause, and the ordinary adolescent, for whom jazz was simply a part of the environment as beach umbrellas are in seaside resorts, there was, and is, a large void. Normally those who make the works of art out of other arts, or out of special professional worlds, are situated in this intermediate space; in the world of jazz it has been almost empty.

On the other hand, this world has had the unique gift of producing articulate artists. Much of the effort of the 'jazz intellectuals' has been devoted to making them articulate, rather than to making themselves articulate about jazz, but this does not alter the fact. The jazz musician does not of course normally paint, or sculpt, or make films, but he does—he can hardly avoid doing so—use words. His prose is embodied in a vast corpus of 'spoken literature', mainly autobiographical, out of which Hentoff and Shapiro have produced a magnificent montage, the book *Hear Me Talkin' to Ya* (the title is borrowed from a record by Louis Armstrong). This sort of prose is not easily quotable in extracts, for it makes its effects, if so purposeful a term has any meaning here, by accumulation. Only now and again, notably in the talk of the blues singers, does it achieve a rhythmic ironic vividness of dialogue for which good dramatists would give much:

> LEROY: 'Yeah. So we had a few Negroes down there that wasn't afraid of white peoples or talk back to them. They called those people crazy. . . .'
> NATCHEZ: '. . . crazy people . . . (LEROY: 'Yeah.') '. . . I wonder why they called them crazy because they speak up for his rights. . . .'
> LEROY: 'Yeah, they call them crazy.'
> NATCHEZ: 'I had an uncle like that and they hung him. . . . They hung him down there because they say he was crazy and he might ruin the other Negroes.' (LEROY: 'That's right.') 'See, and that is why they hung him, see, because he was a man, that he worked he wanted pay; and he could figure as good as the white man, and he had as good an education as some of the white—better than some of the white people down there.' (LEROY: 'Yeah.') '. . . 'cause a lot of them down there would come to him for advice'.[5]

If the prose is just the prose of life—though this is not often found in literature—the poetry is unique, especially when it has what someone called the unique talent of the blacks for making poetry out of words of one syllable. The blues are unquestionably the finest body of living folk-poetry in the modern industrial world. They consist primarily of a large body of five-stressed rhyming couplets with the first line repeated, which are combined, modified, and augmented to taste. Like other folk-poetry, they are concerned almost exclusively with straightforward statements, questions, or appeals, and not at all with literary ornamentation. Even their similes are used for precision and not for evocation:

> *Got the world in a jug, got the stopper in my hand*

or

> *Love is just like a faucet, it turns off and on,*
> *Love is like a faucet, it turns off and on,*
> *Sometimes when you think it's on, baby, it has turned off*
> *and gone.*

Their symbols and poetic props are either straightforward, or standard formulae such as any minstrel uses as fill-ins: the sun which rises and goes down, the railroad, the house, the wind, the graveyard:

> *Sun rises in the east, and I declare it sets in the west.*
> *Sun rises in the east, and I declare it sets in the west.*
> *Ain't it hard to tell, hard to tell, which woman will treat*
> *you the best.*

> *There's three trains ready, but none ain't going my*
> *way,*

*I said there's three trains ready, and none ain't going
  my way.
But the sun's gonna shine in my back door some day.*

*Blow, wind, blow, blow my baby back to me
Blow, wind, blow, blow my baby back to me
Since she's gone, nothing's like it used to be.*

The blues are therefore not poetic because the singer wants to express himself or herself in a poetic manner. He or she wants to say what has to be said as best it can, as in the famous *Make Me a Pallet on the Floor*—the song of a poor New Orleans prostitute—where the only 'technical effect' is that of the repetition of lines and phrases, which, as it happens, makes the content of the song astonishingly poignant; an 'effect' which arises naturally out of the repetitive pattern of ordinary popular speech:

*Make me a pallet on your floor,
Make me a pallet on your floor,
Make me a pallet, baby, a pallet on your floor,
So when your good girl comes, she will never know.*

*Make it very soft and low,
Make it, babe, very soft and low,
Make it, baby, near your kitchen door,
So when your good girl comes, she will never know.*

*I'll get up in the morning and cook you a red hot meal,
I'll get up in the morning and cook you a red hot meal,
To show you, baby, I 'preciate what you done for me
When you made me a pallet on your floor.*

*Make it soft and low,
Make it, baby, soft and low,
If you feel like layin' down, babe, with me on the floor,
When your good girl comes home, she will never know.*

It is remarkable how complex and sophisticated an effect can be achieved simply by the slight variation of repeated lines, in words, rhythm, and context.*

The casual way in which the blues gets its poetic effects, rather as pebbles are shaped by water, may be illustrated by a specific example, the *Red River Blues*, which Mr Sonny Terry, the singer and harmonica player, tells me is the first blues he ever learned:

> *Which way, which way, do that blood red river run?*
> *Which way, which way, do that blood red river run?*
> *Run from my back door to the rising sun.*
>
> *I hate to see that rising sun go down*
> *I hate to see that rising sun go down*
> *It make me feel I'm on my last go roun'.*
>
> *Which way, which way, do that blood red river run?*
> *Which way, which way, do that blood red river run?*
> *Run from my window to the rising sun.*

This is a special development of a widely known genre, the 'river' blues, which normally deals either with the effects of floods on the life of riverside dwellers, or—a familiar poetic conceit—the river which divides a man from his love. (I am informed by an expert, Mr Alexis Korner, that the singer Josh White recognized a song sung by Big Bill Broonzy as the *Red River Blues,* though it runs "Mississippi River is so long, deep, and wide, Can' see my good girl standin' on the other side', and so on in that vein.) The middle stanza of the present version is a familiar blues verse, best known as the opening of the *St Louis Blues,* from which it may very well have been lifted. It is a fair guess that the 'red river' came into the song originally via the

---

* Since the final consonants are very slurred in Southern U.S. speech, the rhymes are true rhymes—e.g. 'flo'—'do'—'know'. I have, so far as possible, spelled out the words in standard form, in order to avoid the impression of 'coon English', which black Americans dislike.

well-known cowboy song *Red River Valley,* which is of course about geography, not colour. At some stage the Red River (which runs from Texas, along the Oklahoma border, through Arkansas and Louisiana into the Mississippi) turned into a coloured river, the colour of blood. How did it link up with the sun? Perhaps because someone remembered the red glow of a river against the sunset? The blood-red river, seen from a house, becomes a symbol of life, the rising and setting sun of its impermanence. A collection of poetic bricks, chipped to size, turns, we do not quite know how, into a reflexion on life and the inevitability of death. Other verses drop off, until what is left is a concentrated lyric song.*

The blues is full of such poetic bricks, to be put together by the singer as he chooses: verses, and particularly standard lines which the minstrel can insert whenever he or she can't think of anything else, or wants to return to familiar ground:

> *You see me laughing, just to keep from cryin'*

or:

> *Take me back, baby, try me one more time*

(no listener will forget the intensity which Bessie Smith puts into this line) or:

> *I looked down the road, as far as I could see*

(a very characteristic line for the travelling singer) or the typically implacable

> *You must reap what you sow:*

> *I told you darling, long time ago*
> *You goin' to reap for what you sow*

---

* The tune is approximately that of the beautiful *Trouble in Mind.* It has been recorded, Alexis Korner informs me, by Brownie McGhee, Sonny Terry, and Leadbelly. A more conventional version by Josh White is available in Britain (*The Josh White Story,* vol. II).

And what you sow, gonna make you reap
And what you reap, gonna make you weep
Someday, sweetheart.★

But behind the elementary, though remarkably effective, poetic apparatus of the blues there lies a view of life, which that apparatus is designed to express with the utmost directness and economy of means. It is this which gives the blues their remarkable power, even when they are little more than doggerel:

I'm going away, babe, just to wear you off my mind
I'm going away, babe, just to wear you off my mind.
If I stay around here, I'll be troubled all the time.

So help me, honey, but I don't love you:
So help me, honey, but I don't love you.
Well, I just don't like them funny old ways you do.

It's raining here, babe, storming on the sea:
Raining here, storming on the sea:
You mistreat a good man when you mistreat me.

I'm sorry, baby, sorry to my heart
Sorry, baby, sorry to my heart
We've been together so long, now we've got to part
                                    (Joe Turner, *Going Away Blues.*)

This view of life is adult, truthful, totally without illusions, and humbug, which is why so much of such poetry sounds remarkably like the verse of Brecht, who in turn drew his inspiration from the directness of popular songs:

Oh, life is like that,
Well, that's what you got to do,
Well, and if you don't understand,
Peoples I'm sorry for you.

★ Brownie McGhee. I need hardly say that I am greatly indebted to Messrs Brownie McGhee, Sonny Terry, Big Bill Broonzy, and James Rushing, all of them fine blues singers, with whom I have been privileged to discuss the blues on their British visits.

Sometimes you'll be held up, sometimes held down,
Sometimes your best friends don't even want you
    round, you know.

Well, life is like that,
Well, that's what you got to do . . .
(From the LP *Blues in the Mississippi Night*, Pye-Nixa.)

Truth is what is in the blues; truth is what the blues singers cherish above all, and the word which recurs time and again in their conversation when they grope for an explanation of what they are after, and attempt to separate their own songs from those which are merely made to earn money.★

This is no doubt why British adolescents listen to the voice of blues singers as they would not to those of parents, teachers, or other poets, taking in 'the truth' in hushed silence in cellar clubs or bedrooms. Nobody beats around the bush in the blues; neither about life, death, drink, money, or even love.

Few things are more ironic, and characteristic, than that the name of this diamond-hard, lucid, and uncompromising idiom has come to be used by Tin Pan Alley to describe the mood of self-pity and superficial maundering which it believes to be characteristic of those who do not immediately succeed in sleeping with their girls (*I'm feeling blue over you*, etc.). For self-pity and sentimentality are not in the blues. On the contrary. Its fundamental assumption is that men and women must live as it comes, or if they cannot stand that they must die. They laugh and cry because they are human, but they know it cannot help them. Nothing can, unless they help themselves; for heaven is rarely in the blues, which is a purely secular song, and there is no God, though sometimes, as in Bessie Smith's *Blue Spirit Blues*, there is

★ Thus Saint Louis Jimmy, a veteran singer, attempting to explain why Europeans like the blues: 'In Europe they like stories, they like the truth; that's why they like the blues, not all this foolishness . . . because the blues is the truth about how they mistreat people, that's what the blues is.' Similar statements are in print or on record by Big Bill Broonzy, Lightning Hopkins, and doubtless others.

hell. In this world 'a good man is hard to find', and when he is found, he won't bring unmixed advantage:

Now it's ashes to ashes, sweet papa, dust to dust,
I said ashes to ashes, I mean dust to dust:
Now show me the man any woman can trust.

Like the world of the disorganized and beaten-down labourers among whom this wonderful idiom grew up, the world of the blues is tragic, and helpless: as Bessie Smith—as usual the definitive voice of the blues—once put it:

You cain' trust nobody, you might as well be alone.

And you remain alone. For when the men and women who sing the blues turn to sing of collective salvation, whether secular through the union, or religious through the churches, they rarely sing in the idiom of the blues, but in the idiom of the hymn or gospel song, which is its spiritual brother. Its poetic achievement is equally real, but except for a few revivalist hymns such as the sadly familiar *When the Saints Go Marching In,* it does not belong so intimately to jazz as the secular blues. Perhaps because there are few saints in jazz.

Like all folk-poetry, the blues is intended to be sung; and nobody who has heard Bessie Smith sing the *Reckless Blues* or Ma Rainey sing *See See Rider,* or the young Chippie Hill *Trouble in Mind,* can read the words as other but a faint shadow of the real poetry of the blues; for it is the timbre of the voice, the passion, and the marvellous flexibility and rhythmic suspension of the vocal line which turn lines like 'When I wasn't nothing but a child' or 'Now that I am growing old' into statements as definitive of their kind as:

Et la mort à mes yeux dérobant la clarté
Rend au jour qu'ils souillaient toute sa pureté.

But even as a verbal skeleton, the blues are a literary achievement of considerable importance, and so far the most important non-musical by-product (or rather non-musical aspect) of jazz.[6]

part three

Business

e i g h t

The Jazz Business

J azz is not only a way of making music, but also one of making profits. Few of the popular arts have been subsidized, whether by public or private patronage. Mostly, like jazz, they have been forms of commercial entertainment by professional artists hired by various kinds of private entrepreneurs. Box-office and sales chart are what determine the movements of such arts and the fate of the artists. What the jazz-lover hears, therefore, depends not only on the creative urges of the musicians and other imponderables, but on the way jazz is organized as a business. In this and the subsequent chapter I shall explain briefly how jazz functions as a business and technical enterprise, and how this affects it musically and in other ways. Readers who believe that records make themselves and that horn players are fed by ravens sent down from heaven, like the prophet Elijah, are advised to pick themselves a less earthbound music to admire.

Jazz musicians are professionals. The prejudice against 'commercialism' among a large section of the jazz public makes it necessary to repeat this obvious truth. Jazz may be in its origins and character a folk-music, but this does not mean that it is an art of amateurs. Even in the countryside much of folk-art is professionalized—the art of minstrels, jugglers, or wandering showmen, not to mention such virtually specialized artists as certain religious functionaries, or the fiddler who gives the tune for capstan shanties, the black convict whose work consists of 'song-leading' for labour gangs. The prehistory of jazz is full of such primitive professionals, of whom one particularly vigorous and murderous one, the late Huddie Ledbetter ('Leadbelly') is widely known thanks to the records he made for the Library of Congress in Washington. Every connoisseur can reel off long lists of the names of such artists, as often as not blind men who, from combining begging with music, graduate, like Homer before them, into full-time art: Blind Blake, Blind Boy Fuller, Blind Lemon Jefferson, Blind Willie Johnson. They are itinerant, because no place in the country provides enough work for the settled professional.

The city however does, and jazz is from its beginnings a music of the city poor. Not only does the city provide such professionalism, it demands it. Its style of life is more specialized, less traditional than country life, where the arts are for the most part closely tied to the various specific occasions and aspects of life, and almost unthinkable apart from them, and therefore perforce largely amateur. It is no accident that the W.P.A. guide book to the state of Mississippi reported in the 1930s that 'because of the increasing influence of the city upon the Negro and the resulting departure from the simple life, the number of social songs has increased with a proportionate decrease in the number of spirituals and work-songs'. The city tends to split the artist from the citizen, and to turn most of the arts into 'entertainment', a special need supplied by specialists. Moreover, the city's demands on entertainment, because more specialized, are much higher than the country's. Ever since ancient Athens it has been a complaint against it that townsmen 'always want something new'; it might with equal justice be observed that the city insists on higher standards, because it has more chance of comparison, and because it does not need to measure the performer by the amateur's capacities. At all events, regular entertainment even in the pre-industrial city is almost invariably professional: * this applies to singers, musicians, sportsmen, showmen, and extra-marital sex, for prostitution is an urban, not a rural phenomenon. Even when an artistic movement begins as a deliberate revolt against commercialism and professionalization, like the 'New Orleans Revival' in America during the war, and in Europe after it, it cannot resist the force of facts, at any rate if it appeals to the public. Within the last few years every successful British 'New Orleans' band leader and musician has had to choose between his normal occupation and his music. Some have chosen their jobs, others have become full-time professional musicians. The ideal of a permanent and widely popular amateur music has not resisted the technical impossibility of bucking the social division of labour.

The folk-artists who made jazz had no romantic nonsense about the virtues of amateurism in them. They became professionals as soon as they could earn a living at their music, when they did not already come from show-business families. In the early days of New Orleans we can still see this group of professionals emerging from part-time music. However, for practical purposes professionalism can be regarded as established from the first decades of the 1900s. As we have seen, this development, the competition of craftsmen within their community and their separation from the rest of the people, has affected the actual musical evolution of jazz very considerably.

These professionals have earned their living in three different, but related, types of economic setting: pre-industrial entertainment, the modern entertainment industry, and the specialized jazz business. The first two of these have no particular connexions with jazz, except that of selling it to the public if there is a demand for it, as they sell the spectacle of bearded ladies imitating steam whistles, girls with big busts kicking or not kicking

* Occasional or limited entertainment, such as guild pageants and passion plays in medieval cities or a coronation today, need not be professionalized to the same extent.

139

their legs, the latest mass murderer, or musical genius. The last deals exclusively in jazz, for it has developed out of the discovery that there is a paying public for this specific type of entertainment. Most of the European jazz musician's living today comes out of the jazz business, though in the U.S.A. this is probably not yet the case.

If we compare the commercial outlets for jazz at the peak of the golden age of 1960 with those in the New Orleans period, we find three major differences: first, some of the traditional ones have declined; second, the new technical media (gramophones, radio, films, TV, etc.) have grown tremendously; third, and most striking, a specialized public for jazz as such has emerged.

A great deal of jazz is still played, economically, in very much the same way as in the days of King Oliver: in night clubs, for dances, and on the stage. Indeed, the honky-tonk, or bar room, or night club—especially the less classy type of joint—still remains an essential pillar of the music, especially in the United States, where the specialist jazz public is less organized than in Europe. New and experimental players can get a start in joints more easily than in most other places. They can be got cheap (in a London joint I know first-rate, but 'uncommercial', musicians will play five or six hours for £3 each), the patrons do not mind what noise comes from the stand so long as there are drinks and girls, and, also, in every entertainment quarter there have always been one or two saloon keepers, club owners, or madams who genuinely liked either musicians or the new kind of music even at the cost of a few bad debts and a certain amount of nerve strain. Such were Tom Turpin in the St Louis or ragtime (himself no mean piano player), Lulu White, Madame Mame de Ware, 'Ready Money', the Countess Willie Piazza, and other notable madams of the early century, 'Pee-Wee' on Beale Street, Memphis, 'The Chief' in Kansas City, Henry Minton in New York (himself an ex-musician and Musicians' Union official). These and other unsung patrons of the lively arts, showed a more enterprising taste than most of their orthodox contemporaries.[1] Similarly, unfashionable players can get a berth in such places. In New York today many of the great names of the thirties manage to make ends meet by playing behind the bar in saloons. On the other hand, that other great standby of the early jazz musicians, the music-hall or vaudeville stage, has declined precipitously. In America it is virtually extinct, and in so far as it survives in Europe, it is as a purely secondary medium which exhibits jazz artists who have made their name elsewhere. In the early thirties the visiting jazz musician normally topped a variety bill (as he still does, if lucky, in the Paris Olympia); today— unless he has special music-hall qualifications—he plays almost entirely for the organized jazz public. No new jazz talent in Europe has been discovered through the 'halls', and none in America since the war.

The new technical media—records, radio, etc.—have been of fundamental importance for jazz, but not—odd though this may seem—for directly financial reasons. Financially, radio, TV, and the films have provided a living for jazzmen as pop-music play-ers, and an occasional windfall, or even bonanza, for bands hired to play jazz, or put into a film. (But the proportion of films containing jazz has been negligible until the middle fifties, and most of them were shorts.) Radio, with its greater capacity to cater for minority taste, has been kinder to live jazzmen, though not as kind as to recorded ones. Though film and, in America, TV fees have been high, especially for name bands, live broad-casting fees in Europe were and are modest. On the other hand, the advertisement value of the mass media has always been so great that any sensible musician is prepared to settle for a non-economic price, if he has to. Since the decline of vaudeville virtually all national and international reputations have been made by or through broadcasting, which in Europe reaches national audiences. A show on the air, a mention by a popular disc jockey, are by far the quickest ways of popularizing musi-cians or pieces of music.

Nor is the gramophone record as lucrative as it seems, at least to the musicians, though it is far and away the most important medium in jazz. The leading American jazz musician who shocked British journalists by claiming not to care or know how

141

many records he sold was not merely putting on an act: his group's main income came from live performances. Jazz musicians, or the ranks of the virtually full-time 'session' players in a small minority of cases, enter the stratosphere of the 'top ten' only by accident. However, the gramophone record is so vital a part of the business that it is worth looking at its economics a little more closely.*

The musician himself normally receives a straight session fee. A British name artist may get a 5 per cent royalty, plus a share of the 6¼ per cent 'mechanical royalties' which bodies like the Performing Rights Society, ASCAP, and BIEM negotiate and collect in complicated ways, assuming that he also gets his name on the labels in some other capacity (as composer, arranger, etc.). These cover the innumerable performances of a record on the air or on jukeboxes, films, etc. A man in steady demand on sessions —sometimes indeed, employed as a regular 'house' or 'studio' musician by a company—can do extremely well. For instance, in America a single drummer, Mr. Osie Johnson, could appear in a single year in 233 tracks made at forty-six different sessions. However, the number of highly prosperous session men is limited. In the same year in America equally useful but less fashionable drummers such as Shadow Wilson and Specs Powell appeared on only four and two sessions respectively,[2] and in Britain the same few dozen names permute and combine on ninety per cent of all native jazz records.

The royalty income (which affects, substantially, only the bandleader, composer, arranger, or star soloist) naturally depends on record sales, as do the profits of the various entrepreneurs. Small though the percentage is at home, and even smaller on foreign rights, a genuine best-seller, or a regular succession of steady sellers, produce a very tidy income. How tidy, those who earn it are reluctant to say, though that downright Lancashire ex-workingman, Jack Hylton, once gave details of how much

* Companies are extraordinarily cagey about producing hard facts and figures, unless they show them to be both *(a)* selling and *(b)* making next to no money. I owe the following estimates—which I reproduce for what they are worth—to a friend with a great deal of experience in the business.

he earned in his heyday in the 1920s and early 1930s: he drew $116,000 from HMV in recording royalties for 1929, and a guaranteed $232,000 for the next two years from Decca.[3] Admittedly Hylton was not only the unchallenged emperor of European dance bands, but a very shrewd man into the bargain. At the other extreme there are jazz records which sell considerably less than the 1,000–1,500 which covers the cost of making an LP in 1957–8; for instance, a record made annually on contract by a modern jazz musician, now turned arranger, sold precisely 386 copies in Britain. The only consolation for all concerned is that the demand for jazz records (unlike ordinary pop discs) is permanent. If a company is willing to tie up space and capital in them, they continue to sell to new generations of fans. There are old-fashioned 78 rpm jazz records which have never been out of print since they were first released ten or twenty years ago, though they have probably never sold more than 2,000 copies on average per year.

Fortunately jazz records have this permanence and are fairly cheap to make,★ since they generally require few musicians:

★ For those who like figures the following estimates may be useful:

A. SHORT-PLAYING RECORD

Selling-price (1958) of copy		$0.84
Cost per copy: Distribution		0.33
Package		0.02
Labels		0.02
Artist's Royalty		0.03
Publisher's Royalty		0.035
Musicians (at 2,000 sales), total $95.20	per copy	0.05
Studio cost ($28.00 a title at 2,000 sales)	per copy	0.03
Purchase Tax		0.21
Maker's margin, overheads, publicity		0.14

$95.20 should have sufficed in 1958 for a half-session at union scale (i.e., $12.60 per player, $19.60 for the leader). Overheads per single record were obviously small, but publicity may have come high.

allowing for retakes, four or five single sides or tracks can be made in a session. It has therefore normally been worth producing relatively uncommercial jazz records, even at inflated prices and production costs. At a guess, even in 1958 a cheap single record would certainly cover its cost with a sale of 2,000 or less and produce a modest profit with a sale of 4,000. Reissues of foreign or old records are naturally a great deal cheaper.

Jazz records therefore become 'commercial' in two ways: either because they are saleable in the open market, like any other pop record, but with the advantage that unsold stock does not become valueless in a month or two; or when there is a sufficiently large public of aficionados existing to guarantee them a steady, if modest sale of, let us say, 1,000 to 1,500 copies. Until the later 1930s this latter possibility depended on convincing the commercial gramophone companies of the existence of a jazz public. This was done, with notable success in Britain, by a combination of pressure from outside—especially from the dance-music press—and from inside, by the fifth column of jazz-lovers in the dance-music business who had the ear of the companies. From the later thirties enthusiastic American amateurs began to reissue old discs and later to record live jazz directly for the aficionado public on small private labels or for 'hot record societies', a practice taken up after the war in Europe. Several of these private labels and catalogues were eventually taken over by the commercial companies, or developed into commercial labels.

The jazz market for gramophone records has also benefited from the peculiar internationalism of the jazz public. To some extent small sales in one country can be supplemented by the accumulated small sales of several others. For instance, records by King Oliver have been issued in the U.S.A., Canada, the Argentine, France, Britain, Germany, Switzerland, Czechoslovakia, Sweden, Denmark, Italy, the Netherlands, Australia, and Japan. His *Blue Blood Blues* was released by Columbia in France, Britain, Australia, and Switzerland; his *Snake Rag* reprinted in America, France, Britain, the Netherlands, and Australia.[4] A record which just breaks even in Britain may therefore still earn decent royalties by Scandinavian, Dutch, or Japanese sales.

B. LONG-PLAYING RECORD

Selling-price (1958)   per copy $4.20
Cost per copy: Distribution (52½%)   1.58
           Sleeve   0.35
           Pressing, material, label   0.28
           Artist's Royalty (5%)   0.15
           Mechanical Royalties (6¼%)   0.19
Musicians (10 men for 2 sessions),
    $291.20 at 1,000 sales   per copy   0.175
Studio costs $224.00 at 1,000 sales   per copy   0.13
Purchase Tax   1.05
Maker's Margin, overheads, publicity   0.30
Break-even point: say 1,200 sales

The cost of printing the sleeve assumes a run of 1,500. The estimates are of course approximate and perhaps pessimistic. They come from a very experienced record producer. An American estimate for 1960 is more ambitious. It sets the actual break-even point for an LP made by a small company at 3,000 sales and for a large one at 7,000. (The average sale, however, is given at only 2,000 copies, which suggests that some LPs can still be made very cheaply.)

Outside and by now perhaps also inside America the most important source of jazz and of livelihood for jazz players is today the specialist jazz public, or the institutions which have grown out of it: the jazz club (which began, essentially, as a club for listening rather than dancing to jazz), the jazz concert, and the specialized jazz record or broadcast. Most of these were first set up on a non-commercial basis by amateurs to meet the demand of other amateurs, or at most by commercial undertakings on the passionate promptings of amateurs. As jazz has become a more paying proposition, a business structure has grown up around this non-commercial nucleus, but it is largely distinct from the normal apparatus of show business. Its entrepreneurs, agents, impresarios, recording advisers, dealers, organizers, etc., are mostly former fans, critics, and musicians who have drifted into business with the tide of jazz popularity, all the more so because the established businessmen in the entertainment world lacked at first the interest, and later the know-how, to tap the jazz market. Collectors of the 1930s look after the jazz catalogues of the big American and British recording companies. The leading agency for jazz musicians in Britain is filled with former collectors, critics, pioneer jazz musicians, and others. A typical 'fan' organization, the National Jazz Federation (non-profit-making), originally a federation of jazz clubs, developed into a major organizer of jazz concerts, tours for visiting artists, and jazz clubs, while in America an *avant-garde* aficionado of considerable shrewdness, Mr Norman Granz, succeeded in the ten years after the war in building himself a sizeable business empire on the dual foundation of a permanent concert road show of front-line musicians ('Jazz at the Philharmonic'), and a cast-iron catalogue of recording artists which he distributed on highly favourable terms (and under his own name and labels) through big companies when they came to need a jazz catalogue. It is rather as though poetry suddenly became a commercial proposition, and former poets, reviewers, and organizers of poetry circles, found themselves putting cigars in their mouths, taking planes to the U.S.A. (or Europe respectively), and indulging in conspicuous expenditure in domestic cocktail bars and hi-fi. Business is business, but the jazz businessmen often still show marked traces of their non-commercial past: a passionate hostility to the colour bar, a marked tendency to sympathize with left-wing politics, and an occasional willingness to subsidize wholly non-commercial music, if it is 'good jazz'.

The extent of the 'specialist' demand for jazz may be gauged by the fact that an issue of the British *Melody Maker,* chosen at random early in 1958, listed *seventy* different clubs or other locations where live jazz was played between one and seven nights weekly in London and the Home Counties; not counting nine other jazz concerts, jazz artists appearing on ordinary music-hall bills, the numerous (unadvertised) sessions of skiffle music and the like in various coffee bars, and various unadvertised clubs which employed jazz musicians. In the same week, and in the same area, there were five live jazz broadcasts on sound radio and none on TV. In America this specialized demand has always been much smaller, and perhaps more concentrated in the universities which have provided the most systematic engagements for adventurous jazz groups, but even there, especially in the later 1930s and 1940s, clubs and other joints combining commercial enterprise with a strong backing by the aficionados were rather important outlets for good jazz: for instance, Café Society Downtown in Greenwich village, which was for long a showcase for new jazz discoveries, and 'Nicks', which catered for the middle-aged intellectuals attempting to recapture their Dixieland youth. In France the aficionado clubs multiplied after 1944 in and around the Saint Germain quarter, though they soon became commercialized, charging very high prices to all except a selected group of students who were let in free to create atmosphere. However, a cheaper alternative, the so-called *discothèque* clubs, which played exclusively jazz records, seem to have been more successful there than in other countries.

The specialist market has also produced a number of institutions patterned on the 'art-music' business, and of varying commercial importance: 'jazz festivals'—in Newport, Conn., in Nice, Cannes, San Remo, and other European holiday resorts—and, more recently in America, the university jazz recital and summer school. From the musician's point of view these are spiritually rather than financially satisfactory, like the occasional recitals in the temples of official music, the Carnegie Hall, the Festival Hall, or the Salle Pleyel. They are a sort of cultural recognition of jazz, but too infrequent to count much. On the other hand, the organized concert tour has become the standby of many a jazz combination. Such tours are today much more speculative propositions than in the happy days before TV, when the touring band might play perhaps a quarter of their time as a variety show in cinemas, sheltered by the wings of the great stars, and the rest of the time strictly for dancing in roadhouses and ballrooms. But the decline of the cinema and of the American ballroom deprived the touring band of its fixed public and largely killed the increasingly expensive big band: during their heyday it was possible to hire a good sideman for the road for about $50 a week, but 1960 scale (i.e. the Musicians' Union minimum) for an eighteen-piece band was $2,700 a week.[5] Given the cost of top talent and the smallness of the jazz public outside a few big cities, the concert tour is risky, even though the wise promoter will reject any deal that will not allow him to make money on a sixty per cent house. In consequence few jazz groups or shows could rely entirely on such tours even if they wanted to.*

It will be evident that the average jazz player gets his income —which is not normally a straight salary—in bits and pieces: a gig here, a longer engagement there, a radio programme, a recording session, with luck a basic band salary to fall back on. Even if he has that, he must move about constantly, for in spite of the great increase in the jazz public, a band can rarely stay more than a few weeks in the same location. Not for the jazz audience the loyalty of the dance-palais, whose customers dance to the same band for decades. In London, at the time of writing, only *two* clubs rely primarily on the same band night after night; and those are profoundly 'traditionalist' jazz clubs, i.e. clubs playing what has by now become chiefly a dancing music. A band, and especially an expensive large band, *must* travel. Casual work and travel are therefore built into the jazzman's economy, especially if he wants to earn more than the barest minimum.

This is all the more so because the foundations of that economy are extremely fragile. The leading player of today, like the leading actor, may be forgotten tomorrow. In America, the small jazz combination has, until recently, *never* lasted for more

* For the financially minded reader an example may be instructive. It is taken from Ralph Gleason's column in the *San Francisco Chronicle* (26 June 1960) and analyses an actual concert by Duke Ellington and Sarah Vaughan:

Capacity of house: $21,000

Expenditure: $10,043. (Rent of hall $435, Lights and light men $150, Public address system $87, Tickets $132, Doormen, etc., $225, Special police $90, Stand-by musicians $314, City licence $10, Advance box office $300, Insurance $50, Advertising and promotion $3000, Talent, $5250.

In fact—such are the risks of the business—the takings were only $5,100.

148

than a few weeks or months, though the post-war tendency to turn jazz into an art-music which appeals to a public analogous to that for classical chamber music, but larger, has produced lasting small groups: the Dave Brubeck Quartet since 1951, the Modern Jazz Quartet since 1954. Norman Granz's road show, aptly named 'Jazz at the Philharmonic', was the first to tap this concert public systematically in 1946. There has so far been only a single example of a permanent large jazz band: Duke Ellington's, which has had a continuous existence since 1926 and includes at least one player who has been with the band since then, and several who have had continuous stretches of ten years or more with it. In all but two big bands the turnover of personnel has been high. (British bands, as one might expect, have been much more stable, being built largely on the 'fan' public: Humphrey Lyttelton has had a band continuously for twelve years, which is about as long as is possible in the short history of British home-made jazz.) There are both economic and psychological reasons for this instability. To run a jazz band, especially a large one, for any length of time as a paying proposition is extremely difficult, and requires gifts of organization, leadership, and business shrewdness which few musicians possess.

Permanent attachment to a band also compels players to live one of the worst of all kinds of professional life, that of the touring artist, often passing through a succession of one-night stands. And even when the constant rootlessness happens to suit musicians, who may hate to be tied down, it is more than offset by the routine and discipline without which no permanent organization can work, but which freely improvising artists don't like. The good and permanent band is normally run by a martinet, or a 'natural' front man with an eye to the public. Few jazz musicians like this for their instincts are anarchist. All 'natural' sidemen dream of a combo in which nobody will be leader, and everybody will always play as he feels, a band of brothers. But this, as long experience has shown, is a certain guarantee of rapid failure and disintegration.

The bulk of jazz players therefore have a footloose and casual playing career, shifting from band to band and place to place, interspersing their temporary attachment to some establishment with periods of freelancing, and combining it all with recording, casual gigs, and anything else that is going. The musical biography of most players shows this pattern. At one extreme are the few solid, steady men who stay with the same band year in year out, headed by Harry Carney whose thirty-three years with Ellington are almost certainly the world record; at the other the anti-organization men like the clarinetist Pee-Wee Russell 'playing with so great a variety of combos that complete documentation would be impossible';[6] in between come the rest, but nearer the Russell end of the spectrum than the Carney end. Financially it is not a bad life for a good musician who is widely known in the profession, and moderately reliable in turning up for work (that is to say who is not too drunk, too much addicted to drugs, or too generally crazy and irresponsible to do so). Irresponsibility is more common among white musicians who have graduated into the profession from being amateur aficionados and among some groups of the 'modernist' revolutionaries than among the old-fashioned black players, or white players with a dance-band background, who have the actor's professional conscientiousness on the job. The heart-rending stories of first-class musicians discovered starving on park benches have normally reflected not so much objective economic conditions, but the lack of foresight of the musicians themselves, or their stubbornness in refusing to play any but their own type of music, or their unemployability. Good unknown musicians have sometimes failed to break in; unadaptable ones playing or singing in an idiom which went out of fashion, have often failed to maintain themselves; and a large cloud of second-rank, semi-professional, and occasional players, such as surrounds the core in any casual profession, have even more frequently known genuinely hard times. But the jazz profession is relatively small, relatively open, and very full indeed of camaraderie and craftsmanship. Every good player is a discoverer of talent. Most good players know one another and put one another in the way of jobs. And jobs—even those out of the limelight—are very reasonably paid when times are good. On the other hand, such reflections miss the point. Secondary poverty is built into the world of jazz, because it is, like acting or other types of show business, a world of casual labour which encourages free spending and discourages rational economic behaviour. Such a world contains men and women who put enough by in times of prosperity to survive, or who have sense enough at the crucial moment to abandon playing in bands for some less impermanent work—arranging, regular studio work, setting up in business. But it also, and in greater numbers, breeds the sort of musician who forgets that $280 a week basic salaries (which is what a first-rate dance-band musician might earn in England in the early thirties) do not last, or who does not care whether they last.

Through this loose, shifting, small-scale, anarchic world the musician makes his way with the help or burden of a complex network of businessmen, whom he carries: agents, managers, publicity men, bookers, and the rest. Before the rise of the specialist jazz public these were normally ordinary entrepreneurs, for whom the musician was a simple 'property'; often entrepreneurs of the shady type which is bred in that zone between the day world and the night world, in which gangsters, gamblers, pimps, fight-promoters, and other purveyors of night-time entertainments and services exist. This is a zone of, at best, a certain boozy paternalism, and at worst, of buyers, sellers, and intermediaries who would make a fast buck out of their sisters, and pretend that they had only made fifty cents. The sullen, wary, but hidden hostility of musicians to the entrepreneurs and intermediaries is the reflection of generations of agents who took thirty per cent and 'managerial' fees, of gangster club-owners who laughed at union scales and hours, of bookers whose black-list could kill an artist, of engagements for women artists which came at the end of a series of beds. One of the leading American entrepreneurs began his professional career as manager of night clubs in Al Capone's Chicago. Any American musician can tell of towns—including New York—in which engagements in the leading night spots and dance halls depended, and in some instances still depend, on the say-so of racketeers: it is a milieu beside which even the classical Hollywood film industry is relatively civilized, and which can be compared only with the milieu in which the fight business flourishes. In Europe the environment of the jazz business, even in its early days, was perhaps less dramatic, but no closer to the business ethics of the Sunday school. The rise of the specialist jazz public, and with it of businessmen who—whatever their other characteristics—have often been brought up as aficionados, has improved the situation somewhat. There are even examples of men who, like John Hammond, Jr, in America, have acted as remarkably efficient talent scouts, advisers, publicity men, and business intermediaries for an army of musicians without making or desiring to make money out of them. But if the worst examples of exploitation have perhaps retreated to the fringes of the jazz field, there is enough left over to preserve the musicians' suspicious and generalized cynicism about those in the business who do not play instruments, but on whose 'goodwill' the player depends. It can be broken down, but not easily. It is hard for the musician to feel that he is not surrounded at all times by fools (the ignorant fans) and knaves (the businessmen, publicists, etc.), all of whom have a right to the business smile, the thousandth pose for the thousandth photograph which looks like all the others, the phoney heartiness which may buy a chance, a job, a raise, a renewal of a contract, or a line of free publicity.

It is therefore natural that so anarchic a business should have developed trade-union and self-defence organizations, though a little surprising that so intractable a body of men and women as the entertainers should have succeeded in building strong ones: and the British Musicians' Union and American Federation of Musicians are very powerful indeed, as are the organizations of composers, writers, and others, ASCAP and the Performing Rights Society. Possibly in Britain the strength of the union derives from the working-class background of the profession, in America from techniques into which it would be best not to inquire; for if the American Federation of Musicians is strong, its leader, James Caesar Petrillo (originally of Chicago) was also one of the more old-fashioned type of craft-union boss with a bare-knuckle strategy. Actually, the jazz musicians themselves—a small and specialized minority within the profession—have done much less to build up the union strength from which they have benefited than the despised pit-bandsmen and light musicians. And the iron hand of the union, where it is established, serves to keep everyone organized as well as to impose the union's will on the business. What difference a powerful organization, capable of imposing minimum scales, could make to the business is obvious. But these advances have been won in Britain and the U.S.A. by a ruthless policy of restrictionism, or the creation of a guaranteed and protected field of jobs for live musicians in the union's area. This has sometimes diverted the entire course of jazz. The rigorous ban on the importation of foreign bands into Britain between 1935 and 1956—solo musicians could get in under the looser rules of the Variety Artistes' Federation—and the two-year shut-down on recordings which Petrillo imposed in America from 1942–4 are landmarks in jazz history. Both almost certainly did much to advance the 'traditionalist' jazz re- vival: the British union's ban by throwing British musicians on to their own resources (i.e. by leaving the British critics and jazz amateurs a clear field of influence), the American ban by bring- ing before the public numerous forgotten recordings from the companies' pre-1942 catalogues, which they were obliged to issue for want of any new ones. On the other hand the British ban almost certainly postponed the further evolution of British jazz by depriving our musicians of the chance of hearing good American artists in the flesh and playing with them: the startling acceleration in the evolution of British 'traditionalist' jazz towards a more ambitious music can almost certainly be put down to the influence of the two visits of Count Basie's band in 1957. The American ban, in its place, held up the evolution of 'modern' jazz, since it deprived the young New York experimenters of the chance of making records, and therefore winning a wider audience, until 1945.

If the musicians and writers formed their organizations, the businessmen developed the usual tendencies towards monopoly, though in so fluid a business as that of popular music, this was and is rarely very stable. The gramophone companies, of course, have long been a small and tight group, though one which does not exclude competition, and indeed encourages it. The point is, that while the production of gramophones and records can be tightly controlled by a small group of firms—in Britain there are two main groups, EMI and Decca—the production of successful artists cannot. There can never be any guarantee that an unknown singer or band, recorded by a marginal enterprise, and fancied by some popular disc jockey, may not turn out a hit and set a fashion, leaving the established companies in frantic search for a new side to their catalogues. For the mass production of such unpredictable and changing commodities as hit tunes and hit artists still depends largely on general vigilance, guesswork, intuition, or plain luck. A label which virtually monopolized the good jazz, or the hits, in 1950 may find itself in 1958 with nothing but a back catalogue of unpopular music. For similar reasons agencies which succeed in cornering most good jazz bands at a time when they can be put under contract cheaply, and then sell them on their own terms, can have no guarantee that they may not be left with an unfashionable set of artists on their hands. The only safe form of monopoly in this business (apart from such technical ones as those in pressing facilities, shellac, record distribution, etc.) is the monopoly of booking. It is among the bookers that the tightest and most lasting controls have been established. Thus the Anglo-American band exchanges since 1956 have been largely handled by one or two British agencies, in close connexion with the American bookers. However, except on the gramophone side, the jazz and pop music business is so fluid, and requires relatively so little long-term investment of capital, that these monopolist tendencies make comparatively little difference to the general picture, which is one of old-fashioned cut-throat competition. Jazz and pop music in general is one of the last frontiers of private enterprise. On these rhythmic waves buccaneers of the old type can still sail their ships as gentlemen of fortune: out-smarting one another and anyone else, greasing palms, steering nimbly through the whirlpools of promoting, record making, publishing, managing, booking, plugging, and the rest. This is still the world in which smart young men can make it. The organization man, the tame psychologist, the economic adviser, are still far away. And so long as the cost of production of the hit tune or song, on which the industry rests, remains as low as it does (and that is a great deal lower than a film, a TV show, or a stage show), the jungle will continue to flourish in it, and the panthers will continue to prowl it, as they do the rather similar garment trade, enjoying the kill as much, and perhaps more, than the actual meal.

An important question remains: what effect on the actual music has this web of business and technology in which jazz is enmeshed? The answer is, a very considerable effect.

This is most easily seen by considering the most important technical medium of jazz, the gramophone record, without which the stylistic evolution of jazz is quite unthinkable. It was (and still is) to this music what art galleries are to the art student and books to the aspiring writer: an essential educational institution. To this day the majority of jazz-lovers and players have learned their jazz largely from records, while musicians choose their style and train themselves by copying admired models on discs. This applies not only to deliberate movements of stylistic imitation like the 'New Orleans revival', which would certainly have been impossible but for the luck which made even very archaic jazz contemporary with the gramophone, and the prosperity of the American twenties, which even made blacks into record buyers. (Few black jazz records of that period would have been recorded then for the white market.) The educational influence of the record is universal. Without it, the living evolution of jazz would have been confined to limited groups of professional players or to particular cities in which there always happened to be good living jazz, as is proved by the failure of 'modern' jazz to exert much influence during the Second World War when, as it happened, recording was temporarily interrupted for a few years. If trumpeters in London and Tokyo are influenced by Armstrong, sax players by Charlie Parker, it is primarily due to the gramophone record.

The gramophone record has also made possible the permanent recording of much more flexible and experimental jazz than would otherwise have been possible. Regular bands, popular or jazz, have their established styles and repertoires which leave little room for dissidents. Paul Whiteman and Ted Lewis in the 1920s, whatever their private sympathies for 'hot' jazz—and both went out of their way to employ 'hot' players—could no more have started to play it officially than they could have started to play symphonies. Their public did not come to them for that. The specialized jazz band has similar problems: a passionate bopper in a Dixieland band, a passionate New Orleans man in a modern group (a much more unlikely contingency), must keep most of their enthusiasm to themselves. Mr Milt Jackson must play in the style of the Modern Jazz Quartet when with that group, whether he wants to or not. Mr. Humphrey Lyttelton, who has been brave enough to change his band from a 'traditionalist' to a 'middle period' unit, is engaged in interminable polemics with former members of his public who regard this change as treasonable. But the recording session with a 'pick-up' band, or with a lasting group of men who normally played with other groups, filled this gap. (It also enabled musicians under exclusive contract somewhere else to play what they liked under pseudonyms, a fact which gives headaches to scholarly discographers. By now jazz expertise and popularity are so widespread that few musicians can get away with this, though recent examples still spring to mind.) Such purely studio groups have speeded up the evolution of jazz considerably, as witness Louis Armstrong's Hot Fives and Hot Sevens in the later 1920s. They have also ensured that artists otherwise buried in clubs or commercial bands became available on proper jazz records; e.g. the late Bix Beiderbecke. During the depression of 1929–34 the recorded history of jazz is largely confined to that of studio groups collected from time to time, like Spike Hughes's Negro Orchestra of 1933. In the 1930s the small *ad hoc* groups collected together by Benny Goodman—sometimes for live performance, sometimes only for sessions—were of equal importance: the trio, quartet, etc. In the early years of the bop revolution the fortunes of the new music depended primarily on studio groups. The jazz-lover must have a soft spot for them not only as an enthusiast but as a citizen, for it was in the studio that the colour bar was first effectively broken, thanks to the courage and initiative of men like Eddie Condon in the 1920s, John Hammond and Benny Goodman in the 1930s. Armstrong's *Knockin' a Jug* (1929) is not merely a superb record and a fine example of the flexibility which the pick-up band gave to jazz, but a monument to human progress as the first major jazz record made by a mixed black-white group.

From a purely commercial point of view the gramophone record also imposed a particular musical form on jazz composition: the three-minute miniature. For until the end of the 1940s the 78-rpm disc with that approximate playing time was virtually the only kind on which jazz was recorded, perhaps because the 12-inch, five-minute record was too expensive, perhaps because longer pieces, which involved changing records and breaking continuity, were unsuitable for dance-music, almost certainly because it was the cheapest economic unit of record production. Now three minutes is a highly artificial time for jazz. The single dance, which is the most obvious unit for such music, would normally last somewhere near ten minutes. A living creative jazz performance, as in a jam session, might—without padding—go on for fifteen or twenty. However, since for more than a quarter of a century permanent jazz performances had to be compressed into the three-minute limit, musicians were obliged to invent an extremely dense, formally strict, concise form. They did so with extraordinary success. The late Constant Lambert was quite right to claim that no orthodox composer could compete with Duke Ellington within this length. But we have only to listen to any good jazz record of the pre-LP age to see that others were quite as successful in producing marvels of unity and shape: Armstrong, Morton, Basie, the Mezzrow-Bechet-Ladnier pick-up band. The classicism which business thus imposed on jazz had its advantages, for recent LPs show that jazz players, when left to themselves, are often tempted to run on—especially on instruments which lend themselves to continuous monologues, like the saxophone. Still, whatever the advantages and disadvantages of the three-minute strait-jacket—and Ellington for one never felt quite happy in it—it illustrates the musical repercussions of purely technological or business considerations.

The more general effects of the structure of the jazz business on the music are less easily described. The simplest way to tackle them is to consider aspects of jazz: the problem of musical education, the problem of style and repertoire, and the problem of musical creation.

The jazz business deals in the distribution of an available product: musicians. It does not deal in their production. Like all show business, it has always assumed that saleable players will just appear on the scene. Nothing like the conservatoire, or the classical ballet-school, has ever existed in jazz. Musicians have got their elementary education in playing instruments wherever they found it and their secondary and higher education by playing with other musicians. The production of a steady supply of first-class and fully mature players therefore depends on the existence of commercial bands which also happen to be sound 'educational' institutions. Consider the career of a jazzman of universally acknowledged 'finish'—the sort of man whom any bandleader is prepared to hire, who can be relied on to turn out an admirable mixture of technique and feeling with any combination, or on any session, the trombonist Vic Dickenson: not a genius, but the type of player without whom jazz could no more flourish than the theatre could flourish without the first-rate character actor. He was born in 1906, began to play commercially at the age of sixteen, and got his education in the bands of Zach Whyte, Blanche Calloway, and Benny Moten and Claude Hopkins. In the forties he established himself as a highly individual talent, and he has since been the foundation stone of a wide stylistic variety of small combinations, studio bands, and superb recordings, and is equally admired by players of all schools.

Let us consider, on the other hand, the young European player who came up exclusively through the jazz movement and the young American player who is arriving today. The young European, if he entered music after say 1945, very likely played exclusively for a specialized jazz public and with specialist 'reviv-

158

alist' or 'traditional' bands composed of other youngsters like himself, who had learned their music from records (older players, who were normally forced to go into ordinary commercial pre-war dance bands, generally received a much better technical training). He would rarely be forced to play alongside musicians who, though less learned about King Oliver, were technically far in advance of the amateurs. He would escape both the grind and the educational value of sight-reading, rehearsals, and the varied routine of dance-band playing. There is no doubt whatever that a number of talented European players have developed more slowly, and in some cases more one-sidedly, than they might have done, for want of such professionalism. The young American player of today suffers in a rather different way from the temporary eclipse of the large band which, in the later 1920s and 1930s, was the chief musical school of jazz. There, and there alone, could men learn that extraordinary capacity which makes a band like Count Basie's produce so dynamic a sound: that which enables a man not simply to be 'carried' by the rhythm of the rhythm instruments, but to swing individually and in sections. For (leaving aside 'traditionalist' jazz, which is virtually defunct in its homeland) small-group work or jam sessions are what emerges from jazz education; if they educate the player at all, it is only at the highest and most sophisticated level. He must be good already if he is to become better by small-group work. Mr Norman Granz, from whom I take some of these reflections, goes so far as to think that no player born after 1940 is likely to be fully 'educated' for this reason. I do not think such pessimism is warranted. Big bands may come back, or other forms of training may evolve. But it is clear that the supply of first-rate musicians must depend on what are essentially commercial phenomena.

The problem of style, repertoire, and creation can be discussed together. Here the essential point is that good jazz requires an audience which does not get in the way of the players too much. If players and public are naturally at one, as in the classic days of New Orleans, there is no problem. If they are not, then the players perform best when providing for the minimum needs of the public—dancing, background noise, atmosphere—while enjoying themselves or experimenting in their own way. This was relatively easy when commercial 'pop' music was the main burden they had to carry. Today, however, a commercial public has grown up which requires jazz as jazz, and as we have seen, this provides for the players' livelihood. They are obliged to play in particular 'styles' even if they may want to play differently. They are besieged with demands for 'request numbers' and therefore forced to repeat, time and again, a limited group of standards until they are sick of them: *When the Saints Go Marching In, Trouble in Mind,* or *The Bucket's Got a Hole in It* among the revivalists; *Cherokee, How High the Moon, Body and Soul* among the modernists. There is not much to be said in favour of the routine pop 'ballad', but it does change all the time. Miserable though the Tin Pan Alley repertoire is, it does at least confront the musician with a constantly new set of challenges: themes which he ought to turn into something interesting and from among which, perhaps, he can select one or two which lend themselves to a more lasting process of transformation. A jazz style and a jazz repertoire imposed by a would-be expert public is as constricting to the musician as an exclusive insistence on Grieg and Tchaikovsky is to classical orchestras.

What is worse, the jazz public insists, against all logic, on the impossible achievement of spontaneous creation to order. Every jazz musician is forced to become a sort of nightly poet laureate, who guarantees a supply of odes on fixed dates and occasions. It is no use pointing out that the phrase 'concert jam session' is a contradiction in terms; that the safest way to turn creation into routine is to announce that it will take place every evening between eight and twelve in a particular cellar. In itself this would not be serious, for it is fairly easy for musicians to dress up routine as spontaneous creation, especially with a little loud blowing and hard drumming in small enclosed spaces. The musicians might well do so, and then go away, as they have long done, and jam for their own pleasure in some after-hours night spot. And yet the very devaluation of creation and improvisation which the rise of the specialist jazz public has imposed in work-

160

ing hours risks devaluing it outside. Musicians may lose interest in it, and flee into carefully rehearsed and arranged jazz (which has its own merits), as many tend to do. Or else they may carry the routine tricks of working hours into the times when they really feel like improvising, or ought to improvise.

The growing flood of jazz which has actually to be performed and recorded to meet the existing demand merely intensifies these problems, particularly on record. After all, the entire output of Louis Armstrong's Hot Five and Hot Seven, which produced a score of masterpieces, consists of sixty sides on a dozen or so sessions spread over four years. In a single year fifty tracks made by Armstrong in 1955 were released in Britain.[7] Mr Ruby Braff, a good trumpeter, produced at least forty tracks between March and October 1955. I do not claim that such over-production produces bad jazz. Good professionals can be relied upon to produce a good average level. But a good average level by musicians playing a good solid routine is merely the bread and butter of jazz. And by the very nature of their changing music, jazz players depend, much more than 'straight' ones, on the chicken in the sandwich: the mood, the inspiration, the combination of circumstances which turn routine into joy.

These remarks are not intended to arouse alarm and despondency, but merely to show that the musical character and prospects of jazz cannot be divorced from its character and prospects as a business. If jazz were ever to be standardized into purely composed and 'executed' forms (when it would cease to be jazz as we know it), it might avoid these difficulties. It might then have no more troubles than the symphony orchestra, which, like the licensed Ford dealer, sells a known and branded commodity for which a permanent and relatively unchanging demand exists. The repertoire which fills halls may be rather more limited, the versions which appeal to the public a shade more florid than musicians might like, but within those limits they play what they consider 'good' music. But the jazz group cannot afford to become a dealer in standardized commodities, partly because its commodity (creating music while it plays) dies once it is standardized, partly because the music itself constantly changes and evolves. The jazz player, if he has any sense, is reconciled to playing standardized stuff most of the time, for that is his business as a professional entertainer; and if he is sensible, he will also enjoy performing as the actor does, though he is less completely dependent on the audience. But he has also generally had a large 'free' margin—inside and out of hours—when he could play as he pleased. Within that margin he could be overheard by the public, with luck, though he was not performing or only half performing for it. It is the gradual conquest of this margin by the jazz business (by you and me, the jazz public) which has led him into a quandary in the past twenty years. He has not escaped from it yet.

part four
People

nine

The Musicians

Jazz is what its musicians and singers make it. The player is the centre of its world. We must therefore try to discover what sort of man, or more rarely woman, the jazz artist is. This is in some respects easy, in others difficult. No aspect of jazz is better documented than its biography. There are, at a guess, biographical data of perhaps two or three thousand musicians, singers, and other jazz entertainers in print somewhere or other. However, though these list the musical careers of their subjects in considerable detail, supplemented by the fantastically laborious and scholarly discographies, they neglect other aspects of their lives almost totally. Unless we know a musician personally we rarely even know whether he was married or when, and whether he has or had children. The biographical information about the social origins of musicians is as casual and unsystematic as the information about their geographical origin is meticulous. Nevertheless, we know enough to reconstruct the portrait of both black and white musicians pretty well, even in the more obscure phases of jazz. The two must be kept apart, although the jazz musician has developed a common pattern of personality, which does not depend on his skin; for the social origins of white and black artists are very different, at least in the earlier phases of jazz, and so is the part they play in their respective communities. Louis Armstrong, like Joe Louis or Sugar Ray Robinson, can become the symbol and hero of all Harlem. No white jazz musician has ever become the symbol and hero of more than a minority of young rebels.

Let us consider the black musician first. The obvious and dominant fact about the earliest jazz is that it was a poor man's music, and a music of the 'undeserving' and unrespectable poor at that. At the turn of the century a respectable black preacher's family in the South, like that of W. C. Handy's father, was at least as shocked at the idea that its son should become a musician as a lower-middle-class or middle-class white family. In the Southern countryside as well as in the towns—perhaps more than in the towns—the line between godly and worldly music was as sharp as in Calvinist Dumfriesshire. The godly man sang gospel songs, and put away Satan's tunes like the blues with horror and disgust. (When John and Alan Lomax collected their folk-songs in the Southern penitentiaries they had the utmost difficult in persuading former worldlings who had become hard-shell Baptists or Pentecostal Holiness people to dig out their morally tainted musical past.) That the modern jazz-lover has made both work-songs and spirituals into part of the jazz repertoire is one of the many ironies of our subject, but one not shared by devout artists like Miss Mahalia Jackson, who has steadfastly refused, through the years, to sing for anything but the glory of the Lord, or in company with reprobate music. Naturally the barriers against jazz were less high among blacks than among whites. Beside the overwhelming barrier of colour in a country of racial discrimination, all others seem small and surmountable: the ghetto breeds its own internal fluidity, as well as its own compartments. Moreover, there have been up to the present so few ways in which American blacks might rise in wealth, achievement, and social status, that even a very plebeian one like jazz was not to be neglected, all the more so as it is a known fact that the world of entertainment for the poor is much more egalitarian than the culture of the rich. Today, at a time when mixed bands under a black leader are a commonplace in jazz, there is hardly yet a single black conductor of an American symphony orchestra or leader of a chamber-music ensemble, and few black symphonic players. It is therefore natural that, from the beginning, some middle-class blacks entered jazz. Indeed, among the musicians for whom a musical training, or general education, or simply an initial degree of relative self-confidence are important assets—composers, arrangers, bandleaders—the middle class black played a disproportionately large part almost from the beginning. Most of the leading jazz composer-arrangers—Handy, Carter, Morton, Redman, Ellington, Sy Oliver—and many of the leaders of the famous early large black bands—Fletcher Henderson, Ellington, Redman, Lunceford, Count Basie—are or were of middle-class origins.* (This is in marked contrast to the leaders of the famous large white jazz or semi-jazz bands, who are mainly of relatively much lower social standing, like the Dorsey brothers, who came from the Pennsylvania mines; Ben Pollack and Benny Goodman, who came from the Chicago Hull House slum settlement school; Harry James, who came from circus life; Glenn Miller, Woody Herman, Ted Lewis, Paul Whiteman. The white equivalents of Ellington or Henderson had other careers open to them than band-leading.)

But on the whole the early jazz was poor men's music, or the music of traditional show folk, whose social standing was not much above vagabonds'. Admittedly even among the black poor there are distinctions. The instrumental players other than guitarists and pianists were perhaps not of quite such humble social origins as the blues singers and players, who clearly represent the most pauperized, oppressed, and vagrant segment of the black people. A foot-loose rural guitar-picker like Leadbelly,

---

* Henderson (born 1898) and Lunceford (born 1902) actually had a university education, which put them among the most exclusive élite of black Americans at the time.

in and out of jail, was despised, if only as a hayseed, even by the poorest street musicians of New Orleans. The 'blind man at the corner singing the *Beale Street Blues*' or the boys who led him along Southern roads, like the now famous Josh White, the itinerant bar-room pianists with flamboyant nicknames like Pinetop Smith, Speckled Red, Cripple Clarence Lofton, or Little Brother, were on the margins of even black society. It is no accident that the first blues player and singer whom W. C. Handy heard in 1903 was 'a lean, loose-jointed Negro (who) had commenced plunking a guitar beside me while I slept. His clothes were in rags; his feet peeped out of his shoes. . . . As he played, he pressed a knife on the strings of the guitar in a manner popularized by Hawaiian guitarists who used steel bars.'

Nor is it an accident that the man sang about

> *Goin' where the Southern cross the Yellow Dog,*

i.e. to Moorehead, Miss., where the Southern and Yazoo Delta railroads cross, where the penitentiary lay, which the singer probably knew from inside. (Handy was later to make one of the classics of jazz, the *Yellow Dog Blues,* out of this memory.) The women singers, though their musical status was to be much higher than the men's, came from comparable social depths. If they came from show-folk families, like Ma Rainey, Ethel Waters, and Billie Holiday, they were lucky. Few great artists have come from such appalling slum poverty as the great Bessie Smith; and the social status (and perhaps the original profession) of many blues singers is indicated by the nickname of Bertha 'Chippie' Hill; for a chippy is a prostitute.

Except for the peculiar group of New Orleans Creoles, the instrumental musicians came from equally modest social backgrounds. The *gens de couleur* were 'bricklayers and carpenters and cigar makers and plasterers. Some had little businesses on their own—coal and wood and vegetable stores',[1] i.e. they were skilled workers and petty artisans, at least until they became full-time professionals. Alphonse Picou (clarinet) was the son of a cigar maker, apprenticed to a tinsmith and later a joiner. Barney

168

Bigard (clarinet) began with cigar-making and engraving. Sidney Bechet knew enough to open a tailor's shop during the slump. But the Creoles, former free men depressed into the ranks of the labourers and immigrants by segregation, were a unique local group, and even in New Orleans those who got their non-musical living driving a coal cart, like Louis Armstrong, or working on the docks, like George Lewis, were at least as numerous as the Creole musicians, though less articulate.* Outside New Orleans those of unskilled status were the vast majority.

At all events, the original jazz players belonged to the working class which, since blacks are largely confined to labouring jobs, meant the unskilled. When they lost their jobs or fell out of fashion, they would naturally drop back into the characteristic occupations of the working-class black. Papa Mutt Carey would

---

* Another factor may account for the apparent prominence of musicians from the skilled working-class in New Orleans: the caste system which kept many of the unskilled immigrant players in the unrespected and unregarded social zone of the blues-singers. Such a one was the trumpeter Chris Kelly 'who played for those blues, cotton-picking Negroes, what they called in the old days "yard and field Negroes".' 'They were real primitive people,' says Danny Barker, the guitarist, related to Creoles, 'who worked in the fields, worked hard. They wore those box-backed suits and hats with two-coloured bands on them, shoes with diamonds in their toe, or a two-dollar gold piece in the toe . . . Chris Kelly played for those people . . . He worked all the little towns. He talked a real broken patois, African almost. The Creoles couldn't understand him. They didn't like him and they didn't want to see him on the street, because he played for what was supposed to be the bad element. When he would play a street parade, mostly advertising, all the kitchen mechanics would come out on the corner, shaking. The Creoles would hate to see that.' Creoles and other old city musicians would have all the townsman's contempt for the country black (Cf. the *American Guides* series for *Arkansas* for this phenomenon in the 1930s.) Old town musicians in New Orleans set the standards, had the connexions which got a man engagements on tour and in other towns, in other words they have decided—*via* the discographers and researchers—which New Orleans musicians live in history and which do not. Buddy Bolden is a legend, though no record of him survives. Chris Kelly is a footnote in history, rescued thanks to the loyal memory of some minor New Orleans musicians. See *Hear Me Talkin' to Ya*. pp. 56–7.

become a postman and porter in California, Albert Nicholas would work on the New York subway and in the post office, Natty Dominique as an airport red-cap, King Oliver as a pool-room attendant, Bunk Johnson, an uptown man (the poorer and less respected blacks lived uptown) returned to the country and the sugar-cane. They were working men and aware of it, for, as Johnny St Cyr (banjo) put it:

> A jazz musician have to be a working-class man, out in the open all the time, healthy and strong. That's what's wrong today; these new guys haven't got the force. They don't *like* to play all night; they don't think they *can* play unless they're loaded. But a working man have the *power* to play hot, whisky or no whisky. You see, the average working man is very musical. Playing music for him is just relaxing. He get as much kick out of playing as other folks get out of dancing.[2]

Perhaps St Cyr's is an idealized picture of the old days of transition to professionalism, even in New Orleans, but the social situation it paints is clear.

The artist sprung from the unskilled poor, and playing for the poor is in a peculiar social position. In the world from which he comes and in which he works 'entertainment' (which means any personal talent, or gift sold for the public to watch, hear, or otherwise enjoy, from one's body to one's soul) is not merely a way of earning a living, but far and away the most important way of making one's individual path in the world, rivalled only by crime and 'politics', with religion, of the type evolved by poor men for themselves, trailing a little behind. It is essential to remember this. The star musician, dancer, singer, comedian, boxer, or bullfighter is not merely a success among this sporting or artist public, but the potential first citizen of his community or his people. A Caruso among the poor of Naples, a Marie Lloyd in the East End, a Gracie Fields in Rochdale, a Jack Johnson, Joe Louis, or Sugar Ray in Harlem, a Louis Armstrong occupy a position far more eminent among 'their' people than a Picasso or Fonteyn in orthodox society. Among oppressed peoples such as blacks and gypsies, the entertainer is often the only member of his group who wins fame outside 'the race'. Even at a less exalted level, the moderately successful entertainer is one of the rare men or women who can escape the curse of poverty and endless unskilled drudgery, if only for a time. For the recipes for 'getting on' which have built respectable Western society since Calvin, thrift, hard work, systematic education, and the life, are not much good to those who genuinely start from bedrock, with no assets but talent, energy, strength, or looks. Every investigation into the social origins of the rich, of business and public executives, or men and women of high intellectual achievements, demonstrates the extraordinary disadvantage at which the genuinely unskilled and illiterate are. In the arts alone can they compete on equal, perhaps on superior terms, for just as 'the best fighter is a hungry fighter', so the best entertainer is the one for whom his art is the only possible way out of squalor and oppression into relative freedom. But for the poor 'the arts' mean commercial entertainment, and commercial entertainment in the nineteenth and early twentieth centuries meant work in one or other of those semi-ghettoes which all great cities develop as 'entertainment districts', and where music halls, brothels, night clubs, saloons, boxers' gymnasiums, variety agencies, and their denizens rubbed shoulders: on Beale Street in Memphis, on Seventh Avenue or Lenox in Harlem, Twelfth and Eighteenth Streets in Kansas City, from Montmartre to the boulevards in Paris, behind the Paralelo in Barcelona, and so on.

The jazz musician was therefore potentially a king or duke, but his Versailles was on the Place Pigalle, his subjects lived in the slums, and his rival potentates or peers were (black) gangsters and crooked politicians, professional gamblers and fighters, fancy women, and occasionally great preachers, lay or religious. He was, of course, a professional and a craftsman; and as we have seen, his professionalism and craftsmanship were by far the most important factors in his life, though even they necessarily threw him into the company of the others who worked by night and slept or relaxed by day, and thus separated him from the ordinary citizen. But his mode of behaviour was at least equally determined by his social origins and his social role in the community of the poor, or more precisely, of the labourers and sub-proletarians of the slums over whom they reigned.

For instance, if he was often bohemian in his ways, it was not on the pattern of the standard bohemia of the nineteenth-century arts, which is at bottom the scale of values of the lower-middle class turned inside out, but on the pattern of the unskilled labourer magnified. He did not have the nineteenth-century bohemians' horror of 'respectable' manual work. When Sidney Bechet, the great reed man was broke in the thirties, he started his tailors's shop, and Tommy Ladnier, whose trumpet could suggest more blues with a single note than any other, shined the shoes of the customers. He did not react against the values of clerks and shopkeepers by neglecting himself or dressing sloppily. On the contrary, he was an enthusiastic and flamboyant dresser, regarding his dress as a symbol of wealth and social status, like the cowboy, the navvy, the sailor, and other casual but occasionally flush labourers. If he was a free spender it was for the same reason—casual earnings breed casual spending—and because his social standing in his world depended on behaving like a king. If he developed the over-life-size gestures and habits of the superman—the limitless appetite for women and whisky, the passions and capriciousness of the *prima donna* (who has herself, as a type, sprung from a similar social milieu)—it was not only because to the successful New Orleans trumpeter or classic blues singer or dancer all the whisky and all the women (or, if she was a woman, all the men) were freely available, but because he had to live up to his part. For the star was what every slum child and drudge might become: the king or queen of the poor, because the poor person writ large. We see him first, surrounded by legendary mist, as Buddy Bolden, the demon barber of Franklin Street, the blackest of black men, as the tale goes, 'a pure Negro' (for darkness means low status, even among blacks), who 'found his cornet on the street.' We hear him knocking with his trumpet on the floor of the Odd Fellows' Hall to give the beat, holding it up, pausing to be sure of his embouchure, and leading his band into the wonderful blues of the poorest of poor prostitutes, *Make me a pallet on your floor,* while the audience yelled out, 'Oh, Mr Bolden (note the Mister), play it for us, oh Buddy, play it!'[3] In the legend he played so loudly that 'on some nights you could hear his horn ten mile away'. He could not read a note of music, and the women fought for the privilege of carrying his cornet. 'He was crazy for wine and women and vice versa.' At the age of twenty-nine he went mad, and lived the rest of his life (until 1931) in a lunatic asylum with *dementia praecox.* We see him again, in the classical version of the over-life-size music-hall star, as Fats Waller, the pianist who started the day with eight fingers of whisky and threw his fantastic talent to the winds. 'I've seen Fats Waller enter a place', says Louis Armstrong, 'and all the people in the joint (I mean the place) would rave, and you could see a gladness in their faces. . . .'[4] He would compose the best part of a musical show while the girls were rehearsing their dance routine, meanwhile 'bubbling over with so many stories and funny remarks that those girls could hardly hoof it for laughing', 'a volcano, alright, alone in his class'. He earned millions and threw them away: 'he kept broke because he was always balling and having a good time and just didn't care'.[5] He laughed and cried louder than anyone, he drank and made love more, he slept less, he was fatter, he welshed on more advances and played more trashy music better than anyone. He died at the age of thirty-nine in 1943, at the peak of his career.

Last, but most important, he did not in the early stages share the most striking characteristic of the orthodox nineteenth-century artist, the contempt for his public. His model was not Rimbaud but Marie Lloyd or Johann Strauss. The frontier between the 'hip' people and the 'squares' (though there is no evidence that these terms were used in New Orleans times) did not run between the artist and the chosen few who could 'dig' him on one side, the idiots and the bourgeois on the other. It ran between the artist and his public, the outcast community of the 'undeserving poor' on one side, and the respectable world on the other. It was the line which, in the 1890s, divided the music-hall artists, the guardees, the prostitutes, and the enthusiasts from the blue-nosed, teetotal, nonconformist spoilsports of the London County Council who wanted to license the halls and get the girls out of the Empire promenade. Why indeed should the artist feel misunderstood? True, the public did not appreciate the technical achievements of the musician and, I dare say, then as now tended to applaud loudness or emotion rather than musicianship. But they liked the music, they danced to it like mad, and there were always plenty of them, from the girls in the honky-tonks after business was over to the audiences in the black theatres, to sway and cry at the blues. When geniuses like Louis Armstrong and Bessie Smith were spontaneously recognized as the king of trumpeters and the 'empress of the blues' by the applause of the public and the sales charts of record companies, there was no strong reason for the artist to feel isolated, except from the 're-spectable' world in which official cultural reputations were made. But about this many of them had not heard, or did not care.★

The divorce between the jazz musician and the public proba-bly began in the later 1920s. At any rate, there are clear signs that from about 1927 the straight old music lost its power to draw: even the black papers began to hint that jazz was 'on its way out'. This change of taste, which has been more fully discussed above, no doubt hit the traditional artists hardest: Bessie Smith drank harder than ever, and supplemented her old-fashioned blues more and more widely with pornography, but even this could not stop her disappearance from the recordings and her miserable decline to the Southern backwoods shows where she had once started. Nothing went right for the great King Oliver after 1928, and his simple goodness and modest Christian resig-nation—Oliver was that rare phenomenon, a pioneer jazz player who was also a copy-book citizen—only make the story of his

---

★ Those who did, were embittered by its neglect. Thus Fats Waller, a musician of sound classical training and superb technique, whose favourite instrument was the organ, and whose main ambition was to excel as an inter-preter of J. S. Bach's ecclesiastical works, was never given the chance to record in this field.

174

last ten years more pathetic. It would be doctrinaire to argue that the new styles now demanded even by the black public were not jazz, even though they were quite certainly much more influenced by the standards of white commercial entertainment; and it would be simply untrue to argue that most musicians minded very much what they played, so long as it swung and gave them the chance to blow out. Plenty of jazz players continued to feel at ease in their world, even when resigning themselves to a more modest place within it. The kings of New Orleans might be cornet players; the queens of Nashville or Atlanta blues singers; but the kings of the Northern black ghettoes, with their more sophisticated tastes, were more likely to be music-hall dancers like Buck and Bubbles or 'Bojangles' Bill Robinson, boxing champions, or, if musicians, band-leaders. The street had given way to the stage. But the musician's world was changed. To succeed under the new conditions he had to be a music-hall personality, like Louis Armstrong and Fats Waller; to have a 'gimmick' like the frenetic Cab Calloway with his nonsense vocals;★ and even in the ordinary bands he needed far better technical equipment and musical knowledge than before, equipment and knowledge only a tiny fraction of which would be appreciated by the public.

And so some players—the less adaptable ones—entered an empty world, where only their own kind appreciated them, and the others played for a public whose applause was largely irrelevant. The musician began to be alone with his music. It is significant that, whereas the kings of the pioneer instrumental jazz got their crowns by public acclamation, Coleman Hawkins, whose supremacy on the tenor sax was virtually unchallenged among musicians from his first appearance in the early twenties for more than a decade, never led a band until 1939, and indeed found it preferable to earn his living in England and Holland for the best part of the thirties. The top player was increasingly a

★ Fortunately for jazz, in Harlem a superlatively vivid rhythm was sometimes gimmick enough. Chick Webb, the crippled little drummer, made his and his band's reputation largely through his 'swing'.

musician's musician, or a star only for the selected and untypical public of 'true' jazz fans. Jazz lived and flourished best no longer where it was acclaimed, but where it was tolerated and left alone, as in the speakeasies and night clubs of Kansas City. As for the old-style musician, only in the holes and corners of the South, or in the poorest Northern slums, where, as on the Chicago South Side, the immigrants congregated, could he hope to get by.

A good deal of jazz thus tended to become a musician's music, and the jazz player to be even more closely confined to a special social and intellectual world. Such was his situation when white intellectuals in the thirties discovered that jazz was intellectually reputable, and when, thanks largely to their systematic championship, it became widely popular among the whites as well as among its old black public.

At this point we must consider a factor in the black jazz musician's life which has steadily grown in conscious importance: race relations. No bar of black jazz has ever made sense to those who do not understand the black's reaction to oppression. But, as we have seen, most of the pioneer jazz musicians did not protest openly against their condition.* Handy and Armstrong could write or sing about 'darkies', 'pickaninnies', and 'coal-black mammies' as if they did not realize that these are insults and fighting words to the self-conscious black. Rarely did they kick against the pricks: they did not compete with the ofays. That an Al Jolson should earn a great deal more than a Bessie Smith even at her peak was as much in the nature of things as that black artists playing the South should accept discrimination. At most a proud man like Fats Waller, whose limousine was persistently sabotaged, would refuse to go on with the tour until his booker hired him a private railway coach; but even he did not refuse to play the zone.

A generation brought up in the Northern ghettoes, a couple of decades playing in the North and West, and the marvellous political awakening of all the oppressed and underprivileged in

* See Chapter 3. The subject is further discussed in Chapter 11.

Roosevelt's America, put a new tone into the jazz-musician's instrument: open resentment. Every line of the autobiography of the old-timer, W. C. Handy, radiated modest optimism and the conviction of gradual progress:

> At the New York World's Fair, 1939–40, I saw, in small degree, a fulfillment of 'No Excellence Without Great Labour'. There, on the American Common, tablets were erected containing the names of six hundred men and women selected from all races who had contributed in some degree to American culture, and among those names I saw mine.[6]

But the new Northern or assimilated generations, those who had flowed north in their millions from 1916 on, and their children, were less contented. They had not escaped discrimination, though they had lost the stable, settled, certain community life of the South, for which even some of the most militant hankered: Big Bill Broonzy, the blues singer, claims to have gone back to his patch of land in Pine Bluff, Arkansas, after every trip north to record or perform. And the inequality they knew was, for the musician, twice as unbearable as in the past, because they now knew that *their* music, black men's music, was not simply entertainment, but serious art; many whites believing (correctly) that it was the most original and important contribution of America to world music.

Jazz, as we have seen, had always attracted a small quota of middle-class and intellectual black players, but with one major exception (Duke Ellington) they had played or arranged the music as it came, and tried neither to intellectualize nor to turn it into art-music, i.e. to compete with white music.★

But from the late thirties the black jazz musician became increasingly ambitious, both to establish his superiority over the

---

★ Among older middle-class musicians, other than those already mentioned, we may note Benny Carter, 1907, clarinet, sax, and arranger (Wilberforce Univ.), Teddy Wilson, 1912, piano (Tuskegee), Billy Eckstine, 1914, pop singer and band-leader (Howard), and Fats Waller, 1904, piano and pop singer.

white musician, as it were officially, and to raise the status of his music by competing with white music on its own ground of elaborate and sophisticated structure and theoretical as well as practical expertise. Jazz did not, indeed, begin to attract young black intellectuals as such in any numbers until the new and ambitious versions of the music had already established themselves. The Modern Jazz Quartet, for instance, three of whose members clearly belong to the black élite (John Lewis: anthropology and music at University of New Mexico; Milt Jackson: music at Michigan State; Percy Heath: fighter pilot and Granoff School of Music, Philadelphia) contains no player whose career began earlier than the last war years. Nevertheless, the urge to intellectualize and turn jazz into an *avant-garde* art-music is clear from the end of the thirties.

The motives for this urge may best be explained in the words of the anonymous and intellectual California musician reported by J. E. Berendt: [7]

You see we need music, we've always needed a music—our own. We have nothing else. Our writers write like the whites, our painters paint like them, our philosophers think like them. Only our musicians don't play like the whites. So we created a music for ourselves. When we had it—the old type of jazz—the whites came, and they liked it and imitated it. Pretty soon it was no longer our music. No Negro can play New Orleans jazz today with a conscience. A few old ones still do, but no coloured man listens to them. They might just play it for the whites. Even though the experts have proved that there's no blacker music.

You see, as soon as we have a music, the white man comes and imitates it. We've now had jazz for fifty years, and in all those fifty years there has been not a single white man, perhaps leaving aside Bix, who has had an idea. Only the coloured men have ideas. But if you see who's got the famous names: they're all white.

What can we do? We must go on inventing something new all the time. When we have it, the whites will take it from us, and we have to start all over again. It is as though we were being hunted.

Such black racialism was not necessarily the only political attitude of the revolutionary young players, but it illustrates the rather emotional and primitive general resentment which almost certainly prevailed among them over more mature and sophisticated views. Very few black jazz artists in and after the 1930s were associated with the labour and communist movements, but even among those few I can think of no pioneers of modern jazz. However, it is possible that some of these may have played, among other symbols of rebellion, with the orthodox left-wing ones. Indeed, I suspect that left-wing politics got among the highly specialized and insulated group of black musicians, especially outside New York, mainly through their contact with the strongly progressive band of jazz enthusiasts and critics; and these, as we shall see in the chapter on the jazz public, were markedly out of sympathy with the new musical developments. However, it is important to remember that the new developments of jazz, however abstract and formal at first sight, expressed a political attitude. The very slogan 'art for art's sake' (or, as the pioneer revolutionary, John Birks Gillespie said, 'I play for musicians') must be translated, at least some of the time, into some such terms as: 'Jazz is an art-music, not just entertainment, and as Negroes we demand attention for it as such.'

The new intellectualism of jazzmen found expression in a variety of ways, some of them surprising. For instance, the fashionable costume of the new player was no longer simply a variant of the full-dress regalia of the labourers' king who is in the money, but a derivation from the dress of nineteenth-century Parisian bohemian intellectuals. Heavily rimmed glasses (even when not needed), a goatee, a beret, perhaps a long cigarette holder or meerschaum pipe were the uniform of the 'bopper' in the middle 1940s. Carelessness and sloppiness in dress—the true 'bop-follower' often systematically avoided pressing his suits—became fashionable.[8] Reading and orthodox culture had never been essential qualifications of the jazz player, but in the new era it became a distinct asset to be able to say, like Thelonious Sphere Monk, a particularly characteristic pioneer of the new music, that 'we liked Ravel, Stravinsky, Debussy, Prokofieff, Schoen-

179

berg, and maybe we were a little influenced by them'.[9] This is the generation of players that started buying Dalis when in funds, and around which talk of psychoanalysis and existentialism flows.

The rebellion against the inferiority of the black and the traditional forms of jazz expression which were identified with it ('Uncle Tom Music') is equally evident in the behaviour of the new players. Among some—especially the latest, most intellectualized generation which has emerged sine 1950—it took the form of a deliberate turning away from the simple extrovert noises, the spontaneous emotions of the traditional musician, and the instruments that had always carried them. Trumpets were played as though they were flutes, drums were reduced to a whisper, wind instruments were sometimes eliminated entirely. Groups like the Modern Jazz Quartet, reacting against the old ways by anti-bohemianism, appear on the stage in faultless morning or evening dress, bowing stiffly and with expressionless faces to applause. Not to play like a music-hall act and a clown, *not* to behave even offstage like the old-style player who looks for a night club and some whisky and a chick, and a band to sit in with, as soon as he comes off the job: such is their ambition. An even more obvious form of revolt against inferiority, which a leading group of the new players shared with other Northern big-city blacks, was mass conversion to Mohammedanism. The new music was played, among others, by Abdullah ibn Buhaina (Art Blakey, the drummer), Sahib Shahab (Edmund Gregory, alto), Abdul Hamid (McKinley Dorham, trumpet, tenor), Liaquat Ali Salaam (Kenny Clarke, drums), Ibrahim ibn Ismail (Walter Bishop Jr, piano) and other sons of the Prophet, though most of the actual founders have done little more than put on an occasional turban. The new Moslems studied the Koran in translation, tried to learn Arabic, and propagated the faith. It would be easy, but wrong, to make fun of such gestures of revolt. The best judgement on them is contained in a small dialogue between Dizzy Gillespie and the arranger Gil Fuller, who watched one such band of Moslem boppers break rehearsal to bow towards Mecca:

180

Dizzy's eyes filled with tears. 'They been hurt', he explained, 'and they're tryin' to get away from it'.

'It's the last resort of guys who don't know which way to turn', said Fuller impatiently.

'East', said Dizzy. 'They turn east'.[10]

The attitude of the new musicians, as well as their music, thus expressed the peculiar ambiguities of this generation of black intellectual rebellion. It was political, but expressed itself in abstraction and formalism. It was black, but expressed itself at least partly in the adoption of the patterns and clichés, the modes of orthodox (i.e. white) culture, a fact which made the task of the jazzman twice as difficult.

The new musician and the new music thus paradoxically undermined the racialism they intended to propagate. It is black, and desperately anxious to compete with the whites as *black* music: the 'respectable' ambition of the modern jazz musician is no longer simply to be accepted as a man who plays Bach, or as a composer of classical music, but as a man who plays a music which is as complex as Bach *but based on a specifically black foundation,* the blues. At the same time his rebellion—even when he attempts to side-step this effect by a flight into Mohammedanism or some other non-white culture—takes him farther away from the specifically black musical idiom of the old jazz, and from the cultural situation of the old jazzman which, though not particularly determined by skin colour, was sharply distinct from orthodox and respectable culture. His paradox is that, though he wishes to be a much more conscious and complete challenger of white cultural supremacy than his predecessors, his very challenge assimilates him to the white pattern. The jazzman of New Orleans, or even of Kansas City, represented a form of art, a way of the creative artist, a pattern of relations between art and society, which were as different from that of the orthodox world of symphonies, chamber music, and opera as the Byzantine painter and mosaicist is from the world of the Venice Biennale, or the heroic bard from the modern novelist. The 'modern' jazzman represents the same type of minority *avant-garde* music

181

as his white equivalents in Paris or New York. He differs from them only as, say, the non-representationalist differs from the expressionist painter. Hence the modern jazzman is rapidly evolving into a figure familiar to anyone who follows the history of twentieth-century Western arts. His 'blackness' (i.e. the special traditions of the culturally unorthodox world from which he has sprung) becomes increasingly irrelevant.

With one exception. The new type of *avant-garde* jazzman may evolve into another version of the modern Western intellectual, but he had evolved out of the old self-made, outcast, entertainer. The startling fact about the 'modern' movement is that all its pioneers are or were jazzmen of the old plebeian type. Dizzy Gillespie (born 1917) is one of nine children of a bricklayer from a hole in South Carolina, who came up through the ordinary jazz-band world. Charlie Parker (1920–55) was a slum-child from Kansas City. Kenny Clarke, Art Blakey, Max Roach, Chico Hamilton, the drummers (born 1914, 1919, 1925, 1921 respectively) learned their music as it came. Charlie Christian (1919–42), who revolutionized the guitar, Fats Navarro, (1923–50), the trumpeter, were just provincial players who came up somewhere in Oklahoma and Florida. No doubt some of them had a better education, including musical training, than the men of Armstrong's generation; but they can in no sense be regarded as people who owe anything substantial to conservatories or to the advantages of a black middle-class background, or even—since their music repelled most jazz intellectuals—to outside influences. It was among such players that the musical and social revolution of the jazz musician began round about 1941–2.

If we are to understand it, we must look at another characteristic phenomenon of the Northern black generations, the 'hipster', whose evolution is intertwined with that of the modern jazzman. There is by now a good deal of literature about the hipster, most of which reads like a psychoanalyst's case diagnoses, and for a good reason: [11] because the hipsters do not explain themselves, and show the world only their symptoms, which have to be interpreted. But the hipster is there all right. He began to appear at the central metropolitan street-corners of

182

Northern ghettoes between the wars, though it is not impossible that he existed in embryo in Harlem even earlier. At any rate, he does not belong to the South. He can, I daresay, still be seen in the American black equivalents of Soho and Saint Germain des Prés, dressed in whatever is the uniform of his fraternity—before the vogue of the bopper's costume it used to be the 'zoot suit', with its epaulette shoulders, its frock coat hanging almost to the pavement, and its peg-bottom trousers. He wore (and perhaps still wears) his face like a mask, for ostensible emotion was taboo. He talked jive-talk which nobody ought to understand. He lived 'for kicks'—jazz, sex, marihuana, or any other stimulants that were going. He was not like other people, the 'squares'. He was beyond the law, beyond human emotion, beyond ambition, and money, beyond good and evil; he was against the white and black *status quo*—the 'Uncle Toms'—but he did not know what he was for.

We are today fairly familiar with the hipster's type of negative, emotional, anarchic revolt: older generations have watched it among the young post-war generations in a number of countries, since the 'existentialists' of the post-liberation Left Bank in Paris gave it its first orthodox habitation and name. (Their American white equivalents, as Norman Mailer has correctly pointed out, have actually borrowed their idiom from the black hipster: 'In Greenwich village a *ménage à trois* was completed—the bohemian and the juvenile delinquent came face-to-face with the Negro, and the [white] hipster was a fact in American life.') The international symbols of this revolt, like the late film star James Dean, are familiar to all. But in spite of this convergence, the original Harlem hipster was not, like the lost generation of Saint Germain des Prés, a derivation from orthodox upper-class culture, such as is still oddly reflected in the Edwardian toff's outfit of English working-class teddy-boys, or the pseudo-art-school styles of East End working-class girls, but a specialized development of the ghetto of labourers and outcasts.

The Harlem hipster 'functioned' in some respects like the jazz player. His social origins were certainly similar: he owed nothing to education or orthodox cultural influence. He was (Mezz

Mezzrow is almost certainly right on this point) the would-be smart and able youngster with ambitions, 'keyed up with the effort to see and hear everything all at once, because that's how bottom-dogs ought to be unless they want to get lost in the shuffle.'[12] His chief achievement, jive-talk—for talk was the hipster's only triumph—is a continuous, ever-renewed virtuoso collective improvisation which depends on talent, on speed, on imagination, and a sort of primitive verbal bravura. Nobody ought to be able to talk jive-talk, even if he learnt all yesterday's or even today's jive vocabulary by heart, just as nobody is able to play like Armstrong or Charlie Parker even with the most painstaking imitation. For the hipster sophistication and light-ning speed on the uptake were everything. His expression, as has been said, was 'the physiognomy of astuteness'. Whoever needed the faintest explanation of even the most cryptic gesture or statement was by definition a square. Like bop jazz, only in verbal terms, jive-talk was a set of variations on themes and rhythms unstated, because assumed. Just so the Max Roach Quintet call their derivation from the well-known song *All the Things You Are, Prince Albert*. Anyone who does not know that the theme played is derived from the harmonies of the (un-named) *All the Things You Are* is a musical square.

Mezzrow is almost certainly right in believing that hipster-dom represented a more urgent, aggressive, and higher ambition than anything in the old South, quite apart from the passionate effort to show 'that they're not the ounce-brained, stuttering, tongue-tied Sambos of the blackface vaudeville routines, the La-zybones of the comic strips, the Old Moses of the Southern plantation'.[13] In his way, the hipster aspired to the white man's status as a professional, an intellectual, in fact to just those achievements which are almost beyond the longest reach of the ghetto boy without money or skill, with a caricature of school-ing, without a background or even a tradition that such ambi-tions are desirable. That is perhaps why the only people who have come close to realizing the hipster's ambition in their own field are the jazz musicians. And that is probably why the ambi-tion of the ordinary hipster, who is far more often a man without career or achievement, turns from breaking out of inferiority into contracting out of it. At all events the hipster described in the post-1945 years is not the same man as the one whose 'fraternal order' Mezz Mezzrow joined around 1930. He is the collective 'outsider'. He does not live in this world, but escapes from it into a world of bop music, which the square cannot understand, and *pot* (marihuana), of 'kicks'—sensations—which the square cannot feel. 'He may earn his living as a petty criminal, a hobo, a roustabout, or a free-lance moving man', it does not matter how, for the hipster (whose very essence in Mezzrow's description was *action*) no longer acts, but simply exists. Even his one triumph, jive-talk, seems to have contracted into a featureless, simplified vocabulary of monosyllables, grunts, and tacit gestures, which serves almost exclusively to differentiate him from the square. Only two things remain of his former self: a total refusal to conform to the squares and a savage integrity about his own standards and the things he likes.

No doubt there are other elements in the hipster's make-up also, on which the more psychologically minded literature has dwelt. In a way the ambitious slum youngster of the second generation of Northern black immigrants is doubly rootless, having lost the subordinate, but fairly obvious, place of the New Orleans slum boy in his community. The obvious, uniformed cohesion of the hipster against the squares is certainly in part due to the desire to be in *some* community, if only that of those without social roots. The observers who note that the hipster classifies what other people would call good as 'solid' or 'in there' (i.e. *somewhere*) and an undesirable state as *nowhere*, may have a point. For in a sense he is nowhere socially or as an individual. If he will succeed, he is nowhere yet; if he fails, or gives up the struggle, he remains nowhere, except in the private world of drugs, or sex, or some other subjective sensation.

It is easy to see how the young revolutionary musicians fit into the general scene of hipsterdom; for the hipster is just such a home-grown ghetto intellectual or artist as they, only less successful. The modes of behaviour of the revolutionaries, deliberately shocking not only to non-musicians but even to older musicians, were those of the hipster: for instance, the refusal to abide by the old-established code of manners which obliges the soloist who is about to finish his chorus to nod to the next man to give him his cue; the apparent boredom with which the most radical musical innovations were played; the habit of playing with one's back to the audience, shuffling on stage anytime and offstage without a look at the end of a solo. If the old players' ideal had been social, the new ones now modelled themselves on the Rimbauds and Modiglianis of orthodox art; or more exactly, they reproduced their ways independently. They doped heavily, to the disgust of the older men, for whom whisky, women, and an occasional stick of tea were all that a decent musician needed. There is little doubt—though again it would be invidious to name names, even those which have come before police courts —that drug addiction was much more widespread among the modernists than among any previous group of jazz players. There are life-histories among them, such as that of the earliest and greatest of the moderns, and perhaps the only genius among them, Charlie 'Yardbird' Parker, which have the horrifying, helpless inevitability of the lone wolves of modern romantic culture. There was no more pleasure or success in the life of Parker than in that of Van Gogh, even though his talent was much more rapidly appreciated. There was merely the total inability to get on any terms with the world, and the compulsion to play what must be played in the face of the world. The artist has become the wild beast, who is by definition caged wherever he is, for every conceivable society must be a prison for him.

Since those early days of the jazz revolution the harshest outlines of revolt have been a little softened, though no doubt somewhere there are still young players who see themselves— jazzwise—in the same defiant and partly self-pitying terms as each new *avant-garde* of orthodox artists. Dizzy Gillespie now undertakes official cultural missions for the U.S. Government. J. J. Johnson, the trombonist, is a long way from the days— from 1952 to 1954—when he had to earn his living as a blueprint inspector, occasionally gigging in his spare time. The Modern Jazz Quartet was reviewed by a classical music critic for the

186

Sunday Times and aroused violent controversy among the readers of the *Observer*. In fact, it has taken the jazz revolutionaries a great deal less time to win orthodox recognition than it ever took a Benny Carter or a Dickie Wells to get accepted as a serious artist outside a tiny circle of unknown enthusiasts. And yet, the revolution cannot be undone. The young jazz musician today is socially and individually a different person from the Armstrongs and Bessie Smiths, and even from the Fats Wallers and Lionel Hamptons of the past.

The white musician in America need not be discussed at such length. In a sense, he has practically from the start been the outsider type, playing a music which he knew to be misunderstood by the public. 'When will we ever be able to earn our living playing hot?' asked Frank Teschemacher, the famous Chicago clarinetist. The question was rhetorical. Teschemacher and his friends knew perfectly well from the moment that they began to imitate the black players that this kind of music was not saleable to the white dancing public for 'jazz' in the 1920s. The most they could hope to do with it was to play a few college dances where some of the students might be for it, to play the kind of night clubs or halls where the manager and the public didn't mind what the noise was, so long as it was loud, and to make an occasional record. If they wanted to earn their living by music, at least after 1927–8 or so, they had to play in 'sweet' or 'pop' bands. The uncompromising white musician thus faced the problem of the misunderstood and isolated artist from the beginning; indeed, who knows how many of them had not chosen to play jazz just because it was their private paradise, which neither fathers nor 'square' friends could share, a protest against the old generation, against the 150 per cent Americanism of the lush decade before 1929? Howard Becker the sociologist has described a group of such young white jazz musicians in the Chicago of the 'cool' era, but the description, with a few changes, could stand for the 1920s also: they were sons of good middle-class Americans. They protested, totally and absolutely, against all aspects of the 'American way of life', by playing their jazz, by frequenting only musicians and night-club girls, by

187

wolfing existentialist or other guaranteed anti-bourgeois philos-ophers.[14] No generation of white jazz players since the start (with the possible exception of the poor New Orleans whites who simply played the New Orleans way and thought no more about it) has been without such a contingent of rebels. And none has been without its quota of self-lacerating and doomed roman-tic artists, drinking themselves quietly into an early death, sur-vived only by their records. Bix Beiderbecke, the greatest of white jazzmen, was such a one in the 1920s, and has even stim-ulated his novel, Dorothy Baker's *Young Man with a Horn*. Bunny Berigan, another trumpeter, paralleled him in the thirties. One lasted twenty-nine years, the other thirty-three.

The classical white jazzman, a pocket Hemingway or Scott Fitzgerald, equally suspended between the whisky bottle, the wisecrack, and the jam session, was a refugee from the bourgeois world. However, there was also the non-classical white jazzman, whose situation was much more like that of the black musician. He was an entertainer or popular music player by trade, and not primarily a crusader or a deliberate castaway. This was certainly the position of most of the original white New Orleans players, the majority of whom came from social strata like the Sicilian immigrants, whose social position in the hierarchy of the old South was not a great deal higher than the blacks': at any rate they were also sometimes lynched.* 'Wingy' Manone, for in-stance, a slum child from New Orleans, and near neighbour of the young Armstrong, played music like Armstrong, worked the habitual circuits of the small-time Delta musician—Louisi-ana, Texas, the middle-Mississippi valley, later Chicago, New York, and the West Coast—and earned his living as a 'comedy personality' as much as by his trumpet.

---

* Among the Italians in early white New Orleans (or 'Dixieland') jazz we note La Rocca and Sbarbaro, Manone, Bonano, Rappolo, and the Loyacanos, who probably have the historic distinction (to which I draw attention for the benefit of the cultural authorities of the Albanian People's Republic) of being the first jazz players in history to come of Albanian stock. Their ancestors fled from the Turks to Sicily, and their home-town still speaks and considers itself Albanian.

Southern or Northern, the genuine professional musician type seems to have lacked something of the hunted purism of the refugee jazzman. George Brunies, for instance, an excellent New Orleans trombonist, seems to have been quite happy in his berth with the terrible band of Ted Lewis from 1923 to 1935, and did not feel his jazz status was jeopardized by lying down on his back with another musician on his stomach, while he operated a trombone slide with his feet. Ray Bauduc (drums), another white New Orleans player of professional stock, seems to have been content to earn his living solidly in three main jobs from 1926 to 1942, with little of that frantic freelance gigging and vagabondage through ephemeral combinations which was so characteristic of the classic purist. However, as we have seen (Chapter 8) the economy of the jazz business is such that a great deal of casual work is inevitable, whatever the tastes or compulsions of musicians, and post-New Orleans white pros, especially those who got their start in the wild 1920s, when jobs were never short, have often had a varied and casual career.

In Europe, where no musician could earn even pocket money, let alone a living, by playing jazz until the rise of a specific jazz public in the 1930s and 40s, the ordinary professional dance-band or variety musician formed an even more important component of jazz. Socially, in Britain at least, he came from either musical or show-business families, or more usually from a working-class background, with the usual admixture of bohemian ex-clerks or students. The working-class background was inevitably strong, since the most obvious school in which the musician learned his trade was one which, both as a professional military and as an amateur civilian institution, has long been part of the British working class, especially the skilled part: the brass band.[15] That is why we frequently find such dance-band musicians as did not turn professional immediately in characteristic proletarian professions like printing, factory work, engineering, as toolmakers' apprentices, in cotton mills, as professional footballers, and the like, and why we find many even among those who started as clerks—mostly, one would guess, the sons of working-class fathers—beginning their careers in brass bands.[16]

These men were not necessarily jazz players, though they were the most likely to come into contact with jazz, through touring players and singers, through the jazz influence in the pop music they had to play, or because the work of dance musicians is so boring that they were quite likely to seize upon jazz as a creative relief from routine. The few early players who came straight to 'rigorous' jazz had naturally to fit into this milieu, since it was the only one in which they could make a living by playing their music at least sometimes. The dance-band profession was thus the earliest nursery of European jazz, and patronized it even while it remained 'commercial'. Thus Jack Hylton's Band, which has had a poor press among the aficionados, because its claim to play 'jazz' in the 1920s and early 30s rightly irritates the purists, not only provided a refuge for several jazz-men of stature, but actually did its best to encourage them whenever possible (e.g. by hiring Philippe Brun the trumpeter, André Ekyan the saxophonist, two uncompromising French performers, and the great Coleman Hawkins). Henry Hall, of the B.B.C. band, hired Benny Carter, the American star, to arrange for him. The dance-band profession, in fact, made possible what jazz there was in Britain—at least until the middle thirties—and provided its first fifth column within commercial music.

Since the end of the thirties, the rise of the specialized jazz public has produced a new kind of white musician: the amateur jazz enthusiast, who has, in the nature of things, often turned into the professional player. Since this type of player shares his origins and approach to jazz with the non-playing aficionado, he can be conveniently discussed in the chapter on the jazz public.

Whatever the character of the white jazz players, one thing has always—until recently at least—separated them from the black ones: their freedom of movement. The blacks could not leave. Playing music (for self-educated players, playing *their* kind of music) or some other form of entertainment were their only ways of earning a living unless they wanted to be unskilled labourers, and their only way of making a way in the world. For most of jazz history the black men, who found jazz jobs

190

hard to get, had not the choice of joining a radio station's staff band or a classical orchestra, or working as a staff composer or arranger in films or on the air, or simply settling down to sell insurance or to journalism or business, like those middle-aged Chicagoan former jazz players who still meet annually, as 'Sons of Bix', to commemorate the idol of their youth. The colour bar stopped them. Most of them could not even retire into ordinary, prosperous pop bands—to bands like Whiteman's, Roger Wolfe Kahn's, or Ted Lewis's—for the black equivalents to the big white pop enterprises were fewer, much less prosperous, and very much less stable. The black musician was therefore obliged to stick to his music, which was his only prop. Perhaps this helps to account for his superiority in execution and in ideas over the white. For white musicians *had* ideas. The group of white New York players who recorded in the later twenties, with or without the addition of brilliant Mid-Westerners like Bix Beiderbecke, shows signs of anticipating many of the musical ideas of 'modern jazz' fifteen years before the blacks, but it did not develop them. For what happened? 'Miff' Mole, the trombonist, went into commercial bands and radio, where he played mainly classical music for a decade. Eddie Lang, the guitarist, went to Hollywood to make a film about Paul Whiteman and then became Bing Crosby's accompanist. Frank Trumbauer, the saxophonist, stayed with Whiteman from 1927 to 1936 and eventually left music altogether for the Civil Aeronautics Administration. And so on. They were good jazzmen, but they did not have the hard compulsion to express themselves and to win their place in the world through developing their jazz, and only through it, which drove the Charlie Parkers, the Gillespies, and the Thelonious Monks. Only those who were congenitally and implacably 'anti-commercial' had this compulsion. But was it, in their case, always a compulsion to make music, or merely one to break away, to recapture their youthful paradise on Lake Michigan, to live the bohemian life of the anti-bourgeois? Perhaps both. But many of those whose compulsion was most clearly that of the dedicated creative musician have died, like Bix, or Berigan, or Lang, or Teschemacher.

Such are the forces which have made jazz musicians what they are. For they do not start as men of a special type. There are certain kinds of human activity, such as a facility for lightning calculation, which are very unevenly distributed by nature: to all intents and purposes either you have them or you have not. But the gift of expressing oneself through music is not among these. As Johnny St Cyr said: 'You see, the average working man is very musical.' Naturally the gap between the best jazz musicians and the worst is immense, and there are very few of the best; but until it was turned into a self-conscious art-music which requires preliminary expertise, jazz was better suited than any other twentieth-century art to give artistic expression to the or-dinary man, and especially (in the blues) the ordinary woman. Everyone has something to say, as the makers of films with non-professional actors discovered. Jazz, which grew up by completely adapting its technique to what ordinary people had to say, even to the point of allowing musical illiterates and those with a rather poor technique to make valid artistic creations, required less preliminary selection among its musicians than any other art. Perhaps it tended to attract those who were inarticulate in any other medium (including words) more than the others, for a man who can say what he wants in prose cannot get the extraordinary sense of happiness and release which comes from becoming eloquent with a trumpet or in a song. Louis Arm-strong without his trumpet is a rather limited man; with it he speaks with the precision and compassion of the recording angel.

The jazz musician was therefore, and still is to a large extent, nearer to the ordinary randomly chosen citizen than most other artists, and jazz has been able to draw upon a wider reservoir of potential artists than any other art in our century; in extreme cases, such as New Orleans, on virtually the whole of the pop-ulation. Only his way of life has tended to set him apart, and has in turn tended to attract certain types of recruits—whether those with a special vocation for music, or with a special taste for the milieu, or those who happened to find the trade particularly convenient. The frontiers of jazz have been open towards the world of the non-musician. This has been one of the causes of its strength and vigour. If it becomes increasingly like the other orthodox arts it is likely that these frontiers will be closed, their passage being allowed only to selected entrants. If this happens, the character of jazz will change fundamentally, though one would not like to guess in what way.

t e n

The Public

*E*very jazz-lover has two or three clear, old-fashioned, rose-tinted pictures in the family album of his hobby. One is of the classic New Orleans street parade: the musicians on their cart, cornet blazing, trombone sitting on the tailgate so that the slide moves freely, 'going to town' as the Basin Street whores leave their cribs to listen, the kitchen mechanics come to the doors tapping and shaking, and the conjure women stop selling their spells. Another is of the dance hall somewhere across the tracks: black faces on snappily dressed bodies, and the throb of the horns over the drum. A third is the 'rent party' in the slums of the Chicago South Side or Harlem: pigs' feet, beer, whisky, and the hypnotic rhythm of the piano:

> *Give the piano player a drink because he's bringing me down.*
> *He's got rhythm: when he stomps his feet*
> *He sends me right off to sleep.*

A fourth is certainly of the honky-tonk: a big man at the upright piano with a derby hat, men with drinks, girls and their pimps

—themselves, as like as not piano players or pool-room sharks, or both—and the cry: 'Play that thing, mister, oh, play that thing.' When the words 'the jazz public' are mentioned, it is images like these which come most naturally into the minds of the aficionados. Mistakenly so. For though it is true that the first and original public for jazz was of this kind, it is also, from our point of view, the least interesting. For jazz is peculiar in having acquired a 'secondary' public far vaster than its primary one. It is rather like the city of Venice, in which the foreign visitors in any year now greatly outnumber the native Venetians. Naturally the relationship of the natives to their city is interesting; but it is much less odd, and for that reason much less puzzling, than the relationship of the outsiders who do not belong there but have taken it to their hearts.

The vast majority of those who have enjoyed jazz since 1914–18, when it became a national American, and subsequently an international, phenomenon, were and are outsiders in one way or another. This applies less to American blacks and a section of Southern whites than to the rest of us, for, as we have seen, poor and uneducated blacks used a primitive or preparatory form of the jazz idiom in their normal folk-music, secular or religious. Hardshell believers from the Carolinas, used to praising the Lord in their way, would find nothing strange in jazz:

> 'When James P. [Johnson] and Fats [Waller] and I would get a romp down shout going', says the famous Harlem pianist Willie 'The Lion' Smith, 'that was playing rocky just like the Baptist people sing. You don't play a chord to that—you got to move it, and the piano players do the same thing in the churches, and there's ragtime in the preaching. Want to see a ring shout? Go out to the Convent Avenue Baptist Church any Sunday.'[1]

It was not jazz, but anyone who spoke this musical idiom would have as little trouble learning jazz as an East Anglian has in learning standard English. In a sense all first-generation urban blacks in the U.S.A. can be regarded as part of the 'primary' public of jazz. For ideological reasons some of them—notably the very religious or respectable—might not like it, but it was their music nevertheless. The black public for jazz therefore presents us with a rather different problem from the white public, at least until it comes to contain a large percentage of second-generation urbanized blacks, or of blacks with social and cultural aspirations which make it look down on the old-fashioned idiom in which it has been brought up, or on the simple jazz which emerged directly out of this idiom.

Not so the whites. In the cities of the North and, *a fortiori,* in those of Europe, jazz was a new language. It is pretty certain that it made its way first and foremost through the ballroom. Until the eve of the Second World War the pioneers of jazz among the secondary public had invariably been the dancers, and, as we have seen, the early history of jazz expansion can virtually be written in terms of the active and rhythmical dances to which it provided a uniquely suitable accompaniment. The cake-walk prepared the way for ragtime; the one-steps, two-steps, and foxtrots for jazz. When Benny Goodman, the 'King of Swing', tried to explain why his style of jazz became so popular, he naturally observed: 'It was a dancing audience—that's why they went for it'.[2] The true-blue jazz-lover, who looks down with contempt on commercial pop music, and would not dream of actually dancing to his favourite music unless his girl insisted on it—and then only as a concession to cultural backwardness—is a late phenomenon. As a type he has emerged out of the mass of swaying couples who did not look for creative art in the places where jazz was played, and whose main reason for liking jazz was that it was good to dance to. If we ask a middle-aged jazz-lover how he came to like the music, we shall very likely get the answer this writer got from a Newcastle schoolmaster in his forties, who has been an amateur since about 1930:

> You see, when I was young, I used to go out dancing a lot, and it got me interested in the music. Of all the dance music I heard, jazz seemed the liveliest, and the one with most to it. Then I started to buy records.

For similar reasons the dance musicians themselves were drawn to 'pure' jazz, even in countries such as Britain, where their native idiom was quite different, and where indeed a peculiarly formal and extremely popular dance style evolved in the 'palais' which sprung up between the wars. 'Strict tempo' dancing, the foundation of the mass ballroom vogue among the British working class, with its contests and championships, grew in a direction diametrically opposed to jazz. Yet when, in 1932, a knowledgeable British journalist wrote about the jazz public, he estimated—no doubt with some exaggeration—that ninety-five per cent of it consisted of dance-band musicians.

For jazz was not merely good to dance to. Of the mass of commercial pop and dance music, whether or not it was coloured by the jazz idiom, 'pure' jazz was the most interesting to play or to listen to, the one least likely to pall. A middle-aged jazz critic has recalled his school-days in 1926–7, when he first aquired a taste for it:

> The father of one of the boys was a director of H.M.V., so we got all the new records as they came out. We played them over and over again, naturally. After a few months I found that I got bored with most of them, but the "hot" records stood up. That is how I first suspected there was something to jazz.

The 'jazz fan' emerged from the run of the popular music mill, because 'hot' jazz itself emerged from the competition with ordinary semi-jazz dance music as something worth special attention.

The jazz-lover in the strict sense of the word thus emerged from the mass of the ordinary public for dance and pop music by a sort of natural selection; but he is no more like that public than men are like the apes from which they have evolved, a comparison which, though unfair, springs readily to the mind. As a type he has always and everywhere had clearly recognizable characteristics, the first of which is his stubborn refusal to be confused with the 'pop' fan. He is passionately 'anti-commercial', to the point where the mere fact that an artist attracts the larger box-office is often regarded as *prima facie* evidence of musical treason, or even where the musician who dresses properly for his stage appearance may get black looks from the more incorruptible fans. The fan is not normally happy except among initiates. To quote a characteristic passage from two of them:

> The collector, despite the revival [of interest in jazz—EJH] can *still take some solace* from the fact that if you seriously ask the head clerk of any large record store, he will tell you that John Q. Public might be getting a little more hep, but there has been no sweeping change for the better—the huge majority still come out starry-eyed for the latest Dinah Shore. The collector's clubhouse at the private country club is a lot more crowded than before *but it still has a homely atmosphere* [my emphasis—EJH].[3]

Perhaps for this reason the fan, even within jazz, has limited tastes. Middle age, history, and vested interest have by now created a certain number of catholic or eclectic jazz-lovers, but this does not come naturally. For the characteristic fan, jazz, like the ideal blood of an aristocratic family, is a sharply defined stream in constant danger of pollution from the muddy floods which surround it. 'What is jazz?' is the single question which crops up most frequently in the discussions of the aficionados. It is neither pop music nor 'straight' music. Normally it is not even everything which falls between these two territories, assuming the jazz fan to have defined their vague boundaries to his satisfaction. There is also a particular type of the 'true' jazz which must be defended against its impure, or deviationist, or obsolete competitors. In the 1920s and early 1930s 'white' jazz fought 'black' jazz; in the middle and late thirties 'big-band jazz' also fought 'small-combo jazz'. Since the Second World War this civil war has become institutionalized in the battle between the traditionalists and the modernists, each camp also containing sub-camps whose members have the firm conviction that most of their colleagues have sold the pass. The rights and wrongs of these

198

discussions need not concern us here: they are not all stupid. It is their Calvinist spirit that counts, whether expressed in the sophisticated accents of the critics or the simple cries of 'Treason' by teenagers whose favourite jazz bands decide to play in a different style.

Jazz, for the fan, is therefore not simply a music to be enjoyed as one enjoys apples, or drinks, or girls, but one to be studied and absorbed in a spirit of dedication. Jazz fans do not listen to their music to dance, and often avoid dancing, unless pressed into it by their girl friends, whose approach to the music is normally more utilitarian. They stand or sit by the bandstand, soaking in the music, nodding and smiling at one another in a conspiracy of appreciation, and tapping their feet unless the expression of any overt emotion is conventionally frowned on. (In the peak days of the feud between ancients and moderns, a reliable way of telling one from the other in Anglo-Saxon countries was by the fact that the ancients favoured a more Bacchic style of appreciation, while the moderns, imitating the *avant-garde* musicians, kept a dead face; however, among traditionalists the aficionados of the blues have always tended towards a rather church-like gravity. In Latin countries, and notably in France, the contrast was less, owing to the traditional enthusiasm of all local art-lovers for demonstrating their cultural allegiance by breaking up the concerts of rival art-lovers.) Jazz, for the true fan, is not merely to be listened to, but to be analysed, studied, and discussed. The quintessential location of the fan is not the dance hall, the night club, or even the jazz concert or club, but the private room in which a group of young men play one another records, repeating crucial passages until they are worn out, and then endlessly discussing their comparative merits. For every jazz fan is a collector of records, within his financial means. Flourishing communities of fans have come into being in countries such as Britain, at times when virtually no live jazz of interest was to be heard at all, almost purely on the basis of records, and there are many fans (such as this writer) who at an earlier stage of their career listened to no live jazz at all for something like ten years on end.

Moreover, the fan is not exclusively interested in jazz as music. For him jazz is a world, and often a cause of which the actual sound emerging from the instruments is only one aspect. The lives of the musicians, the environment in which jazz evolved, the political and philosophical implications of the music, the scholarly or sporting details of discography, are equally part of it. It is not merely due to the lack of musical literacy among jazz fans that technical discussions of jazz in musical terms have been so rare, nor to the strong Marxist influence of the 1930s that so much of jazz criticism and jazz appreciation consists, in effect, of writing or studying the social history of jazz 'up the river from New Orleans', or even more fundamentally 'across the water from West Africa'. This mixture of aesthetic, social, philosophical, and historical interests is part of the make-up of the jazz fan. Only since the Second World War has something like 'pure' musical or aesthetic appreciation or criticism of jazz emerged as a serious force, and then only among one school of jazz-lovers. Biographical and historical material, studies of individual bands, discographies, discussions about the nature of jazz, impressions of the jazz scene, re-creations of the social atmosphere of jazz, and record reviews have always provided the bulk of the content of the specialist jazz magazine, in the pages of which a line of music-print is as rare as Hebrew or Chinese characters in the ordinary book.*

The jazz fan is therefore rarely a musician himself. (Periodicals addressed to the amateur and professional musician are recognizable by the spate of articles of the type 'How to get the best out of your trumpet', 'How to improvise a chorus', and the like; these do not often occur in the specialist magazines.) It is true that enthusiasm for jazz has always been rife among amateur and professional dance musicians, that is, among a fairly large public, for the American Federation of Musicians, aided by an insurance expert, estimated that in 1953–4 there were 19,114 jazz pianists busy every night in the U.S.A., not counting amateurs. (In case this figure should mislead, it may be mentioned that the number

---

* In America this is ceasing to be the case.

200

of 'classical' or academic pianists of 'superior ability' at this time was estimated as 114,684.) [4] It is also true that an enthusiasm for jazz has always tempted a good many fans to try their hand at playing: the 'revivalist' movement in jazz was primarily a movement of amateurs, even if many of them have since become professionals. Lastly, it may be true that in the early stages of the jazz movement, the proportion of fans who were also players, or who became players, was high: much higher than that of lovers of painting who paint, lovers of classical music who play, though perhaps not higher than that of lovers of poetry who also write verse, which is a rather unskilled occupation. We do not really know, for there are no figures, but it is not at all unlikely. However, it seems quite clear, both from experience and from the contents of the specialist literature, that the practising or aspiring musician rapidly became a small minority of the jazz public, which consisted, and consists, overwhelmingly of 'appreciators'. *

Broadly speaking, this description is true of the jazz public anywhere and at any time: I have no doubt that it applies to the hot and cool communities of Tokyo, Rejkjavik, and Buenos Aires as much as to those of Los Angeles and London. But who composes these communities?

Statistics are difficult to come by. Among the few we have are those of a sample collected by a gramophone company in the Paris region in 1948 (at the height of the local jazz boom). [5] According to this inquiry twelve per cent of the record-buying public were in the market for jazz (thirty per cent of those under the age of thirty), sixty-nine per cent of the jazz-record buyers

* If the readership of *Downbeat* is typical of U.S. jazz fans, this is not true in America. According to the magazine's readership survey (15 September 1960), sixty-five per cent of its readers own and play two instruments each, while seventy-three per cent describe themselves as amateur musicians; an admirable state of affairs. Incidentally, the unmarried among these young men spent $172 a year on records, eighty per cent of them jazz, eleven per cent classical, and only nine per cent pops. However, *Downbeat* has always been a musicians' as well as a fans' journal. Even today musicians form the third largest group of its readers (after office-workers and students).

were young—under thirty—and their social composition was as follows:

	Per cent
Middle class	34
White-collar	22
Tradesmen, shopkeepers	7
Students	4
Working class	26
'Collectors'	4
Musicians	2
Foreigners	1

In brief, jazz in France was (and, to judge by subsequent inquiries such as those of the review *Arts,* is) a minority addiction, the addicts being in majority young—though with a surprisingly high proportion of older people—and overwhelmingly members of the lower-middle and middle classes.

On the whole this impression is probably universally true, though with considerable national variations. There is no doubt at all that jazz is, and has always been, a minority taste, even allowing for those who appreciate hybrid and jazz-influenced music which the purists refuse to admit. This is true not only of France, where jazz-record buyers lagged far behind those of classical and operatic music (twenty-three per cent) and even farther behind such native European forms of light entertainment as *chansons,* variety, accordion and *bal musette* music, and operetta (a total of fifty per cent), and only just equalled 'dance music' (twelve per cent). It is equally true in Britain where (before the jazz boom of the last five years) the best-known British 'revivalist' jazz band could reckon with an average sale of only 5,000 copies of each of its 78-rpm records, and the company which released the works of Jelly-Roll Morton was surprised and gratified to find that this acknowledged and advertised hero of old New Orleans sold 3,000 to 4,000 copies per (78-rpm) disc. Jazz has until recently simply not been big business in Britain, in the terms in which those who prepare records for the 'hit parade' of the 'top ten' or 'top twenty' think of it; or even normally in the terms in which a regular steady seller in the popular music market—say Mr Victor Silvester, Mr Stanley Black, or Mr Jimmy Shand of the Scottish music, think of it. This is why it has so largely been left to marginal or amateur enterprise, and even today, when it has become profitable, it can at best be described as small to medium business. We may estimate the size of the 'strict' jazz public as somewhere between the 25,000 or so who buy *Jazz news* (specialist jazz books sell 8,000 or so) and the 115,000 who buy the traditional weekly of the jazz-lover, the *Melody Maker.*[6] True, these are the hard core of the strict jazz public, and they are surrounded by a penumbra of people who, though neither regular readers nor record buyers, probably go to the occasional concert or buy the occasional record. But even if we assume that all those who visit the concerts of a famous American band, say Count Basie's, are jazz-lovers, and that such a band plays to capacity throughout its tour, the national jazz public at present hardly amounts to more than 100,000 or so: say 20,000 in London, 60,000 in the rest of the big cities covered, and the balance in the neglected towns.[7] Such figures are not negligible, but they are those of a minority public. this does not mean that such a minority may not become a majority, though this is unlikely, for the young people, among whom the great bulk of the jazz addicts are to be found, are themselves always a minority, except in rather exceptional demographic situations. Britain is a fairly extreme example, for the jazz public here is proportionately much larger than in most other countries, with the exception of the Scandinavian ones and perhaps the Dutch; proportionately larger than in France, and certainly than in the U.S.A.

Admittedly, both in Britain and in the U.S.A. jazz-tinged idioms of popular music are very much more popular than in France, Germany, or Italy, where the native forms of light music have—at least until the rise of rock-and-roll—been much more resistant, because quite differently based. It may even happen that strict jazz artists or records become temporary best-sellers in the Anglo-Saxon world for this reason (i.e. that in America they sell upwards to 250,000, in Britain upwards of 100,000 copies, as things stood in 1958). However, though jazz-influenced pop music must belong to the world of jazz as the historian sees it, it is not jazz as either the musician, the sociologist, or the business-man sees it. It has the same relation to jazz as Palm Court string groups have to classical music: at best the low-brow version of the high-brow article, at worst a mere background noise. As the children in a California high school, devotees of pop music in its most heavily rhythmical versions, put it: 'Jazz is a sophisticated kind of entertainment, isn't it?'

The second equally undeniable fact is that the jazz public is overwhelmingly young—and masculine. Among whites, jazz is essentially a music appealing to boys and young men between the ages of, say, fifteen and twenty-five.* (The post-war com-mercial offensive against school children may have lowered this age-level a little, but probably not much. Instrumental jazz is not children's but young adults' music, and the children influenced by it are more likely to take to simple vocal music of the rhythm-and-blues or country-and-Western type.) This observation re-quires no statistics. In jazz clubs and at jazz concerts young men invariably preponderate, because very few girls go there except with boy friends, while very many boys also go there alone or with other boys. The actual community of addicts is almost totally masculine. Though there are enthusiastic and knowledge-able aficionadas among women—normally on the fringes of the intellectual or artistic occupations, or of night life—closer re-search will almost always show that they have acquired the taste through an earlier boy friend among musicians or fans. This is fairly easy, for the jazzman is both a passionate proselytizer, and a keen follower of the women. Of all the arts in mid-twentieth-century Britain, this is so far the one with the overwhelmingly strongest heterosexual tradition and ethos, in spite of the almost unlimited toleration of jazzmen for deviations and idiosyncrasies in people's private lives.†

* Ninety-two per cent of the readers of *Downbeat* in 1960 were males.

† As usual, this applies less to the *avant-garde* of 'modern' jazz, whose fringe followers—perhaps less in Britain than in some big American cities—contained

It is equally clear that a good many youthful jazz-lovers abandon their enthusiasm once they reach maturity. This may be
partly for material reasons: married men cannot afford to buy
records on the scale of single men, nor are they encouraged to
go to all-night dances, clubs, and other jazz occasions. But there
is more to it than this. The wild passion and effervescence of jazz
fits in with adolescence. Young people find it easier than mature
ones to overlook the formal and emotional limitations of jazz, or
even its frequent mediocrity, for they pour into it their own
emotion, vitality, and dedication to make up for the shortcom-
ings of the music. To the eye of passion, coloured glass can look
like diamonds, and much of jazz (though not the best of it) is no
more than musical glass cut in so suitable a form as to reflect the
light of its public with the utmost brilliance. At all events, the
curve of jazz enthusiasm in men's lives takes a sharp turn down-
wards from about the middle twenties on. Older men either
drop their interest in jazz entirely—the records are played increasingly rarely, and perhaps eventually sold—or settle down
into a less passionate pattern of appreciation; unless they become
professionally concerned with jazz in some way or another.

The older fan exists, for even on the most pessimistic assump-
tions each generation of addicts formed since the late 1920s is
bound to have left some residue of permanent jazz-lovers. Often,
indeed, a flare of jazz enthusiasm among the young may awaken
the dormant enthusiasm of the middle-aged: jazz is not old
enough to have really ancient addicts. Normally, the older jazz-
lover has a less exclusive and demanding allegiance to his music:
he can take it or leave it alone. An occasional concert or club—
provided the audiences are not so overwhelmingly adolescent as
to make him feel alone—an occasional session playing and dis-

---

a number of declassed types who affected at least sexual ambivalence. See
Norman Mailer and the San Francisco 'beat' generation on the hipster. A very
few homosexual musicians are known even among the pioneer jazzmen—for
instance, Tony Jackson, the brothel pianist of New Orleans who inspired Jelly-
Roll Morton—and it is easy to see why the social milieu of night-club jazz
would attract them. This only makes the overwhelmingly heterosexual atmosphere of the art more striking. By tradition the jazz musician (and by imitation, the jazz fan) goes for women just like the traditional Italian operatic tenor.

cussing old records with contemporaries ('just like old times'), arguments with his children on their unaccountably bad jazz taste, a quiet quarter of an hour with the American Forces Network jazz broadcasts late at night: these are about his limits. The stuff can still move him. At worst, the sound is pleasant and part of his life, at best he knows that for certain moods and emotions there is no more poignant equivalent than a good jazz record. Jazz, for the older amateur, is like the occasional dose of lyric poetry for the man who has long ceased to read poetry systematically, a nucleus of surviving youth. The older jazz-lover is not simply, as André Hodeir suggests, young at heart. He may quite well, like Yeats, know that he is not, but also know what youth (including his own) is about:

> Labour is blossoming or dancing where
> The body is not bruised to pleasure soul,
> Nor beauty born out of its own despair,
> Nor blear-eyed wisdom out of midnight oil.
> O chestnut tree, great rooted blossomer,
> Are you the leaf, the blossom, or the bole?
> O body swayed to music, O brightening glance,
> How can we tell the dancer from the dance?

The social composition of the jazz public presents a more complicated problem and national variations of greater significance. It may be worth looking at a few countries in greater detail.[8]

Paradoxical though it may seem, the specialized jazz public in the U.S.A. has always been relatively, and probably absolutely, smaller than in Europe, though the public exposed to some kind or other of jazz has been much larger. The sales of the British *Melody Maker* are considerably higher than those of the equivalent American weeklies. As for the demand for jazz records, *Billboard* gives the following statistics for the early 1950s.[9]

	Per cent
Popular music	49.1
Classical music	18.9
Country and Western	13.2
Rhythm and blues	5.7
Children's records	10.2
Foreign folk-music	1.1
Latin-American	1.0
Hot jazz	0.8

Virtually only the last item represents the 'pure' jazz public for while most of rhythm and blues (the ancestor of the recent rock-and-roll craze) is jazz, its normal public is among the unself-conscious black buyers, not the self-conscious jazz appreciators. The same is true of the very much less jazz-tinged, but very 'folky' country and Western music (hill-billy, cowboy music, and the like). Admittedly it is likely that 'popular music' includes a certain amount of jazz of the more saleable kind, but even so the jazz public must trail a very long way indeed behind the public for classical music. The American jazz fan is therefore a rather exceptional specimen.

In the U.S.A. the (white) jazz-lovers seem to have come first, as a group, from among the Northern middle-class youth, that class being defined as those who went to college between the wars. The South has produced proportionately very much fewer fans and collectors, no doubt for the obvious reasons. At all events American universities have played a disproportionately large part as nurseries of jazz music. The history of the white 'Chicago' musicians of the 1920s can be written in terms of college dances, and notably of student taste at Indiana University. Eastern colleges provided the staple public for the earliest 'swing' bands, notably the Casa Loma Orchestra. The students of the University of California (Los Angeles) turned Goodman's first tour into a success, and those of Berkeley and Stanford were later to provide the backbone of the early West Coast 'revival' bands.[10] Since the war it has become axiomatic in the business that blues and high-brow jazz can be made to sell best on the 'college circuit' but even in the colleges jazz still remains a minority taste, though a large one.*

There is equally little doubt that the first group in history which shows most of the characteristics of the modern aficionados, the white 'Chicago' musicians of the middle 1920s, was primarily a white-collar or middle-class group. (They differ from the modern fan chiefly in that most of them became actual players.) Bix Beiderbecke, Hoagy Carmichael, the 'Austin High School Gang' (McPartland, Teschemacher, Lanigan), Dave Tough, Floyd O'Brien, Pee-Wee Russell were from the right side of the tracks, as is indicated by the absence of Italian and Slavonic names among them. Mid-Western jazz was not confined to middle-class boys, though it is significant that the only working-class school to have produced a marked jazz tradition of its own was the highly untypical Hull House School, the Toynbee Hall of Chicago, i.e. a foundation of middle-class social workers.† At all events, the young Chicagoans had all the essential fan's stigmata: the desire to play and hear, not jazz but the only true jazz, the painstaking and dedicated copying of an entire

* The following is the chart of gramophone record preference in colleges, as reported in *Billboard*, 1960:

Category	All students per cent	Male per cent	Female per cent
Classical	36.8	30.4	51.8
Popular	34.2	27.0	51.2
Jazz	22.3	20.0	27.7
Show	6.0	2.4	14.2
Opera	3.5	3.8	2.6
Semi-classical	2.4	1.4	4.6
Folk	2.1	1.8	2.6
Mood Music	0.8	0.7	1.0

As students recorded more than one preference, the percentages may add up to more than 100. The figures for folk-music are today almost certainly rising. The tendency of the girls to express multiple preferences (their choices add up to over 150 per cent) makes their taste for jazz a little less impressive than it looks.

† This produced, among others, Benny Goodman and Ben Pollack.

style, the occasional idealization of the black (most notably in Milton Mesirow, who at least claims middle-class origin),[11] the occasional deliberate declassment, the intellectual interests and pretensions—Bix fancied Debussy and Schoenberg—and the obvious revolt against middle-class respectability:

> 'It was little Dave (Tough)', writes Mezzrow, 'who gave me the knock-down to George Jean Nathan and H. L. Mencken. . . . Dave used to read *The American Mercury* from cover to cover, especially the section called *Americana* where all the bluenoses, bigots, and two-face killjoys in this land-of-the-free got the going-over they never forgot. That *Mercury* really got to be the Austin High Gang's Bible. It looked to us like Mencken was yelling the same message in his magazine that we were trying to get across in our music; his words were practically lyrics to our hot jazz.'[12]

Systematic record collecting first seems to have begun among the 'college crowd' in the later 1920s.[13] The pillars of the early hot clubs in the middle thirties were middle-class intellectuals— the daughter of a wealthy Canadian manufacturer, a lawyer, a future English don, and the like. The most influential and active patron of jazz in the thirties was (and is) a radical offshoot of an extremely wealthy and respectable Eastern family. Similarly Howard Becker, who has described a group of modern Chicago jazz aficionados in one of the few sociological studies on the subject, correctly draws attention to their middle-class character-istics: they are sons of old, respectable, comfortable Anglo-Saxon American families who deny their birthright for the company of horn players and honky-tonk girls and the aesthetics of low life. Theirs is a political protest, for 'they reject the American way of life *in toto*', though without substituting anything for it but music, *avant-garde* existentialist philosophy, and a personal anarchism, which is perhaps why those of them who do not wreck themselves by this life and die early will probably end, like their predecessors, as respectable bourgeois, except for a few who become musicians, or revolutionaries. Jazz was, and is, for deviant American members of the middle class what surrealism and existentialism were for deviant French members of it.

These were the handful of pioneers. A larger American public of pure jazz enthusiasts only appeared among the high school youths in the middle 1930s rather later, and probably on a rather smaller scale, than the comparable public in Europe. Both the first journals appealing specifically to the jazz public *(Down Beat,* 1934) and the first Hot Clubs (Chicago 1935) were younger than their European opposite numbers. The jazz revival of the war years added another batch of recruits, so that by 1944–5 the American record collectors' community consisted mainly of two sectors: those in their later twenties, who had been converted in the middle thirties, and those just about twenty, who had been converted in 1942–4.[14] It is certainly still overwhelmingly middle class and overwhelmingly between the ages of twenty and forty, the younger group supporting mainly rhythmic pop music, the older ones never having been fully exposed to jazz or having abandoned it. A market research report (1960) on a California radio station which plays jazz exclusively makes this quite clear: 79.4 per cent of its listeners were between twenty and forty, 90 per cent had attended or were attending college, only 6.6 per cent were craftsmen, 4.5 per cent 'operatives and kindred workers'.[15] Whether this public is as overwhelmingly on the political left as the jazz fans of the New Deal vintage, among whom there were probably very few Republicans, we do not know.

Apart from the political and ideological changes among the young post-war Americans of the age-groups which produce most jazz fans, there is no great evidence that the composition of the jazz community has changed much.

However, the American jazz public has two important peculiarities. In the first place it contains a far larger and wealthier section of adults than the European. These lawyers, doctors, business executives, scientists, or newspapermen, now on the verge of middle age, have never recovered from the musical infection of their youth. While the kids maintain the jazz club or concert, it is people of this kind who maintain the 'Dixieland' clubs where elderly men also play as though the world were young, and who give to the American night-club an atmosphere so different from the European, breeding jazz-impregnated singers, jazz-impregnated and socially corrosive satirists. They also provide that most adult of jazz artists, Duke Ellington, with the public he needs; for his appeal to the adolescents is not too strong. Such men give to jazz the nearest thing to patronage it possesses. Is it accidental that some clubs most firmly associated with middle-aged mobsters systematically hire good jazz groups, not because they give better profits, but because they *like* jazz? Nor is this public negligible. Even in 1960, when the pop music market was largely determined by the teenagers, twenty to thirty per cent of the selections on American juke-boxes were 'composed of records by artists who appeal through nostalgia and familiarity to the strictly adult market' and 'most of the records of these bands—Glenn Miller, Artie Shaw, Benny Goodman, the Dorseys—are between fifteen and twenty years old.'[16]

This leads us to the second peculiarity of the American jazz public. It is this. Whereas jazz came to Europe through the regulated channels of American record imports, which were in turn controlled by the pioneer aficionados and critics, who therefore imposed their own tastes and standards on the wider public, jazz in America was live music, which altogether escaped minority intellectual control. Except for very small groups of rigid sectarians, the line between the 'pop' and the 'jazz' public in America was therefore much hazier than elsewhere, the power of commercial advertisement to interest a marginal public in whatever band or style happened to be in vogue was immeasurably greater. To judge by the periodic 'polls' which the jazz press has conducted since the middle 1930s, European taste has (until the later 1950s) fairly consistently reflected the taste of the critics, even to the point of remaining faithful throughout the years to artists whose achievement in jazz critics believe to be permanent. American taste, on the other hand—perhaps because it depends less on records and more on the temporary prominence of live musicians—has been notoriously changing and fickle: in fact, even the American 'true' jazz public has behaved far more like a pop public than has the European.

This may be illustrated by the choice of the best trumpeter. Virtually every European poll since the beginning has consistently placed Louis Armstrong first, and even after the split between the 'traditionalists' and the 'modernists', has bracketed him with the leading modern trumpeters Gillespie or Miles Davis. American polls have successively placed a variety of trumpeters of very uneven merit at the top, in some instances even failing to place Armstrong in the first ten.★

The Continental public has also been markedly middle-class and intellectual, probably more so than in America. It is also by far the oldest consistent and organized jazz public in the world. The first Norwegian jazz club seems to have been founded as long ago as 1928, and though the journal Le Jazz Hot did not appear in France until 1935, by 1933 there were magazines dealing mainly or wholly with jazz at least in Holland, Sweden, Belgium, Switzerland, France, and Germany. On the Continent jazz had the advantage of fitting smoothly into the ordinary pattern of avant-garde intellectualism, among the dadaists and surrealists, the big city romantics, the idealizers of the machine age, the expressionists, and their like. Thus in France Jean Cocteau and Max Jacob patronized Le Jazz Hot, while Marianne Oswald, the favourite diseuse of the intellectuals, singing poems about down-and-outs and prostitutes by Prévert, did so to 'serious' jazz accompaniments. After the war the theoreticians of modern jazz published their discussions about it in Sartre's Les Temps modernes. This self-confidence, and the Latin proclivity for writing manifestoes, probably explains why France became the intellectual headquarters of jazz criticism before the middle thirties, dominating the taste of jazz-lovers through the periodically revised writings of M. Hugues Panassié and the activities of

---

★ Seven European polls between 1937 and 1957, taken in four countries, name Armstrong seven times, Gillespie twice, Miles Davis once. In the same period the American Metronome poll chose at least six other trumpeters, not including Armstrong (Berigan, James, Eldridge, Gillespie, Davis, Chet Baker).

collectors through the *Hot Discography* of M. Delaunay, as today it does the aesthetics of modern jazz criticism through M. André Hodeir. The French might know a great deal less about actual jazz than the Americans who were on the spot; they might indeed patently know too little to write full-dress books, as was the case with M. Panassié's pioneer *Le Jazz Hot* (1934), virtually all of which was abandoned by its author within five years. But the proverbial Gallic certainty and lucidity saw them through, and the rest of the world listened.

In Britain the situation was rather different, and in many ways more interesting. Here too, the growth of the jazz public passed through the usual stages. Until 1927 the 'true' jazz fans were merely a handful of scattered individuals, but in 1927–8 a recognizable jazz public emerged, strong enough to make it worth the gramophone companies' while to release a regular supply of American 'hot' records, mainly of the white New York variety. An attempt to issue a series of primarily black records failed, since even the 'hottest' aficionados found them too strong for their tastes, at least if we are to judge by the contemporary record reviews.★ Again, to judge by the record releases, this public remained steady and grew throughout the next years, apparently quite unaffected by the slump which for a time virtually destroyed recorded jazz in the United States. Indeed, as we have seen, some of what little survived in America was virtually commissioned for the European—i.e. mainly the British—market. By 1933 the British jazz public was large enough to make a large-scale London recital for 'serious' jazz fans, by a visiting American band, financially possible: Duke Ellington's London concert at the Trocadero, Elephant and Castle. Until then, and for a long time thereafter, visiting artists relied on ordinary music-hall and dance bookings, i.e. on attracting a much wider

---

★ *Melody Maker* 1927, p. 469. The records published by a small company Levaphone-Oriole included Lil's Hot Shots (Louis Armstrong), Jelly-Roll Morton piano solos, Russell's Hot Six, and others received with marked lack of enthusiasm by the contemporary critic. Still, the publication of such a selection of records in 1927 is itself significant.

public than that of the jazz aficionado: the appearance of the jazz concert, like the specific jazz club, marks the emergence of the jazz public as an independent force.

Large or small, the British jazz-lovers became increasingly self-confident during these years. Their first articulate prophet had been an energetic young Spaniard, Fred Elizalde, who formed the first 'pure' British jazz band from among Cambridge undergraduates in 1927; Oxford, as usual the home of lost causes, held back. Their second, and far more influential one, was a cosmopolitan young Irishman with a fortunate combination of musical and literary talent, who has described his early career charmingly and fully.[17] Mr. Patrick 'Spike' Hughes formed a recording band, played, composed and, most important of all, in 1930 took over the jazz-record reviewing in the *Melody Maker,* which henceforth became the bible of every British jazz-lover. At about the same time the British fans also began to develop the characteristic institution of the 'Rhythm Clubs' which multiplied rapidly after 1933. By the end of 1935 ninety-eight had been formed, of which perhaps fifty were really active. Their main centre was in and around London (which alone contained upwards of twenty), in the south, and in a few scattered large cities. They do not seem to have penetrated the north and Scotland in force until rather later, and Wales hardly at all.* The middle thirties also saw the first of those little specialist journals which are as much part of the world of jazz as of that of poetry.

The jazz public was small. I do not suppose many jazz records sold more than 1,500 copies. It was also, in spite of the impeccable social setting of prophets like Elizalde and Hughes, over-

* I have summarized these data from various issues of the *Melody Maker* in 1934 and 1935. The London areas which founded Rhythm Clubs up to the middle of 1935 were: Central London, North Middlesex, Croydon, Forest Gate, Ealing, East Ham, Barking, Richmond, Willesden, Sutton, Walthamstow, Greenwich, Uxbridge, Edgware, Muswell Hill, Lewisham, Edmonton, South Norwood, Carshalton, Hornsey, Wembley, Woodford Green. The student will observe the absence of Rhythm Clubs in Hampstead, Kensington, or Chelsea.

whelmingly drawn from the lower-middle and working classes. The established upper and middle classes—those who went to public schools and universities—were far less important in it than their opposite numbers were in America and on the Continent. The working-class contingent among British jazz-lovers came chiefly from among, or turned rapidly into, dance-band musicians. These were, as we have seen, a group of markedly proletarian origins, which always contained a core of jazz enthusiasts. Indeed, their trade journal complained in 1927 that they 'pandered to their own tastes rather than the public's in playing too much "hot" music'.[18]

Probably, however, the people to whom jazz made its strongest and most direct appeal came from that social zone in which the sons of skilled workers, probably themselves in office jobs, met the sons of white-collar workers, shopkeepers, small business men, and the like: from the 'lower-middle class'. Clerking, small business, the drawing-board, accountancy, commercial art, the lower reaches of journalism, the fringes of show business, provided the jazz-lover's professions: anyone who knows 'fans' of the 1930s, can immediately think of three or four accountants or commercial artists. They were cultural self-made men. The respectability against which they revolted was that of the semi-detached suburban three-bed, two-reception house; but they also resented, and revolted against, the world of upper-class culture, as reached through the public school and 'varsity. If H. G. Wells had been in his teens in the early 1930s, he would have attended the first Rhythm Clubs, and met others like himself, for the jazz fans came from his world. This is probably why the young post-1945 writers, who, led by Kingsley Amis and John Wain, gloried in what purported to be 'provincialism', wrote jazz among the many other rude words on their banners. They were fifteen or twenty years late in discovering it, but their instinct was right.

Theirs was, by and large, the world of the grammar school and public library rather than the public school and university; of the teashop and Chinese restaurant, rather than the sherry party; and when times were bad, as they were in the thirties, sometimes of the fish-and-chip shop. They were not against official culture. Jazz for them was not, as for many Continental intellectuals who took to it, a retreat into unintellectualism. On the contrary, it was part of achieving intellectualism the independent way (and often the hard way) by self-education. American and Continental 'hot' and 'rhythm' clubs spent much of their energy making or sponsoring live jazz. The British ones were not so interested in this—there is no British equivalent to the Quintet of the Hot Club of France or the Dutch Swing College Orchestra of the thirties—but they spent a great deal of time discussing jazz and its social background and history. The early fans' taste in the orthodox arts did not differ significantly from the official taste: if 'high-brow', they read their Eliot, Pound, and Empson and their D. H. Lawrence, though also their Oscar Wilde and Bernard Shaw and, as like as not fifteen years before the rest of the high-brows, their science fiction in pulp magazines. No doubt jazz appealed to them because it was *their* discovery and art, not that of the upper-class cultured; but it also appealed to them because, thanks to its immediate appeal, it was an ideal introduction to serious music for people with no previous qualifications and training. If they progressed to classical music, as like as not they did so via Delius, whose sensuous appeal is equally direct, and especially Debussy, whose *Aprè-midi* provided the bridge to the classics for more than one fan. It is easy for those who come from intellectual environments, and have gone through the full educational treatment, to forget that even the teenage sons of Oxford dons start on Bach and Piero della Francesca not because these have a powerful appeal to their age-group, or even make much sense, but because there is considerable tacit pressure to the effect that they are high-class things, which one ought to think well of.

The pioneer jazz fan was therefore culturally active, energetic, often with ambitions to create: perhaps one reason why commercial artists, journalists, people on the fringes of the theatrical and film business were so frequently found in his ranks. A Mr Clifford Kellerby, a bus conductor, was not at all untypical in his extra-curricular activities: he played in both jazz and military

216

bands, edited the *Leeds Transport Magazine,* drew posters, painted (we owe our information about him to a large, and, alas, not very successful symbolic painting on the past, present, and future of jazz) [19], and 'travelled on the Continent'. I have very little doubt that he also composed a fair amount of poetry in free verse. If less ambitious, he very likely still had the hobbyist's and collector's itch, which found an outlet in the compilation of elaborate and scholarly discographies, the collection of biographical material, and experiments (if he had the money) with elaborate gramophone equipment. He was almost certainly politically conscious, because the appreciation of jazz implied, at its minimum, views about racial discrimination, i.e. Fascism. In the 1930s this meant almost invariably that he was on the extreme left, being joined in this situation by the young, unemployed musicians who were pushed there by unemployment, the young Jewish ones who were pushed there by Hitler. Not that the left recognized the jazz fan as a type; but he was in it all right and gave all jazz made in the pre-Second World War mould a permanent slant to the extreme left.★

★ It is not the business of this book to compile statistical tables or social surveys, but the following notes, taken from an analysis of the contributors to a British jazz magazine in the middle forties give a pretty good impression of the atmosphere of this first generation of active fans: (1) draughtsman; (2) free-lance journalist; (3) editor of a Scottish literary journal, poet and writer; (4) 'collector'; (5) journalist; (6) artist; (7) 'has done experimental writing' (subsequently journalist, record-dealer); (8) jazz and dance band journalist, 'student of philosophy'; (9) dance band journalist; (10) agricultural expert, writer for Young Communist journal; (11) small business, 'very interested in literature'; (12) draughtsman, 'interested in literature, art, modern poetry, music'; (13) first wrote on jazz in Young Communist journal; (14) surrealist Bohemian; (15) 'student of American history, sociology, and economics, active in Rhythm Club movement', first wrote on jazz in Young Communist journal; (16) anarchist, 'interested in modern poetry, literature, surrealism, classical music, and Eastern philosophy'; (17) actor and journalist (connected with Communist activities); (18) ex-Cambridge poet; (19) physicist; (20) farmer; (21) doctor; (22) London student; (23) film technician; (24) journalist; (25) free-lance journalist, broadcaster; (26) free-lance (commercial radio scripts, material for Windmill Theatre shows, etc.); (27) surrealist, painter, writer; (28) anarchist journalist, writer (Jazz Music, *passim*).

From the middle thirties jazz began to permeate upwards into higher society, and notably into some of the public schools and the old universities. To judge by my own memories of Cambridge in the last pre-war years, its conquests were modest. An enthusiasm for jazz or the blues was a respectable eccentricity, but nevertheless neither normal nor socially particularly cherished. It affected some (but not all) of those who idealized Roosevelt's America and most of what came out of it, but not to anything like the extent to which, say, American films gripped us. It did not belong markedly to the Auden-Spender-Isherwood-*New Writing* phase of literary enthusiasm, which dominated the Spanish Civil War years. The first really jazz-struck bunch I can recall at Cambridge were those in or on the fringes of the Communist Party in the immediate pre-war years, but whose tastes took them towards the neo-romantic, quasi-surrealist kind of poetry (the 'New Apocalypse', Dylan Thomas, etc.) which was to dominate the forties: the Rousseauists, rather than the Voltaireans among us. It is among friends of this kind that I remember sitting entranced, not only by Mahler (another of their 'discoveries'), but by Basie and Rushing, Turner and Johnson, and above all by Billie Holiday's *Strange Fruit:* by the jazz of 1938–9 vintage.

This modest expansion of the jazz public reflected the vogue for 'swing' which swept the United States after 1935 as well as the political currents of the times. But swing put the older, and more quintessential, British jazz-lovers into a quandary. The jazz community exists largely, as we have seen, by its exclusiveness and its hostility to commercialism. Swing was popular and commercially successful. The ranks of the aficionados were therefore shattered by ideological civil wars between purists and impurists, a war as usual easily won by the purists. Their taste—which came to dominate the taste of the jazz public, for the pioneer fans became in their turn the writers and critics—can be roughly defined as favouring any jazz appreciated by them before 1935, or made in a pre-1930 idiom, with a marked preference for that played by black players. Mr Rex Harris's Pelican books on jazz still reflect this attitude, heightened by the later New Orleans fanaticism, with remarkable accuracy. The strength of this purism was all the more remarkable, because it was not only rationally and musically indefensible, but not shared by the leading critics and sponsors of jazz. M. Panassié, with all his increasing passion for the pure gospel of New Orleans, welcomed every new discovery of the swing era with his customary ebullience and good taste: Billie Holiday, Lionel Hampton, the Lunceford Orchestra. Mr John Hammond in America, who discovered and launched virtually every musician and band of importance in the swing era, was himself a bitter opponent of commercialization. The Purists were pure, not because they were told to be, or because they could justify themselves, but because sectarian exclusiveness was in their blood.

It was therefore natural that the extraordinary expansion of the jazz public which took place everywhere during the war, was not the direct prolongation of swing, but a reaction against it: the 'New Orleans Revival'. In Britain, and indeed everywhere else, this is difficult to analyse in purely social terms. It was an age-group, rather than a particular social stratum, which received the revelation from Jelly-Roll Morton and King Oliver: the boys who were between fifteen and twenty-two years around 1945, though some of their leaders, and all their critical mentors, belonged to the generation of the 1930s. Out of fifteen leading British 'revivalist' musicians one (the first of them all) was born in 1917, three in 1920–1, two in 1926, and nine in 1928–32—six of them in 1928–9.* All of them came from among the jazz fans, none from among the professional musicians. Their social origins were mixed: public schoolboys and university students took to 'revivalism' as readily as anyone else. However, the centre of gravity of the movement undoubtedly lay in the suburbs, especially those of London, increasingly infiltrated by the skilled working class. The 'revivalist' jazz bands formed on the

* George Webb 1917; Wally Fawkes, Pat Hawes 1920; Humphrey Lyttelton 1921; Cy Laurie, Eric Silk 1926; Ken Colyer, Mick Mulligan 1928; Alex Welsh, Sandy Brown, George Melly, Johnny Parker 1929; Chris Barber 1930; Lonnie Donegan 1931; Ottilie Patterson 1932.

outskirts and marched upon the centre of the city, like rebellious armies deposing Roman emperors. George Webb's Dixielanders raised the banner of revolt in the Red Barn at Bexleyheath, Kent, in 1944, the 'Crane River Jazz Band'—nursery of numerous New Orleans prophets—came from Cranford, Middlesex, while to this day the Jazz Club Calendar of the *Melody Maker* records the strongholds of the music in Chadwell Heath and Southall, Croydon and Wood Green, Ealing, Hanwell, Harringay, and Dagenham. Soon Leeds produced the Yorkshire Jazz Band, Manchester the 'Saints' (named after the tune which may best be described as the national anthem of the revivalists, *When the Saints Go Marching In),* Liverpool the [*sic*] 'Merseysippi Band', while from Scotland there came, as usual, a stream of musicians. Why the Scots have taken to jazz so much more readily than any other part of Britain is obscure, but the fact is not in dispute: ever since the early and middle thirties they have provided by far the largest single contingent of good jazz musicians in these islands.

To judge by the character of the London fans, the lower-middle-class youth pretty certainly remained the main pillar of the jazz public. Nevertheless the general atmosphere of revivalism in this country (as distinct from America and the Continent) was rather more 'proletarian' than that of earlier jazz fashions.* Possibly this is due to the fact that—as we have seen —the revival movement was much more of a *playing* movement than earlier fashions, and much more home-based. Its heroes were not so much the great and often defunct New Orleans black players. These were rather gods whom mortals discerned as through a glass, darkly, for their battered acoustical records of the 1920s often sounded so appalling that a great deal of faith was needed to recognize their merits. (This was even more true of some of the old men who were resuscitated for the benefit of the young white public: nobody except a historian would have listened twice to poor Bunk Johnson's recordings, which were to be an inspiration to countless youngsters.) The public for

* See Appendix 1.

revivalist jazz in Britain was soon built of admirers of Humphrey Lyttelton, Ken Colyer, and Chris Barber rather than of King Oliver and George Lewis, of those who knew Ottilie Patterson (of Newtownards, Northern Ireland) and Lonnie Donegan (of Glasgow) rather than Bessie Smith and Huddie Ledbetter, whom these singers imitated scrupulously. And the 'jazz club' of the 1940s and 50s was not, like the Rhythm Club of the thirties, a place of self-education, where records were heard and dissected, but essentially a place where live jazz by British musicians was encouraged and admired. The revivalist public was therefore less 'learned' than its predecessors, and less 'intellectual'.

At all events, the social tone of the movement was set by the amateur and semi-professional musician, and the ordinary inexpert fan, generally of schoolboy or student age. This kind of simple, non-intellectual music had its appeal to the intellectuals, not to mention young aristocrats from the gossip-column zone. It captured the art students, the young actors, the young writers, especially those who also discerned in it the latent but undefined revolt which they themselves felt. It is no accident that revivalist jazz provides the incidental music to John Osborne's *Look Back in Anger,* whose hero, it will be remembered, occasionally goes off-stage to practise the trumpet and once had ambitions to become a jazz trumpeter. However, for quite different reasons, it also increasingly and obviously captured the provincial working-class youth. In Glasgow, in Belfast, in Newcastle, the Mississippi, musically speaking, was in full flood, and those who swam in it were primarily working-class youngsters.★

Revivalism remained a minority phenomenon, though by the middle fifties there were probably few grammar schoolboys, attenders of youth clubs, and other youth organizations who had not become familiar with it. Oddly enough, in spite of the general change in the political climate, it retained strong links with the Communist left, partly no doubt for historical reasons. Few

★ Intelligent impresarios in the provinces soon learned to time their early performances so as to give the fans a chance to come off shift or after the day's work.

of the leading revivalist bands were without some Communists, and several were led by young men who came out of, or from the neighbourhood of, the small Communist youth movement, while the International Youth Festivals of 1947–57 were also international rallies and propaganda platforms for revivalist jazz. However, an equally, if not more strongly, leftist offshoot of the revival gave birth to a virtually universal musical vogue among young Britons: 'skiffle' (1956–8). This may best be regarded as a modification of revivalist jazz to suit an even more completely unqualified and lay public. The movement was quite spontaneous. Left-wingers had long pioneered 'ballads and blues' sessions on both sides of the Atlantic, and produced a modest cabaret political and *avant-garde* vogue for artists like Josh White, Leadbelly, Burl Ives, Woodie Guthrie, Pete Seeger—or in Britain, Ewan McColl and Isla Cameron. Revivalist bands in Britain had taken to allowing a guitarist-singer with rhythm accompaniment to sing such blues and songs (mainly from the Leadbelly repertoire) between band sets: the arrangement was called 'skiffle', a term dug up from the obscurer recesses of American jazz history, and virtually without meaning for anyone in the U.S.A. A taste for the blues had long been part of a sound revivalist approach, though commercially a hopeless proposition. Of all jazz fans, the blues-lover has been the most consistently esoteric. To this day the admirer of Sonny Boy Williamson or Bessie Jackson, Roosevelt Sykes 'The Honeydripper', or Lightning Hopkins, must rely on imported and second-hand American records, for it has not been commercially worthwhile to release a representative selection of blues records in Britain.★

How and why this sort of material, hitherto confined to folksong collections and the 'rhythm and blues' catalogues of American record companies, conquered the public, is obscure, but by the middle of the 1950s it had done so both in America and in Britain (under the respective names of 'rock-and-roll' and 'skiffle'). Nobody created or anticipated the fashion: Mr Lonnie Donegan in Britain, whose *Rock Island Line*—originally a black

★ By 1960 this situation had improved somewhat.

prison-camp song—exploded into the big time in the spring of 1956, had made the record as part of his routine duties with a leading revivalist band. His version of the song had been available for almost two years. Indeed, Leadbelly's original record had been available for the better part of a decade. The rise of the rock-and-roll stars in America was similarly unpremeditated, though premeditation by astute business men like Colonel 'Tennessee' Tom Parker and Mr Hank Saperstein (who took in hand the fortunes of Mr Elvis Presley) soon came. However, if the general trend of taste was similar on both sides of the Atlantic, the British version showed two important peculiarities. Firstly, it was much more patently an outgrowth of the revivalist jazz movement. Second, it became as much a movement for amateur music-making as for listening; indeed, the largest movement of its kind within living memory. Within a few months the country was covered with a network of skiffle groups, consisting of guitars and rhythm instruments improvised out of washboards, thimbles, tea-chests, and the like, and accompanying youngsters who shouted the songs of Tennessee prostitutes, Mississippi convicts, and Alabama gamblers in what would have been a hybrid accent if the listener could have recognized it. Skiffle was unquestionably the most universally popular music of our generation. It broke through all barriers except those of age. Between the ages of eight and eighteen there can have been few inhabitants of Britain, whatever their class, education, or intelligence—down to the half-wits—who did not, for however short a period, take some active pleasure in it. The mind of the student reels as he attempts vainly to chart the frontiers of the appeal made by simple, shouting, thumping music of this type; for a Welsh farmer, who substituted rock-and-roll records for the classical ones with which he had always soothed his Friesians, discovered that their milk-yield went up by five gallons a day.[20]

Revivalist jazz, as we see, progressed steadily, and with increasing speed, from minority to majority status. By the later fifties it had virtually ceased to be minority music: skiffle was triumphant. But even after it had exhausted its short vogue, the old-fashioned instrumental jazz of New Orleans remained stronger than ever. It had, indeed, insensibly turned into standard popular dance music for youngsters between fifteen and twenty-five, who, if asked, would have guessed that King Oliver was the monarch of Denmark. This tendency was not confined to Britain.[21] Inevitably, therefore, the true aficionados searched for more esoteric positions to occupy. Some fled farther back into the recesses of black folk-music, until smoked out of them by the cloud of rock-and-roll shouters. Others fled forward, into the unexplored territories of 'modern' or 'cool' jazz.

Modern jazz had been on the American and European scene since the middle forties. Its sectarian appeal would no doubt have made itself felt earlier but for two facts: it was much harder to listen to than the older kind, and the bulk of the established critics and jazz intellectuals, formed in the school of the thirties, were bitterly hostile to it, for political and social reasons. What they cherished in jazz was a 'people's music'—that is, a music which both appealed to ordinary people and, in its nature, provided an alternative pattern of the arts to that of the esoteric minority culture of our age. Modern jazz seemed to them to sell the pass: a jazz version of esoteric *avant-garde* music might have its own merits, but they were not the ones they had come to jazz for. Often they were also, and understandably, repelled by the demoralized and asocial atmosphere which frequently surrounded the modernist revolutionaries—the drug taking and peddling, the hipsterdom, and the general atmosphere of a cut-price 1919 Montparnasse. Nor did the fact that commercially-minded men with an eye to the cash value of novelty took up 'bop' as a slogan for 'up-to-date' jazz, encourage them, even though the advertising types failed. In spite of a good deal of American drumbeating in the later forties, 'bop,' 'cool' or 'modern' jazz proved incapable of being turned into a widely saleable music. A 'king of swing' could be built in the 1930s, but not even Mr Woody Herman, who favoured the modern idiom and modern musicians in the later forties, could get himself recognized as 'king of bop'.

Modern jazz won itself a public of sorts, drawn partly from among professional musicians (always ready to appreciate a technically interesting music), partly from among the various national equivalents of the hipsters and St-Germain–type layabouts, partly from among that stratum of young intellectuals, who, as in France, are given to accepting anything in the arts which can plausibly claim to be revolutionary. But it seems pretty clear, in Europe at least, that its major expansion occurred only in the middle and later fifties, when revivalist and traditional jazz had become too widely accepted for comfort. I do not suppose the process was always deliberate. Among musicians in Britain it often took the form of a vague malaise, a boredom with the traditionalist music whose limits they felt they had explored pretty completely, a desire to play something more interesting. (Characteristically it often took the compromise form of moving from the 'traditional' music of the twenties to the 'mainstream' music of the thirties and early forties, a halfway house to modernism.) But the trend was unmistakable, and it was greatly aided by two American developments: the virtual drying up of the American source of 'traditional' records (except for the perennial blues), and the swelling stream of modern records which British companies either had to release under contract or thought it worth releasing because of the established principle that what sells in America will soon sell in Europe. For in the U.S.A. modern jazz, by the middle fifties, acquired recognized cultural standing, perhaps because the line between hipsterdom and intellectualism grew faint in the period of McCarthy and the apotheosis of General Motors. Where every intellectual risked being an outsider or a secret dissident hidden underneath a crew-cut and grey flannel suit, an outsider's music might well come into its own.

The evolution of the jazz public is no more finished than that of jazz. However, it is not too soon to draw a few general conclusions from its history so far. The first is, that, in spite of considerable national differences, it is surprisingly similar in all countries. It is invariably a predominantly young public, for jazz, with its capacity to express unequivocal emotions in the most direct manner and its gallery of potential heroes and symbols, is a music ideally suited to adolescence. Except perhaps in Britain, the original nucleus of fans always contains a very large element of 'sons of good families', students, and the like, in rebellion against the world and their elders. This is so even in Socialist countries, where jazz (thanks to the official opposition to it) has often become a banner of rebellion for such groups as the *stilyagi* in the U.S.S.R., who are very often the sons of highly placed and conventional parents. Because it is rebellious, the aficionado community finds affinities with movements and ideologies of opposition, and sometimes, as in the Anglo-Saxon countries in the 1930s and after, may become impregnated with it. But normally, being vague and individualist, it remains on the margins of activity, and tends to attract those who want to contract out of convention as much as those who wish to overthrow it. The jazz of the 1920s was non-political; that of the 1930s and 40s attached itself to the left, and no doubt overlapped a little with its activists, just as it is likely that in some Socialist countries it is vaguely anti-Socialist, and may overlap a little with anti-Socialist activities. But on the whole we shall not expect many fans or amateur trumpet players to build, or perhaps even to man, the barricades. Mostly they will eventually retire into one form or another of official orthodoxy, remembering their turbulent past only as the proverbial young American executive of the post-war films remembers the little Italian girl with whom he had a passionate affair in Rome before returning home to the rat-race and the battle of the sexes.

In Britain (and possibly in other countries about which I am uninformed) the core of the jazz public represented another kind of rebellion, and a more serious one: the aspirations of the culturally and educationally underprivileged young for official recognition. Perhaps this is one reason why its political connexions and activities have been much more persistent here than elsewhere.

Round this nucleus, another wider and vaguer jazz public has emerged, as jazz has become better known. For these young people jazz has been not so much a cause and a banner (though all adolescents make themselves symbols of their separation from their elders), as a fashion and a convention. It is part of their life at a certain age, like playing tennis or going camping or going to espresso bars. There is a wide difference between the atmosphere of the jazz rebel, with his penchant for low life as much as for music, and the atmosphere of the characteristic British mass jazz club of the early and middle 1950s, where nobody drank, or wanted to drink, anything stronger than Coca-Cola, or smoke anything stronger than tobacco, and where the songs about whores, fancy-men, gamblers, and tough men echoed through an atmosphere which was much less like that of Storyville than like that of an old-fashioned youth club, minus the organizers. In a way this sort of public was and is a great deal more like the public jazz was made for than any other. Few jazz occasions recaptured the New Orleans spirit (as distinct from the New Orleans environment) better than the 'river-boat shuffles' or 'jazz carnivals' which came to be organized in Britain: one or two steamers would be hired to go to Margate and back, a selection of bands playing, or relays of musicians would play for an Albert Hall filled to the brim with working-class adolescents having the time of their lives. By aficionado standards, few of these were serious jazz fans. It was simply that for them jazz had become what Viennese waltzes were for their grandparents, and shimmies or foxtrots for their parents: the normal kind of music for dancing and a good time.

A third form of jazz public (if it can be so called) has also developed round the original nucleus of the fans: those who take no particular interest in jazz, but recognize that it has become part of the cultural scene, and must be treated as such. Jazz has been slow thus to establish itself, except in the Scandinavian countries where (in Denmark at least) jazz classes appear to have been organized in schools, and jazz concerts officially subsidized even in the early 1930s. Even in America official recognition of the fact that jazz is the most original musical contribution to civilization made in that country has been slow. (Fortunately, for it is very doubtful whether jazz flourishes any more than folk-song in an atmosphere of academic music schools and seminars or symphony concerts.) However, little by little the patent appeal of jazz has been reflected in the institutions of orthodox culture. Jazz reviews have appeared in serious journals, jazz programmes on serious broadcasts. At bottom all this amounts to no more than the recognition that jazz is now something about which the well-informed person ought to know enough to hide his ignorance. But even that is something.

eleven

Jazz as a Protest

The atmosphere which has surrounded jazz almost since the beginning is so overcharged with emotion as to make it extremely difficult to explain in purely musical terms. The first English writer to deal seriously, if inadequately, with jazz, R. W. S. Mendl, observed this as early as 1926. Unlike earlier light music, he noted, jazz was actively disliked and 'subject to the most violent and slashing attacks',[1] and this, he thought, probably accounted for the failure of any composer of the front rank to take it up. It was so strongly disliked, he argued, because it 'upset' us more and stirred us emotionally more than older kinds of light music had done. So it does, but the upsetting is by no means only musical.

Let us simply consider the extraordinary fervour which jazz has been able to rouse fairly consistently among its devotees, and which leads young jazz-lovers to treat famous musicians as something like models, heroes, or saints, and more mature ones to leap over the barriers of non-musical loyalty with astonishing ease. Lt Dietrich Schulz-Koehn of the German army spent his war leaves in Paris working on the 1942 edition of M. Delaunay's *Hot Discography,* though the French jazz-lovers' community was, for obvious reasons, extremely anti-German. When captured at Lorient he interrupted the negotiations for the surrender of the local German troops by asking whether anyone collected Benny Goodman records. It is difficult to see the devotees of other widespread international hobbies pursuing their passion quite so far. Again, the views of the Soviet authorities on jazz have been known at least since the middle 1930s. They disliked it, and regarded it (sometimes not unjustifiably) as a phenomenon of bourgeois decadence. When views on such matters were expressed by the leaders of world Socialism, Communists in Western countries normally assumed that they were sensible or justifiable and often made extraordinary efforts to convince themselves and others of this, sometimes in the teeth of their own previous liking for, say, Rilke, Braque, or Alban Berg. At all events they normally made few attempts to express contrary views in public. Yet it is no exaggeration to say that no Communist jazz-lover—and there has been a disproportionately large number of them—has ever taken serious notice of Soviet hostility to his music. This was regarded as an aberration, due to ignorance, or at best as something due to purely local Russian conditions, an attitude which Communists might profitably have adopted on other questions also. So far from taking notice of Russian views, British Communist journals printed serious jazz reviews continuously even in the peak years of 'Zhdanovism'. Clearly, jazz rouses remarkably powerful and tenacious emotions among both its supporters and opponents.

In this chapter I wish to suggest that this is due to the fact that jazz is not simply an ordinary music, light or heavy, but also a music of protest and rebellion. It is not necessarily or always a music of conscious and overt *political* protest, let alone any particular brand of political protest; though in the West, in so far as it has had political links, they have been pretty invariably with the left. (It is hard to see how it could be otherwise, since even the most apolitical jazz-lover must be committed to opposing racial discrimination, which is publicly defended only on the right.) But a good many of the protests and rebellions which jazz has at one time or another embodied leave politicians cold and unsympathetic. The French boys and girls who, in 1942, were arrested by the Germans in the Paris Métro dressed in 'flash, impertinent, provocative suits and dresses, and wearing a badge with the words *"une France* swing *dans une Europe* zazoue",' can only just be fitted into the category of the anti-Nazi resistance, even though several of the poor things ended in labour camps.[2] Such protests may become political because the people against whom jazz-lovers protest (for instance, fathers, mothers, uncles, and aunts) happen to hold certain conventional views, some of which are political (for instance, Republicanism in the U.S.A. Or they may be labelled subversive chiefly because those against whom they are directed cannot conceive of a rebellion against some of their conventions as anything but a rebellion against all their views: for example, as 'un-American'. The point is not that the jazz protests can be fitted into this or that pigeonhole of orthodox politics, though it often can—mostly into a left-wing one—but that the music lends itself to any kind of protest and rebelliousness much better than most other forms of the arts. There is historic justice in the story of the seven striking Nottinghamshire miners who, at the end of 1926, were fined £3 each for 'forming a jazz band' and making life difficult with it for a blackleg.[3] It is a music for expressing strong feelings of dislike.

This is due, in the first place, to an element jazz shares, alas, with Tin Pan Alley: it is democratic music. As the organ of the British popular musicians wrote in one of its first editorials, at the beginning of a career of consistent and passionate championship of jazz:

> Jazz is a new cult. It is probably a grand new art, and it has this advantage over 'straight' music that it appeals not only to the fauteuils but to the gallery also. It considers no class distinction.

231

Jazz was originally music designed to be enjoyed by the least intellectual or expert, the least privileged, educated, or experienced citizen, as well as by others; though the specialist jazz aficionados have been much more reluctant to admit this than the players. It was also designed to be played by men who have 'picked it up' any way. The jazz listener does not require the sort of preparation which is needed to listen profitably to a fugue, the jazz player can perform without the sort of training which is needed to sing coloratura, though this does not mean that either fails to benefit from training. More than this: jazz is a musical manifesto of populism. *The Merry Widow* might be the musically modest citizen's grand opera, but the jazz band, real or pseudo, was in no sense an imitation of a culturally more ambitious or respectable genre. Loud, raucous, sounding (even without the pseudo-jazz additions of tin pans, motor horns, and funny hats) like nothing on Earth except an undisciplined brass band playing in a room too small for it, the pioneer jazz band nailed the colours of its 'vulgarity' firmly to the mast. It appeared not simply because people liked the sound, but because it was a conquest of popular over minority culture, like that of the Marx Brothers who break up a performance of Grand Opera by getting the band to play *Take Me Out to the Ballgame*.

Several things may flow from such populism, good and bad: for those of us who are for popular art as for popular government must be prepared to recognize its considerable drawbacks. At its best the democracy of jazz produced an ideal of art in society wider and socially sounder than that of the orthodox minority culture, though recognizing and admiring its achievements. For instance, it gave people who, in terms of classical music, would have been doomed to remain pure listeners or simple executants, the chance actually to make (i.e. to create, not merely to reproduce) music. It has produced scholarship and serious critical discussion of art among people whom the orthodox arts could never bring to this point: audiences whom gossip columnists contemptuously describe as 'not the most intelligent that have been seen', who listen, with absolute attention, in absolute silence, and in their thousands, to what would in orthodox terms be considered a reasonably difficult chamber-music recital; and what is more, who discuss them as the old Viennese musical public would discuss the rival merits of Furtwängler and Bruno Walter. It has come nearer to breaking down class lines than any other art. At least I know of no other which could produce a table full of sax players from a West Indian orphanage, American soldiers from a black neighbourhood in Cleveland, journalists, dons, salesmen, and souteneurs single-mindedly debating the stylistic differences between the East and West coast schools of jazz. At its best the democratic protest of jazz merely means that this music stakes a claim to a serious participation in the arts for people who would, but for it, be mostly debarred from such participation; and its appeal for such people is therefore strong.

At its worst it degenerates into philistinism. For if jazz is designed for the least intellectual or expert, the least prepared, privileged, or experienced citizens as well as for others, this also means that it appeals to the most stupid, ignorant, lazy, and inexpert, who do not like what they cannot understand, or what requires effort, or knowledge, or expertise. It is true that this sort of philistinism surrounds the jazz-influenced kinds of pop music much more than jazz itself, whose strict devotees are generally shocked by the prospect of simply sitting back and enjoying themselves; the critics more than the musicians. The Hollywood films in which the hero, after a disgusted flirtation with 'long-hair' music, lifts the saxophone to his lips, pushes his body into convulsions, and finds the girl, the money, and the way forward, are about the stars of Tin Pan Alley. For these the contempt of the strict jazz public is often as boundless as that of the classicist. But if jazz *has* influenced and coloured pop music to the extent it has, it is largely because the pop public took so readily to an idiom which flaunted its 'vulgarity'; for exactly the same reason that *Take Me Out to the Ballgame* played in the middle of Grand Opera sounds much more 'outrageous' when played by a brass band than by a string orchestra. Nor is it any use denying that even many jazzmen have regarded their music

233

not as an addition to serious music but as a straight competitor to the 'classics'.

In the second place jazz is a music of protest, because it was originally the music of an oppressed people and of oppressed classes: of the latter perhaps more obviously than of the former, though the two cannot be kept rigidly separate. It has, of course, made perhaps its most powerful appeal to middle- and upper-class aficionados because of these social origins: nobody has ever started a movement of emotional commitment to Czerny's exercises, which are not less interesting than some boogie-woogie piano (though in a different way), because nobody has ever felt like idealizing the nineteenth-century lower-middle classes *en masse*. But blacks have been so idealized, much to their justified disgust.

The belief that the American black in some sense represented desirable elements which white civilization lacked has been widespread in America and Britain since the black-faced minstrel shows first became a standard type of popular entertainment in the second third of the nineteenth century. The search for the pure, the innocent, the 'natural' counterpart of modern Western bourgeois society is as old as that society itself, for it reflects the permanent awareness of its fundamental flaws. Sometimes it took the form of simple exoticism and primitivism: the search for the noble savage, who might be located, according to taste, in Tahiti or the Corsican highlands, in the Caucasus or on the Arabian deserts. Sometimes, especially among members of the middle and upper classes, it took the more complex form of a sort of partial idealization of social groups who were, in other respects, hated, despised, and oppressed: workers (especially un-skilled ones) and peasants, women, social outcasts like criminals and prostitutes, oppressed pariah peoples like blacks and gypsies. In such cases admiration was mixed with contempt, sometimes with fear which is often only an unacknowledged form of admiration for something we cannot do ourselves. The gypsy was filthy, thieving, superstitious, and treacherous, but 'spontaneous' and 'free' as in Mérimée and Bizet's *Carmen,* which is the textbook example of this attitude; the Southern black is for William

Faulkner a rightly dominated subman, but also, by his very strength, emotional fervour, and 'simplicity' a sort of reproach.★ Among the more rebellious minorities, mainly of intellectuals and artists, the idealization was much more simple: the mileu of gangsters, pimps, and prostitutes, as represented in, say, Becker's film *Casque d'or,* was quite simply more heroic, free, innocent, and in its roundabout way, just *because* it was one of outcasts and protesters against social convention. In terms of jazz, jazz is good music because it is believed to derive not simply from blacks but from the red-light district of New Orleans.

The emotional, and often quite irrational, bias in favour of blacks and black low life has always been extremely strong among serious jazz-lovers. Politically left-wing aficionados have attempted to counter it with the argument that jazz is a people's music of both black and white oppressed, though for historic reasons the blacks have formed and advanced it most, and practised it best, and for sociological ones the low-life zone of large cities has provided its best nurseries. But though this view has won some intellectual assent, at least when not put forward in its more extremist forms, it has not really disturbed the fundamental 'black' bias of most of the older jazz-lovers.[4] This bias, especially among some traditionalist zealots, can reach the point of mania as when one (white) historian of jazz writes that 'white men cannot even play it', or another argues that:

> I may say that authentic jazz can be created only by Negroes; any other jazz by white men . . . is not authentic. They cannot emulate the feeling and expression of their Negro contemporaries, because they are alien to the mystical and profound inspirations which motivate the Negro musician.[5]

The desire to become a 'white Negro', of which Mezzrow's *Really the Blues* is the best literary expression, is merely the most

★ Since these are subjects on which a lot of people are ultra-sensitive, it is probably necessary to state formally that anyone who thinks these descriptions of gypsies and Southern blacks or any other national and social groups represent reality, or the author's opinions, is mistaken.

extreme form of this attitude. It may be as well to remember that this is merely an inverted version of the more orthodox type of racialism, such as that of the people 'whose hostile reaction to syncopated dance music is attributed by them to everything connected with the nigger'.[6] The fact that the one attitude leads to civilized behaviour between peoples and the other to Nazi or South African barbarism should not obscure the equal irrationality of both. A good deal of jazz criticism is permeated by less extreme versions of the same pro-black race feeling, and this sometimes affects critical standards.

Colour prejudice in reverse (what black intellectuals used to call 'Crow Jim') must not be confused with the obvious recognition, which implies no belief in mysticism or blood, that the origins and evolution of jazz are more closely linked with the history of American blacks than with any other group of people, and that up to the present the supremacy of black players in jazz is about as obvious and perhaps even more unchallenged than that of Jews in chess playing. (Of course it may be argued that this is partly due to the practice of critics, since about 1930, of establishing the criteria of good jazz in terms of the achievements of black players, but I do not think the general superiority of, say, Armstrong, Bessie Smith, and Charlie Parker over any of their white contemporaries and predecessors can be wholly explained away in this manner.) The point I wish to make is not that the role of blacks in jazz has been exaggerated, for it has not; but that the appeal of jazz for many white middle-class admirers is that it is a music of those who, by middle-class ranking, are socially below them. The lady leaves her castle with the raggletaggle gypsies, not because they play so sweet, but because they are *not* ladies and gentlemen—they are in fact gypsies.

Apart from this, the protesting element in jazz owes less than one might suppose to its actual black character. For, paradoxically, the black's own musical protest against his fate was one of the less important elements in the appeal of jazz, and one of the latest to become influential. All American blacks, like all members of oppressed and underprivileged peoples everywhere, are always protesting against their situation in one way or another, by the very modes of their behaviour, even if not consciously and deliberately. However, in times of relative political stability such as those when jazz was evolved, such protests are often indirect, allusive, complex, esoteric, and extremely difficult for outsiders to recognize as protests, because they are not addressed to them. Jewish jokes, often of a type which, if told by an outsider, would be regarded as anti-semitic, are an extremely elaborate form of expressing resentment against the old ghetto Jews' position, but quite unadapted to become the basis of rebelliousness by non-Jews. Just so the innumerable self-deprecating in-group allusions of traditional Southern black culture are likely to be regarded by outsiders, and indeed by politically more advanced blacks, not as protests but as 'Uncle Tomism'. And not wholly without reason, for one of the functions of such protests is to blow off steam without producing the explosions—lynchings and pogroms—which incautious practical rebelliousness might always provoke. At all events, the early phase of jazz, which is the one with the greatest general influence, the 'New Orleans style' and its derivations and dilutions, is almost certainly the socially best 'adjusted' music ever evolved by American blacks, the product of a cruel and unjust society, but one in which the black was allowed considerable emotional certainty and security so long as he 'kept his place' within the ghetto where he played for other blacks. 'Unembattled, happy, almost complacent' is not a bad description of old-style New Orleans jazz.[7] This did not last, but its influence on white pop music, serious jazz, and the jazz public cannot be described as one of social protest. Only in the fervour of the spirituals and in the heart-breaking, but unselfpitying blues, did a note of genuine protest sound. But the vogue for these did not make substantial progress until the socially conscious 1930s.

But even the unembattled kind of common people's music has the elements of protest in it; nor are these confined to the black people. It is not only their type of music which speaks directly from and to the ordinary untrained man or woman, in which people play as men speak, or laugh, or cry, only more so; and which, by virtue of this directness is a standing protest against the cultural and social orthodoxies from which it is so sharply distinct. It is any music *specifically* made by and for the poor, which however little intention of political protest. This may be illustrated by the example of an institution which has affinities with art and, incidentally, has had the most profound influence on the evolution of jazz, the 'poor man's church'.

The labouring poor have often, in Protestant countries, developed their own kinds of religion separate from, and in some respects opposed to, those of the upper classes.[8] These almost invariably have certain characteristics. They play down the things at which poor and ignorant people are bad—for instance, intellectualism, elaborate theologies, and the like—and stress those in which they compete on equal and superior terms—for instance, emotional fervour, moral enthusiasm, austerity. The educated preacher who appealed to Episcopalian and Presbyterian congregations among the New England (or Midland) middle classes, was unpopular among frontiersmen, mill-hands, miners, or sailors, who admired the man or woman who punched the Bible and preached blood and hell-fire in the style of the hot-gospelling actor-orator-singer. Every poor man's Protestant sect, white or black, is essentially a 'ranting' sect, whether it consists of Durham Primitive Methodists in the nineteenth century, or hillbilly Baptists, or the modern Pentecostal Holiness churches, Adventists, and Jehovah's Witnesses. Again, such sects were much given to democracy. The congregation took an active part in the proceedings, by choral singing, amens, and hallelujahs, by 'speaking with voices' and 'testifying' whenever the spirit moved a member, not to mention other means. The official gap between the preacher and the public was as small as possible, and the actual gap was no larger, since virtually any member who was 'moved' and had fervour and eloquence—and who has not, at certain moments?—could become a preacher himself or herself. Again, for very much the same reasons, religious worship was unformalized and unritualized, spontaneous and collective. Once again these characteristics appear in their purest form in black churches, and may be heard on the invaluable records of their services and music, but they may equally be found in white ones of whatever nationality, provided these reflect similar social situations. Such religion, even when not intended as a social or political gesture, *was* a protest. Every element in it exalted the ways and aspirations of the poor, the ignorant and oppressed, the labourers, and depreciated the standards of the rich, the educated, the powerful, the upper ranks.

The parallel of such church services with primitive jazz is not arbitrary, even if we leave out of account the very close links between the 'hot-gospelling' black churches and the rhythmic blues, which makes a childhood among the Pentecostal Holiness people or the Churches of God in Christ so valuable an education for the future jazz musician. Like such churches, jazz was systematically *not* like orthodox culture, and exalted the gifts and ways of untrained and ignorant musicians and dancer-listeners in very similar ways. Like them, it went 'straight to the heart' of ordinary people, because its technique was designed to do so. The most remarkable technical achievement of the blues, its capacity to sweep the listener to the right emotional mood literally within the first bar, sometimes by the first note, is one it shares with the gospel song. The techniques of the hot-gospeller in prose, of the gospel singer in song, and of the improvising soloist in jazz are (as the word 'hot' implies) fundamentally similar. These techniques have only occasional parallels in the orthodox arts, which rely on a much more elaborate and complex system of gears and transmission belts between the artist's emotion and its artistic expression. Only when we get an artist (himself, by the way, also a poor man's evangelist) like Van Gogh, who aims at immediate impact of emotion, do we find a procedure analogous to jazz.

But its very nature and origins jazz therefore expresses some kinds of protest and heterodoxy and lends itself to the expression of others. The mere fact that it originates among oppressed and unconsidered people, and is looked down upon by orthodox society, can make the simple listening to jazz records into a gesture of social dissent; perhaps—as generations of teenagers have discovered—the cheapest of all such gestures. What they would do if jazz were ever to become domesticated and officially accepted, like ballet, makes for entertaining speculation.

I do not propose to survey the various kinds of protest which jazz has helped to express in the course of its history.* The subject has been treated by psychologists, and may be left to them. My object has been to show, not why people require some way of making musical protests, or blowing off steam, but why, having these requirements, they should find jazz so eminently suitable. It is because it is 'common people's music', which, both by its social origins and associations and by its musical peculiarities, lends itself to such interpretation even where it is not designed for it. If jazz had not been on the American scene, some other form of the American popular tradition would unquestionably have come to take its place as a vehicle for protest, though hillbilly songs, cowboy music, or the vigorous and 'democratic' products of the early, half-folky Tin Pan Alley, would not have made perfect substitutes. For jazz owes at least this to its black origins and associations, that it is not merely 'common people's music', but common people's music at its most concentrated and emotionally powerful. Because blacks are and were oppressed even among the poor and powerless, their cries of protest are more poignant and more overwhelming, their cries of hope are more earth-shaking, than other peoples', and have found, even in words, the most unanswerable expression: 'Nobody knows the trouble I've seen', 'Sometimes I feel like a motherless child', 'Good morning, blues, Blues, how do you do?' Because the musical language of jazz is Afro-American, it is more heterodox, and owes less even to the echoes of orthodoxy than other kinds of popular music. Moreover, because of its musical origins, it has used that most potent of musical devices for inducing powerful physical emotion, rhythm, as no other music familiar to our society has. It is not merely a voice of protest: it is a natural loudspeaker.

What jazz protests about or against is, for our purposes, secondary. The protests which white intellectual Californian

* Chapters 3, 9, 10 contain some relevant material on this point.

240

tramps, or British teenagers, or Johannesburg Africans, or Moscow *stilyagi,* seek to express through it differ from one another, and from those of various groups of American blacks. They are also, incidentally, of unequal seriousness. It would be foolish to reduce them all to a single denominator. They do, however, have this in common. Jazz *by itself* is not politically conscious or revolutionary. The voice of men shouting 'We do not like this' must not be misunderstood for the cry of 'This cannot last', let alone for the slogan 'This must be revolutionized'. Nor should artistic unorthodoxy be held to imply unorthodoxy all round, any more than the thief's unorthodoxy about the criminal law implies unconventional views about politics. In fact, until adopted by groups of intellectuals, jazz has lent itself to political revolutionism rather less well than other kinds of popular music, for instance, religious hymns. There is a sound reason for this.

The origins of jazz lay among that section of the poor which, though extremely oppressed, is least given to collective organization and political consciousness, and which finds its 'freedom' by side-stepping oppression rather than by facing it; the unskilled, pre-industrial, big-city labouring poor. Being poor and oppressed, they sing and play about poverty and oppression as a matter of course. Folk-song experts of the left have never had any difficulty in discovering flamenco songs expressing bitter hatred of policemen and judges, Neapolitan ballads idealizing brigand-rebels, or blues of left-wing social significance. But equally, they have never been able to deny that the great majority of such songs, however persistent the undertone of resentment against poverty and oppression, are songs of private life and personal relations: the characteristic blues is and remains the song of the troubles between a woman and her man or a man and his woman. In a sense the strength of the slums, the brothels, the music halls, as nurseries of the popular arts derives from the fact that those who live in them and frequent them have no other *regular* outlet for their unhappiness than the making and experiencing of aesthetic impressions, 'living for kicks', as the phrase goes. For those who organize and fight, ecstasy is often a by-product of collective action, art a part of it, like the choral song, which, as hymn or in a secular form, is so characteristic of such movements, with their frequent—possibly their general—tendency to puritanism. But jazz is anti-puritan, and the choral song plays no part whatever in it. It is the critics who have classified secular jazz and blues and the gospel song under the same heading: historically and socially the 'gospel people' among the blacks have been strongly opposed to jazz and all it stood for, many jazz musicians and blues singers resentful and contemptuous of church groups. In much the same way the labour movements of Britain have generally been unenthusiastic about the old music halls, while the old music hall artists, in spite of their marked prejudice for the poor against the rich, were rarely political militants. The old British contrast between the 'pub miner' (who was, more often than not, the less organized type) and the 'chapel miner' (who provided the cadre of union organizers) has its less formalized parallels in the world of jazz. Few politically militant blacks were genuine admirers of jazz, at least until it had been borne in upon them (often by the propaganda of white intellectuals) that this music was 'an achievement of the race' of which blacks should be proud.

It was easy to associate jazz with radical and revolutionary politics, and in times of political ferment American jazz musicians were quite willing so to be associated: after all, if the poor, however unorganized and demoralized, have any politics, they must be 'on the side of the poor'. (In other countries, where the jazz movement had different social bases and often grew out of the political left, the links were sometimes closer.) However, when left to itself, the jazz protest remained vague and ambiguous, because what it is against is far clearer than what it is for. It is against oppression, against poverty, against inequality and unfreedom, against unhappiness. It is, in a vague and anarchic way which has been misunderstood by the anarchist intellectuals who have taken jazz to their bosoms, against policemen and judges, prisons, armies, and war. (There are no traditional blues in praise of battle, however pacific; only spirituals.) The hatred of these things does not imply militancy. Very many American jazz musicians have expressed hatred and resentment of an unjust society, if only privately. Very few have been associated even with the active and organized fight against racial inequality in the way in which a good many prominent figures from more commercial popular entertainment—notably from Hollywood—have been.* Europe in the post-1945 period has known many American intellectual and artistic expatriates; but though several black players have settled here, largely because they are treated with greater human dignity in the old world, I cannot think of any 'political' jazz refugees of either colour to set beside the numerous 'political' refugees from Hollywood or New York in the other fields of art.

What jazz is *against* may be reasonably clear in theory, though it may find only a rather passive, evasive, and individualist expression outside music. The most notable of such expressions are perhaps the savage diatribes of the jazz-steeped night-club satirists who became prominent in the later fifties, Mort Sahl, Lennie Bruce, and the rest. What it is *for* is much less clear. No doubt, liberty, equality, fraternity, and a chicken in the pot every Sunday, or every day, allowing for the American standard of living. However, these great slogans are less self-explanatory than even some who are not jazz musicians or jazz fans believe. And this has always beset the protest of jazz, like a good many other individualist and spontaneous protests, with a great temptation: that of settling for very small positive gains—for official recognition, for personal satisfaction. Or, to be more precise, of oscillating between a discontent which can never be satisfied because, like the 'blue flower' of the German romantics or the crock of gold at the foot of the rainbow, it is so defined as to be beyond satisfaction, and one which can be rather easily satisfied, by growing up, by being sent on a tour as 'cultural ambassador' for the U.S. Government, by playing with the New York Philharmonic, or earning a lot of money.

The yearning for official recognition is perhaps the most dan-

---

* There is the excuse that black jazz musicians are much more easily victimized than white popular entertainers who have made a great deal of money. But, as the McCarthy period has shown, this is not a wholly valid excuse.

gerous part of this temptation, because it affects not only the general appeal of jazz but also the music. It has always existed, even when the jazz players were perfectly content to blow out their souls as ordinary entertainers of a popular dancing audience, and the fans most vociferous in their contempt for the 'long-hair' arts. It is this which has caused jazz musicians of all styles time and again to insist on playing with string sections (for violins symbolize accepted cultural status in music), in spite of the uniformly disastrous results of such experiments. The film *St Louis Blues,* which, like so many American films, is a compendium of widely accepted fictions, all equally miserable, illustrates this very clearly: like the film about Louis Armstrong's world tour, it ends in the apotheosis of jazz being played in a Philharmonic auditorium by a lot of fiddlers.★ The rebels of the arts in jazz settle for admission to their version of the Royal Academy, unlike the rebels in more sophisticated arts, who have learned better. Similarly, jazz-lovers in both Britain and America have shown quite disproportionate resentment against the neglect of their music by the guardians of orthodox sound. Generations of them have grown up to repeat the same rare crumbs of praise for jazz by classical musicians (first- or second-rate), and to hail with touching gratitude the occasional recognition of jazz by the Third Programme of the BBC or similar established cultural institutions.† The jazz fan, the jazz critic, have hitherto been hunted creatures. Few books about jazz fail to begin with, or to contain, a defence of jazz against its detractors.

This feeling of inferiority, whether acknowledged or not, has been part of the jazz protest. It has produced such phenomena as the attempt to turn jazz into something equivalent to 'straight music'—the 'symphonic jazz' of the 1920s, the devices lifted from Bach and Milhaud in modern jazz, the dressing up in

★ That intelligent impresario Norman Granz knew what he was about when he baptized his touring jazz show *Jazz at the Philharmonic.*

† Thus during the thirties a casual appreciation of Duke Ellington by Percy Grainger was almost invariably quoted, just as Ernest Ansermet's much more acute appreciation of Sidney Bechet in 1919 occurs in every discussion of 'traditionalist' jazz.

morning coats and acknowledging applause by stiff bows, the systematic refusal to behave in any way like an old-fashioned extrovert entertainer. All this is understandable, perhaps inevitable, but it is to be regretted, for the strength of jazz is not the strength of the feeling of inferiority among its musicians or admirers, but that of an idiom which is, however limited, radically different from the orthodox minority culture. The British stage did not necessarily become better because actors have come to be given knighthoods. In one sense, the influx of the sons and daughters of the middle and upper classes has unquestionably weakened it, as Bernard Shaw recognized: how many British actors or actresses today can take King Lear, Othello, Cleopatra, or Lady Macbeth in their stride, as the unknighted troupers of the nineteenth century could?

Paradoxically, it is the simplest and least 'political' jazz which has best resisted the temptations of compromise, respectability, and official recognition. Bessie Smith, who never sang in white theatres and would not have changed her style if she had, is—like the blues—the least corrupted and corruptible part of jazz, and therefore the purest carrier of the jazz protest. (It may be significant that of all the biographies and auto-biographies of jazz artists, those of the women singers express the irreconcilable bitterness of the underdog most persistently.°) This is not because such artists are more immune to temptation. Often, indeed, the primitive and elemental musicians are far more willing than the sophisticated and emancipated ones to play what the public wants or to act as the public wants them to act. It is probably because they simply cannot sing or play any differently, being too unadaptable. If Armstrong were to play the Purcell Trumpet Voluntary, it would still come out like the blues.)

But this fact makes it harder for those who have no feeling of inferiority about jazz to champion its unique and radical merits. They can be easily accused of idealizing the simple, illiterate, and unemancipated. 'You want us to stay inferior' is a charge readily brought against those who merely want to keep jazz independent. This is inevitable. The logic of the struggle for emancipation and equality makes those who fight for it try to demonstrate two things first and foremost: (*a*) that they can compete successfully with those who claim superiority on their own ground, and (*b*) that they can abandon a way of life which has hitherto been associated with inferiority. The early feminists tried to show not only that they could pass university examinations as well as the men, but that they could do without 'feminine fripperies'—dressing elegantly, make-up, and the rest. Zionist Jews tried to show that Jews were good at farming and fighting, which had not hitherto been regarded as typically Jewish occupations, and rejected the valuable Yiddish culture of their East European ghettoes as the badge of the inferior past. Those organizing African universities are highly suspicious of European advisers who suggest that they need not pay much attention to Greek and Latin. Do not the classics belong to the higher education of the Europeans, and is not the plan to cut them out merely a reflection of the desire to deprive Africans, even now, of the best education?

There is some sense in such suspicions and such rejections, however exaggerated their practical results. After all, those who kept women in inferiority did very often idealize those parts of feminine behaviour which happened not to compete with male achievements: Be pretty, sweet maid, and let who will be clever. Anti-semites never denied that Jews were clever or good at business, only that they were brave, hard-working, or honest. The champions of African inferiority are the first to idealize the 'unspoiled tribesman' as against the 'half-educated intellectual'. The cries 'Up the Pathan, down the Bengali Baboo!' 'Up the noble Beduin, down the Egyptian schoolmaster!' 'Up the brave and stupid Masai, down the corrupt Kikuyu!' ring through the history of racial oppression, just as aristocrats and employers are never tired of contrasting the simple old retainer or the loyal old operative with the inferior specimens of the peasantry and workers on the modern political scene. It is natural, and necessary, for those who feel themselves to have been kept under to resent this, and to demonstrate their equality by doing what they have been regarded as incapable of doing.

But if it is natural that babies should be emptied with the bath water, care must be taken that they can also be put back. (There is no technical reason why they should not, unless they have been dropped on their heads in the process.) Probably they will be. Emancipated women have long stopped avoiding pretty dresses, emancipated Jews despising Yiddish stories and jokes. In due course, no doubt, emancipated American blacks will have their own 'New Orleans revival', being sufficiently distant from the old South to separate the original cultural achievement of their people from the conditions of oppression in which it took place.* Very likely by the time this happens the critics will be ready to warn them that a return to a dead past is not the same as the development of a living tradition, a warning which has hitherto had to be addressed mainly to young white musicians. In the meantime those who have no feeling of inferiority about liking or playing jazz can only continue to defend its genuine originality and achievements, even when they are combined with things which others would prefer to forget or put behind them. They can, however, also do something else. They can assist the emancipation of those who are oppressed and unprivileged, and feel themselves to be inferior. For that is probably the quickest way of making their point.

* It is pleasant to record successful prophecy. Though a 'New Orleans revival' in the strict sense has not yet taken place, there has been since 1958 a striking return to 'the roots'—blues and gospel song—especially among the most race-conscious black musicians. It is precisely the most folky qualities which are now (1960) being idealized, perhaps excessively so, as 'funky' or 'soul'. However, the large tract of jazz which lies between proto-jazz and the bop revolution still remains to be discovered by many modernists.

part five

Selections from Writings
for *The New Statesman*
and *The New York
Review of Books*

twelve

From
The New Statesman,
1958–1965

Basie

Like all artists, jazz musicians play chiefly for the only public whose judgment they respect, that of other musicians. Like all artists, they run their art into trouble if they get too far beyond the control of the ordinary paying public which knows what it likes: provided it does not pay too much or know too much. If it pays too much, the temptation of tin pan alley may be too great: Mr. Bill Haley's rock and rollers *may* be competent jazz-players, but they can't show it in public. If it thinks it knows too much, it will get in the musicians' way. Far and away the best kind of public is one which does not much mind what the musicians play, so long as, speaking broadly, they make the right sort of noise and perhaps loose off a few fireworks now and then; a public which will incidentally allow players and arrangers to satisfy their own consciences.

251

Few places have provided better conditions of this sort than Kansas City in the years between 1920 and 1940, a hard bitten and remarkably "wide-open" town which has revolutionised the world of jazz, largely through the agency of Count Basie's band, which emerged from it in 1936, and arrived at the Festival Hall on Tuesday. Let us be thankful for Kansas City. Count Basie and his sixteen men are the finest jazz orchestra that has visited this country since Duke Ellington came here in 1933. Two of the British bandleaders who reported in force at the *première* were heard to say to one another in the interval, that they proposed to take their bands off Waterloo Bridge into the river. One sympathises with them, though the situation hardly calls for such extreme steps. Jazz as it is played by the Basie band is simply out of the reach of British musicians, and when they are again reconciled to the fact, they can continue to entertain themselves and us in their more modest way, as before.

The band appeared in a decor which looked like a design for a sea-lions' pool, and was supposed to symbolise its music. Anyone who saw the players, greyish and relaxed with fatigue after their journey, face the press a few hours before going unrehearsed on the stand, will appreciate their mere achievement in getting through the evening. Heaven knows what these soft-spoken and far from simple men with poker-faced publicity smiles think, as the cameras take the photos which look exactly like those taken in a hundred other cities, or as they play *Low Life* admirably for yet another time. But they don't show it. A combination of extraordinary natural rhythm, supple, controlled and easy, and of equally extraordinary craftsmanship, makes this band not only a superb rhythmic and blowing machine—perhaps the best in the world today—but unforced and alive. This is probably due to the men's complete confidence in their own technical equipment and in one another. There is no doubt that this band comes to us as a team near the peak of its collective form. Some of it is also due to excellent arrangements written for this combination of players and for no other; though lack of rehearsal with the microphones exaggerated the brass somewhat. But the band does not depend on routines, for a group of them semi-improvised the traditional *Royal Garden Blues,* which is far from their normal repertoire, with almost contemptuous effort-lessness.

Any way one likes to look at it, this is a very high-class band indeed. Its rhythm spreads with wonderful ease from the few deceptively simply chords with which Count Basie himself opens on the piano, to the rest of the rhythm section and thence to the brass and reeds until, as one admiring British musician said, "every man seems to be his own rhythm section." The soloists are superbly stylish, notably Joe Newman, a slim and elegant trumpet, Frank Foster, a boyish saxophone sporting the small goatee of the avant-garde coloured musician, and the trombone of Henry Coker. And the entire band refrains, with an almost insolent confidence in its powers, from the vulgar and simple tricks of the trade which set the teenagers rocking and rolling. It does not need them. At most it allows itself to batter at their emotions with a mass of brazen sound, but its best numbers are not its loudest, and the band knows it. Apart from a couple of bravura pieces for the drummer and the bass player, Basie makes only one major concession to his singer, Joe Williams, an impassive tall man who hides his thoughts. Williams is a jazz-singer of considerable talent, who has greatly increased the band's popularity in America, but for one critic at least he cannot make Basie play the blues as James Rushing could in the distant days when he and the band first moved us with *Sent for You Yesterday.*

Anyone who wants to listen to a really first-rate coloured band at the peak of its present form ought to hear Basie. Until Duke Ellington returns to this country, British jazz-lovers will be lucky to hear anything which achieves or surpasses this standard of excellence.

Parisian Jazz

Artistically jazz, like *haute couture,* is a rather de-nationalised product. To the casual listener a 'New Orleans' band sounds much the same whether composed of Scotsmen or Japanese, a 'cool' quartet, whether composed of Singhalese or Swedes, which is natural enough since all are essentially imitating Americans. (The only local school of jazz which appears to behave with real stylistic autonomy is that of the *jive bands* in the Johannesburg slums.) Musically, therefore, the British jazz-lover who visits Paris crosses no frontiers. The 'traditional' jazz to be heard there is mostly worse than ours, the middle period and modern jazz rather better—thanks to the constant presence of expatriate American musicians of top rank—but otherwise there are few surprises. Mr Kenny Clarke, the drummer, holds together a variety of modern combinations at the *Club Saint Germain,* as he did in New York (including a startlingly good French pianist, Martial Solal). Michel Hausser, Henri Renaud and their partners at the *Chat Qi Pèche* sounds like the Modern Jazz Quartet, only not so good, because they are an imitation Modern Jazz Quartet. M. Guy Laffitte, as good a tenor-player as any in Europe, audibly echoes the Parisian expatriate Don Byas. As for the airy swinging trumpet of the veteran Bill Coleman and the blues-playing Mezz Mezzrow, who hold up the *Trois Mailletz,* they belong to Paris only because they live there; and owe most of their international reputation to the championship of French critics in the 1930s.

Socially, on the other hand, nothing could be more strikingly different from the jazz world of London than that of Paris. Though jazz has penetrated a long way into the zone of the certified and OK British intellectuals, the characteristic jazz fan here is still an adolescent electrician or apprentice tool-maker, a draughtsman or lab technician, a compositor, bank-clerk or junior technologist. If H. G. Wells were young today, he would almost certainly belong to some jazz club, and it is not without relevance that science fiction has been an extra-curricular interest of British jazzmen since before the war.

Not so in France, where jazz is almost exclusively an annexe of Left Bank intellectualism, and the sale of records dips sharply and regularly every June during the examination season, when the *lycéens* and students have other things to think about. There it has long been strictly OK. Jean Cocteau and Max Jacob patronised the review *Le Jazz Hot* in its early days, Sartre's *Les Temps modernes* has long opened its columns to André Hodeir and Lucien Malson—needless to say, a *professeur de philosophie*—and at least one able professional bass-player began his musical life as a graduate sociologist. When a group of avant-gardists wish to make a documentary film about the *Palais Idéal* of the postman Cheval—a backyard Xanadu constructed by a Provençal Douanier Rousseau with Blakeian leanings, which has long been a hobby of the ex-surrealists—they naturally add a modern jazz sound-track. A very good one too, by André Hodeir. Except when they are tourists, the French jazz audiences look as though they have been rounded up from the terraces of the Quartier. Except when they are black Americans, French jazz players look like the intellectuals they are: that is to say either like the young Clemenceau or (allowing for glasses and the absence of the tonsure) like the young Abelard in a blue cardigan.

The Parisian jazz world has a few remote outliers on the right bank, survivals of its origins around Montmartre, but fundamentally it exists between the river and St Sulpice. virtually all the jazz worth listening to is to be found between the *Club Saint Germain* (neatly placed ten yards from both the *Flore* and *Deux Magots* cafés) and the *Troil Mailletz* in the Rue Galande, where the intellectuals border on the North Africans. If Jazz were not played in cellars one might well going from one to the other within earshot of some drummer or other: via the *Tabou* (Rue Dauphine) where players go after hours, flanked by posters advertising German abstract art, the *Caméléon* (Rue St André des Arts), and the Rue de la Huchette, which has come a long way since Elliott Paul's *A Narrow Street,* for it now contains both the headquarters of M. Ionesco's drama and the heaviest concentration of jazz clubs in the city, including the *Chat Qui Pêche* and Maxim's Saury's *Caveau de la Huchette,* the liveliest of the dying tribe of 'New Orleans' cellars. Explorers may tackle the *Cigale* (Bd Rochechouart), a street café where African musicians honk it out with more noise than finesse, visiting players drop in at the *Mars* (Rue Robert-Estienne) for news of what goes on, but at bottom it is all on the Left Bank.

It is a narrow, economically untenable world, which has

ceased to expand: three years ago the French radio abandoned its annual amateur jazz contests. The provinces and the working classes have not yet come to its rescue, and in so far as they have turned to jazz, it is to the New Orleans music of Sidney Bechet, who gives 250 provincial concerts a year in a style despised by the Parisian avant-garde. The clubs charge excessive prices and are fast being replaced by *discothèque* joints without live musicians; the musicians, unless (American) stars, compete for casual work at 3–5,000 francs a night and may have to play for 1,500. No doubt the present depression—which local observers put down to politics, though it also affects Britain, which has no Algerian colonels—makes matters worse, but not much. Parisian jazz therefore retreats into marginal professionalism: occasional concerts, and film scores, which have lately multiplied, thanks to the commercial success of Vadim's film with John Lewis's score, and Louis Malle's *Ascenseur à l'echafaud* with Miles Davis. The most ambitious experimental jazz orchestra, André Hodeir's *Jazz Groupe de Paris* (2 trumpets, trombone, 3 saxes, vibes, bass, drums) has failed to establish itself commercially and remains a spare-time group whose members earn their living elsewhere.

In fact, like Parisian dressmaking, Parisian avant-garde jazz is a minority taste which must depend either on those who can pay a luxury price for it or on the export trade. But the French jazz public is not rich, even though its parents sometimes are, and the only real export market is for the excellent books of French jazz critics and theorists: it is surprising how few French jazz records are released in this country. There remains the tourist trade, a natural sucker for cellar clip-joints, on which the jazz clubs can continue to rely, at least until the visitors begin to demand girls and floorshows. And yet: while French jazz maintains its intense intellectual liveliness and Paris its attraction for American musicians, somehow or other the horns will continue to blow in whatever is the most advanced style of the times.

Whenever Duke Ellington is mentioned, the jazz critics dust off their superlatives. Since most of them have already been used up to celebrate his present visit, a few categorical statements will do for the purpose of briefing the squarer readers of the NEW STATESMAN. They may, therefore, take it that Ellington is certainly the most ducal figure in jazz—he has worn his title by right of elegance since the age of eight—and probably the most original composer in the U.S.A. His band is not only the finest but the oldest jazz orchestra, having functioned continuously since 1926—an awe-inspiring record for those who know the business—chiefly performing its leader's compositions. All these things are almost as surprising to the convinced Ellington admirers as to the outsider, for though there is no doubt about his achievements, they are as enigmatic as his public charm, or as the behaviour of his chief soloist, who looks and behaves like the most impassive of Orozco's Indians until he lifts his horn to produce the most lyrical invention in the history of the alto saxophone.

The stature of a mountaineer is judged not by the height of mountains he climbs but by their difficulty. Jazz critics admire Ellington so profoundly because they know the nature of the musical rock-faces he scales. He is more than merely Constant Lambert's *petit-maître,* a painter of musical pictures with a remarkable technical mastery in the precise mixing of orchestral sound and the interplay of solo and orchestra. He is the man who first recognised and solved the unbelievably difficult problem of turning a living, shifting and improvised folk-music into composition without losing its spontaneity. Anyone can use jazz devices in orthodox composition or leave cadenzas blank for solo improvisation. Nobody but the Duke (in a peculiarly anarchically controlled symbiosis with his musicians) has produced music which is *both* created by the players *and* fully shaped by the composer. He has been so unique and so far ahead of his time that even jazz musicians sometimes fail to appreciate his originality, surprised to find some revolutionary device of modern jazz anticipated in the early 1930s, and that by a man who sees no reason to break with jazz tradition. For example, Ellington, alone in this as in so many other things, has consistently kept in his music two of the oldest sounds in jazz: the liquid New Orleans clarinet and the heart-rending vocalisations of the southern blues trumpet.

This remarkable man is now with us again for thee weeks. A lifetime in the nightworld of show business, where blacks are acts and not men and only folding money is counted, has taught him to hide his intellectualism behind the mask of a courtly dresser and an expert on the women. It emerges in a certain bland ambiguity of his style (Ellington is a gift to students of ambiguity) and in his persistent musical wit. Perhaps it has also taught him to underrate his public, for at the Festival Hall he gave us the jazz equivalent of what a symphony orchestra would do if called to perform at a Butlin camp. But British jazz fans are probably more highbrow than the Ellington band, or perhaps more aware of a distinction which the Duke, who has an occasional fondness for cream-chocolate music, does not recognise. However, as the band has no prepared programme, it will no doubt adapt itself to the local demands. It is still unique and marvellous, though one of the Ellington musicians felt that, after a week's break, it was not yet quite played in again. This was, I think, a mistaken and unnecessary modesty. The Ellington musicians play, as the Moscow Art Theater acts, in a class of their own.

Blue Note

At a time when New York reports that 'religio-LPs enter big-time stakes' ('album interest has suddenly focused on the religious kick') we are apt to search nervously for grains of comfort in the stubbly fields of jazz and pop music. We may find some in the fact that the current list of the ten best-selling jazz LPs/EPs in Britain contains two discs of authentic, uncompromising and uncompromised blues singers: the late Leroy Carr (*Treasures of*

North American Negro Music, and the Terry-McGhee team, accompanied by Chris Barber. This advance of the blues is not unexpected. It is nevertheless a triumph for the small if influential band of fanatics which has for years systematically set out to infect an indifferent public with its own devotion to this difficult art; among them Humphrey Lyttelton, who has twice combined with Jimmy Rushing, and Chris Barber, who has pursued a fixed policy of importing blues and gospel singers for his band. So far as one can see Mr Barber gets nothing but spiritual satisfaction from these imports: it is the blues-singers who benefit by the chance to sing with what is (to the puzzlement of several critics) the most successful band in show business today. Few of those who came to hear the Barber band at the St Pancras Town Hall on Monday had ever heard, or even heard of, McKinlay Morganfield ('Muddy Waters') who also appeared on the bill. But it is a safe bet that henceforth this blues-singer, like his predecessors, will have a public of his own.

Muddy Waters, as his flamboyant trade-name suggests, practices a type of singing as yet unfamiliar over here. Rushing stands four-square on the floor, swaying his mighty bulk gently, and calling out his beautifully swung lines with ease, relaxation and equanimity preferably against a big band (*Little Jimmy Rushing and the Big Brass,* Philips LP). The late Big Bill Broonzy sang for the feeling of the words. Muddy Waters is a mannered, not to say a mannerist, singer who constructs patterns of voice and electric guitar, which make their emotional effect by systematically bombarding the audience with the loudest and bluest of blue sounds: a flamenco-sounding blues man. He is a large sleek-haired gypsy-like artist; at any rate he has the calculating air of the gypsy musician bending over the audience figuring how far and in what direction to let out the emotional stops. Not so his accompanist and half-brother, Mr Otis Spand, a chubby little player designed by nature to play the blues on a piano if ever a man was, and who ravishes us by nature as Muddy Waters does by artifice. An impressive team.

There is no getting away from the blues: the most sophisticated and modern players return to it. The fascinating Thelonious Monk drags a somewhat intimidated Gerry Mulligan into them on *Mulligan Meets Monk*. The late Art Tatum's *Trio Blues* can only be described as the *haute école* of piano blues, like Ulanova dancing Russian folk-dances: the whole of this sensational record belongs in every collection. There is no getting away from the blues: and a good thing too.

Count Three

The wise man who enters a formal jazz concert crosses himself, knocks on wood, or, if a rationalist, merely hopes against hope that this time it will come off. But generally it won't. There are very few jazz combinations which can be guaranteed to produce exactly what the public expects when buying its tickets; that is, if the public's expectations are high. One of them is once again among us, and this critic, a natural pessimist, took his seat in the Festival Hall with perfect, and justified, confidence. Count Basie's band did not let us down. What it does is musically modest, even by jazz standards. The 'Kansas City' formula for big band jazz, of which Basie is the master, and which is quite plainly the most workable yet discovered, is based on simplification and not complexity. (I am not struck by some of the cuter arrangements by Neal Hefti.) Out of the 'riff', the simple repeated blues phrase against which the soloist improvises, has come what André Hodeir calls the 'massive phrase', which is the foundation of all the Basie does. There may be higher things in jazz, but if it comes to ensemble swing, there is not, and perhaps never has been, anything like this band. Individually the soloists are often not of the first class. Indeed, they are generally well below Basie's classic early band. But as a team they have relentless rhythmic perfection. That band, even playing pianissimo, can lift people out of their seats like a crane.

To compare it with Ellington's, as superficial observers have done, is grotesque. Beyond the fact that both are 'big bands' by jazz standards—sixteen men in this case—they have nothing in common. Basie is no more like Ellington than Cobbett as a

260

stylist is like James Joyce. Both write prose well, but the one is trying to do a much more difficult thing with it than the other. Ellington is a subtle composer, Basie the leader of a group which has evolved a foolproof version of the big band blues. Ellington's band is a group of touchy prima donnas, Basie's a team of superlative craftsmen, with the collective pride of an élite regiment. (It must be the only band which itself fines players who turn up late). On its day the Ellington band is peerless, but its day is unpredictable. The Basie band, more modest in its ambitions, is utterly predictable, and consequently more consistently praised. What is equally to the point, Ellington is an individualist, Basie in the main stream of jazz. The most remarkable thing about his success is that it is achieved by playing straight unadulterated jazz, without gimmicks and acrobatics, a jazz independent of style in so far as it can absorb players of any style (e.g. the markedly modern Thad Jones and Joe Newman) with perfect ease. Even Joe Williams, with whom I was not much struck on the first visit two years ago, has developed into a first-class big-band ballad singer, though he is still not my ideal of a blues singer.

Travellin' All Alone

Billie Holiday died a few weeks ago. I have been unable until now to write about her, but since she will survive many who receive longer obituaries, a short delay in one small appreciation will not harm her or us. When she died we—the musicians, critics, all who were ever transfixed by the most heart-rending voice of the past generation—grieved bitterly. There was no reason to. Few people pursued self-destruction more wholeheartedly than she, and when the pursuit was at an end, at the age of forty-four, she had turned herself into a physical and artistic wreck. Some of us tried gallantly to pretend otherwise, taking comfort in the occasional moments when she still sounded like a ravaged echo of her greatness. Others had not even the heart to see and listen anymore. We preferred to stay

261

home and, if old and lucky enough to own the incomparable records of her hey-day from 1937 to 1946, many of which are not even available on British LP, to recreate those coarse-textured, sinuous, sensual and unbearable sad noises which gave her a sure corner of immortality. Her physical death called, if anything, for relief rather than sorrow. What sort of middle age would she have faced without the voice to earn money for her drinks and fixes, without the looks—and in her day she was hauntingly beautiful—to attract the men she needed, without business sense, without anything but the disinterested worship of ageing men who had heard and seen her in her glory?

And yet, irrational though it is, our grief expressed Billie Holiday's art, that of a woman for whom one must be sorry. The great blues-singers, to whom she may be justly compared, played their game from strength. Lionesses, though often wounded or at bay (did not Bessie Smith call herself 'a tiger, ready to jump'?), their tragic equivalents were Cleopatra and Phaedra; Billie's was an embittered Ophelia. She was the Puccini heroine among blues-singers, or rather among jazz-singers, for though she sang a cabaret version of the blues incomparably, her natural idiom was the pop song. Her unique achievement was to have twisted this into a genuine expression of the major passions by means of a total disregard of its sugary tunes, or indeed of any tune other than her own few delicately crying elongated notes, phrased like Bessie Smith or Louis Armstrong in sackcloth, sung in a thin, gritty, haunting voice whose natural mood was an unresigned and voluptuous welcome for the pains of love. Nobody has sung, or will sing, Bess's songs from *Porgy* as she did. It was this combination of bitterness and physical submission, as of someone lying still while watching his legs being amputated; which gives such a blood-curdling quality to her *Strange Fruit,* the anti-lynching poem which she turned into an unforgettable art song. (I need hardly say that this superb record, with its companion blues *Fine and Mellow,* is not available on British discs.) Suffering was her profession; but she did not accept it.

Little need be said about her horrifying life, which she de-

262

scribed with emotional, though hardly with factual, truth in her autobiography *Lady Sings the Blues*. After an adolescence in which self-respect was measured by a girl's insistence on picking up the coins thrown to her by clients with her hands, she was plainly beyond help. She did not lack it, for she had the flair and scrupulous honesty of John Hammond to launch her, the best musicians of the Thirties to accompany her—notably Teddy Wilson, Frankie Newton and Lester Young—the boundless devotion of all serious connoisseurs, and much public success. It was too late to arrest a career of systematic embittered self-immolation. To be born with both beauty and self-respect in the Negro ghetto of Baltimore in 1915 was too much of a handicap, even without rape at the age of ten and drug-addiction in her teens. But while she destroyed herself, she sang, unmelodious, profound and heartbreaking. It is impossible not to weep for her, or not to hate the world which made her what she was.

Status Seeking

Every day jazz is becoming culturally more respectable. To be precise, two quite different things are happening simultaneously. One the one hand, there are the usual attempts—more common, for obvious reasons, in the U.S.A. than elsewhere—to give jazz the accolade of accepted culture by putting it into symphonic programmes, summer schools, university courses and the like. On the other, there are the more numerous and significant attempts to make other cultural articles more attractive by borrowing jazz appeal; of which the Sunday TV programme known in the trade as 'Jumping with Jesus' is the most obvious. Messrs Christopher Logue and Charles Fox, whose jazz-and-poetry experiments still re-echo on record, frankly use jazz, among other things, to increase the sparse audience for poetry, though probably without success. But by far the most systematic attempt to draw jazz into the orbit of other arts has been made by the films. In the past two or three years the practice of commissioning film-scores from serious jazz musicians has become almost as fashionable as that of making socially conscious musicals. Several examples are before us now: Ellington's sound-track—his first—for *Anatomy of a Murder,* Mandel-Mulligan's for *I Want to Live,* and, of course, the French ones, of which the most recent and unsuccessful is Thelonious Monk's sound track for Vadim and Vailland's *Les Liaisons dangereuses.*

What has gone wrong with this at first sight exciting collaboration is simple and instructive. Roger Vadim is a technically bright director who, in spite of a good elementary feel for the moods of weather, sex and decadence, has always lacked any sensitiveness to the world around him. He has merely observed that the people he makes films about listen to jazz in between, and sometimes while, making love, and therefore appear to regard jazz as little more than a suitably chosen background noise. So no doubt it is for them, but that is not enough for a film-score, especially not for one of *Les Liaisons dangereuses,* even for a version deprived of most of what made that book terrible and haunting in its original version, the transposition of revolutionary crisis into sexual terms. When Vadim commissioned the Modern Jazz Quartet to do the music for *Sait-on jamais,* John Lewis did the job of fitting the music to the sense and movement of the film for him. But, unlike John Lewis, Thelonious Monk, an eccentric and original composer, is also an almost purely self-contained one, who, one may guess, is not greatly interested in expressing or following moods other than his own, even if he were capable of understanding, or sympathizing with, what the characters in this film are after. In brief, all we observe is the pursuit of absolute logic by means of sex to the occasional accompaniment of music by Thelonious Monk. Good music: Monk is invariably worth listening to. But not a film-score.

Culture makes only a few tentative incursions into the massive programme of *Newport Festival Jazz* which opened at the Festival Hall last Saturday, and that mainly in the performance of Dave Brubeck, whose piano borrows heavily from classical techniques which are perhaps unfamiliar to jazz audiences but otherwise not striking. I am told that at a subsequent concert the Brubeck Quartet came to life. My own view, that its merits are modest, is not modified by a second hearing, though one cannot deny talent and devotion in Paul Desmond, who lectures mildly down his saxophone like an economics don evolving a theory of international trade. However, Joe Morello is a beautifully delicate and elegant drummer, if a very academic one. Brubeck was followed by Dizzy Gillespie in a Somali cap, light-grey suit, hornrimmed glasses and bent trumpet. Mr Gillespie (nobody who plays an instrument with such effortless technical command and musical intelligence should be patronised, even by reviewers) is as old-fashioned and vulgar a showman as Louis Armstrong: a mugger, scene-stealer, a music-hall comedian. He is at the same time an intellectual, and doubtless the only reason why he is no longer, as he once was, the acknowledged chief of the *avant-garde,* is because the fashion there is for a more serious, introverted and humourless type of behaviour. He played everybody else in the programme under the table with contemptuous ease. I rather think that he is a great man.

The Buck Clayton All Stars, who are a seasoned band of campaigners from way back in the Thirties, had some difficulty in establishing themselves after Gillespie, but within a short time their straightforward professional swinging reconquered the audience. Buck Clayton himself, blowing lightly and strongly, a master-craftsman with feeling; Dickie Wells, still a wonderful trombonist; Emmett Berry, clear as only a jazz trumpet can be, and the rest, stood round on the stage like people at a cocktail party, moving casually into an old-fashioned front line to blow the audience out of their seats. The noble Jimmy Rushing after a poor start, finished strongly with the immortal blues *Goin' to Chicago* and *Sent for You Yesterday.* The old stuff is still irresistible.

Culture enters hardly at all into the music of Brownie McGhee and Sonny Terry, the blues-singers who are once again with us. Anyone who does not go to hear them is a fool.

Too Cool

For those of us who are Hindus, Jews or (like so many American jazz modernists) Muslim, the 1950s did not exist. By our own calendars we have a few more years to wait before generalising about the 'character' of the past decade. Still, as we are surrounded by men trying to sum up the past ten years, it is perhaps impolite to advertise our heterodoxy. Very well: what, from the jazz critic's point of view, has been happening since 1950?

Let me make no bones about it. Artistically the Fifties, though producing a far greater quantity of jazz in a far greater number of countries than in any previous decade, were disappointing. American jazz, which is still the only one that really counts, remained parasitic on the achievements of earlier years. The young modernists experimented aimlessly and eclectically, with the incidental results (familiar to students of modern painting and poetry) of making one 'cool' experimenter indistinguishable from several dozen others; but the only innovations which retained their power were those of Parker, Gillespie, Monk, and the men of the Forties. The most important jazzplayer of the decade, and the one who best typifies it—Miles Davis—is an altogether lesser man than those who dominated earlier: an Armstrong or a Parker. He is a beautiful, melancholy, technically rather limited individualist, but no *chef d'école,* though the leader of an exceptionally fruitful small group. The most talented composer-leader of the period, John Lewis of the Modern Jazz Quartet, has confined his great gifts to the interior decoration of a few musical drawing-rooms. Compared to the vast mansions which were still being built and furnished by that old lion of the Twenties, Duke Ellington, and the ruthless *Bauhaus* explorations of that pioneer of the Forties, Thelonious Monk, Lewis's structures look pretty flimsy.

The Fifties did not even produce many new musicians of stature, a fact underlined by the long list of eminent obituaries during the decade: Bechet, Lester Young, Billie Holiday, Tatum, Catlett, Baby Dodds, among the older styles; Parker, Navarro, Clifford Brown among the moderns. Old talents were rediscovered or appreciated—Monk among the moderns, Buck Clayton, Vic Dickenson and several veterans of the Thirties—but there were few genuinely new faces.

Most of this sterility was due to a wholly disastrous desire to intellectualize jazz, to make it academically respectable, and at

266

ease among the conservatoires, summer schools and biennales. Respectability is the death of a music which exists because it is a protest against artistic and social orthodoxy, and which operates in a way wholly different from 'straight' music. (Respectability does not even pay dividends: the man who, in the Fifties, became—with Paul Robeson and Kwame Nkrumah—the best-respected black in the world, was an old-fashioned jazz entertainer, Louis Armstrong.) Fortunately for jazz the musical failure of status-seeking became steadily more obvious. The jazz tradition, expelled by the front door, re-entered by the back. The reputation of the Fifties has been at least partly saved by what will, in retrospect, seem the most important phenomenon of their jazz history: the return to the blues.

Unlike the 'revival' movement of the Forties, which petered out in the Fifties (except among the young European public), this was no archeological reconstruction of the past. The blues which fertilised jazz, including the most experimental and 'far out', was the contemporary urbanised black folk-music and gospel song which, thanks to the vast teenage commercial boom of the middle Fifties, enjoyed a fantastic popular vogue in the debased form of rock and roll. It is no accident that many of the 'hard blowers' among modern saxophonists play close to this style, that new musicians (like Coltrane and Ray Charles) have been drawn from the rhythm-and-blues field, and that connections with hot gospelling sects are today a valuable qualification for a jazz-player. Jazz is when men blow out their souls, and not merely musical figures. That is why Bix Beiderbecke is remembered, not because he 'used higher intervals of a chord as a melody line and backed them with appropriately related changes', thus anticipating Bird Parker. It is to the credit of the Fifties' jazz that, while not abandoning any of its technical sophistication, it began to rediscover this fact.

Miles Away

The most elusive of jazz musicians has once again escaped us. The trumpeter Miles Davis, who was recently to have opened a

British tour, remains the only major living jazz artist whom we have not heard in the flesh, for reasons which are as vague and complex as all excuses for not turning up in show-business. Under normal circumstances this would be no reason for writing about him, but Davis is the sort of wraith-like artist whose characteristics are merely emphasised by his absence. What the devil is there to him? Something, clearly, or else he would not have topped numerous popularity and critics' polls in various countries—lately even in traditional Britain—ahead of Louis Armstrong or even the technically far superior Dizzy Gillespie. But what? The question is in its way as difficult to answer about him as about Lawrence of Arabia, and for analogous reasons. The 'image' of both men seems so much bigger than their measurable achievement.

Davis is a player of surprisingly narrow technical and emotional range; perhaps outside traditional blues-players the most limited artist to have achieved so high a reputation. Moreover, as has been pointed out, even within that range most of his records are not very good. A handful of tracks in 1949–50 established him. A series of carefully spaced records since 1957 confirmed him; but even this latest, and by common consent most fruitful, phase of his art contains some notable failures such as his leaden and dragging *Porgy and Bess.* (On the other hand, on much of *Milestones* and some of *Kind of Blue,* it contains genuinely imperishable stuff.) And yet, what even the worst of his mature records radiate, and what almost certainly explains Miles's remarkable success, is an absolutely unmistakable sound and mood. The sound, at its most characteristic, is a very slow, ghostly, muted, faraway lyricism rather like what we might have expected if Tennyson had blown a jazz solo instead of writing 'Tithonus.' The mood, as one might expect, is one of total introversion and ranges from a reflective melancholy to naked desolation; but these sound as though felt by someone who, though not suffering from nightmares, is never quite awake. It is a sleepwalker's art, a lonely sound which plays before, after and beside, but rarely *with* other players. It is quite unforgettable. Film-critics have an almost infinite capacity for

268

not noticing sound-tracks, but when Miles Davis did the accompaniment to a recent French thriller (recorded as *Lift to the Scaffold,* as usual on Fontana), Miss C. A. Lejeune did notice it. She said there was too much brass. It is a genuine if unorthodox tribute to Miles's power to project himself, all the more so as there is only one trumpet on the film-track and as Miles rarely raises it above his customary remote echo-sound.

What else is there besides this strange personality whose power lies in Davis's uncompromising hostility to the outer world? A genuine talent for improvising long, simple, often hauntingly beautiful arias, sometimes against backgrounds scored by Gil Evans. A gift, unexpected in so essentially uncooperative an artist, for inspiring the musicians who play with him in the small groups which are his natural habitat. The rare ability to suggest vistas beyond the sound of his horn, stretching into some sad sort of infinity. I do not think that he is a great artist, because as yet he lacks both the tragic and the comic dimension. But there are few more genuine poets in jazz, and no player who would make better background music for an exhibition of romantic art. The present vogue for him is justified; but I should feel happier if the young men and women for whom jazz is the only adequate expression of their view of life, chose for their symbol a player whose art was less close to self-pity and the denial of life.

Manhattan Solo

When good Americans die they go to Paris, but when good jazz-fans die they unquestionably go to New York; it is to be hoped with a lot of celestial folding-money in their pocket, for this city is no bargain. On any given evening, somewhere between the Battery and the Harlem River, about three quarters of all living jazz musicians whose names are known to the foreigner can be heard or seen. Like everything else in this astonishing stone battleship of a city—the twin peaks of the midtown and downtown skyscrapers are its turrets—the concentration of jazz is awe-inspiring. And yet like so much else in New York, it has little organic connection with the city. Jazz is just there, a minority among the other minorities whose sum-total makes up the town, though the increasing conversion of Manhattan into a black and Puerto Rican borough will make it sound louder as time goes on.

To be precise, New York jazz is at least two minorities; and it is disturbing that they have so little relation with each other. Uptown there is the jazz of Harlem (the one that does not even get advertised in *The New Yorker,* otherwise a faithful guide to the music). This is the sort of noise you hear coming out of the dark belly of the *L Bar* on Broadway and West 148th, the visceral sound of Marlowe Morris's rhythmic organ-playing, rather like crystallised glue, or in the *Top Club* on West 145th, which is a simple minded place where men to go drink, girls to hustle and bartenders to give short measure. A little band, led by a former dancer, operates on the stand between the bar and the tables with two poorish sax players, a splendid swinging trombone called Buster Cooper and a handsome sweating shaven-headed entertainer, Titus Turner, who sings ballads, shuffles, but above all shouts some very gratifying fast city blues with comedy effects. It is not very ambitious music, but by God the place jumps and the clients at the bar laugh and stomp their feet as men ought to do when they are enjoying themselves. Those who listen to this music are not 'fans'; they are just people who like to have some entertainment while they drink. Those who play it are craftsmen and showmen, who accept the facts of life in the jungle with disconcerting calm. 'The best drummers', says an eminent trumpeter over a drink, 'are either working or in jail'. Maybe they are, but this is the kind of statement which visiting Englishmen have to take time to digest.

A few miles downtown is the other kind of jazz, the *avant-garde.* Let me make no bones about it. This is by far the most impressive jazz played in New York today. Much of it is no doubt disappointing. John Coltrane at the *Jazz Gallery* is, like so many sax players, in urgent need of sub-editing. Dizzy Gillespie, at the same place, makes his concessions to the higher culture by not actually clowning, but he still refrains from using those incomparable gifts which make him potentially the greatest jazz musician alive. But Ornette Coleman at the *Five Spot* (in the confines of the Bowery) is a deeply impressive artist. The far-out boys do him an injustice by insisting on the revolutionary character of the sounds which, in defiance of all the rules of all musical games, he produces out of his plastic alto-sax, and which can only be described in words which carry unwanted overtones of depreciation: squeaking, neighing, honking and suchlike. Widening the technical range of an instrument is not enough to make a player more than a freak. The unforgettable thing about this very dark, soft-handed man playing with a vertical fold over his nose. Is the passion with which he blows. I have heard nothing like it in modern jazz since Parker. He can and does play the chorus of a standard straight—with an intense, voiced, lamenting feeling for the blues which lays this critic flat on his back. He swings. Beside him his trumpeter and pupil Don Cherry sounds a thin piper of experimental exercises. Coleman is a big thing in jazz, and it is to the credit of New York that it has recognised him in a few months, after years of lonely playing in the wilderness of the West.

But who has recognised him? The public at the *Five Spot* is overwhelmingly young, white, and intellectual or bohemian. Here are the jazz fans (white or black) with the 'Draft Stevenson' buttons, lost over their $1.50 beer. If Coleman were to blow in *Small's Paradise* in Harlem, it would clear the place in five minutes. Musicians such as he are, it seems, as cut off now from the common listeners among their people as Webern is from the public at the Filey Butlin's. They depend on those who are themselves alienated, the internal emigrants of America. And their tragic paradox is, that the value of what they blow lies not where they are going, but where they are coming from. The tragedy of modern jazz, as of most modern art, is that it moves further away from its roots.

271

Intellectuals are at present more strongly in favour of San Francisco than ever before. It is very beautiful and, as American cities go, untypical. Krushchev was welcomed here, the local students have organised demonstrations both against the un-American Committee and the American Legion (which has retaliated by reaffirming the guilt of Sacco and Vanzetti), and across the bay in Berkeley they have actually bred a strain of courteous cops. Instead of mobsters. San Francisco has a water-side union run by reds. Its beats, looking indistinguishable from their European equivalents, produce the largest amount of bad poetry for any square mile of the world, but still, poetry. By common consent, it is a good place to live in and a holiday from the rat-race; a place still haunted by the shades of the age before 'togetherness', by the giant robber barons of the Pacific, the over-lifesize labour heroes of the Thirties. Why, in defiance of all right-thinking sociology, at least one local radio station still angles its commercials frankly at 'the working-man'. (I need hardly say that it plays, not jazz, but 24 hours a day of hill-billy music.)

Whether another aspect of San Francisco, which affects the jazz-lover, rouses sympathy or not, depends on taste: it is 'a tight city'. There was a time when this place was as wide-open as any in the West. The citizens still take pride in recalling the occasion when Eisenhower, returning from Korea, gave a special salute to a particularly delirious group of female voters who happened to be the girls from the city's leading brothel. For there was action along the bay, plenty of action. This is so no longer. Mayor Christopher (a Greek—the cops and the graft are Irish) has shut the place down, and the far-seeing elements are already worrying whether the combined pressure of Reno and Las Vegas, which have every interest in seeing other towns moral, will keep the lid permanently half-closed. But it is a well-known fact that jazz flourishes best in wide-open towns, for that is where there is most employment for musicians.

For a city which enjoys a world reputation as a jazz centre.

San Francisco therefore possesses surprisingly few, and not very outstanding, resident musicians, and not much more than half-a-dozen jazz clubs, including the North Beach jazz-and-poetry type joints. What it does possess is a massive, enthusiastic and knowledgeable jazz public—mostly young, intellectual or bohemian—and therefore a power to make reputations which is much appreciated in the business. It made Brubeck and Cannonball Adderley. More recently (and characteristically) it has made chiefly the stars of the savage, jazz-impregnated social satire which flourishes, of all places, in night-clubs, Mort Sahl and Lennie Bruce. Sahl stands for wit, intellect, self-consciousness and hatred of the Right; Bruce who disappears behind his mimicries—for emotion, no self-criticism, horror and hatred of the squares. Sahl can, at a pinch, be understood by anyone who knows about America and psychoanalysis: Bruce is almost incomprehensible except to those who are steeped in the world of what Bernard Wolfe's Broadway novel called the 'late risers': the agents and acts, the musicians and junkies, the hustlers. But, like the other artists made by San Francisco, these too have followed the money east and are now only occasional visitors.

There is one exception to this exodus, San Francisco made the New Orleans revival in the early 1940s, but the musicians are still here, living off expense-account advertising men and the solid, but thinning, ranks of those who were young in 1940: a closed and passionate community. This public has provided a haven for meritorious oldtimers who have made their homes here: Kid Ory on the Embarcadero, Marty Marsala at the *Kewpie Doll* and the marvellously undimmed Earl Hines at the *Hangover*, though he has had to camouflage himself as a Basin Street type, which suits his piano-style about as well as the Petrushka music would suit a real fun-fair. But there is no limit to what a public with preconceived notions will impose on an artist. I have lately watched the legendary blues-shouter Sam 'Lightning' Hopkins performing to a packed, young, washed and wholesome house at the University of California Folk Music Festival. Hopkins, a lean, quietly wolfish character in very light slacks, white-and-black shoes, dark jacket, bow tie and dark glasses, was clearly at

273

a loss. They had given him a proper folky guitar instead of an electric one. They were selecting a repertoire for him, in tune with the folkniks. He hadn't quite settled down to the new act, which was shaping towards the elderly frail black preacher from the South, full of folky wisdom. He sang well, though not juiced up enough to be in really high gear, casually, in a voice both gravelly and soft, with a light, lifting guitar. Occasionally the voice bit like a pick. But he did not holler. That blue, rebellious and desperate shout from across the Texas tracks was no longer there.

For the rest, jazz in San Francisco is what happens in the beat joints (far-out, but not so good as London), what is on the two local all-jazz radio stations, and what comes on tour—chiefly the Ellington band, which followed the girls with the 44 inch bust in *Facks II* (business is business) until the place was closed down for non-payment of taxes. This was the jazz of our dreams, in the place where it belongs, melting a hard assembly of middle-aged lawyers, doctors, journalists and fixers like traditional brides. It reconciles me to much of the U.S., even to the memory of Louis Armstrong, on the eve of his sixtieth birthday, giving the Studebaker commercial over the air, 'tomming' as they say 'from the heart.'

The Old School

In America they would have had it the other way round, but in our tradition-minded country Jazz at the Philharmonic (Festival Hall) respects seniority. Cannonball Adderley's Quintet opened: an up-and-coming group led by a good saxophonist who has made modern jazz palatable to a mass public and is capable of more than he has yet given us. A collection of venerable and famous names closed the show. The most dazzling among them were Jo Jones, a bald extrovert drummer of vast and merited reputation, and unshakable rhythmic reliability, who ought to inspire several new clichés ('light as the touch of Jo Jones brushes'), and Benny Carter. Jazz critics feel about Carter as artists feel about some master of line like, say, Ingres: boundless, but vaguely cool, admiration. This is why he has rarely of late had his full critical due. He stood before us, watching the audience across his alto like a Latin maître d'hotel his dining-room, and blew a single, firm perfectly judged line of sound at us the way a champion skater performs his figures. If Haydn's Prince Esterhazy had ever required a jazz player to liven up his musical entertainments, he might have done worse than choose someone like this cool, gentlemanly, extra-ordinarily original artist, who last stayed with us before the war, when *The New Statesman* did not yet report jazz concerts.

Coleman Hawkins, looking like an ambassador in a vodka advertisement who happens to be holding a tenor-sax, blew like a young man dissatisfied with all previous approaches to the instrument, even to some extent his own; and he practically invented it. This evening it didn't quite come off, but greatness must be saluted. Unlike him, Don Byas did not fight the natural lyricism of the tenor. Roy Eldridge, perhaps below his best, was on trumpet.

The most impressive performers of the evening, technically, were J. J. Johnson who plays the trombone as if it were a trumpet, and the unique Dizzy Gillespie (trumpet), the mystery man of jazz. Nothing is beyond this fantastically talented and intelligent musician, the first *chef d'école* of the modern jazz revolutionaries. Then why is it that his dead contemporary, Charlie Parker, is a legend, and his live co-revolutionary, Thelonious Monk, is once again an acknowledged musical innovator of stature, while Dizzy is merely the most dazzling trumpeter in the world? Why did Miles Davis, who is a beginner on his instrument compared to Gillespie, impress critics and public on his recent British tour as few other visitors have done, while Gillespie merely creates an impression of unsurpassable brilliance? Is it because this extremely reticent and devious artist hesitates to do the one thing which can raise a jazz musician to the very top, to reveal his soul? I do not know. But if ever he were to give us what is in him, a great many prevailing critical judgments would be sharply revised.

275

The age of Billy Graham and MRA is not the ideal one for a great religious artist. At any rate after Mahalia Jackson's third song two elderly ladies, who looked more familiar with church services than the rest of the audience, walked out, leaving the Albert Hall to the sinners who can recognise the most majestic voice of faith they are likely to hear in our generation.

Mahalia Jackson, a huge, firm-fleshed woman whose face, radiating an internal beauty in repose, contorts with the love of the Lord when she sings, is one of those artists who are beyond good or bad taste. Musically and textually most gospel songs are sorry doggerel and distinctly inferior to the godless blues which Miss Jackson steadfastly refuses to sing. There are many musicians who would give her a more swinging accompaniment than Miss Mildred Falls, whose large light-blue figure sits by Miss Jackson's broad expanse of shining mauve. None of this matters, for Mahalia has the awe-inspiring gift of communicating the original and true meaning of words. When she sings the word 'soul', we know what it is. When she sings 'Oh Lord my God', sending out her leonine contralto like a gigantic whip, or 'You never walk alone', placing each syllable separately like a pillar of steel, we are with her in Zion. When she sings *I Found the Answer* ('Now the sun is shining for me each day'), we believe her.

Her answer is joy, a much rarer emotion than one might think, for it requires us not merely to accept life (which most of us eventually do) but to believe that it is or could be good. Mahalia's repertoire, which is very much her own, though as a solid show-woman she listens to advice about audience preferences, contains little at present about heaven and nothing about hell, but plenty about trust, certainty and exaltation. Even the traditional spirituals she sings at present, with the rocking drive of a big band, are those of confidence rather than longing; *Down by the Riverside, Joshua Fit the Battle of Jericho, Elijah, Jesus Met a Woman at the Well,* and especially that gospel cavalry charge, *Oh Didn't It Rain.* No doubt the joy of the gospel song is all the more massive because it contrasts with the uncertainty of real life. No doubt it is religious, because only in the spirit can the poor and mistreated be really free. As Mahalia sings (varying a familiar verse of English folksong): 'If religion was a thing that money could buy, the rich would live and the poor would die'. But it is joy nevertheless. It is unequivocally for life, a rare trumpet which gives a certain sound.

Her astonishing voice can produce anything from a small, round, convinced sound in the upper register to a deep, soft chest-tone of immediately communicated ecstasy and that unforgettable jubilant archangel call. As a good professional she knows her instrument, tending to finish each song with a characteristic effect—generally a deep-smeared, rough-edged, bent sound placed somehow obliquely to the note it represents. As a good blues singer, she sings exclusively for the words, guided only by the basic pulse of the gospel beat. She is perhaps a shade less florid and more tranquil than in the past, with less of a tendency to build her solo as a series of increasingly hot choruses. But her native sense of swing is an unerring as ever, her power to announce the good news in the idiom of our century best designed for the communication of emotion as great as ever. We can congratulate ourselves on two things: that this very great woman and artist is universally appreciated as the queen of gospel singers, and that she has done us the honour of visiting this country.

Reluctant Monk

In France the hall would have been wrecked. As this was London, those who plainly regarded Mr Thelonious Monk as a clumsy bore merely walked out in a well-bred but marked manner. This was comprehensible, for Mr Monk, a sardonic and fey person at best, ostentatiously lost interest very soon, or else retired behind his private fortifications. Yet anyone who fails to hear him will miss one of the few original achievements in jazz.

Of the three or four real jazz composers Monk is the most primitive and limited, because nearest to the improvising soloist. Some great players, especially technically successful ones, soon

277

discover what they can do and go on doing it, like Johnny Hodges, who plays today as he did in 1931. Luckily. Some, like Parker or the Beiderbecke of bop—Fats Navarro, suffer physically from their inability to leap over the chasm which separates the man who blows from the man who can also get others to express his ideas. Monk, perhaps because his piano technique is inadequate for his ideas, has had to leap that chasm. But what preoccupies him as a composer is what fascinates the innovating soloist: experiments in timing—such as that extraordinary retarded, limping rhythm of his; instrumental adventures—he makes his bass play, at excessive length, like a blues guitar; but above all the ceaseless exploration of phrase and harmony. Fortunately his own compositions are mostly based on simple themes, which do not lose their shape even when taken to pieces in every conceivable way. He is not unaffected by current fashion, as witness his return to the oldest and most elemental figures of the piano blues. It is merely his curiosity, his search for new, even accidental, effects that never changes.

All this we knew and sometimes regretted, for the line between planned experiment and artistic abdication or incompetence is hazy, as in modern painting; and Monk has neither the technical mastery nor the staying power which enables an Ellington or John Lewis to maintain a steady level. Nor has he their orchestral sense. But what Monk's Quartet revealed at the Festival Hall in at least two pieces was a self-discipline, a taut classicism (greatly assisted by the admirable Lester Youngish tenor of Charlie Rouse) and a capacity not merely to indicate the directions of jazz advance, but to occupy, in a formally satisfying way, some of the new territory. And how many people are there today who can do this?

Not Art Blakey's Jazz Messengers who shared the bill with Monk. They are a first-class group with the strength and weakness of the 'blowing session': drive and virtuosity, on one hand, undisciplined trailing solos, rudimentary arrangements or clichés on the other. A properly arranged 'Dat There', one of the finest modern numbers I have heard in a long time, showed what they can do. Their chief asset is Art Blakey, a fantastic but somewhat obtrusive drummer who keeps an iron control over the rest, and a cadaverous young trumpeter of great promise, Lee Morgan.

Hello, Satan

Who writes the bony poetry of the blues? Nobody knows. A sung blues is a selection and combination of lines and phrases, polished and fitted together by a succession of singers into an aesthetic whole as unplanned and coherent as an old-fashioned small-town square. To seek a single author is to miss the point. Except with Robert Johnson, the greatest of the Mississippi singers, and the only blues shouter whose voice is identifiably that of an individual poet. Virtually nothing is known of him except that he was born and raised on a plantation in Robinsville in the Delta, was probably killed by a woman at the age of 21 (or, as some claim, 30) and recorded 29 blues at two sessions in 1936–37 before disappearing from sight. Sixteen of them, including the fantastic ones from the second session, have now been reissued on a long-awaited disc in the Classic Jazz Masters series (BBL 7539) by Philips, the big company which reissues the most interesting jazz at present, and to which we also owe the marvellous John Hammond's *Spirituals to Swing* concert of 1938 (TFL 5187-8) and the Bessie Smith Blues of 1923–4. Johnson is not easily appreciated, for his Deep Southern accent is almost incomprehensible without repeated listening. One would willingly trade the anecdotage of the sleeve-notes for the only information which really matters—the text of his haunted songs.

The special and identifiable tone of Johnson's poetry is that of a man driven by fate and his own emotions. Both are personified in symbols and monsters standing by his side:

> *I got to keep moving, I got to keep moving.*
> *Blues falling down like hail, blues falling down like hail.*
> *I can't keep no money, hellhound on my trail,*
> *Hellhound on my trail, hellhound on my trail.*

His technique is not original. Visionary passion presses the usual worn images to a factual precision which gives them life. The blues is not merely personified ('Good morning blues, blues how do you do?'), it is a real figure—'Blues walking like a man'. The singer is not merely a man on the road, like any other:

> *I got stones in my passway and my road seem dark at night,*
> *Got stones in my passway and my road seem dark at night.*
> *I have pains in my heart, they have taken my appetite.*

For Johnson is doomed. His day is spent in the company of the devil:

> *Early this morning when you knocked upon my door—*
> *I said 'Hello Satan, I believe it's time to go'.*

He knows he is not only unhappy but evil, as the mentally enslaved black believes himself not merely oppressed but rightly oppressed, for white is good and dark bad. Like that of the medieval vagabond artists, his tragedy is the Christian one of damnation. The cruelty of his god is the price he pays for his poetry, the brief and uncertain pleasure of women his only relief:

> *I can tell the wind is running, leaves shaking on the tree,*
> *   shaking on the tree.*
> *I can tell the wind is running, leaves shaking on the tree.*
> *All I need's my little sweet woman to keep me company.*

Johnson sings in a high African voice, neither fast nor dragging, accompanying himself with those frighteningly definitive blues sounds on the guitar. There is energy in his song but no hope. The world and the soul are his jail; and though he does not say so, his people's. He has been dead these 25 years, but attention must still be paid to such a man. He has written his own epitaph:

> *You may bury my body, ooh, down by the highway side.*
> *So my old evil spirit can get a Greyhound bus and ride.*

God

Ray Charles comes to us with a greater preliminary flourish of typewriters than any previous jazz artist from the U.S.A. not excepting Louis Armstrong. He comes not as one but as three persons: a jazz and blues man, a pop star and a hipster saint, fourth in line to Lester Young, Billie Holiday and Charlie Parker. (All he still lacks is a holy nickname like Prez, Lady or Bird, though I understand in extremist circles a claim is being staked for 'God'.) The combination is not only powerful but unique. Charles as a pop star is *big* by the standards of real size in that field, which are financial. He is said to make more than £300,000 a year, and even when we make allowances for publicity agents' attitudes to figures, he is a very rich artist, and quite certainly the biggest pop seller among those formed purely in the jazz mould, and the richest of those unhappy outsider figures whom the hipsters choose as their culture-heroes. It is the combination of the minority and majority elements in him which makes him so significant a phenomenon, though also one very difficult to judge lucidly.

Fortunately Charles's rise to the top has been so rapid that it is still possible to recall him clearly in his pre-mythical phase. I experienced him first in 1960, in Oakland, California, when he was already as big a draw as anyone in the black market—especially among the 'down home' immigrants from the South and South-West—but still totally unknown to all whites except a tiny handful of jazz and blues-lovers and some teenagers. His rapport with the black middle class was slight. I heard him at a function organised for this king of public, which approximately recalled the atmosphere at a Golders Green *bar mitzvah* party, and he went dead. On the other hand, in the same town, among the 4,000 at a rock-and-roll dance, who treated our contingent of a couple of dozen whites politely as unpersons, his performance was sensational.

The dance was in effect a secular revival meeting to celebrate sex instead of God, and even today his strongest numbers deliberately use the tried hot-gospel machine for whipping up divine

281

ecstasy, to heat the bedrooms of our imagination. A pure gospel-number, shared between the call of Charles at the piano and the response of the four very undivine-looking Raelets, and apparently about the Lord, will end with the consciously shocking words: 'I'm talking about my baby'. Old-fashioned worldly blues-singers like Big Bill Broonzy disapproved of this tearing down of moral frontiers. 'He's a mess,' he said, with some justification. 'He's a-crying sanctified. He's mixing the blues with the spirituals. I *know* that's wrong. You shouldn't mix them. He's got a good voice, but it's a church voice.' At all events the congregation in Oakland reacted as though a prophet were present. There was not much dancing, merely a general, silent, massed slow heaving, broken by occasional cries of assent and release. It was an extraordinary experience, deeply moving and disturbing.

The audience at the Finsbury Astoria was not like that—although, since Charles has never quite captured the *Jukebox Jury* public over here, it had some affinities with Oakland, being largely an audience of jazz-lovers rather than pop fans. The tension was lower, and Charles had also diluted his material with the pop-market numbers which have made him such a wide seller, such as ballads and a sort of lachrymose hipster hillbilly. It was possible to judge him dispassionately for about half the time. He is, let us make no mistake about it, a very great star. His alto-playing is undistinguished and his piano-playing far from outstanding. Nor is he technically a great blues-singer, though he is an entirely genuine one. But his voice has star quality to an astonishing degree. Since Charles is blind and therefore virtually immobile—except for a few tentative jerky steps and a shifting of his dark glasses—it must carry the entire burden of his communication with the audience. (The big band is, or was on this occasion, nowhere near as tight and electric as such a talented group should be, and the Raelets are mere adjuncts to Ray.) But the voice is remarkable, soft and furry or abrasive at will, at times high, clear and ecstatic, keeling over into the strangled frenzy of the top-gear preacher, or full of a hot desperation. It would not be right to say that he manages it with the light, contemptuous certainty of a champion, though his professionalism with a microphone is obvious. Ray Charles exists in that border world of the great performers in which the distinction between sincerity and insincerity, between deliberate effect and living emotion, has lost its meaning. What he does coolly, plays on his emotions as well as ours; what he does in passion, comes out as showmanship. The *monstre sacré* is a frightening spectacle. The hunched, thin, unhappy blind man who can sing 'Careless Love' (which is about something quite different), milking all the public's emotion out of the repeated, dragged out, at once ambiguous and clear lines 'Once I was blind, but now I can see', can make even the insensitive shiver.

There is no mystery about why he has maintained the full loyalty of the jazzmen from among whom he has sprung. What he sings and plays is the blues, ancient and modern, and they can comfort themselves with the thought that he proves what they have always known, that what they feel in jazz and the blues can capture the millions. There is no mystery about his popular appeal. Once the masses have become acclimatised to the idiom of the blues, as they have been, thanks to rock-and-roll, it is inconceivable that a man of Charles's gifts should not mow down like grass any audience with the slightest experience of adult emotions. And there is no mystery about his cult among the hipsters, for a blind orphan black, in trouble about narcotics and putting down authentic jazz, exactly fits their specifications. It must be said, however, that he is neither as original nor as great an artist as the other gods in the hipster pantheon. Unlike Billie Holiday and Parker, and in spite of the publicity, he is *not* a genius, and is intelligent enough to be the first to admit it.

What links the audience at the Finsbury Astoria with the Oakland immigrants and the American teenage record-buyers is not merely the quality of the voice. It is the idiom of the black big-city ghetto, which has become, through jazz and its influence on popular music, the idiom of our modern Western urban sub-civilisations. It is the nature of the song: the cry of the victim, the defeated, the outcast, the lost and isolated individual for whom nothing of real value remains except private intensities of feeling. For them the senses have replaced the sense of life, and Ray Charles is what Marx said of religion, the heart of a heartless world—our own. One must salute talent when one sees it. Charles is a star. But one cannot escape the thought that a world in which he is a star is an unhappy and a sick world.

Duke

Duke Ellington has at last decided that the English are grown up, at any rate those numerous English who are prepared to cancel even their skiing holidays to listen to him. Slowly, because he is as used to morons as anyone else in the business of popular entertainment, of which he has formed part for 40 years, he has realised that London need not be fed violin solos of *Autumn Leaves,* or even pot-pourris of past Ellingtoniana. His present programme does contain one casually strung together medley and (luckily) a few of those simple, sophisticated and indestructible tunes which for many of us mean Ellington: 'Things Ain't What They Used to Be' (superlatively carried by Johnny Hodges), 'Caravan', 'Stompy Jones'. But most of his programme was new, unfamiliar and, which shows an even greater confidence in the audience, high-brow. The band plays four pieces from a new and as yet uncompleted *Far Eastern Suite,* the product of last year's government-sponsored tour to Asia, two pieces from Ellington's incidental music to the Stratford, Ontario *Timon of Athens* and, above all, the rarely heard *Tone Parallel to Harlem,* a long suite which is, by common agreement, Ellington's most ambitious and successful composition.

Possibly the old master has extended his admirers—an unvoguish assembly with a high proportion of spectacles and adults and a low quota of beards and girls—a little too far. 'It's more like an LP,' was one opinion overheard in the foyer, and the applause was sometimes dutiful rather than mad. Yet the professional musicians, students and young technicians, the now middle-aged accountants, salesmen, doctors and teachers, who make up the hard core of the Duke's British public, are used to getting a sense of solid satisfaction rather than bacchantic revelry from him—few of them, alas, have heard him on his home ground, a night-club stand—and that certainly is what they all felt. They are wrong. Nothing but wild enthusiasm will do for what Ellington gave us.

His present band, except for the reeds, is not without weaknesses on the solo side. There is no trombone voice to balance the sentimental Lawrence Brown, nor the sort of trumpet note which Shorty Baker provided so well. Cootie Williams, back in the band after many years, brings to it an intense, introverted, primitive blues-cry, an echo of golden-age Armstrong, but what he now plays seems specialised and technically undemanding. Rolf Ericson, a Swede, plays brisk but colourless flugelhorn. Yet the quality of the music and the novelty, which keeps the players on their mettle, more than offset these weaknesses. The Duke, plainly, is in one of his creative periods and the band knows it.

Ellington's strength and weakness is that he is essentially a pop composer. He thinks in images and memories. The word Harlem suggests the first theme of his suite, the bass 'walks' us through our conducted tour of the place, pretty girls turn into pretty tunes. His Far East has much of the Orient of cabarets called Soraya and cinema mood music. He brings to this pop world the astringency—as well as the sentimentality—of the man-about-town, a marvellous cool and skipping wit, and the entire tradition of black music: what is elsewhere mere archaeological excavation, the down-home blues, the creole clarinet of New Orleans, the stride piano of the Twenties, is the living matter of music in the Ellington band of 1964. He brings to it his peculiar genius for orchestral writing. How many composers, live or dead, can get the precise—and planned—effect of the passage in the Harlem suite in which the bass alternates first with Hamilton's liquid clarinet, then with Procope's huskier one, backed by Gonsalves, until the strong entry of the trombones precisely pointed up with the trumpets? Pop-based music does not fly high; emotionally—except where the fate of Ellington's people is at stake—it has its limitations, which come out in the Shakespeare scores. But his pop roots do not prevent him from writing serious music—perhaps the most serious being written in the U.S. Duke Ellington is a great man, a unique figure in the history of modern music. His orchestra will eventually die with him, and records alone will preserve his irreproducible works. Can we afford not to listen to him when he does us the honour to treat us as an audience worthy of him?

New Thing

The penalty of 'art' in our time is that it is supposed to progress, and consequently to develop an avant-garde. The penalty of salesmanship in our time is fashion-change. Since jazz has, for better or worse, come to consider itself an art, and since it has always had to sell itself on the market, it has developed both a belief in the importance of progress, and of an avant-garde, and a cycle of fashion-change. You have got, as they say, to pay your dues.

Jazz began to suffer the consequences of this adjustment to modern culture about the time of the Second World War. Before then its low social status had preserved its independence. There was no special prestige in being a jazz musician, for even within the black ghetto it was not a respectable, though it could be a very prosperous, occupation. The jazz musician was an entertainer, and if his private inspiration did not coincide with the taste of the public or the bookers, he would not be an artist, but merely a janitor or postman. The most eminent of older black musicians still preserve the pattern of behaviour of this professionalism, though sometimes with a considerable admixture of irony. Duke Ellington knows, and knows that by now most of his public knows, that he is a great deal more than a sort of glorified musical valet of the leisure-classes, as in the Cotton Club days, but his public comportment is still that of a Jeeves who humours a public of Bertie Woosters.

Again, though jazz undoubtedly evolved—and much faster than any other kind of music in the twentieth century—it is extremely dangerous to think of its changes as analogous to those of the orthodox arts. Its framework was that of working craftsmen, their object to start with perfection and not novelty as such. For a great many of the older artists, perfection came with personal maturity. Once they had developed 'their' style, they might vary and deepen it, but they hardly thought of changing it, and when they were tempted to do so (as the great Coleman Hawkins was at one time by Bebop), the results were not usually encouraging. That is why the jazz of 1935–40, when the music first reached a satisfactory stage of technical maturity, is still practised by virtually all the musicians who had made their reputations by that period. The lessons and novelties of the later period have been absorbed, but have not been allowed to swamp the basic 'classical' styles: Ellington is once again the great example. Fortunately, they may be heard to this day—from the saxophone of Ben Webster, now on a welcome return visit to this country, from the trumpet of Buck Clayton or the trombone of Vic Dickenson, who have also come back to us, and of course from the mouths of the simpler and older blues-singers like the indestructible Joe Turner. For out of the Kansas City of the 1930s, with which all these excellent visitors are associated, came the most lasting formula for orchestral jazz so far evolved. None of these artists has any bias against more modern developments in jazz, but none of them has the slightest feeling that somehow they ought to have kept up.

The jazz revolution of the early 1940s changed all that, though not quite as radically as it seemed in the great days of Minton's. Dizzy Gillespie himself has quietly returned from the furthest outposts of the avant-garde to a renovated version of classic Swing; but then Gillespie, a remarkably intelligent, ironic and well-balanced artist without the slightest tendency to self-destruction, has always had more in common with the older professional virtuosos than the Charlie Parker Rimbaudians who set the pace for the new movement. Still, from the early 1940s there was for the first time in jazz an avant-garde which cherished its musical revolutionism as such, saw itself as doing the peasantry a favour.

The novelty of the Boppers lay not in the mere fact of experiment. It lay (to quote Sidney Finkelstein) in working out a conscious, sometimes rigid system from the new elements, which in turn reflected a new generation of jazz-players' claim to special status as revolutionary artists. Before Parker, men played jazz, sometimes in older, sometimes in newer ways. After Parker, some of them played 'modern jazz' until new generations of rebels made *them* old-fashioned.

The curious thing is that it took 20 years for this to happen, though not for want of trying. None of the jazz experiments of the late 1940s and 50s produced an accepted corpus of ultra-revolutionism. The most successful of them produced self-contained adaptations of the 'modern' idiom, such as Miles Davis's or the Modern Jazz Quartet's, but not—with the possible brief exception of the 'cool jazz' of the early 1950s—schools. The more deliberately 'progressive' fell flat, though there is now a renewed interest in people like Lennie Tristano as precursors of the 'new thing' of the 1960s. Neither did the attempts to fuse jazz with modern orthodox music ('third stream') start any general stampede in the direction of the symphony orchestra. By the end of the 1950s modern jazz appeared to have settled down, after its exploratory youth, into its own form of traditionalism —hard-swinging, blues- and gospel-influenced neo-Bopping. What passed for novelty was often the rediscovery of long-underrated artists like Thelonious Monk.

Since 1960 a new official avant-garde has appeared. At all events it now has a label, the rather despairing one of 'the new thing', a number of young players in New York following in the steps of the masters (Ornette Coleman, Cecil Taylor, the late Eric Dolphy), a number of sceptics among both musicians and critics, and some non-playing champions like the militant black writer LeRoi Jones, whose book on the blues has attracted deserved praise. As usual, everybody finds it a lot easier to say what the rebellion is against than what it is for. 'It sets aside tonality, the unwavering beat, the conventional chord structure, and improvisation that is chiefly based on chord progressions.' Such definitions are no more helpful than the sibylline statements which jazz avant-gardists have now taken over from the avant-garde painters who used to have a quasi-monopoly of such non-sense, such as: 'For musicians only: time is not speed; it's distance, and sound is measured motion.' If 'the new thing' lasts, we shall no doubt retrospectively discover the rules of the game, since without rules there is no game. 'Freedom' is not a programme, but simply a declaration of the intent to secede.

Meanwhile those of us who do not claim to understand 'the new thing'—including this critic—can merely grasp at two fairly substantial straws. The first is the fact that there *is* a new movement in New York, though very little of it is heard over here except on a few Blue Note or EMI records, and not much is heard in Manhattan because the public does not want to pay for it. We are now clearly past the point when anything that sounded vaguely unfamiliar, like the gimmicky multi-instrumentalism of Roland Kirk, was hailed as a step forward, since the exhaustion of the 1940s idiom was evident.

The second, and more substantial, is the sheer quality of some of the new musicians, such as Ornette Coleman and the more intellectual Cecil Taylor. There is in the best of the new music a ferocious passion (in Coleman often recognisably based on the blues of his native habitat), just as in the worst there is lots of excessively long, loud and undisciplined doodling. There is at its best an ability to find genuinely original and suitable noises for a recognisable human predicament: so much so that 'the new thing' has been called (wrongly) a music of social protest—a musical equivalent, maybe, of Harlem Maoism.

On the other hand, one must make two obvious reservations. The first is that the present 'school' will not necessarily turn out to be the main vehicle for the new departure in jazz. Some of its stars may have neither the technical nor the emotional staying-power to hold a movement together: neither Ornette Coleman nor Sonny Rollins, for instance, have returned audibly better than before from their self-imposed retreats into silence and re-thinking. Some of the more widely publicised 'new thingers', like the saxophonist Archie Shepp, have yet to prove themselves. (Still, it is a promising sign that there are new saxes, for the history of modern jazz can almost be written in terms of a succession of boss reed-players.) Older innovators, who somehow just missed being elevated into *chefs d'école*, like Mingus or Bill Evans, may retrospectively turn out to be equally important.

Finally, 'the new thing' won't determine the future of jazz until the ordinary non-avant-garde players absorb its innovations. Unlike the painting avant-garde, which rests on the prices fetched by individual works, and on patronage, the jazz avant-garde cannot yet be parlayed into prosperity by a few dealers and critics. It has to sell records, and it has to attract a paying public, and so far it is doing neither. Above all, it has to be played by the craftsmen, the way 'modern' jazz was played by the frustrated musicians in rock-and-roll bands. Perhaps it will be, perhaps not. But it does look as though, for the first time since Parker, a fresh phase has begun.

t h i r t e e n

From *The New York Review of Books, 1986–1989*

'Playing for Ourselves' ★

Sometime in the 1950s American popular music committed parricide. Rock murdered jazz. Count Basie describes a moment of the murder in his autobiography. There was

> a heck of a thing going on at a theater down on Fourteenth Street somewhere, and we used to get down there at around eleven o'clock and you couldn't get near the place for the crowd. . . . I remember this and I also remember how things went. The first acts would go on, and the kids would all be

★ This essay originally appeared in *The New York Review of Books* on January 16, 1986, as a review of *Good Morning Blues: The Autobiography of Count Basie* as told to Albert Murray (New York: Random House, 1986) and *The World of Count Basie* by Stanley Dance (New York: Da Capo, 1985).

jammed in there having a ball and applauding and whistling.
Then when it came time for us to go on, just about all of
them would get up and go outside and get their popcorn and
ice cream and everything, and we just played our act to an
almost empty house. Then when we finished our set they
would all come back in. No kidding.

So we would just go downstairs and play poker till it was
time to go on again. That's the way it actually went. Those
kids didn't care anything about jazz. Some of them would
stay and come down front and stand and listen and try to
hear it as long as they could, and we would try fast and slow,
and it made no difference. That was not what they came to
hear. To them we were just an intermission act. That's what
that was. It didn't mean anything but just that. You had to
face it.

If anyone wanted to turn *Good Morning Blues* into a play, this
image of the aging bandleader stoically accepting a deeply resented defeat might make a good curtain. But Basie's career
continued for another thirty years, though his memoir rather
races through them. He did not quite see the current resuscitation
of jazz as the American classical music of the professional middle
class and the dinner music of lower Manhattan Yuppie restaurants. (One can hardly speak of a real revival until the music
ceases to rely primarily on survivors of the days before the
1960s.)

These last decades before he died in 1984 were not the most
distinguished in the career of what was not the greatest big band
in jazz—Basie himself constantly stresses the supremacy of Ellington—but was, in many ways, the quintessential expression
of the populism of jazz; and jazz remains much the most serious
musical contribution of the United States to world culture. Basie
is a central figure both in the golden age of the music which
coincided with the New Deal years and in the discovery of
jazz, hitherto a music of unrespectable poor blacks and hip-flask-
swigging white dancers, as an art to be taken with the utmost
seriousness, and a breeding ground of great artists. The discovery was largely the achievement of political radicals who devoted

themselves passionately and selflessly to the joint cause of the blacks and their music, without, as Basie underlines, exploiting them.[1] In the debates about the history of the American left in the Roosevelt period that are now raging, this achievement in music of the Reds and fellow travelers of the time has not been sufficiently appreciated.

Until it loses itself in the repetitive details of touring and personnel changes, *Good Morning Blues* is therefore of considerable interest to anyone who wishes to understand the evolution of one of the few twentieth-century arts that owe nothing to middle-class culture. And the original Basie band, recognized as the purest expression of big-band swing as soon as it roared out of Kansas City, owed less to the middle class and intellectuals than any other—except, of course, its discovery and training for fame.

It was not much of a "reading band" at its best. In its heyday it used little except head arrangements. "I don't think we had over four or five sheets of music up there at that time," Basie recalls. It was not a respectable band, even by jazz standards. The arranger Eddie Durham, used to the college men in the Lunceford band, found Basie's group too much for him. They "didn't believe in going out with steady black people," in the words of Gene Ramey, whose sketch of the Kansas City atmosphere in Stanley Dance's invaluable collection of interviews, now republished, is one of the best:

> They'd head straight for the pimps and prostitutes and hang out with them. Those people were like a great advertisement for Basie. They didn't dig Andy Kirk. They said he was too uppity. But Basie was down there, lying in the gutter, getting drunk with them. He'd have patches in his pants and everything. All of his band was like that.

This is not the image stressed in *Good Morning Blues,* a notably reticent work in many ways, though in fact the attraction of the milieu of gambling, good times, women, and, not least, whiskey, constantly shines through the cracks in the autobiographical façade of the elder jazz statesman. His book brings out, perhaps more clearly than any other memoir, both how attractive and how important to the development of the music was that floating, nomadic community of professional black musicians, living on the self-contained and self-sufficient little islands of the popular entertainers and other night people—a street or two where the action was, rooming houses, bars, clubs—which were scattered like a Micronesian archipelago across the U.S.

For that is where players found a milieu that accepted the overriding importance of professionalism, of getting the music right, of the strange marriage between group cooperation and ferocious competitive testing of individuals, which is analogous to the milieu of that other creation of working-class culture, professional sports. Once again Basie's understatements and exceptional—indeed for the autobiographer excessive—modesty muffle his account. The most he allows himself to say in the way of hype is "I don't mean to pat myself on the back, but that band was strutting, really strutting." He is much more likely to record occasions when he suffered or evaded defeat than to exult in public. The band's true sound of locker-room triumph is to be heard elsewhere:

> We were only Count Basie's band, and we got out of a ragged bus, but when we got on that bandstand we started jumping and showering down. . . . We put a hurting on them that night and washed Lunceford out of the dance hall.
>
> (the trumpeter Harry "Sweets" Edison, quoted in Stanley Dance's *The World of Count Basie*)

The conviction of the early Basie band lay in this capacity to exult. For the professional musician of Basie's day, as he himself puts it, "playing music has never really been work." It was more even than a way of having a good time. It was, as sport is for the athlete, a continuous means of asserting oneself as a human being, as an agent in the world and not the subject of others' actions, as a discipline of the soul, a daily testing, an expression of the value and sense of life, a way to perfection. Athletes cannot use their voices to say this, but musicians can, without having to formulate it in words. So the working-class athlete's conviction produced a great art in the form of jazz; and, thanks to the phonograph, a permanent art.

Basie's strength as a bandleader lay in his capacity to distill the essence of jazz as black players felt it. That is why this inarticulate dropout from New Jersey was doubly lucky to find himself stranded, in the mid-Twenties, in Kansas City. First, because it allowed him to recognize his vocation. Till then he had merely been a poor black youngster who liked playing piano and chose the only form of freedom available to his kind, the gypsy life of show business. Liberation and not money was the object ("I don't think I ever came into contact with any rich entertainers when I grew up") and he neither made nor kept money. "I liked playing music and I liked the life." *Good Morning Blues* is a superb evocation of the underside of black show biz in the 1920s—the casts of burlesque shows like "Hippity-Hop" thirsting for some action in the desert of Omaha, Gonzelle White and her Big Jazz Jamboree slowly foundering as she sailed along the TOBA circuit of black vaudeville theaters, finally sinking in KC. After the wreck Basie drifted into full-time jazz "without quite being aware of the big change I was making." It was his first stroke of luck.

The second was finding himself in Kansas City, capital of that apparent cultural desert southwest of the Missouri which even blacks bypassed en route from the Delta to the bright lights of Chicago and Detroit, and which even the black vaudeville circuit still wrote off. KC was long its westernmost point, which is why shows like Gonzelle White's disbanded there if not turned around, rerouted, or re-formed. Kansas and Oklahoma were not meccas of show biz. Apart from KC and Texas, the entire Southwest had only small and scattered black populations. The first tour of the newly formed Basie band was a row of one-nighters through places like Tulsa, Muskogee, Okmulgee, Oklahoma City, and Wichita.

Yet this was the region that produced two major developments in jazz. It fused the down-home blues with popular dance-band music, and the arranged performance with the jam session, to create both the classic swing band and the most powerful experimental laboratory of jazz. Kansas City produced not only Count Basie but also Charlie Parker.

Much has been written about this apparent paradox. Most of it has concentrated on the peculiar character of Kansas City (Missouri), in the wide-open, free-spending days of Boss Pendergast, whose gang-run nighttime municipal Keynesianism kept KC in the Depression an oasis where black musicians could at least eat. (It would be too much to call the player's life of hot dogs, plates of beans, jugs of whiskey, perhaps with a little subsidy from a girl, prosperity.) But in fact, though *Good Morning Blues* makes little of it, there was little regular work in Kansas City. As one of Basie's pioneers puts it, "the work was around, out on the road," though in Kansas City itself there was an enormous amount of ill-paid casual gigging with tips, and even more unpaid jamming.

Most of the talent seems to have come out of the territory, with relatively little direct recruitment from the deep South and even less from the East. Walter Page's Blue Devils, the foundation and inspiration of Basie's team, was a territory band working in Oklahoma. And the down-home blues that Kansas City integrated into band jazz was not a big-city product; nor, at this stage, were band-accompanied male blues shouters, who became Basie's trademark, of any interest to a white public.

The KC musicians, in short, played what came naturally to southwestern blacks and largely what a segregated audience wanted. The blues was imposed on them by the ghetto. Independently, Basie and Jimmy Rushing observe of each other that in the mid-Twenties Basie "couldn't play the blues then," and Rushing, who could, "wasn't really a blues singer in those days." Ten years later they sang and played little else.

The gems mined in the dance halls of places like Muskogee, were cut and polished in the countless nightclubs and after-hours sessions of Kansas City by an unusually large community of professional musicians. But in spite of the KC myth which insists on battles won with visiting stars, and admiration from outsiders, this community thought of itself as in some sense marooned:

> We were really behind the Iron Curtain. There was no chance for us. So there was nothing for us to do but play for ourselves.
>
> (the great drummer Jo Jones, quoted in
The World of Count Basie)

It could have been said about the Kansas City scene as a whole. It was said about its most characteristic product, the Basie band.

Yet at first sight Basie himself had few qualifications for eminence. By jazz standards he was not a top-class pianist, especially when compared to the New York stride-piano giants in whose style he had been formed and against whom he constantly measured himself—to his disadvantage. As one of his arrangers said: "He knew he couldn't challenge Fats Waller or Earl Hines. He didn't have the same kind of gift from above."

Nor was he a particularly literate musician, unlike most of the big-band leaders, who tended to come from a schooled black background. He came into the big time with little more than a number of head-arrangements and blues, not only because he did not lead a reading band, but because he himself was not a writer or arranger in the ordinary sense. Even his ideas had short breath: "He'd only go about four measures," says his arranger Eddie Durham. His provincial ignorance, even within the limits of commercial dance music, was startling. In 1936 he risked his booking in a great New York ballroom because, he claims, "I don't believe I even knew what a goddamn tango was." There was nothing original about the format of his band, except perhaps using two saxophones in contest. And any reader of his memoir will wonder how this easygoing, frequently drunk, tongue-tied man managed the job of holding his team together.

In short, on paper he had no qualifications to be anything except another adequate jazz player. And with the modesty, or honesty, which is his trademark, he says as much in his tribute to John Hammond, who heard his broadcast from the Reno

Club on a shortwave car radio in 1935 as he drove through the Middle West, was bowled over by it, and made Basie into a national figure:

> Without him I probably would still be back in Kansas City, if I still happened to be alive. Or back in New York . . . trying to be in somebody's band, and then worrying about getting fired.

But what was it that Hammond, and later the rest of the world, recognized in Basie? Once again, the best descriptions come from others:

> He was and is [says Harry "Sweets" Edison] the greatest for stomping off the tempo. He noodles around on the piano until he gets it just right. Just like you were mixing mash and yeast to make whiskey, and you keep tasting and tasting it. . . . Freddie Green and Jo Jones would follow him until he hit the right tempo, and when he started it they kept it.

That "tempo" was the clue to Basie, and *Good Morning Blues* begins with his discovery in, of all places, Tulsa, Oklahoma, of what Albert Murray elsewhere calls "that ever-steady, yet always flexible transcontinental locomotive-like drive of the Kansas City 4/4"[2] in Walter Page's Blue Devils, who are by common consent the pioneers of that lovely, easy, lilting rhythm both driving and relaxed. They were to form the core of his early band.

Having set the tempo, Basie would next

> set a rhythm for the saxes first, . . . then he'd set one for the bones and we'd pick that up. Now it's our rhythm against theirs. The third rhythm would be for the trumpets. . . . The solos would fall in between the ensembles, but that's how the piece would begin, and that's how Basie put his tunes together.

(Dicky Wells, trombonist, quoted in *The World of Count Basie*)

The great waves of ensemble riffs, hitting the audience like Atlantic rollers, were therefore—initially at least—not stylistic
tricks or ends in themselves. They were the essential ground-
swell of the music, the setting for what the musicians themselves, in the great days, did not see as an ensemble band, but
(apart from the self-effacing members of the stupendous rhythm
section) as a company of creative soloists. Alas, it eventually
declined into an ensemble band in response to the public. Self-
effacement was also the secret of Basie's minimalist arrangements
and his increasingly sparse piano interventions, whose purpose
was entirely to keep the music moving.

Whatever the origin of an arrangement, it was whittled down
into the Basie version by ruthless selection and cutting. Basie,
who "never wrote down anything on paper," composed by
editing, in other words by fitting his numbers to his musicians.
But unlike Ellington, who had precise musical ideas and picked
his players to fit them—even if some had originally been suggested by listening to other musicians—the less articulate Basie
was fundamentally a selector. What he heard in his head was the
shapes and patterns of numbers, the rhythm and dynamics, the
stage mechanics and effects rather than the plot or words of
the play. ("I have my own little ideas about how to get certain
guys into certain numbers and how to get them out. I had my
own way of opening the door for them to let them come in and
sit around awhile. Then I would exit them.") But none of this
became real until he heard musicians play and recognized in the
sound what he had in mind. Listening was his essential talent.
That is how the Basie band in its prime—between 1936 and
1950—came to be built up and shaped by apparently haphazard
recruitment and playing.

The only time during this period that Basie groped and
showed uncertainty was when he came into the big time and his
booking agent, the devoted Willard Alexander, told him that for
commercial reasons he had to double the size of his band. He
floundered, and almost failed. Fortunately both his backers and
other musicians (Fletcher Henderson generously gave him his
own arrangements) were so convinced of the band's merits that
he had time to adjust.

299

Consequently the Basie band was a marvelous combination of solo creation and collective exhilaration. It attracted and held a remarkable collection of individual talent. The intense joy of being in the early Basie band, a band of brothers, shines through the reminiscences of hardbitten and jealous pros. Some of that joy was owing to the temperament and tact of the leader who led, as it were, like the headman of a traditional Russian village commune, by articulating and crystallizing consensus. Even more was owed to the players' sense of equality, fraternity, and above all liberty to create, controlled only by their own collective sense of what sounded "right." And to the end of his days Basie liked to present himself not as leader or driver, but as the fulcrum of his band, the small still center: "keep your eye on the fellow at the piano. The sparrow. He don't know nothing, but you just keep your eyes on him and we'll all know what's going down." It was not entirely an affectation.

Those who were young in the 1930s and first heard the unanswerable sound of the early Basie band rolling across continent and oceans are tempted, like Yeats with the Easter Rising, to call the muster roll of heroes: Basie, Page, Jones, and Green, Herschel Evans and Lester Young, Buck Clayton and Harry Edison, Benny Morton, Dicky Wells, and Jimmy Rushing singing the blues. But in retrospect these were not only men who produced remarkable music and helped to create what is in fact the classic music of the U.S., but who did so in an extraordinary and unprecedented way. *Good Morning Blues* and *The World of Count Basie* are not works of cultural sociology. (Perhaps luckily: Adorno wrote some of the most stupid pages ever written about jazz.) Nevertheless, they should be read by all who want to explore the obscure zone that links society with the creation of art.

Stanley Dance's book is a collection of interviews by one of the oldest and most knowledgeable jazz lovers in the world. *Good Morning Blues* is more than a ghosted autobiography. Albert Murray, a distinguished black writer who worked with Basie on the book for years and backed it—as all good oral history should be backed—by research far more extensive than the actual interviewing, deserves credit for a remarkable achievement. He has, like his subject, effaced himself to let someone else speak as he would have wanted to, but, without his help, could not have done. He has respected Basie's reticence, and neither concealed nor disguised the limitations of a man of great gifts, but with all the reluctance to commit himself publicly that one would expect of a black entertainer who grew up in the days when they were still called "sepia." The man who emerges is a man to respect. Basie was always good at finding others to voice his ideas. *Good Morning Blues* is his last success in doing so.

The Jazz Comeback *

Until recently jazz has occupied a curiously marginal position in the official culture of its native country, and even within the black community. The public for it has been tiny: far smaller than the public for classical music. Record producers, who probably contain a much higher proportion of jazz buffs than the American people at large, can hardly be expected to invest much in music that nowadays sells less then 4 percent of discs and tapes.[1]

The jazz public is enormously serious, even a public of connoisseurs. Since the 1930s it has certainly contained a considerable

* This essay originally appeared in *The New York Review of Books* on February 12, 1987, as a review of *Sitting In: Selected Writings on Jazz, Blues and Related Topics* by Hayden Carruth (Iowa City: University of Iowa Press, 1986), *His Way: The Unauthorized Biography of Frank Sinatra* by Kitty Kelley (New York: Bantam Books, 1987), *'Round Midnight* a film by Bernard Tavernier, *La Tristesse de Saint Louis: Jazz Under the Nazis* by Mike Zwerin (Beech Tree Books/William Morrow, 1987), *American Musicians: Fifty-six Portraits in Jazz* by Whitney Balliett (New York: Oxford University Press, 1986), *In the Moment: Jazz in the 1980s* by Francis Davis (New York: Oxford University Press, 1986), *A Life in Jazz* by Danny Barker, edited by Alyn Shipton (New York: Oxford University Press, 1986), and *Up From the Cradle of Jazz: New Orleans Music Since World War II* by Jason Berry, Jonathan Foose and Tad Jones (Athens, Georgia: University of Georgia Press, 1986).

number of intellectuals with wide cultural interests. And yet official high culture in the U.S. was extraordinarily slow to take note of what is probably the most serious home-grown American contribution to the twentieth-century arts. Hayden Carruth, poet, professor, and, since the early Thirties, an informed and thoughtful jazz enthusiast, observes that

> as a poet I never met another poet older than I who understood jazz as music. . . . Among poets of my own age I have met one or two who love and understand jazz, but none who has written intelligently about it. Most of my contemporaries have only a kind of nostalgic feeling for the "swing era.". . . Only when I come to poets whose musical education began after 1945, do I find any number, though still comparatively few, who write about jazz with understanding. . . . For some in the baby-boom generation the beginning of jazz is the work of Charlie Parker. For most it is the work of Miles Davis.[2]

Not that jazz was hard to find for twentieth-century urban or, through radio, any, Americans. Its sound was familiar and not difficult of access, at any rate for those who first heard it in their teens. The problem was exactly the opposite. Jazz, or more generally the music of North American blacks, was and is so deeply embedded in popular entertainment in the cities of the U.S. that it was almost impossible to separate it out as a special kind of art.

Even in the black ghettos it had no separate existence, except for the communities of professional players who, like all professionals, whether physicists, economists, or musicians, live by and for peer judgment, even when they are being paid by people who cannot tell the difference between trumpet and trombone, or who think Kenneth Arrow makes shirts. As Carruth observes, even the late Malcolm X, who was a champion ballroom dancer in Boston and New York in the late 1930s, does not in his autobiography speak of the jazz to which he danced as music. He treats it as "a cultural adjunct."

A striking example of the impossibility of recognizing the jazz threads within American popular culture is Kitty Kelley's scandal-mongering biography of Frank Sinatra, who was in his day undeniably an excellent jazz singer. This is not surprising, since he learned his craft in the big-band "swing" era, when jazz briefly became the mainstream of youthful pop music, and began his career as a vocalist in the Harry James and Tommy Dorsey bands. In fact Ms. Kelley, though primarily interested in her subject's nonmusical activities, is sufficiently conscientious to record how Dorsey instructed him in jazz phrasing.

Yet it is evident that Sinatra, raised among New Jersey working-class Italian immigrants, came from a milieu that had about as little relation to black music as it was possible to have in urban America. He showed no interest in jazz as such: few jazz names appear in the ample index of *His Way*. He was simply a young Sicilian of some talent and boundless ambitions who wanted to make the big time as a singer of sentimental songs, and did so, thanks not least to a sexual magnetism that attracted audiences at all distances. Luckily for him (and for Sinatra's admirers) the jazz idiom, to which a young man in the Hoboken of the 1940s took as naturally as he would to the company of Italian mobsters, gave sentimentality an interesting musical edge, and a sort of offhand distancing. Ten years older, and he might with equal conviction have sung "O Sole Mio." Moreover, for all his immersion in jazz, for most of us Sinatra is no more primarily a jazz artist than was Bing Crosby, whose superb and relaxed jazz phrasing Dorsey urged Sinatra to imitate. His phrasing survived and protected him to some extent from the vocal erosion of age. He deservedly became and remains a star of show business, and his songs have probably accompanied and subsequently recalled more seductions than any other singer's. But his relation to jazz is peripheral.

The very omnipresence of the jazz element in American popular music, and especially dance and show music, after the First World War meant that for most Americans it had no precise location or independent existence. It also meant that jazz was more easily recognized as an original form of art, and its practitioners as original artists of serious stature, by a public which came to it as to a foreign land: the Europeans.

The fact that jazz was thus taken seriously in Europe earlier than in the U.S. has always rankled in its native country. It still does, if the American critical reception of Bernard Tavernier's moving film *'Round Midnight* is anything to go by. Pauline Kael's grumpy reaction ("The French are pretty hard to take when they celebrate just how much they love American art") is not uncharacteristic. But what is hard for Americans to take is not the self-congratulation of Europeans, but that in this instance they have something to congratulate themselves about.

For it is undeniable that, from the early 1930s on, musicians who were seen by official high culture in their homeland as vaudeville acts or something to dance to were in Europe acclaimed by intellectuals, artists, and high society. Hitler destroyed the Central European avant-garde that was attracted by jazz, and the early links between Soviet culture and jazz have only lately been disinterred by the scholarly labors of the president of Oberlin College.[3] But nobody who knows anything about French culture will be surprised that Cocteau compared jazz to Stravinsky, while Stravinsky drew on jazz, that the man who started the world's first pure jazz magazine, Charles Delaunay, was the child of Cubist painters in the heyday of the Ecole de Paris, and that Jean-Paul Sartre, though seeming no more likely to tap his feet than his cousin Albert Schweitzer, knew that he ought to take jazz seriously. Perhaps because Boris Vian, as avant-garde as the next man, doubled as a Dixieland trumpeter in Paris clubs.

It is equally undeniable that the first book to survey and assess the leading jazz artists and "put jazz on the map in Europe and in its own country"[4] was written by a twenty-two-year old Frenchman, Hugues Panassié, in 1934; or, for that matter, that then as now the European public, small as it was, could at times be the only public for which it was worth producing *American* jazz. A leading producer of the stateside jazz avant-garde's records today is in Milan, and 70 percent of his modest sales go outside the U.S.[5] For that matter, why did we have to wait for a Frenchman to make the first full-length feature film which takes a black musician seriously as a creative artist, and, what is more, casts a black jazz musician in this role—Dexter Gordon, whose performance in *'Round Midnight* is astonishing, more moving than his music?

None of this alters the fact that, then as now, the U.S. is where the action is, and where a jazz musician would want to be, appreciated or not, so long as he could earn a living there.

As it happens, Tavernier's film raises a more interesting question. Like almost all we know about jazz except the sounds themselves, it is jazz from the fan's point of view: naturally enough, cameras are not instruments through which musicians express themselves. Indeed, Gallophiles will recognize the special flavor of the French intellectual jazz fan, always ready to discover a *poète maudit* even in blackface, loving jazz not only for itself but because it leads him to Rimbaud, and flattered by the proclaimed taste of older jazz musicians for Debussy.

No musician would make a film essentially about his relation with an admiring fan, but that is the central theme of *'Round Midnight*. It is based on the case of a real Frenchman who did his best to protect the great but declining bebop pianist Bud Powell against himself in Paris. Tavernier's protagonist takes in a famous but alcoholic sax player, briefly nurses him back to respect and creativity through selfless care and immersion in the slow rhythms of French family life, perhaps seen here as unduly reticent and gentle; but he cannot prevent him from returning to New York where he dies. It is almost certainly the best feature film made about jazz, and illuminating both about the people and the music—for jazz fans are equally interested in both.

However, the fan sees his hero in a retrospective sentimental haze. Bud Powell in Paris was an altogether more frightening and inaccessible phenomenon than the gentle somnambulist self-destroyer whom Dexter Gordon plays so well. (The present writer, who saw Powell in Paris, speaks from personal memory.) The film combines the fans' resentment at the world's failure to accept the greatness of jazz with their reluctance to share it with outsiders. It is full of esoteric references—to Charlie

Parker's wife, to Lester Young's tricks of language—whose very opaqueness confirms the aficionado's monopoly. Tavernier, justifiably, makes no attempt to distance himself from sentiment and cliché which are essential to fandom. (But then, neither did he do so in that other splendid film about art, artists, and, not incidentally, fathers and daughters, *A Sunday in the Country*.)

But the jazz fan, however knowledgeable, is fundamentally a lover. While old-style pop music, as everyone knows, crystallized and preserved the relation of human beings in love ("They're playing our song"), jazz, more often than not, is itself the love object for its devotees. The Czech novelist Josef Skvorecky has compared its initial impact to the first love of teen-agers in the era when such emotions, however fleeting, were still supposed to be unforgettable. "It had begun as a love affair like the others." This is the description of how jazz was discovered by Dr. Dietrich Schulz-Koehn, who occupies a small niche in the informal pantheon of jazz lovers' history as the German officer captured at St. Nazaire in 1944, whose first question to his American captors was: "Do you have any Count Basie records?"[6] The metaphor of love or falling in love keeps pushing its way into Mike Zwerin's enthusiastic but superficial account of jazz in Nazi-occupied Europe, itself a work of autobiography, sentiment, and piety rather than scholarship. ("Accuracy came first, but when there was a choice between poetry and journalism, I picked poetry."[7]

Few jazz fans are in a position to make films, though they have, in jazz photography, created a library of marvelous images. A number of young white men—and a small but growing number of women—also graduate from fans to players, though opinions about the musical interest of their activities have generally been divided. Fortunately a modest number have, over the years, compensated for the lack of commercial and institutional interest in jazz by turning themselves into impresarios or record producers. The recently repolished Blue Note label, founded and long maintained by two German refugee jazz fans, is a case in point. But what do they do with words?

Relatively few fans write poetry to or about the beloved, and when they do, it tends to rely excessively on the magic of names which vibrate only for other lovers. ("Oh I loved you Pete Brown. And you were a brother to me, Joe Marsala. And you too, sweet Billy Kyle."[8] Rather more of them, belonging to the large underground of jazz lovers in academia, now write books of serious scholarship about the object of their passion. Characteristically, most of the books noted here are published by university presses. But very few indeed practice the extraordinarily difficult art of communicating in prose what musicians are and do.

Probably the only writer who has actually succeeded is Whitney Balliett of *The New Yorker*, whose *American Musicians* collects together twenty-four years of "jazz profiles." As a writer of *New Yorker* profiles he is distinguished but not exceptional. His unique strength as a descriptive writer on jazz lies in a musically informed combination of watchful, precise observation with ear and eye, a sort of Audubon-like impartiality, and an uncanny instinct for words which not only are but *sound* right. Very few listen and observe as exactly as he does, and nobody reports more exactly. Balliett's descriptions of solo improvisations—he is particularly good on drummers—are, as nearly as is possible, translations of the movement of music into language; as can be verified by checking his report of, say, Jess Stacy's famous 1938 piano solo at Carnegie Hall against the record.

After a Goodman–Gene Krupa duet, there was a treading-water pause, and Stacy, suddenly given the nod by Goodman, took off. The solo lasted over two minutes, which was remarkable at a time when most solos were measured in seconds. One wonders how many people understood what they were hearing that night, for no one had ever played a piano solo like it. From the opening measures, it had an exalted, almost ecstatic quality, as if it were playing Stacy. It didn't, with its Debussy glints and ghosts, seem of its time and place. It was also revolutionary in that it was more of a cadenza than a series of improvised choruses. There were no divisions or seams, and it had a spiralling structure, an organic struc-

307

ture, in which each phrase evolved from its predecessor. See-sawing middle-register chords gave way to double-time runs, which gave way to dreaming rests, which gave way to sing-song chords, which gave way to oblique runs. A climax would be reached only to recede before a still stronger one. Piling grace upon grace, the solo moved gradually but inex-orably up the keyboard, at last ending in a superbly restrained cluster of upper-register single notes. There was an instant of stunned silence before Krupa came thundering back.

Unlike most jazz writers, he never gushes or conceals the weaknesses even of his favorites. His range of sympathy is un-usually wide, from King Oliver to Cecil Taylor, though it does not entirely include Miles Davis and hard bop, about which (in this book) he is very reticent. In short, he is the ideal writer for the literate jazz lover who is forced to recollect emotion in tran-quillity, far from records and tapes. What, except admiration for a first-class craftsman in words, he communicates to those who do not like jazz, it is impossible for a jazz lover to say.

Since so much of what we know about jazz comes to us through the selfless but not unbiased devotion of the aficionados, not least as collectors, genealogists, chroniclers, or—as in Danny Barker's *A Life in Jazz*—translators of spoken reminiscence into print,[9] we ought to know a good deal more about the public for jazz and its evolution than we actually do. However, writers on jazz have tended to be as incurious about the listeners as they have been endlessly fascinated by the tiniest details about the musicians. The reception of jazz, especially in the U.S., still has to be seriously studied, although several of the books under review do provide incidental materials for such a study.

And yet, the future of jazz depends almost entirely on what happens to the public for it, as was clear during the fifteen or so years from the early 1960s on, when this public virtually van-ished as the mass of the young stampeded to follow the rock fashions, in this as in several other respects a disaster decade for Western culture. (The rhythm-and-blues of the 1950s had still allowed a kind of amicable symbiosis between jazz and pop.[10]) The best that could be said about jazz in the early 1970s, even in

New York—as usual it was said by Whitney Balliett—was that it had stopped collapsing. Its condition was "parlous but persuasive."[11] Once again, this is jazz as seen by fans or critics. For musicians who could no longer make a living by playing jazz it was the first rather than the second.

In spite of the (qualified) gloom of Francis Davis, whose *In the Moment* reports on the jazz scene of the 1980s, interest in jazz began to revive in the late 1970s with the visible exhaustion of rock music, and has been growing at an impressive pace recently. "The bins are bursting with reissues and clubs are suddenly doing record business," wrote a jazz journal at the end of 1986,[12] and the phenomenon appears to be international. It is once again becoming possible for more than a handful of musicians to earn a living playing jazz. Long-dissolved groups are reconstituted, musicians return from California studios and European exile and answer the question, "Where is jazz going right now?" with, "I don't know where it's going, but it's healthy."[13] Even if the revival lasts, jazz will certainly not be more than a minority taste, like reading poetry, as it has generally been; but it may once again be an economically workable one.

Given our ignorance of the public which is now turning to jazz, little can be said about it except that, as is obvious, "jazz audiences are generally up-scale in income, well-educated and more white than black,"[14] Nevertheless, the growing body of middle-class and professional blacks may now also consider, as their fathers did not, an educated admiration for jazz as a badge of race pride as well as of cultural status.[15]

Apart from the nucleus of gnarled long-time jazz buffs, this is a new and relatively young audience, often strikingly ignorant, but, in a peculiar way, highbrow. The one branch of jazz which seems to have been left out of the revival is the simple fun music that once appealed so powerfully, especially to white youth, and that resisted the decline of jazz longest: Dixieland. In New York itself, those strongholds of white middle-class males recalling their youth, Eddie Condon's and Jimmy Ryan's, have now gone even as new locations for more advanced live jazz multiplied and flourished.

The decline of Dixieland is clearly not due to a lack of audience appeal, but to critics' and musicians' combined boredom with, and contempt for, "the same old ninety-three tunes in the standard early repertoire" of New Orleans and Chicago, played in unvarying versions by "fourth-rate musicians." [16] Moreover, to many young black musicians, traditional New Orleans music was uncomfortably close to Uncle Tom. Only perceptive and open-minded jazz lovers like Balliett and Carruth are today prepared to say a good word for Dixieland music, or rather for jazz played in pre-1940 style. Carruth (who incidentally suggests, with some exaggeration, that "the number of inferior imitators of post-bop jazz today is greater by far than the number of Dixielanders") reminds his

> younger friends that when they hear records—made by real jazz musicians trained in the modes that came before bop, whether black or white, northern or southern, they are hearing jazz, not Dixieland, and it makes no difference whether the opening and closing choruses are played in harmonic riffs or contrapuntal improvisations.

Nor does he exclude the possibility that even "work taken verbatim, so to speak, from old records" could be "done with such purity of musical devotion and such sensitivity to phrasing" that it could be taken for real jazz.

Indeed, Berry, Foose, and Jones's learned and instructive study of New Orleans music since 1945 goes so far as to omit all mention of what most of the world, including the tourists visiting the French Quarter, would regard as the typical sound of New Orleans. Theirs is New Orleans as represented by the Marsalis family (one of the clans of practitioners on which the popular musical life of the city is still based [17] rather than the New Orleans of Buddy Bolden's ghost, Preservation Hall, and ceaseless clones of *South Ramparts Street Parade*. And the success of *'Round Midnight,* epic of bebop, underlines the failure, a few months earlier, of *The Gig,* a charming film about that characteristic phenomenon of the older jazz scene, the white middle-class amateur Dixieland musicians enjoying themselves, a species still occasionally represented by Woody Allen. It came and went, not of course silently, but rather unperceived. (It is mentioned in passing in Davis's book on page 86.)

The fact that the repertoire of the jazz revival now looks like including the noises people are told by the arbiters of jazz taste to enjoy, as well as some they actually do, may at last give a chance to the young avant-garde musicians who slogged their way despairingly through the darkness of the 1960s and 1970s, and to whom Francis Davis pays particular attention. It is at least possible that bookers will no longer give automatic priority to any of the diminishing band of veterans who can be associated with some remote and prestigious name of which even the johns have heard, even though their only obvious merit is physical survival. And it is certainly the case that jazz musicians like the pianist Ellis Marsalis, who brought up their sons in the true faith of Ornette Coleman and John Coltrane while unbelief raged all round them, are now indirectly coming into their own.

But it is also possible that the revival of some public interest in jazz has had the effect of leading some of the musicians who, in the dark years, made themselves even more inaccessible (to spite those who refused to listen to them anyway), back toward a mainstream music genuinely capable of appealing to audiences, or at least not actively alienating them. Such integration of musical revolutionaries in the mainstream was what created the last golden age of jazz between 1955 and 1960. Francis Davis notes, not without melancholy, that the flag carrier of the 1980s revival, the young trumpeter Wynton Marsalis, is a "resolutely conservative" musician. There are times today when the World Saxophone Quartet not only sounds like Ellington, but actually tries to. Some will welcome this development.

In these circumstances it is possible that jazz may finally be adopted into the postmodernist American establishment as part of the cultural ambiance of the new graduate professional classes. It has become intellectually respectable. Its players are likely to be formally trained in music, or even, like Wynton Marsalis, equally distinguished as classical and jazz performers. It can be readily combined with other consumer expenditures, as has been

311

recognised in the now familiar bonding of jazz and cookery in Manhattan supper clubs and restaurants. Practicing gastronomy to the accompaniment of what good authorities claim to be the classical music of the twentieth-century U.S. is culturally reassuring, even when one is not listening to it closely. It is even, in a modest way, a guarantee of economic exclusiveness, at least so long as the size of the jazz public and the capacity of clubs make it cheaper to buy a modest opera seat than to hear a live set in the Village.

However, among the many whom the new respectability of jazz excludes are those who made this music in the past, and on whom its creative future must rest: young men and women from the black ghetto. Not many of the very young have yet been drawn into the jazz revival in its native country. The degree in Jazz and Contemporary Music recently inaugurated at the New School in New York is now taught by a predominantly black faculty of distinguished older musicians to a largely white student body. For every black student who has joined the course so far there are six whites. Jazz may have established its cultural credentials, but the real rejuvenation of the music has a long way to go.

Slyest of the Foxes *

Of the great figures in twentieth-century culture, Edward Kennedy Ellington is one of the most mysterious. On the evidence of James Lincoln Collier's excellent book, he must also be one of the least likable—cold to his son, ruthless in his dealings with women, and unscrupulous in his use of the work of other musicians. But there can be no denying the extraordinary fascination he plainly exercised over the people he mistreated and was loyal to at the same time, including those who allowed him

* This essay originally appeared in *The New York Review of Books* on November 19, 1987, as a review of *Duke Ellington* by James Lincoln Collier (New York: Oxford University Press, 1987).

312

to establish power over them, i.e., most of his colleagues and lovers.

There was nothing blatant about what must strike impartial observers as his appalling behavior. He was the opposite of the short-fused brawlers who briefly joined so many bands of his time, including his own, though his habit of stealing his musicians' tunes and, occasionally, their women, must have put a strain on even the more placid among them. However, the only people who actually took a knife or a gun to him, so far as the record shows, were legal or de facto wives, who had more than adequate provocation.

In fact, nothing was obvious about Duke Ellington the man, except the mask he invariably wore in public and behind which his personality became invisible: that of a handsome, debonair, and seductive man about town, whose verbal communications with his public, and very likely with the startlingly large numbers of his female conquests, consisted of vapid phrases of flattery and endearment ("I love you madly"). The autobiography he wrote shortly before his death, *Music Is My Mistress*,[1] is a singularly uninformative document as well as a mistitled one. For while he probably despised and tried to subjugate his lovers, indeed all women except his mother and sister, both of whom he idealized and regarded as asexual—at least this is the view of his humiliated son[2]—his relationship to music was entirely different. Even so, music was not his mistress in the original sense of someone exercising dominion. Ellington liked to keep control.

Here, in fact, lies the heart of the mystery that James Lincoln Collier has tried to elucidate in his book. For Ellington, who has been called, with Charles Ives, the most important figure in American music,[3] utterly fails to conform to the criteria of the conventional idea of "the artist," just as his improvised productions fail to conform to the conventional idea of "the work of art." As it happens, unlike most of his jazz contemporaries, Ellington saw himself as an "artist" in this sense and took to composing "works" for the concert hall, where they were periodically performed. In the black middle-class milieu of the El-

313

lingtons, which Collier rightly insists was important, the conception of the "great artist" was familiar, whereas it was meaningless to someone like Louis Armstrong, who came from a less self-conscious and entirely unbourgeois world.

When Ellington, on his triumphant visit to England in 1933, discovered that for British intellectuals he was not just a band-leader but an artist like Ravel or Delius, he took to the role of "composer" as he conceived it. However, hardly anyone claims that his reputation rests on the thirty-odd ill-organized mini-suites of program music, and still less on the "sacred concerts" to which he devoted much of his final years. As an orthodox composer, Ellington simply does not rate highly.

And yet there is no doubt that the corpus of his work in jazz, which, in Collier's words, "includes hundreds of complete com-positions, many of them almost flawless," is one of the major accomplishments in music—*any* American music—of his era (1899–1974). And that but for Ellington this music would not exist, even though almost every page of Collier's admiring but demystifying book bears witness to his musical deficiencies. El-lington was a good but not brilliant pianist. He lacked both a technical knowledge of music and the self-discipline to acquire it. He had trouble reading sheet music, let alone more elaborate scores. After 1939 he relied heavily for arrangements and musical advice on Billy Strayhorn, who acted as his alter ego in running the band and who became something like an adopted son. The musically trained and immensely sophisticated Strayhorn was better able to judge from a score how the music would sound.

Apart from some informal tips in the 1920s from formally trained black musical professionals like Will Vodery, Ziegfeld's musical director, he learned little except by a process of trying it out in practice. He was too lazy, and perhaps not sufficiently intellectual, to read much, nor did he listen intently to other people's music. He did not even, if Collier is to be believed, make any special efforts to find the right kind of musicians for his band, but accepted the first vaguely suitable ones to fill va-cancies; though this does not account for the majestic brass and reed lineups of the Ellington band between the later Twenties and early Forties. He was certainly not a great songwriter, if we follow Collier's demonstration that "of all the songs on which Ellington's reputation as a songwriter—and his ASCAP royalties as well—is based, only 'Solitude' appears to have been entirely his work. For the rest he was at best a collaborator, at worst merely the arranger of a band version of the tune." And at least one of his sidemen told him, at a characteristic moment of mutual irritation: "I don't consider you a composer. You are a compiler."

Last, and perhaps most damaging of all, is Collier's justified observation that he neither had the talent, the "raw natural gift" of other great jazz musicians, nor was "drawn, indeed driven, to [jazz] by an intense feeling for the music itself." Unlike many other great jazz musicians, he showed little promise until he was nearly thirty, and he did not start doing his best work until he was forty.

Here lies the chief interest of Collier's book. In broad outline his judgments are not new. It has long been accepted that Ellington was essentially an improvising musician whose "instrument was a whole band," and that he could not even think about his music except through the particular voices of its members. That he was musically short-winded and therefore incapable of developing a musical idea at length was always obvious, but conversely it was already known in 1933 that no other composer, classical or otherwise, could beat him over the distance of a 78-rpm record—i.e., three minutes. He has been called by a critic of both jazz and classical music "art's major miniaturist."[4] Collier's comments on particular works and phases of the Ellington *oeuvre* are, as usual, knowledgeable, perceptive, and illuminating, but his general judgment could hardly differ from what may be regarded as the general consensus.

Only through jazz could a man of Ellington's evident limitations have produced a significant contribution to twentieth-century music. Only a black American, and probably a black middleclass American of Ellington's generation, would have sought to do so as a bandleader. Only a person of Ellington's unusual character would have actually achieved this result. The

315

merit of Collier's book lies in showing what the music owes to the man, but its novelty is to see the man as formed by his social and musical milieu.

The pecularities of Ellington's personality have often been described with varying degrees of indulgence. He saw himself, with total and unforced conviction, as "uniquely gifted by God, uniquely guided through life by some mysterious light, uniquely directed by the Divine to make certain decisions at certain points in his life," and consequently entitled to total power. The critic Alexander Coleman tried to sum up Ellington's inner thoughts as follows: "I must be able to give and to take away. I command the world because I am ever lucky, careful beyond compare, the slyest fox among all the foxes of this world."[5]

This is substantially also Collier's reading of the man, though the present book insists less than it might on the imperatives of street-smart survival and success that the Duke—the name was given to him early in life—acquired as a smooth young black hustler: the deviousness, the refusal to give anything about himself away, the power strategies of manipulation, the godfather-like insistence on "commanding respect." In this regard Mercer Ellington's memoir of life with his father may usefully supplement Collier's book.

In short, Ellington, as he himself recognized,[6] was a spoiled child who succeeded in maintaining something of the infant's sense of omnipotence throughout life. In Washington, D.C., his father worked his way up from coachman to butler in the service of Dr. M.F. Cuthburt, "reputedly a society doctor who tended Morgenthaus and Du Ponts," according to Collier. From this family background and from the relatively large number of politically sheltered or college-educated blacks he knew in his parents' Washington milieu, he acquired self-respect, self-assurance, and strong pride in his race—and a sense of superiority within it. "I don't know how many castes of Negroes there were in the city at that time," he once said, "but I do know that if you decided to mix carelessly with another you would be told that one just did not do that sort of thing." He preferred not to have a racially mixed band even when this was possible. The charisma that surrounded him derived largely from the consequent, and very striking, air of being a *grand seigneur* who expected to be deferred to, and this impression was reinforced by charm, good looks, and an indefinable magnetic quality.

However, the spoiled child began as an idle and ignorant failure at school, looking for a good time, who never acquired the knack of learning, hard work, or self-discipline, yet never abandoned his sense of status or his ambition. Music, which he seems to have seen originally merely as an adjunct to having a good time, became an obvious as well as an easy way of earning a living, given the enormous demand of the jazz age, and the position of blacks in the dance bands, which was still strong, in spite of the influx of whites. If educated and college-trained blacks made their way as musicians—often becoming band-leaders or arrangers, as did Fletcher Henderson and Don Redman—it was even more natural for a middle-class ne'er-do-well without qualifications to do so, especially one who had recently been pressured into marriage. In the early 1920s good money was to be made in music, probably more readily than by commercial art, for which the young Ellington seems to have shown some gift.

It was Ellington's good luck that he entered jazz at the moment when the music was discovering itself, and he was able to discover himself as he grew into it. There is no sign that he particularly wanted to compose, until he formed a partnership with Irving Mills, who, as a music publisher, knew the financial payoff of songs in the world of show business. There is no sign that Ellington wanted to be more than a very successful band-leader.

His band moved from the rough-and-ready syncopated music played by an army of nondescript young groups into "hot" jazz in the middle Twenties, because that was the general trend. Indeed the typical Ellington style may well have been worked out for commercial reasons by means of the "jungle music" that fitted in with the expectations of the Cotton Club clientele. "During one period at the Cotton Club," Ellington said, "much attention was paid to acts with an African setting, and to accom-

pany these we developed what was termed a 'jungle style' jazz."
This had the advantage both of building on the talents of some
valued members of the band and of providing the band with an
immediately recognizable "sound" or trademark.

Collier also argues that the size and instrumentation of the
band grew, because Ellington's competitors had more brass than
he. The models for the big band were white. The arranged
music they used was built around what Collier calls a "saxophone choir," a coordinated reed section pioneered by Art Hick-
man and Ferde Grofé around 1914 and developed by Grofé and
the "King of Jazz" Paul Whiteman in the 1920s. Fletcher Henderson and Don Redman created a black version by means of a
complex interplay between soloists and band sections.

Ellington thus became a "composer" because the future of
successful bands in the 1920s lay not with freewheeling small
groups of blowers but with larger bands playing arranged music.
He was in no position to imitate Henderson, whom he admired
and from whom, Collier argues, he took over the "system of
punctuating, answering, supporting everything with something," because he was incapable of writing complex music and
his men could not read complex orchestration. On the other
hand the combination of jazz rhythms with harmonic devices
taken from or similar to those of classical music, which Whiteman had pioneered, was easier to follow, and came naturally to
a man who lived and breathed the atmosphere of New York
show business, and, in fact, did not much like being called a jazz
musician. As Collier rightly points out, the real triumph of
"symphonic jazz" is not Gershwin's *Rhapsody in Blue* (commissioned by Whiteman) but the band music of Duke Ellington.

Once Ellington found himself responsible for his own band's
repertoire, he was forced to discover himself as a musician. His
personal method of creating compositions is well described by
Collier:

He would begin by bringing into the recording studio or
rehearsal hall a few musical ideas—scraps of melodies, harmonies, and chord sequences usually clothed in the sound of

318

particular instrumentalists in the band. On the spot he would sit down at the piano and quickly rough out a section—four, eight, sixteen bars. The band would play it; Duke would repeat it; the band would play it again until everybody got it. Years later, the pianist Jimmy Jones said: "What he does is like a chain reaction. Here's a section, here's a section and here's another and, in between, he begins putting in the connecting links—the amazing thing about Ellington is that he can think so fast on the spot and create so quickly." Along the way, members of the band would make suggestions. . . . As a piece was developing, it would frequently be up to the men in the sections to work out the harmonies, usually from chords Duke would supply. When the trombonist Lawrence Brown came into the band . . . to make a third trombone, he was expected to manufacture for himself a third part to everything. "I had to compose my own parts . . . you just went along and whatever you heard was missing, that's where you were."

It is obvious that Ellington brought something to this mode of music making beyond his usual disinclination for planning and preparation. He brought natural and growing fascination for the mixing of different sounds and timbres, a growing taste for pushing harmony to the edge of dissonance, a tendency to break the rules, and a great deal of confidence in his unorthodoxies if they "sounded right" to him. He also brought a tonal sense that is usually compared—by Collier also—to a painter's colors, but is better thought of as a feeling for show-business effects. Ellington, an unabashed composer of program music, seems not to have thought in colors, which occur hardly at all in the titles of his records (except for the nonpictorial "black" and "blue"), but to have drawn on "a sensory experience, a physical memory," as in "Harlem Airshaft," "Daybreak Express" a mood, as in "Mood Indigo" or "Solitude"; or sentimental stories, like those preferred by traditional choreographers as in "Black and Tan Fantasy" or many of his longer pieces.

None of this would have amounted to much except in and through a group of creative musicians with independent personalities and unmistakable voices: in short, except in jazz. Unquestionably every piece of Ellington's music was or is unmistakably the Duke's, whatever the composition of his band at any moment. Indeed he achieved the same, or analogous, effects through very different combinations of players, even though the band benefited from the long presence of certain quintessential Ellington voices: Cootie Williams, Johnny Hodges, Joe Nanton, Barney Bigard, Harry Carney. (But they developed their style because of what the Duke heard in them.) Moreover, it is undeniable that the musical impressionism that reminded classically educated listeners of Debussy, and the consistently brilliant form of the band's three-minute recorded pieces—beyond that length they tended to sag or fall apart—are Ellington's alone.

Nevertheless, his music is important above all because of the way it was made. Duke, the devious manipulator, knew that each musician in the band had to make the music his own. He might do so by being left deliberately without instructions, discovering on his own what Ellington had intended him to—as Cootie Williams was made to see himself as the successor to Bubber Miley's "growling" trumpet. Or he might be needled by Duke's deliberate insults into showing what he could really do. There was a method behind the apparently chaotic indiscipline of the band.

Conversely, Ellington was nourished by his musicians, not only because he drew on their ideas and tunes but because their voices were what gave him his own. He was, of course, lucky in his time. Being mostly untrained as well as highly competitive, players developed individual voices, which made possible the most exciting and original combinations. Collier and just about everyone else agrees that the discovery of one such voice, Bubber Miley's, began the transformation of the Ellington band, and enabled Duke to form those endlessly varied liaisons between the rough and the smooth, the raw and the cooked, which are among his characteristics. It was lucky that the masters of the new hot jazz so often came from New Orleans—Sidney Bechet himself briefly joined the band before it officially became Ellington's. This almost certainly gave Ellington the taste for mellow and sinuous reeds, the sounds of the saxophonist Johnny Hodges and the clarinetist Barney Bigard.

But Ellington's dependence on his musicians is most convincingly demonstrated by the fact that he kept the band going to the end of his life although it lost money. Whether with better management it could have paid for itself is unclear, but there is no doubt that Duke poured his own royalties into keeping it on the road. It was his voice. Ellington showed no interest in making or keeping scores of his works, not because he did not have their sound and shape in his mind but because his numbers had no meaning for him except as played, and, as in all jazz, they varied with the players, the occasion, and the mood. There could be no such thing as a definitive version, only a preferred but provisional one. Constant Lambert, an early classical admirer, was wrong in arguing that the record was Ellington's equivalent for the straight composer's score.[7]

It is evident that works created in this manner do not fit into the conventional category of the "artist" as the individual creator and only begetter, but of course this conventional pattern has never been applicable to the necessarily cooperative or collective forms of creation that fill our stages and screens, and are more characteristic of the twentieth-century arts than the individual in his studio or at his desk. The problem of situating Ellington as an "artist" is in principle no different from that of describing great choreographers, directors, or others who impress their character as individuals on team products. It is merely rather unusual in musical composition.

But this undoubtedly raises serious questions about the accepted definition or description of art and artistic creation. Patently the term "composer" fits Ellington as badly as the term "author" fits the Hollywood directors to whom it was applied by French critics with the national penchant for bourgeois and Cartesian reductionism. But Ellington produced cooperative works of serious art that were also his own, just as film and stage directors can, and unlike the megalomaniacs he knew himself to be engaged in a genuinely collective creation.

Collier asks such questions, but is sidetracked by his understandable conviction that Ellington allowed his talents to be diverted from what he did best into "music in emulation of models from the past, which in many cases he did not really understand," and which was not very good. Whether this "drew him away from developing the form he was at home with" is less certain. After all, by this book's estimate, he produced upwards of 120 hours of recorded jazz, which is a large enough corpus for most composers, and he developed and innovated to the end of his life. If he produced fewer masterpieces after the age of fifty, the pull of Carnegie Hall is less to blame than the business troubles afflicting his instrument, the big band.

All the same, Ellington will live through music like "Ko-Ko" and not through compositions like the *Liberian Suite*. But Collier is surely wrong to contrast jazz, as a sort of *Gebrauchsmusik* "to accompany dancing, to support singers or dancers, or to excite and entertain audiences," with "art as a special practice with its own principles existing in the abstract, apart from an audience," and not "created out of a wish to act directly and immediately on the real feelings of people." Whatever the relation of the accepted conventional arts to the public, which has undoubtedly been a difficult one for avant-garde artists since the beginning of this century, this oversimplifies the relation of jazz musicians to their audience, even if we leave aside the musicians who, since the birth of bebop, have defied the audience to follow them.

For while it is quite true that Ellington's finest work was created for cabarets and ballrooms, for the purposes of much of the audience schlock music would have done just as well or better; and in fact the same audiences were content with third-rate bands. Like most jazz organizations of its generation, the Ellington band earned its living playing dances, but did not play *for* the dancers. The band members played for each other. Undoubtedly their ideal audience accepted their kind of music and was excited by it, but above all it did not get in the way.

The present reviewer, at the age of sixteen, lost his heart for good to the Ellington band at its most imperial, playing what was called a "breakfast dance" in a suburban London ballroom to an uncomprehending audience entirely irrelevant to it, except

322

that a swaying mass of dancers was what the band was used to seeing in front of them. Those who have never heard Ellington playing a dance or, even better, a supper room of sophisticated night people where the real applause consisted in the falling silent of table conversations, cannot know what the greatest band in the history of jazz was really like, playing at ease in its own environment.

On the other hand the people who expected Ellington to "act directly and immediately on the real feelings" did get in the way. In his later years most Americans and all foreigners heard Ellington live only on concert tours. The hushed or applauding halls full of fans waiting for the revelation rarely brought out the best in the band. They brought out the Ellington who knew that enough honking (mostly by Paul Gonsalves) would bring the house down.

Nor is it sufficient to say, as Collier does, "When jazz becomes confounded with art, passion flies out and pretension flies in." The reason why jazz is important is not that it is passionate and unpretentious. So is most romantic fiction. It is not that, unlike the art Collier dislikes, "millions of people care about it." It is and has always been a minority art, even by the standards of classical music and serious literature, let alone the real public of millions. It is certainly not a mass art in the U.S., where New York jazz clubs (like British theater managers) count on the tourist trade as well as the local jazz audience.

Jazz is important in the history of the modern arts because it developed an alternative way of creating art to that of the high-culture avant-garde, whose exhaustion has left so much of the conventional "serious" arts as adjuncts to university teaching programs, speculative capital investment, or philanthropy. That is why the tendency of jazz to turn itself into yet another avant-garde is to be deplored.

More than any other person, Ellington represented this ability of jazz to turn people who are unconcerned with "culture" and pursuing their passions, ambitions, and interests in their own way, into creators of serious and, on a small scale, of great art. He demonstrated this both through his own evolution into a composer and by the integrated works of art he created with his band; a band containing fewer utterly brilliant individual talents than other bands—until the late 1930s perhaps only one, Hodges —but in which extraordinary individual performance was the foundation of collective achievement. There is no other flow of musical creation by a collective to compare with it. Certainly he, and they, acted directly and immediately on the feelings of listeners, but this itself does not explain why, as Collier notes, their music was so much more complex than that of other jazz groups. In short, the author is at times tempted into populist theory of the arts, by which the artist not only "rejoices to concur with the common reader" (to use Dr. Johnson's phrase) but takes the common reader's preferences as a guide. That the theory is inadequate is shown, among other examples, by comparing the American to the German phases of the careers of both George Grosz and Kurt Weill.

However, Collier is entirely right in the belief that the great achievements of jazz, of which Ellington's music is in some ways the most impressive, grew in a soil quite different from that which produced high art. It was a music of professional entertainers of modest expectations, made in the community of night people with folk roots. It was not supposed to be "art" like chamber music; it did not benefit by being treated as "art" and it tended to get as lost as the high arts when its practitioners turned themselves into yet another avant-garde. Its major contribution to music was made in a social setting that no longer exists. It is difficult to imagine that a great musician of the future will be able to say, like one of Ellington's major soloists: "All I wanted to be was a successful pimp, and then I found I could make it on the horn."

Today's jazz, played largely by educated musicians, often with classical training, essentially for a listening public, by a generation whose links with the blues are largely mediated through rock and musically impoverished gospel sounds, will have to find another way, if it can, to make a mark as great as the jazz of those who grew up in the first half of this century. But all of its players, without exception, will continue to listen to the records of Ellington, about whom Collier has written the best book we have: spare, lucid, perceptive about the man, good criticism, and good history.

The Caruso of Jazz *

He was the first among the players of the barely baptized "jazz" to be identified as "an artist of genius." Very few jazz musicians are as well known as Sidney Bechet, especially among people not particularly familiar with the music. No one has a voice more easily and immediately recognizable. Within months of his death in 1959 a statue of him was unveiled on the French Riviera and, thanks to the labors of his biographer, we now know that his face is on postage stamps of the republics of Chad and Gabon. The poet Philip Larkin wrote about him:

> On me your voice falls as they say love should
> Like an enormous yes.

Equally to the point, in the 1920s Bechet was admired by other musicians, including men of considerable discernment like Duke Ellington and Benny Carter. And small wonder. He was, after all, one of the first, if not the first, to turn the saxophone into a major jazz instrument.

Why is it, then, that the career of Sidney Joseph Bechet (1897– 1959) is, or rather became, peripheral to the mainstream of jazz development? He was strategically placed, and had more than enough originality and talent to become a model and inspiration for other musicians, or a permanent model for those playing an instrument: like Louis Armstrong, Coleman Hawkins, Django

* This essay originally appeared in *The New York Review of Books* on May 12, 1988, as a review of *Sidney Bechet: The Wizard of Jazz* by John Chilton (New York: Oxford University Press, 1988) and *Jazz Odyssey: The Autobiography of Joe Darensbourg* as told to Peter Vacher (Baton Rouge: Louisiana State University Press, 1988).

Reinhardt, Charlie Parker, Charlie Christian, John Coltrane. Yet, while he had inspired Johnny Hodges of the Ellington band, his impact during his lifetime is otherwise hard to trace except on white Dixieland disciples. When white fans launched the Bechet vogue in the late 1930s, he was not even particularly well-known among the musicians themselves.

John Chilton's book, one of those monuments of devoted and scholarly data-collection which jazz has so often inspired among its loyalists, probably provides as much material for understanding Bechet's isolation as we are now likely to get. It certainly replaces the romances that passed as Bechet's autobiography.[1] It will provide the indispensable basis for any subsequent exploration of an extraordinary life, which will sooner or later find its way onto film or television. For how many men can claim to have been expelled from both Britain and France (the former after an arrest for rape, the latter after a gunfight in Montmartre), to have had affairs with both Bessie Smith and Josephine Baker and a long, passionate, if intermittent, relationship with Tallulah Bankhead, to have been the toast of Moscow in the mid-1920s after having taught the clarinet to the man who is supposed to be the original for James Bond's *M*? He also, later, played a couple of seasons at a Communist summer camp in the Berkshires, oblivious to the warnings of Willie "The Lion" Smith, who could not stand it for more than a week, on the grounds that "it was the most mixed-up camp I ever saw or heard about—the races, the sexes, and the religions were all mixed."

Unlike most other jazz musicians of his generation, Sidney Bechet was essentially a loner and, in the opinions of those who had business with him, which almost invariably ended in acrimony, a man to handle with great care. At the more egomaniacal end of the entertainment business, where a number of jazz musicians are also to be found, those who have dealings with artists are inclined to regard them (privately) as monsters rather than human beings, but the critical consensus about the difficulties of life with Bechet goes well beyond the complaints of bookers and managers.

"He was *dangerous* if he thought you didn't like him," observed Sammy Price, the Texas blues pianist, who came from a milieu where mere shortness of temper would not necessarily warrant this adjective. He could be "a fiend" admits his biographer. "A very difficult person to work with, self-centered and inconsiderate of others, and never happy to share a spotlight," observed one of his many bookers. Even his admiring pupil Bob Wilber concedes that "he could be evil and, it's not too strong a word, paranoic [sic]." Others were constantly conspiring against him—on at least one occasion, he was convinced, by witchcraft, against which he took appropriate action by setting the Twenty-third Psalm to music. He was so worried that he did so without payment.

In short, as in Cocteau's joke about Victor Hugo, Sidney Bechet was pretty close to being a madman who imagined he was Sidney Bechet. In both cases the illusion was justified by the man's undeniably extraordinary talents. Moreover, in both cases illusion became reality. The French reopened the Pantheon for the dead Hugo and they put up a statue to the dead Bechet. Bechet took this for granted. "My most durable memory," wrote a musician of a week's gig, "is of seeing Sidney sitting backstage, as though he were a king on a throne. He received his loyal subjects, and there were quite a few, with imperious acknowledgments. Alfred Lion of Blue Note records came and feted Sidney with champagne, which he accepted with an egocentric but regal bow."

These characteristics are probably enough to explain his musical isolation. By and large, in the structured and expensive forms of stage and screen entertainment the excesses of solipsism were (until the rise of rock-and-roll) kept under some control. And jazz is a democratic art, shaped by those who play together, which imposes limits on all participants: no skater, however brilliant, has as much scope for personal display in a hockey game as in figure skating.

But Bechet, while naturally recognizing the collective nature of his music, seems to have resented any version of jazz which did not either build the collective round his central and dominant

327

voice, or at least provide him with a regular virtuoso showcase. Indeed, he switched from his original instrument, the clarinet, to the soprano saxophone, in which hardly anyone else specialized in his lifetime, most certainly because of its greater capacity to lead, or to impose itself on, an ensemble. Bechet could not stand trumpeters who took the lead which conventionally belonged to their instrument, especially not those like Louis Armstrong, who might have outshone him, and of whom he was acutely jealous. He worked best with good and even-tempered partners who did not compete for first place, like the trumpeters/cornetists Tommy Ladnier and Muggsy Spanier, with both of whom he produced ravishing records. In such cases he made adequate room for their solos. He was even more at ease with instruments that complemented his, such as the piano, as with Earl Hines in the famous "Blues in Thirds."

However, basically he had the instincts, but not the talents, of a commanding officer; or perhaps of the old-fashioned actor-manager who took it for granted that his shows were about *him*. That is why in later years he felt at ease with young, less talented, and less experienced French musicians, for whom he was the honored *sensei* or master, even when he cut out the solos of those who had eyes for the girls he fancied himself.

But Bill Coleman, the delicate expatriate trumpeter, was unfair to accuse Bechet of being "only happy when he can bark orders at amateurs." The most one can say is that he needed more control than he liked or, usually, got. His finest work was done in small groups of players who took each other's talent, and, above all, professionalism for granted. He played some marvelous sides in 1949 with the bop drummer Kenny Clarke, though neither had much sympathy or feeling for the other's music. He was even better when he shared the basic ideas on format and procedure with his partners, as a former sideman recalled:

Bechet and [the bass player Wellman] Braud arrived wearing big old coats and hats; I think Bechet had a beret on. They sat down opposite one another and exchanged pleasantries. It was like an ancient ritual between chieftains. Muggsy [Spanier] joined in whilst he was warming up—same sort of approach. Being used to the razzmatazz [of his swing band preparations] I wondered what was going to happen: one, two, three, four, and wham! This music explodes all around me.

However, Bechet's isolation was not only personal but also geographical. Jazz is, among other things, diaspora music. Its history is part of the mass migration out of the Old South, and it is, for economic as well as often for psychological reasons, made by footloose people who spend a lot of time on the road. It would certainly not have become a national American music as early as it did if men with horns had not physically brought it into places where it had not previously been known. Joe Darensbourg's autobiography *Jazz Odyssey* illustrates this diffusion of New Orleans jazz excellently, and in doing so it throws light on the pioneer generation to which Bechet belongs. It takes its hero in the 1920s from Baton Rouge, via Los Angeles, Mississippi, Tennessee, St. Louis and Harrisburg, Illinois back to the West Coast and up to the Pacific Northwest which he helped to open up to jazz. In the history of this music, cities like Seattle, Portland, and Spokane have hardly counted for much, but Darensbourg demonstrates that at least social historians of jazz should take the Northwest seriously. ("Word spread round among musicians that you could make money in Seattle. It was a money town," Darensbourg says.)

Nevertheless, most migratory jazzmen stayed in the U.S., which was, in any case, the place where the action was. Bechet belonged to the minority who, from the start looked to the global market for black artists: women like Josephine Baker, who was discovered by Paris, men like the pianist Teddy Weatherford who, from the mid-1920s, operated mainly in the great Asian port cities like Shanghai and Calcutta; or the trumpeter Bill Coleman who lived mainly in France from the early 1930s. Bechet himself spent only three years of the 1920s in the U.S. (1922–1925) and the rest in England, France, Germany, Russia, and a number of lesser European countries, which explains both why he recorded much less in that decade than musicians of lesser talents, and why, when he returned to the U.S. in 1931, younger players thought of him as passé, compared to influential sax players like Hawkins and Benny Carter. A great deal had happened to the fast-evolving music in the almost six years since he had left. Probably a lot of the younger musicians of the Swing Era continued to think of him as a strong but old-fashioned player, if they thought about him at all.

Indeed, Bechet's position was so marginal that he and Tommy Ladnier left full-time music to open a clothes-repair and cleaning shop in Harlem in 1933 (unsuccessfully, like all business projects of Bechet, who mistakenly saw himself as an entrepreneur), and as late as 1939 he considered quitting music again to open a hash house in Philadelphia. In short, the man who had been a major figure and influence in the early 1920s, at forty-two seemed an exhausted talent, an impression reinforced by his looking older than his years.

Admittedly he returned to the U.S. at a bad time for jazz. It was not so much that the slump knocked the bottom out of the market for jazz records, which were hardly yet money spinners for sidemen, as that hot jazz, somehow tied to the mood of the Roaring Twenties, fell victim to the depressed atmosphere as well as the money problems of the slump years. The shift of public taste away from the fast and loud and toward dreamland —it has not been much noted by jazz historians—was international in the early Thirties. German music critics observed it, mainly with satisfaction, between 1931 and 1933. Chilton demonstrates that it was equally marked in Harlem. In 1932 Rudy Vallee pulled in 2,800 customers a night in a leading ballroom, but Ellington only a quarter of that; Guy Lombardo 2,200, but Cab Calloway 500; Ben Bernie 2,000 but Louis Armstrong 350. Bechet was not the only player for whom the times were out of joint in the early 1930s, but it must have been particularly hard for a man so conscious of his gifts to lack both money and reputation among his peers.

What saved him was the strange and unexpected phenomenon of jazz antiquarianism in the form of the search for the true music of New Orleans by impassioned groups of young white fans for whom jazz was not only a music but also a symbol and a cause. The Dixieland revival, which grew out of this search, has been dismissed (in *The New Grove*) as "the longest-lasting movement in jazz but . . . the only one to have produced no music of value."[2] However, if it had done no more than to recover Bechet for the main jazz tradition, it would have justified its existence.

Bechet had always attracted the musical cognoscenti. Ernest Ansermet wrote his universally quoted panegyric in 1919, when Edward J. Dent, the champion of Mozartian opera, also singled him out favorably from among the rest of the Southern Syncopated Orchestra, which he otherwise considered "nightmare entertainment." Ansermet's forgotten praise ("I wish to set down the name of this artist of genius; as for myself, I shall never forget it, it is Sidney Bechet") was given general circulation after 1938 when it was republished in the (French) *Le Jazz Hot* and the (British) *Melody Maker*.[3]

The small but select group of knowledgeable jazz lovers had no trouble in recognizing his quality, but few others listened to fugitive groups like the New Orleans Feetwarmers of 1932–1933 and the half-dozen sides they recorded. After a market for jazz developed again in the mid-1930s these aficionados managed to get Bechet a few small-group sessions which for the first time brought him before the main jazz public and made his reputation: the 1937 tracks on the Variety label (initiated by Helen Oakley, supported by Bechet's old admirers Ellington and Hodges), the classic 1938 Bechet-Ladnier records organized by the French pioneer critic Hugues Panassié, and, of course, John Hammond and *New Masses'* famous 1938 Carnegie Hall concert "From Spirituals to Swing." These inspired the 1939 recordings of Bechet by a recent refugee jazz-enthusiast from Berlin, Alfred Lion, which established the fortunes of his new Blue Note label as well as confirming those of Bechet.

While Bechet's Euro-American rescuers appreciated the New Orleans tradition—how could any jazz lover fail to do so?—and were always anxious to bring back unjustly forgotten artists, they were not New Orleans buffs. Even the Bechet-Ladnier sessions which, it has been claimed, "had more to do with the Dixieland revival than any others" were distinguished for their artistry more than their authenticity. Yet behind them an obscure tide of nostalgia was rising, especially among young middle-class whites, for the pure, the beautiful, the only *true* music of jazz which had somehow been betrayed when Storyville was shut down and the players moved up the Mississippi, though the survivors of the 1920s doing their own thing in small groups were better than nothing, especially if they were black.

Dixieland or the New Orleans revival was essentially a non-musical phenomenon, though it was to enable vast numbers of amateurs to enjoy themselves playing "Muskrat Ramble" and similar numbers. It belongs to cultural and intellectual history, which is why it deserves the serious investigation it has not yet received. It was a purely white movement, though naturally welcomed by aging Creole musicians, especially those down on their luck. "New Orleans" became a multiple myth and symbol: anticommercial, anti-racist, proletarian-populist, New Deal radical, or just anti-respectable and anti-parental, depending on taste.

In the U.S. and other English-speaking countries, its ideological center was unquestionably located on the borders between the New Deal and the Communist party, though for most of the young fans it was probably just something that spoke straight to even uninformed hearts. The internationally influential book *Jazzmen* of 1939, the first American history of the music based on research, which established the "up the river from Storyville" version in its purest form, was co-edited by a music critic on the *Daily Worker*. Revivalism linked the cause of the blacks and the (minority) taste for jazz, with folk song and folk music, ancient and modern, which were and long remained the central pillars of the left-wing subculture that merged into the New Deal culture.

So Bechet, "a man of catholic musical tastes," found that he "had somehow been swept into the dixieland world." For him Dixieland was in the first instance the key to recognition. The

1940 recordings on which he shared the bill with Louis Armstrong were the proof that he had won it, and (granting his late restart) with remarkable speed. From then on no short list of "the jazz greats" would ever leave him out. In the second instance, the Dixieland movement gave him a license to go on doing what he had done all along, since he had told Ansermet in 1919 that he followed "his own way," without taking much notice of others. His age made him an undeniable founding father of New Orleans jazz, and his style was therefore ipso facto beyond criticism. In fact, Bechet felt quite at home within the limited Dixieland format, for he was primarily a linear improviser and melodist, and not much interested in harmonic games as such. In any case he was only too pleased that his strong, fluent, looping, and pulsating ropes of beautiful sound ("a jugful of golden honey" Armstrong called his tone) were easily accessible even to the nonmusical, except for those—they always existed—who found his striking vibrato intolerable. He was not, and did not have to be, a purist, but neither did he have to keep up with the times, this did not stop him from playing superbly with any first-rate musician irrespective of style.

How far did Dixieland provide him with a living, the question that was undoubtedly uppermost in his mind? It is certain that he relied heavily on the public for the rediscovered small-group jazz of the 1920s players, which found a Greenwich Village home at Nick's and its public relations man in Eddie Condon. He clearly also relied on the left-wing connection for gigs, though it is not clear how far this was purely commercial. (Still, in spite of suggestions of communist sympathies, and his undoubted fond memories of Russia, it is hard to see Bechet as a political figure, still less a Red among black jazz players.) As for the New Orleans revival, he recognized its potential for a certified charter member of the Crescent City. Whatever the motives, his 1945 partnership with Bunk Johnson, an ancient trumpeter disinterred by the purists and turned into an icon of authenticity, showed the fans where he stood. Like earlier partnerships, this one also ended in bad feelings.

Yet none of these jobs provided him with an adequate income

at the level Bechet thought appropriate to his standing, though by the late 1940s he now had reasonable record royalties. What finally solved his problems was the invitation to France in 1949. In that country, where jazz had enormous intellectual and cultural prestige and Resistance associations, he discovered what he had always dreamed of—a vast public for whom the man with a French name and sponsored by French critics was a certified genius of jazz, and a community of young fan-musicians whose hearts beat faster at the very thought that he would honor them by stepping into their cellars. France became his permanent home. He became a cultural mascot as Josephine Baker had been. It did his music little good, but his finances no harm at all. It removed him from the personal and entrepreneurial frictions that had always complicated his life in the U.S. He lived out his life as a happy expatriate.

The man who emerges from Chilton's admirable researches was both a typical product of New Orleans and a very odd character. As a member of the Creoles of color, members of the (Francophone) free mulatto artisan and lower middle class, pressed back toward the blacks by post–Civil War segregation, he acquired the musical and professional skills of his community. Throughout his life he could do tailoring and cook, although he refused to be apprenticed to a craftsman's trade as most Creole players were. But then he also, and quite uncharacteristically, refused to learn to read music, initially no doubt because it seemed unnecessary for so brilliant a natural musician, later out of rebellion, in the end perhaps out of defensive pride.

He shared the New Orleans Creole social courtesy, their taste for dressing respectably, their justified pride in the city's musical tradition, and perhaps the unusual lack of interest in race relations that seems to have been characteristic of New Orleans musicians. From Joe Darensbourg's autobiography it is impossible to discover whether he was white or black. Bechet himself frequently said he was more interested in a man's musical talent than in the color of his skin and—apropos of Mezz Mezzrow, a white champion of black superiority, that "race does not matter—it is hitting the notes right that counts."

And perhaps the intense interest in classical music that he had a chance to develop in Moscow—on free days he would regularly go to symphony concerts before hitting the nightclubs—was based on the pre-1914 musical culture which lower-middle-class Louisiana Creole families shared with James Joyce's Dublin equivalents. Caruso, from whom Bechet claimed to derive his vibrato, was part of both. At all events Bechet, a great man for the *espressivo,* put a quote from *Pagliacci* into a solo as readily as he put Beethoven's picture on his wall.

And yet, there can be no denying that he was a man who stood at a fairly acute angle to his universe. Jazz players are more tolerant of the vagaries of human behavior than any other group of people, but while nobody who played with him failed to admire his marvelous musicianship, the general view about Bechet from the bandstands was distinctly unenthusiastic, whether he was with or without the dog and the knife that often accompanied him. Even his admirer Ellington, who seriously considered bringing him into the band again in 1932, in the end chose not to. He must plainly have been a hard man to get along with for any length of time, although with women he found it easier to maintain his soft-spoken and courteous New Orleans charm.

He remains an extraordinary figure in jazz: a role-player who was not good at choosing his roles, a man often living in a world of fantasy, a wayfaring stranger who rode into and out of town, nowhere at home except on the throne he thought of as his right, loyal to nobody except himself; but he was an astonishing, unforgettable artist, utterly original in spite of remaining firmly within an obsolescent tradition. After his death he acquired a reputation even among the modernists, as shown by the spread of the soprano saxophone among them. It had been virtually Bechet's monopoly. Coltrane took to it from 1961. He became a posthumous classic.

And yet, if it were not for the handful of jazz intellectuals who rescued him, the small jazz labels of the late 1930s, the white kids in basement clubs, the French who made his dreams come true, what would have happened to him? He would not have fitted into the big swing bands. He would have been around, but why should younger musicians have made space for an old man with a voice from the past who seemed to take no interest in new ideas, and had the reputation of being a self-centered, truculent, and tightfisted son of a bitch? Perhaps after his death some musicians might, by sheer accident, have discovered the forgotten six sides from 1932 and, listening to that astonishing "Maple Leaf Rag," have felt what Coltrane said apropos of the same session: "Did all of those old guys swing like that?" No, but Bechet did.

Thanks to middle-class whites we do not have to recover a handful of old 78s from beyond the grave. We were lucky to recover a classic while he was still alive. There is some justification for the jazz-fans after all, even the ones who don't know much about jazz. When they heard it, they had no trouble recognizing the eloquence, the lyrical passion, the swinging joy, and the blues that came out of Bechet's horn whenever he blew into it. Fans do not always fall in love with the best in the arts, but this time they did.

Some Like It Hot ★

"It seems quite clear today in retrospect," writes Gunther Schuller, who was at the time entering his teens, "that the Depression years and their aftermath were culturally and artistically the richest this nation has experienced in this century." Probably many more people would today agree with this proposition than would dissent from it, but not many would be convinced by the author's comment that this was so because

★ This essay originally appeared in *The New York Review of Books* on April 13, 1989, as a review of *The Swing Era: The Development of Jazz, 1930–1945* by Gunther Schuller (New York: Oxford University Press, 1989), *Early Jazz: Its Roots and Musical Development* by Gunther Schuller (New York: Oxford University Press, 1989), and *Meet Me at Jim & Andy's: Jazz Musicians and Their World* by Gene Lees (New York: Oxford University Press, 1988).

with financial and material acquisition virtually at a standstill, those lean years forced most Americans to turn to themselves —to rely upon and appreciate more their own creative imaginative instincts and impulses. Self-expression, whatever personal form it might take, became almost of necessity more important than commerce and career.

For the American arts and culture that in retrospect we regard as the glory of the Thirties were essentially commercial, if only because the huge apparatus of patronage and public subsidy, which has made so many writers and composers into dependents of the system of higher education in the late twentieth century, was not yet in place. Federal money undoubtedly became important in the Roosevelt years, but how much of the extraordinary achievement of that period would be lost if we imagined that everything financed, say, by the WPA, suddenly disappeared from the record? True, the work it sponsored was substantial, and the creative talents it helped to keep alive were numerous and impressive; but even in the field in which public patronage made its greatest impact, in the recording of folk culture and folk music (notably by Alan Lomax at the Library of Congress), its essential function was conservation and salvage rather than construction. Even so, if we would not have the work of Leadbelly but for Alan Lomax, and his father, John Lomax, who found him serving his prison sentence in Angola, Louisiana, we would still have the likes of Robert Johnson, who was recorded by a commercial company.

The major cultural achievements of the 1930s undoubtedly belong essentially to a box-office culture, if only because in the U.S. there was no alternative to it. This applies not only to the arts for which *Variety* made itself the spokesman, than as now concerned with grosses rather than immortality, but to serious literature, to an extent that surprises observers accustomed to the self-contained literary milieus of the old world and of contemporary America. Moreover, whatever the state of the U.S. economy, show business generally was anything but depressed, though like American society as a whole, it rested (and still rests)

337

on an unusually deep foundation of marginal, insecure, expendable men, women, and styles. Since students of jazz history have been largely concerned with black performers, most of whom, by the nature of their skin, lived, as Bessie Smith's *Back Water Blues* put it, in permanent danger of submersion, incidents like the temporary collapse of the jazz and race-record market in the early 1930s have attracted much attention. Nevertheless, by and large, as readers of Studs Terkel's marvelous *Hard Times* will recall, poverty, and insecurity, and prosperity for entertainment went together.

This does not mean that the box office can claim responsibility for the cultural accomplishments of the period, some of whose most striking glories Gunther Schuller analyzes in the second volume of his history of jazz, *The Swing Years*. The net effect of subordinating creation to commerce, then as now, was to degrade, to corrupt, and to infantilize, as a product of the search for what would appeal to the widest public. That is no doubt the reason why jazz ceased to satisfy both its creative musicians and its devoted lovers almost from the moment it briefly *became* mass popular music as "swing"; the most interesting musicians, Charlie Parker, Dizzy Gillespie, and Thelonious Monk among them, advanced toward what would become bebop; many jazz lovers (barely noticed by Schuller) retreated to Dixie.

Schuller, who notes how the swing bands succumbed more or less rapidly to the lures or pressures of the market, knows better than most what that sort of market does to art. As he points out, strings in commercial music do not have to sound "soggy and syrupy," but in jazz/commercial arrangements they do, unlike any of the "several 100,000 classical symphonic pieces from Corelli to the present, none of which—even those by, say, Rachmaninov, Ravel [and] Delius," sound remotely like that. It is no mystery why even writers who were quite happy to write for less money for commercial magazines apologized to each other for accepting the gold-lined degradation of Hollywood scriptwriting.

Yet this does not explain why serious and self-respecting work emerged on this commercial scene or was compatible with it, i.e., why artists found themselves able, with all qualifications, to do their thing at least partly within the system. They had not yet accepted its incompatibility with artistic creation by the public gestures of defeatism and abdication that pictures of Campbell Soup cans, and indeed all Warhol's career, exemplify. Here Gunther Schuller provides some more positive if imprecise suggestions. What he detects in this era is the "special identity between a people and its music," which, he argues, has since been fragmented by the complexities of the postwar period, "not to mention the disunity and strife brought into our national experience since then by a cold war, McCarthyism, the Vietnam War, various crises relating to minority self-identity." This former unity he associates not only with past innocence, that familiar illusion of those who are growing old, but also with the fact that "the thirties were for many people a new beginning," not least for black musicians, who could, for the first time, see jazz as a profession.

On the reason for this sense of new times, the author is nebulous, except for the suggestion that the vogue for "swing" attracted a good many talented musicians. Did the growth of jazz and its audience in the 1930s take place "despite the Depression—or perhaps because of it?" Where does the Roosevelt era fit in? Nevertheless, it is clear to him that this remarkable period in the development of American jazz, with its "unexpected musical-sociological alliances," cannot be adequately analyzed in purely musicological terms. Mr. Schuller's book is an implicit call for a social, economic, and cultural history of jazz in the New Deal years.

However, this is not where the author's heart lies. Though his book derives its value from his own theoretical and practical expertise as an instrumentalist and composer, he approaches the subject mainly as a fan. Those whose memory of jazz enthusiasts goes back to the years when this young classical horn player acquired his passion will recognize the characteristics of the period to which he belonged and about which he writes. Aficionados were and had to be self-taught, or taught from one or two books, like Hugues Panassié's *Hot Jazz,* which "introduced many an American to this music, this writer included." They developed their often impressive erudition by talking at length to musicians or anyone else connected with the business, by unceasing and sometimes polemical debate with other real jazz fans—the ones who would not be seen dead *dancing* to a jazz orchestra—but above all by concentrated and repeated listening to every 78 rpm record available. No "close reading" of poems in English literature classes can compare in intensity with the scrutiny of every moment of those magic three-and-a-half minutes.

Like its distinguished predecessor *Early Jazz, The Swing Era* will bring back the mood of early jazz writing and criticism of jazz: the weighing of bands and soloists against each other, the attention to every line written by other pioneers, the preoccupation with impassioned debates about what exactly "swing" is, and precisely how vital blacks or African influence are to jazz. Above all, like the earlier literature (but on an incomparably higher level of musical competence), the book is addressed to a readership as passionately involved in the subject as the author, and ready to follow him through more than 850 pages.

Essentially Schuller has written a series of monographs of bands and artists under classificatory headings (The Great Black Bands, The Great Soloists, The White Bands, Small Groups, etc.). They range in length from the 111 pages devoted to Ellington; through the forty or so for Basie, Armstrong, and, more surprising, if historically justifiable, Goodman; to ten to twenty each for most of some fifty others. The general format is a chronological critical commentary on the recorded *oeuvre,* preceded by general observations, and concluding with a brief and firm judgment. The argument is addressed to the musically literate.

Some readers may be tempted to regard this book as a work of critical reference for the moments when one is expected to show more knowledge of the likes of Claude Hopkins, the Mills Blue Rhythm Band, and the Casa Loma Orchestra than is reasonably expected in anyone not yet a senior citizen. (A work that fails to take an interest in boogie-woogie, country and city blues, and gospel can hardly claim to be encyclopedic.) Certainly

340

this is not a volume likely to be read at one sitting, or designed for this purpose. The numerous musical illustrations are ideally intended to supplement the actual records from which they are transcribed. Yet *The Swing Era* should not be interred on the reference shelf with the fanfares, in this case justified, that usually greet the publication of any musically literate book about jazz.

For what makes this book important is not the author's erudition—there are others who are equally learned about jazz—or even his critical discrimination, formidable though that is. There are other musically expert critics, even though few will want lightly to disagree with Schuller's considered judgments, even when, as in the case of Art Tatum, he shows less enthusiasm than most of us. What makes Schuller invaluable is, first, that he writes as a man equally versed in classical music and jazz—after all, he is best known for championing a fusion of both in the Sixties under the name "Third Stream"—and, above all, that he is a lifelong, professional, practicing instrumentalist as well as a composer. (He played the French horn with the Miles Davis Nonet of 1949, which recorded *The Birth of the Cool.*)

The uniqueness of Schuller's books lies in his awareness, based on his practical experience, of what musicians actually do on the bandstand and how they see their problems. The insight is central, since it is the democratic community of musicians that, after all, made and developed jazz, powered, as Schuller sees so well, by each artist's "desire to learn and improve, . . . so powerful that new ideas . . . were gobbled up and digested in no time, everyone eager to push ahead to still newer discoveries." He knows how much work was necessary to reach competitive instrumental supremacy, and what a strain the high Fs were on even Armstrong's embouchure. He appreciates the desire to excel, to reach unclimbed peaks of virtuosity, and at the same time to create, the basic problem of the improviser being that he cannot command the highest flights of his imagination, but can only "bring his capacity for instantaneous invention to such a high level that it is never less than adequate unto the task, all the while hoping for (and occasionally being able to count on) those special days when he is particularly articulate."

It takes a practicing musician to recognize what it means for a

341

creative jazz singer to learn, rapidly and impeccably, hundreds of songs, most of them—in the 1930s—hot off the press. For "it is not possible to so thoroughly recompose and improvise upon that many songs without knowing them completely. You can only intelligently deviate from something . . . if you know it deeply." How does the repertoire of "standards" for improvising musicians come into being? Schuller immediately shows, by listing the songs Armstrong recorded in 1930–1931, that his taste "was virtually infallible, considering the temptations to be otherwise; and apparently his choices were made rather instantaneously." Of the "right" songs he missed a few—Gershwin's "But Not for Me" and "Embraceable You" and Porter's "Love for Sale"—but not many.

Only musicians do not need to be told that "by playing virtuoso eight-note solos at top tempos, one can hide one's tone deficiencies," which explains why excellent saxophonists who wanted to play like Coleman Hawkins but couldn't were tempted to become "speed" players. Schuller's experience in the business enables him to show that many stylistic characteristics of early jazz were imposed by the technical limitations of recording, or ballroom acoustics and noise. The sharp ear of the bandstand readily tells the difference between players with a genuine bent for improvisation and those who, having created a satisfactory composition, stick to it. Billie Holiday "did not *really* improvise, in the truest sense. Her performances were fixed beforehand. . . . Deviations from a first take will invariably be infinitesimal, cosmetic."

Such observations, often incidental or even in footnotes, not only are among the chief pleasures of Schuller's book, but give it its special value. Hardly anyone else can write on jazz with this authority. *The Swing Era* is indispensable to serious jazz lovers. If any are in doubt about this, Schuller's twenty pages on Billie Holiday, a model of what first-rate jazz criticism should be, will decide the matter. However, the book is not what it claims to be, namely a study of the development of jazz from 1933 to 1945, though it contains a good deal of material for such a study. For this we would need to be told much more about the music

342

business and its changes, the transformation of the record industry, including the rise of specialized aficionado labels, about the college and noncollege dancing public, the rise of the specialist jazz/pop press, and a number of other matters which are assumed as background information by those of Mr. Schuller's generation, but cannot be taken for granted—perhaps even by those who rely on their memory. Above all, such a study calls for an inquiry into the political and cultural milieu of the Roosevelt era, which shaped the development of jazz to a considerable extent, often in a concrete way.

Take, for instance, the late John Hammond, "the most influential (non-performing) individual in the field . . . [whose] name—and good deeds on behalf of jazz—will run like a constant thread through this entire history." And so they should. But how was it possible for any single person, however devoted to the black cause and to jazz, however well-connected and with however amazing a nose for talent, to exercise so much influence single-handedly? Because Hammond placed himself at the point of intersection of four forces: black popular music; the New York–centered (and politically open) music and record industry and its associated structure of bookers and agents; the Europeans, who formed the first nucleus of a specifically jazz record market; and above all, the culture of the New Deal progressives and the left, to which he passionately assented.

For Hammond unquestionably saw his major contribution as bringing black talent out of the ghetto, and to win for it not simply the honor that was its due, but work and careers in a white, or ideally an integrated, world. But to convince white musicians to play or even record publicly with black ones, to open integrated clubs like Café Society as metropolitan showcases for (black) talent, even to get a roughneck band from Kansas City like Basie's accepted by a major agency, took more in the 1930s than merely artistic or commercial decisions, even once it had been demonstrated that black swing was saleable. (And even this, as Schuller shows, had been partly engineered by Hammond, who persuaded Benny Goodman—whose band became the show window of so many later discoveries—to take over the material of the Fletcher Henderson band, which was to help make his fortune as the "King of Swing.")

For jazz to go so far, it needed impresarios and entrepreneurs also committed to a cause, like the late Barney Josephson of Café Society (later driven out of business by the witch hunt). It required a certain public relaxation of an apartheid far stronger than we can now imagine. It needed the political and cultural populism so characteristic of the New Deal era, which generated a paying public for what could be publicized as coming from genuine poor folks: the musical equivalent of Steinbeck's readers. It needed both selfless and expert enthusiasts, and welcoming receivers of the gospel like those who filled Carnegie Hall for the famous "Spirituals to Swing" concert.

In short, as the career of Billie Holiday demonstrates, the artistic development of jazz in the Thirties cannot be separated from its political and social setting, and Schuller's book itself makes this clear. For whatever the mass success of a few big bands and singers, most jazz appealed to a specialized minority.

But for John Hammond's commitment (and, of course, discernment), Billie Holiday would never have been discovered in a Harlem dive singing for tips in the intervals between hustling. But for disinterested guidance and help from sympathizers, she would not have been recorded adequately, or perhaps at all. But for a New York middle-class public with intellectual and populist inclinations, she would never have become a cabaret star in a politically hip Greenwich Village room run by the brother of a Comintern agent, and attended by the sort of writers who asked her to sing about lynching, a subject every commercial agent would have warned her against. "Strange Fruit," which haunts everyone who has ever heard her sing it, may have tempted her into excessive later mannerisms. (Here Schuller and Hammond agree.) But it transformed her standing in the world, as well as among the "Leftwing and Park Avenue liberals, Greenwich Village intellectuals and bohemians" who idolized her, while "most Middle-America white swing fans never heard it and went on discovering Glenn Miller instead." Which discovery has lasted better? If this unique artist is today universally recognized as a genius, it is in part because of the particular constellation of political and social tendencies of the late 1930s, without which none of us would even know that such a woman had ever lived.

Gunther Schuller, of course, knows all this. He has simply chosen to write about something else. To say that *The Swing Era* is not much of a contribution to the social and cultural history of the U.S. or of jazz is not to criticize it, though one hopes that the author may one day find time to recall his memories and impressions of the musicians he plainly knew and observed so closely. The genre of the "jazz profile" has its pitfalls, such as the temptation to string together anecdotes, but such a book by Schuller would be enormously rewarding. In the meanwhile Gene Lees's lively *Meet Me at Jim and Andy's,* though dealing mainly with a later period, overlaps with *The Swing Era* with its portraits of Artie Shaw and Duke Ellington, the latter exceptionally perceptive.

No doubt others will write the history of the Swing Era, on which much remains to be said. Others will provide the balanced encyclopedic survey to which this author, with all his knowledge, prefers his personal choices, (In deference to critics who pointed out the virtual omission of Red Nichols's kind of jazz from *Early Jazz,* Schuller has added some appreciative but anachronistic pages to the present volume.) *The Swing Era* is a labor of learning, of critical discernment and respect, of profound knowledge of how jazz and jazz musicians work. Together with the volume on jazz since the bop revolution that Schuller is now preparing, *Early Jazz* and *The Swing Era* will stand as a monumental contribution to jazz literature. What more, except readers, can any author hope for?

Appendix 1: The British Jazz Fan, 1958

A few thousand young Britons, of whom about half live in London and the Home Counties and thirty per cent in the London postal area, belong to the *National Jazz Federation* which undertakes various activities designed to foster jazz. It is reasonable to regard them as a cross-section of the community of British jazz enthusiasts, though not necessarily of the larger marginal jazz public. Thanks to the foresight of this organization, intending members are asked to state their occupation. The following information is based on a random sample of 820 filing cards. I am greatly obliged to Mr Harold Pendleton of the N.J.F. and to his colleagues for making these invaluable records available to me.

Only about sixty out of the 820 sample jazz enthusiasts are girls: the public of enthusiasts is overwhelmingly male. The remainder of this analysis is therefore confined to the boys and young men, for though no ages are given, it is evident that virtually all N.J.F. members are young. There are too few girls to allow us to draw any conclusions about their occupations and social classes, but as we might expect, the majority seem to be office workers and shop assistants, with a sprinkling of students, nurses, and technicians.

'Occupation' for most jazz fans means 'future occupation', since so many of them are still being educated, apprenticed, or trained, and many are in military service. Where a precise civilian occupation is indicated, I have listed it: i.e. when a card says 'soldier, civilian occupation clerk' it has been counted as clerk; when it says 'architectural student' it has been counted among architects and not students. However, this still leaves several imprecise occupational labels, e.g. 'student', which may well include a number of school children or the troublesome 'engineer', which may indicate anything between a fitter's mate and a future civil engineer. The following table, which lists the main occupational groups in order of size, is therefore rather rough-and-ready. Since this book is not addressed to specialist sociologists, I have cut technical notes and explanations to the minimum.

Occupations of Male Members of N.J.F.

I. TOTAL NUMBER 758

II. UNCLASSIFIABLE
1. Schoolboys and students — 91
2. Occupation unstated — 59
3. National service and armed forces (a) — 39

III. CLASSIFIABLE OCCUPATIONS
4. Engineers and electricians (b) — 120
5. Clerks (incl. bank clerks) — 105
6. Other skilled workers:
   Printing trades (c) — 33
   Building trades (d) — 23
   Other skilled workers — 17 73
7. Draughtsmen, surveyors, etc. — 36
8. Business and commerce (e) — 32
9. Transport (f) — 25
10. Scientific workers (g) — 23
11. Semi- and unskilled workers (h) — 25
12. Technologists and technicians (i) — 21
13. Higher engineering (j) — 17

14.	Artists, writers, journalists, advertising, etc.	15	19. Photographers	6
			20. Articled clerks	5
15.	Civil servants, local government, etc.	12	21. Teachers, social workers, librarian	5
16.	Accountants	11	22. Agricultural and forestry	4
17.	Mining, iron and steel	9	23. Policemen	3
18.	Post and telegraph *(k)*	9	24. Doctors and dentists	2
			25. Miscellaneous	11

Notes:

(*a*) Regular and national servicemen cannot be distinguished. Probably 'Occupation unstated' includes several conscripts.

(*b*) This includes all who describe themselves as engineers, electricians, unless there is reason to believe that they belong to Group 13, and all who describe themselves as *fitter, turner, toolmaker, radar-tester, shuttle-maker* or the like, or as apprentice to any such trades.

(*c*) Compositors (the largest group), 'printers', lithographers, process engravers, etc. Virtually all seem to be skilled.

(*d*) The usual building trades, among whom carpenter/joiners and plumbers are the most numerous.

(*e*) Salesmen, commercial travellers, buyers, shop managers, shopkeepers, insurance brokers, and the like, a few shop assistants.

(*f*) Including 11 motor drivers, 5 railwaymen—4 of them signalmen—6 Covent Garden porters, draymen, lightermen, and the like.

(*g*) 8 lab. assistants/technicians, 5 research workers, 10 'chemists' and 'physicists' not describing themselves as research workers.

(*h*) A very miscellaneous group.

(*i*) All who describe themselves as such and a few others such as *mining student, apprentice metallurgist,* and the like.

(*j*) All who describe themselves as *student engineer,* or in sufficiently specialized terms, e.g. *civil, work study, production, textile design engineer.*

(*k*) A number of people belonging here have already been listed under Group 4. The rest are mainly telegraph operators.

This table may be summarized as follows:

1. The main bulk of the fans lies somewhere between the skilled workers, technicians, and technologists. Rather over 300 of the 539 people in Group III belong to this middle range, which may include groups 4, 6, 7, 10, 12, 13, 19, perhaps also 16 and 20. Even if we assume that all the 73 students will eventually have different occupations, the middle range still covers almost half the sample.

2. Unskilled, semi-skilled, and dead-end occupations are remarkably rare. All, or nearly all, random samples of 60–80 cards contain at least one draughtsman, printer, or lab technician and a large handful of the ubiquitous engineers and electricians, but the lorry or van driver, porter and railwayman occur only sporadically, the labourer, factory worker, millhand, hardly at all.

3. Certain industries are remarkably under-represented. There is almost nobody from the textile and clothing trades (except a few attached engineers and technicians), from food and drink, and the general service industries. For instance: *printing and publishing,* which in 1954 employed 311,000 people, supplies about 40 jazz enthusiasts: *textile and clothing,* which employed 1,633,000 does not provide 5, apart from the technicians; *road transport and railways* (just over one million) provide 22, excluding clerks.

4. Among the non-technical and non-working-class group, we note the relatively high number of office workers, mostly clerks.

5. The students are comparatively well represented.

It is quite safe to conclude that the jazz enthusiasts as a group are distinctly above the national average in education, skill, and technical qualification, and abnormally well represented in the characteristic occupations of the twentieth century. The first part of this conclusion can be demonstrated by the following table, which compares the social class distribution of occupied males under twenty-five years of age in 1951 with that in our sample. The "social classes' of the census are rather odd categories, but they are all we have in the statistics. Roughly Class I includes the higher professions, directors, and higher managers; Class II the less well-paid professions, shopkeepers, farmers, etc.: Class III foremen and supervisory workers, black-coated workers, shop assistants, and skilled manual workers; Class IV semi-skilled; and Class V unskilled manual workers. As it is impossible to do so, I have made no attempt to separate Classes I and II, and Classes

IV and V in the sample. Obviously, for reasons of age, very few members would be in Class I. How many will eventually end there nobody can tell.

Social classes in the population and among jazz fans:
in approximate percentages

Census Class	Occupied males under 25 years, 1951	N.J.F. sample 1958 (a)
I and II	8	36
III	64	53
IV and V	28	11
Total	100	100

(a) All 73 students and the relevant occupational groups have been allocated to Classes I and II. As the allocation necessarily contains some guesswork, not too much should be read into the difference between the two columns of Class III, but the higher percentages for I and II, the lower one for IV and V, are beyond dispute. Schoolboys and servicemen have not been allocated to any class.

For those unused to reading statistical tables, this one shows (a) that the jazz fans contain a far higher percentage of people in Classes I and II than the national population of occupied young men, and (b) that they contain a far lower percentage of the semi- and unskilled.

These figures confirm the general account of the British jazz public in Chapter 10, which was written before I had seen them. Only one thing seems odd. The 'arts' people (as against the scientifically, technically and vocationally educated) clearly play a much smaller part in the *organized* jazz community than they did at one time in the general popularization of jazz. Where are all the art students, journalists, commercial artists, film technicians, actors, and general bohemians? Either they are no longer so important, or else they don't join organizations, even of jazz enthusiasts, other than jazz clubs, about whose social composition nothing reliable is known.

Appendix 2: Jazz Language

*T*his note does not set out to provide a glossary of jazz terms or jazz slang. Such lists may be found elsewhere, e.g. in Feather's *Encyclopedia,* and are almost always out-of-date by the time they are printed. Rather, it asks how the jazz vocabulary is formed. It consists of three rather different things: (*a*) technical terms, (*b*) jive-talk, and (*c*) names.

Since the founders of jazz were mainly illiterate, at least musically, their technical and critical terminology owes little to orthodoxy except the names of the instruments and of certain elementary musical concepts such as keys and chords. Technical terms either duplicate existing, but unfamiliar, ones—e.g. *slide, smear,* for glissando, *slapping* for pizzicato playing, *changes* for the harmonic progression of a tune—or they describe things for which no proper academic equivalent exists, e.g. *shake* (an extreme form of vibrato), *chase* (a series of choruses by two or more players each playing several bars in turn), *breaks* (open passages in the performance when the rhythm is suspended, more generally, solo passages), or *blue notes*. Most of these terms are formed by analogy, except a few of obscure origin, such as *gig* (a casual job, notably a one-night stand) or *riff* (a repeated two- or four-bar phrase). A virtually self-explanatory term from ordinary language is given a specialized meaning; or else a simple metaphor is used, e.g. *dirty* for a kind of instrumental sound. The vocabulary is utilitarian and, until recently, when musicians have begun to use musical jargon, unpretentious. The earlier jazz musicians did not feel the need to call themselves by a socially more respectable name, as undertakers call themselves morticians or press agents public relations experts. Louis Armstrong had his Hot Five, not his Hot Quintet. An orchestra was and is a *band* if large, a *combo* (combination) when small. A melody or theme is (or was) a *tune*; a composition an *arrangement*, a band's repertoire, its *book*. Its leader is the *front man*, its members *sidemen*. Pretentiousness only began to creep in since the later 1930s when the trios and sextets arrived.

This simple method of forming technical terms will not do for more complex concepts such as musical styles. These cannot be self-explanatory, though *bop, (be-bop* or obs. *re-bop)* is said to copy a rhythmic phrase. Mostly the names of jazz styles have been formed in exactly the same way as those of the Lake Poets, the Euston Road School, or the Fauves, i.e. by association: *barrelhouse, boogie-woogie, Dixieland, Kansas City.*

The formation of a technical vocabulary for critical appreciation, value-judgments, and other imprecise concepts is even harder. Since the only jazz critics were for long the musicians and the public, neither very articulate in words, the critical vocabulary is simple and adapted from non-musical experience. It has been argued that the terms which express success in playing jazz, or the player's sensation when he thinks he is playing well, or the appreciation of both, are borrowed from the most pleasurable sensations of ordinary life. Sex is an obvious source, as in *jazz* itself (apparently a Delta word for coitus), in *to send* (to induce ecstasy or orgasm, obs. to sweep away the listener), or perhaps in *hot,* which has well-established sexual associations. Drink and drugs are others, their sensations being in some respects more suitable analogues of jazz experience, since they

353

provide continuous exaltation rather than periodic climaxes; not to mention the fact that they can be combined with playing. Perhaps the modern, but uninviting, fashion of using terms taken from mental derangement for praise (*crazy, insane, nutty*) is merely an extension of the metaphors taken from drugging (*real gone, out of this world*). Perhaps it marks the increasing turn of certain schools of jazz from normality, the rise of anti-social jazz. At all events the fashion cannot be traced back beyond the later 1930s.

In a more general sense the terms for emotion were formed by metaphor, e.g. by the widespread practice of equating joy with height ('exaltation') and grief with depth; or with the colours red and blue, or with fast and slow. Thus the quality most desired in the old blues is that it should be *low-down* or *dragging*. (The modern term *funky*—smelly—compares with the orthodox 'earthy'.) On the other hand *hot* and *cool* have the associations, excited and relaxed. Much the most difficult linguistic job is to find words for the two connected but indefinable things, the 'right' mood when the playing goes well, and the rhythm. Rhythm (and since bands depend on it, the playing of the entire band) is described in terms of two kinds of movement: to-and-fro and forwards. A band *moves* or *drives* or just *goes*; it *swings, jumps,* or *rocks.* It moves and stays in one place, which is the essence of good jazz rhythm. The metaphors for the 'right' mood of the band are merely ways of expressing approval: it may be real hot or real cool, depending on style, *solid, groovy* (obs. *in the groove*), or merely *right*.

Obviously this critical vocabulary is very feeble and crude, though less so than the modern inarticulateness of the 'fans' for whom criticism is exhausted in a few mumbles: *the greatest, the most, wild.* This poverty is not only due to the fact that words are not the instrument of jazz musicians, but also to the fact that, being both players and critics, they are merely an ancillary to instrumental demonstration. The following passage by a famous New Orleans drummer sounds vague enough to the layman, but much less so to musicians used to playing in front of drummers:

354

Each man has a solo, I give him a different beat. It may sound to someone that's listening close by the same, but it's not. I would say it's a different *sound* to it, because I give every man a chance of his opening. In other words, like a guy is going to come in, I give him something for him to come in on, and it makes it different from the fellow that's got through. . . . Even if it's piano or trumpet or clarinet, I give some kind of indication that something's coming, and *that* a lot of drummers don't do, because you've got to *think*. . . .

(Quoted in *The Jazz Makers,* ed. Shapiro and Hentoff, p. 41.)

———

The second kind of jazz language, *jive-talk* or hipster-talk is not a technical terminology but an argot or cant designed to set the group apart from outsiders. Its foundation is the distinction between those who are *hip* or 'in', and the *squares* who are not. The player as such calls his instrument a clarinet, which identifies it well enough; *qua* hipster he may call it by some name which only the initiate can understand, e.g. the obs. *gobstick*. In the past most such private argots have relied on a fair amount of isolation, and thus maintained themselves fairly easily. But the hipster is not set aside from the rest, and since the later 1930s the publicity boys have constantly broadcast his exclusive terms to the world at large, on the perennial advertising theory that exclusiveness can be sold ready-made to the millions. Thanks to the 'swing' craze localized Harlem terms like *jitterbug* became nationally familiar to American teenagers, and internationally familiar enough for the late Neville Chamberlain to commit a memorable howler by using them.* Naturally, therefore, jive-talk protects itself against the seepage of its 'secrets' to the uninitiated by constantly changing, or else by finding expressions so ambiguous, allusive, or untranslatable, as to be beyond the reach of the squares. More than other argots, therefore, jive-talk puts a premium on linguistic creativeness and slipperiness.

* Older readers may recall that he used *jitterbug* for a 'frightened or panicky person', presumably on the analogy of 'jitters'. It merely meant somebody who danced in a particularly active manner or liked to jive in the aisles during a jazz concert.

355

It contains all the fancy-dress devices of private languages: rhyming slang (*Jack the Bear* for nowhere), the double disguise (*bread* for *dough* for money), and the like; the never-ending substitution of new passwords into the group for the old codes (e.g. new names for marihuana—*reefer, muggles, weed, tea, grass, muta, grefa, charge, gauge, hemp, hay, pot*); the use of neutral and general words for highly specific things (e.g. *on the stuff,* or simply *on* for drug addiction). But it also contained the deliberate use of language as a game, or perhaps (to use the obvious parallel) as a joint and collective improvisation, rather than a simple means of communication. Hence the odd, lilting, rhyming phrases some of which have been made familiar through the rock-and-roll craze, which has had similar effects to the swing craze of the later thirties: 'see you later, alligator, in a while, crocodile', or 'zoot suit'. Hence the peculiar poker-faced phrases which, depending on the situation, may mean the opposite of what they say: 'he's terrible, he plays some awful horn.' Hence, among blacks, the constant, half-defiant, half-self-deprecating, entirely anti-white allusions to and improvisations upon the theme of 'the race' and its internal stratifications. (Cf. the obs. *gate-mouthed,* shortened to *gate,* which used to be a mode of address among earlier hipsters: taken from the loose, half-open mouth of the black lounger.) In the nature of things a glossary of jive-talk is invariably out-of-date and incomplete. The most accessible description of one of its phrases is in Mezzrow and Wolfe's *Really The Blues.* The following passages may be quoted, though partly out-of-date and a little coloured up:

FIRST CAT: Hey there, poppa Mezz, is you anywhere?
ME: Man, I'm down with it, stinking like a honky.
F.C.: Lay a trey on me, ole man.
M.: Got to do it, slot. Gun the snatcher on your left raise— the head mixer laid a bundle his ways, he's posin' back like crime sure pays.
F.C.: Father, grab him. I ain't payin' him no rabbit. Jim, this jive you got is a gasser. I'm goin' up to my dommy and dig that new mess Pops laid down for Okey.

Various 'dictionaries' of jive-talk were published between 1938 and 1945, mostly compiled and tricked out by press agents and the like: the *New Cab Calloway Hepster's Dictionary* (N.Y. 1938 and later editions), Dan Burley's *Original Handbook of Harlem Jive* (N.Y. 1944), Louis Shelly's *Hepcat's Jive Talk Dictionary* (Derby, Conn., 1945). Their discrimination and value is uneven. I know of no specific dictionary of hipster slang for the 1950s, perhaps because the jazz fellow-travelling adolescents of the hipster type have reduced their vocabulary to a few dozen painfully imprecise words.

In so far as jive words are not made by analogy or metaphor, or some similar technique, their derivation is often very obscure. It is probably best sought in the specialized argots of the black ghetto, and the borderline zone between entertainment, petty crime, prostitution, drug-pushing, and the like, in which musicians earn their living. How far musicians, as distinct from 'hipsters', use this slang—except for its original purpose of *jiving,* i.e. kidding talk, word-play, and the like—is another question.

———

Two other aspects of jazz language are worth a brief mention: the names of musicians and of pieces of music.

Musicians have two sorts of nicknames, their own and the ones publicity agents give them. Nobody who plays with Louis Armstrong ever calls him *Satchmo* or *Satchelmouth,* a label much fancied for advertising purposes. He is merely called Pops. Musicians' real nicknames are no more interesting than anybody else's and are almost invariably non-musical: Rabbit (Johnny Hodges), Bubber (Miley), Pres(ident) (Lester Young), Bird or Yardbird (Charlie Parker), Dizzy (Gillespie), Klook (Kenny Clarke), Bean (Coleman Hawkins), and so on. Of the publicity names only one group is really interesting, the *noms-de-guerre* of the old-fashioned blues singers, which have the battered concreteness of the anonymous tramp, or the Homeric grandiloquence of the old-fashioned circus barker and Mississippi boatman. A list of them makes inspiring reading: Pinetop Smith, Cow-Cow Davenport, Montana Taylor, Speckled Red, Cripple Clarence Lofton, Alabama Slim, Arkansas Shorty, Big

Maceo, Kansas Joe, Creole Gayno; and in a more splendiferous mood: Easy Papa Johnson, Howlin' Wolf, Lightning Hopkins, Homer the Great, Bat the Humming Bird, Red Hot Shakin' Davis, Devil's Daddy-in-law, Leadbelly, King Solomon Hill. The women can rarely compete with the Black Ivory Kings, Bumble Bee Slims, and Black Spider Dumplings. Normally they merely change their names, though there are a few proper examples of war paint: Big Sister, Cryin' Ellen, the Yas-Yas Girl.

The naming of pieces of music is a specialized activity, halfway between jive-talk and the naming of race horses. There is rarely any particular reason why a piece should bear one name rather than another. On the other hand musicians and others in the business are under constant pressure to find names for an unceasing flow of new numbers. A great many are named by association with places or people: Royal Garden Blues, Mahogany Hall Stomp, Moten Swing (after Benny Moten, a Kansas City band-leader), Sir Charles At Home (after Sir Charles Thompson, pianist, without benefit of honours list). Increasingly musicians have taken to giving such pieces allusive slang names, often obscure to the outsider, sometimes funny, sometimes obscene, sometimes merely sounding good. The modernists, as might be expected, have been particularly drawn to puzzle corner, often inventing meaningless or trick titles: Compulsory, Blue Room, Zec, Illusive, Sombre Intrusion, Bitty Ditty, Chazzanova (all by Thad Jones groups). In recent times a disagreeable tendency towards pretentiousness has also been observable among the *avant-garde*: Purple Heart, Gregorian Chant, Eulogy for Rudy Williams (all by Charlie Mingus). There is really very little to be said about the principles of inventing jazz titles except that they are increasingly the same as the principles of inventing brand names for products, advertising slogans, or other words and phrases designed to stick in the memory.

The number of books on jazz is now so large that no brief
guide to reading can cover it. On the other hand we now have
superb works of reference, which include bibliographies, especially *The New Grove Dictionary of Jazz,* ed. Barry Kernfeld (2
vols., 1988) and *The New Grove: Gospel, Blues and Jazz,* which
reprints the relevant articles from the famous musical encyclopedia and should also be consulted for the pieces by Paul Oliver
and Max Harrison.

A list of the best half-dozen books on jazz has not changed
entirely since this work was first published. In my opinion it
would contain:

1. N. HENTOFF and N. SHAPIRO, eds., *Hear Me Talkin' to Ya*
   (London 1955). Jazz from New Orleans to the cool period
   as seen by the musicians, in their own words. The best
   single book on the subject.
2. S. FINKELSTEIN, *Jazz, A People's Music* (New York 1948,
   1975). Non-sectarian, clear, perceptive on the sociological

as well as the musical side, and addressed to the layman.

3. JAMES LINCOLN COLLIER, *The Making of Jazz: A Comprehensive History* (London 1978). That the author has both jazz knowledge and historical training helps make this bulky paperback the best single-volume history available, but the bibliography is inadequate.

4. ANDRÉ HODEIR, *Jazz, Its Evolution and Essence* (London 1956, 1975) is no longer the only major work of criticism for the musically educated—readers can now be referred to Max Harrison (e.g. in *The New Grove*) and to various works by Martin Williams (e.g. *The Jazz Tradition,* New York 1970, 1983)—but a work by a Frenchman deserves to remain in a shortlist, given the role of French writers in putting jazz on the critical map.

5. WHITNEY BALLIETT, *American Musicians: 56 Portraits in Jazz* (New York–Oxford 1986). These profiles, written over twenty-four years by the jazz critic of *The New Yorker,* contain the best verbal descriptions of what jazz musicians do and sound like.

6. W. BROONZY and Y. BRUYNOGHE, *Big Bill Blues* (London 1955). A superb introduction to the world of the minstrel blues singer, half myth, half saga. A more realistic life of the modern bluesman is Helen Oakley Dance, *Stormy Monday: The T-Bone Walker Story* (1987).

Who can tell what record or tapes are available at the time you read this book, or will be available within a year or two, or under what labels? It is therefore pointless to refer readers to general discographies which must be out-of-date. The reference books mentioned above are invaluable, but unfortunately no guide to availability.

Jazz biography and (ghosted or semi-ghosted) autobiography is a popular branch of the literature, though often it consists of insufficiently shaped compilations of the material. John Chilton is among the most productive of the biographical scholars, author of valuable works on Billie Holiday (*Billie's Blues,* 1975),

Louis Armstrong (with Max Jones: *Louis, The Louis Armstrong Story,* 1971) and most recently *Sidney Bechet* (1987). Alan Lomax, *Mister Jelly-Roll* (1950, 1973), more readable than most such works, is about the life and times of a Creole Benvenuto Cellini. Though controversial, I recommend James Lincoln Collier's *Duke Ellington* (1987). A. B. Spelman, *Four Lives in the Bebop Business* (1985), deals with the *avant-garde.* Ross Russell, *Bird Lives* (repr. 1988), is the best life of Parker.

Jazz history is not so highly developed yet, except for a quite superb piece of social history: S. Frederick Starr, *Red and Hot: The Fate of Jazz in the Soviet Union* (1983). For British amateurs Jim Godbolt, *A History of Jazz in Britain 1919–1950* (1984), and —with Alun Morgan—*A History of Jazz in Great Britain 1950– 1970,* provide a record.

Until the completion of Gunther Schuller's great critical study, only his *Early Jazz: Its Roots and Musical Development* (1986) and his *The Swing Era: The Development of Jazz, 1930– 1945* are available. They should be taken in small doses, but you can't fail to find illumination in these books.

In the first edition of this book I said: "The less said about jazz novels, short stories, or poems, the better. There is a possible exception, John Clellon Holmes's *The Horn.*" This judgment still stands, if I may add Josef Skvorecky's novella *The Bass Saxophone,* which also contains a first-rate autobiographical–cum-critical introduction by the author, an émigré Czech novelist now teaching in Toronto. On the other hand there is a marvelous lot of jazz photographs (for a list of iconographies see *The New Grove*) and, at last, a genuine full-length story film about jazz, Bertrand Tavernier's splendid 'Round Midnight,' with a superb performance by the saxophonist Dexter Gordon and very reasonable music.

Notes

Introduction

1. Interviews in *Rhythm,* June 1939.

How to Recognize Jazz

1. C. Chilton, Jackson and the Oliver Band (*Jazz Music* III, 6, 1947); N. Shapiro and N. Hentoff, *The Jazz Makers* (London 1958), 263.

Prehistory

1. Marshall Stearns, *The Story of Jazz* (London 1957), 32.
2. Samuel B. Charters, *The Country Blues* (1960), 23–5.
3. Alan Lomax, *Mr Jelly-Roll* (New York 1950), 21n.
4. Stearns, 32.
5. C. D. Stuart and A. D. Park, *The Variety Stage* (London 1895).
6. A. Zevaes, *Aristide Bruant* (Paris 1943).
7. Fernando el de Triana, *Arte y artistas flamencos* (Madrid 1952), 140–1.

8. *Some Notes on Negro Crime* (ed. W. E. B. du Bois, Atlanta 1904), 51.

9. A. Green and J. Laurie, *Show Biz from Vaude to Video* (New York 1951), 39; R. Blesh and H. Janis, *They All Played Ragtime* (London 1958), 261–2.

10. Alan Lomax, *Mr Jelly-Roll*, 86.

11. Stearns, 61.

Expansion

1. W. C. Handy, *Father of the Blues* (London 1957), 64.

2. Blesh and Janis, 190–1.

3. Bertha Wood, Paul Leroy Howard (*Jazz Journal*, November 1957).

4. Figures from Franklin Frazier, *The Negro in the United States* (revised edn New York 1957).

5. Barry Ulanov, *Duke Ellington* (New York 1946), 279.

6. Iain Lang, *Background to the Blues* (London n.d.), 13.

7. The only general history of race records is S. B. Charters's *The Country Blues* (1960), but the specialist periodicals contain several learned explorations.

8. S. Spaeth, *A History of Popular Music in America* (New York 1948), 369.

9. Green and Laurie, 36, 39, Chapter 17.

10. For different and unconvincing etymologies, see *Jazz, A Quarterly of American Music,* October 1958, and *Jazz Review*, March–August 1960.

11. D. Boulton, *Jazz in Britain* (London 1958), 34–5.

12. Handy, 63.

13. Chilton in *Jazz Music* III, 6.

14. Dates and titles from Spaeth.

15. Quoted from Blesh, *Shining Trumpets* (New York 1946), 327–8. See also Neil Leonard Jr, The Opposition to Jazz in the U.S. 1918–29 (*Jazz Monthly*, June, July 1958).

16. Blesh, 329.

17. Green and Laurie, 317; E. Borneman, *A Critic Looks at Jazz* (London, Jazz Music Books, 1946), 50–1, for details of the effect of the slump.

18. Boulton, 59.

19. *Melody Maker,* 1930, 155; 1935, 2 February; *Jazz Monthly,* March 1956, 30.

20. Green and Laurie, 457.

21. F. Ramsey Jr and C. E. Smith, *Jazzmen* (British edn, London 1957).

22. E. Condon and R. Gehman, *Eddie Condon's Treasury of Jazz* (London 1957), 200.

23. *Jazz* by E. F. Burian, the Czech *avant-gardist* theatrical producer (Prague 1928), is perhaps the first book on the subject by a Western leftist. The most important works issued by Marxists or under left-wing auspices are S. Finkel-

stein, *Jazz, A People's Music* (New York 1948), and Iain Lang, *Background to the Blues,* both excellent; but a Marxist approach is widespread in Anglo-Saxon jazz criticism. Ernst Meyer, the Marxist musicologist, is one of the few writers in Eastern Europe to give jazz at least a qualified approval in the cold-war era in *Musik im Zeitgeschehen* (Berlin 1952); but he spent his emigration in England. However, the Soviet attitude since 1956 is no longer one of general hostility.

Transformation

1. Y. Bruynoghe, Blues Today in *Just Jazz* (ed. S. Traill, G. Lascelles, London 1957), 175.

2. Cf. his interview in *Melody Maker,* 22 February 1958.

3. N. Shapiro and N. Hentoff, *Hear Me Talkin' to Ya* (London 1955), 306.

4. *Hear Me . . . ,* 264–5.

5. *Ibid.,* 264.

6. *Ibid.,* 300. The date is wrong. The period must be in the late thirties, for Webb died in 1939, and Hawkins returned from Europe the same year.

7. Franklin Frazier, *Black Bourgeoisie,* is the best discussion of this sad subject.

8. Cf. Margaret Just Butcher, *The Negro in American Culture* (Mentor Books 1957), which has got around to Armstrong, Ellington, Bessie Smith, etc., but is apparently unaware of Gillespie and Parker.

9. A. Hodeir, *Jazz, Its Evolution and Essence* (London 1956), 267.

Blues and Orchestral Jazz

1. Sleeve note to Jazz Messengers: *Hard Bop* (Philips BBL 7220).

2. Dark Road, on *Brownie McGhee and Sonny Terry* (Topic 12T29).

3. E. Borneman, Boogie Woogie, in *Just Jazz* I, p. 29.

4. Winthrop Sargeant, *Jazz, Hot and Hybrid* (New York 1946), discusses this problem at length, with many musical illustrations.

5. No adequate history as yet exists, but see Paul Oliver, *Blues Fell This Morning* (1960), Samuel B. Charters, *The Country Blues* (1960), and monographs in the specialist periodicals and on LP sleeves.

6. For the classic blues singers, Francis Newton [Eric Hobsbawm] in *The Decca Book of Jazz* (1958). For Bessie Smith, Paul Oliver, *Bessie Smith* (1960), George Hoefer in Hentoff and Shapiro (eds.), *The Jazz Makers* (1958), George Avakian in Martin B. Williams (ed.), *The Art of Jazz* (1960).

7. C. E. Smith in *The Jazz Makers* and the artist's unreliable autobiogra-

phy (with W. Dufty), *Lady Sings the Blues.* A good critical study by Glenn Coulter in *The Art of Jazz.*

8. Stearns, 7.

9. R. Blesh and H. Janis. *They All Played Ragtime* (1958) for history; Guy Waterman in *The Art of Jazz* and in Hentoff and McCarthy (eds.), *Jazz* (1960), for more detailed technical discussion.

10. Rudi Blesh, *Shining Trumpets,* and Rex Harris, *Jazz,* for general accounts, W. C. Allen and B. Rust, *King Oliver* (1958), H. O. Brunn, *The Story of the Original Dixieland Jazz Band* (1960), for individual groups, Martin B. Williams, *King Oliver* (1960), for a critical appreciation.

11. Stearns, 157.

12. Alan Lomax, *Mr Jelly-Roll* (1950), Orrin Keepnews in *The Jazz Makers,* for life and times; William Russell in *The Art of Jazz,* Martin Williams in Hentoff and McCarthy, *op. cit.,* for critical discussion.

13. M. Mezzrow and B. Wolfe, *Really the Blues* (London 1957), Appendix 1; Borneman, *A Critic Looks at Jazz;* C. Fox, Chicago Jazz, A Reassessment (*Jazz Monthly,* August 1955); John Steiner in Hentoff and McCarthy, *op. cit.*

14. Shapiro and Hentoff, *Jazz Makers,* 246.

15. S. Finkelstein, *Jazz, A People's Music* (New York 1948), 184.

16. John S. Wilson in *The Jazz Makers.*

17. P. Gammond (ed.), *Duke Ellington, His Life and Music* (1958), Barry Ulanov, *Duke Ellington* (New York 1946), Gunther Schuller in Hentoff and McCarthy, *op. cit.*

18. Finkelstein, 197. Throughout this chapter I have greatly relied on this first-rate book.

19. Finkelstein, 193.

20. R. Horricks, *Count Basie* (1957), Franklin Driggs in Hentoff and McCarthy, *op. cit.*

21. J. Berendt, *Das Jazzbuch* (Frankfurt/Hamburg 1953), 80.

22. There is no adequate discussion of the Harlem style, but see Charles Fox in *The Decca Book of Jazz* (1958) and Hsiao Wen Shih in Hentoff and McCarthy, *op. cit.*

23. The bibliography of modern jazz is large. Leonard Feather, *Jazz* (Trend Books, Los Angeles 1959), and A. Morgan and R. Horricks, *Modern Jazz* (1956), are general surveys. R. Horricks (ed.), *These Jazzmen of Our Time* (1959), Michael James, *Ten Modern Jazzmen* (1960), discuss individual musicians. For criticism see *The Art of Jazz,* Hentoff and McCarthy, but especially A. Hodeir, *Jazz, Its Evolution and Essence* (1956).

24. *Arts* (Paris), 23–29 April 1958, 9, for France. Personal information from M. Charles Delaunay tends to confirm this. It is certainly also the case in Britain, but not in the U.S.A. However, for the peculiarities of the jazz public there see below, Chapter 12.

25. Hodeir, 198.

26. Finkelstein 227. My account of the 'modern' transformation of the ballad is also based on this book.

27. See N. Hentoff, Lester Young in *The Jazz Makers*.

The Instruments

1. E.g. J. Berendt's diagrams, which are as good as any.

2. Sidney Bechet, *Treat It Gentle* (1960); Whitney Balliett, *The Sound of Surprise* (1960), 179–82; C. E. Smith, Pee-Wee Russell in *The Jazz Makers*, Whitney Balliett, 227–32; Nat Shapiro, Benny Goodman in *The Jazz Makers*.

3. A. J. McCarthy, *Louis Armstrong,* (1959); Louis Armstrong, *My Life in New Orleans* (1955).

4. A. Hodeir, *op. cit.,* Whitney Balliett, 83–5 (Cootie Williams); Whitney Balliett, 103–4 (Red Allen); Nat Hentoff, Roy Eldridge in *The Jazz Makers;* L. Feather, Dizzy Gillespie in *The Jazz Makers;* Michael James, *Ten Modern Jazzmen* for Gillespie, Miles Davis, R. Horricks; *These Jazzmen of Our Time* for Davis; Whitney Balliett, 143–5 (Davis).

5. Burnett James, *Bix Beiderbecke* (1959); George Hoefer in *The Jazz Makers;* George Avakian in *The Art of Jazz*. There is an exhaustive chronicle by C. H. Wareing and G. Garlick, *Bugles for Bix* (1958)

6. A. Hodeir, *op. cit.* (Wells); Whitney Balliett, 120–2 (Dickenson); J. D. Smith and L. Guttridge, *Jack Teagarden* (1960), also C. E. Smith in *The Jazz Makers;* R. Horricks, *These Jazzmen . . .* (J. J. Johnson).

7. L. Feather in *The Jazz Makers* (Hawkins, Young); *These Jazzmen . . .* (Mulligan, Rollins); *Ten Modern Jazzmen* (Getz, Gray, Mulligan).

8. *Ten Modern Jazzmen* (Konitz).

9. Max Harrison, *Charlie Parker* (1960); also the same, in Hentoff and McCarthy; Orrin Keepnews in *The Jazz Makers; Ten Modern Jazzmen*.

10. Berendt, 168.

11. L. Feather, *Encyclopedia of Jazz,* 106.

12. Bill Simon, Charlie Christian, in *The Jazz Makers;* Al Avakian and George Prince in *The Art of Jazz*.

13. Ross Russell in *The Art of Jazz* (James P. Johnson); Charles Fox, *Fats Waller* (1960); John S. Wilson in *The Jazz Makers* (Waller, Hines); Orrin Keepnews, *ibid.* (Art Tatum); *These Jazzmen . . .* (Monk, Powell, John Lewis); *Ten Modern Jazzmen* (Monk, Powell).

14. Max Harrison in Hentoff and McCarthy, Ernest Borneman in *Just Jazz* I (1957) on boogie-woogie. Blues pianists are mostly discussed in connexion with the history of the blues.

15. By far the best description of what jazz drummers do is in Whitney Balliett, especially pp. 159–64, 233–44.

16. Nat Hentoff, Warren 'Baby' Dodds in *The Jazz Makers;* Whitney Balliett on Sid Catlett, Max Roach, Art Blakey, Philly Joe Jones.

17. *Hear Me Talkin'* . . . , 309–310.
18. *These Jazzmen* . . . (Milt Jackson).

The Musical Achievement

1. Stearns, 228.
2. Cf. also *Echoes of Harlem*—for Williams—and *Clarinet Lament*—for Bigard.
3. On Philips BBL 7190 (American), Atlantic LP 134, and London LTZ-K 15053 respectively.

Jazz and the Other Arts

1. Rex Harris, *Jazz* (Penguin Books).
2. Hodeir, 263.
3. From *Fine Clothes to the Jew* (New York 1927). I have written the stanzas out in the usual three-line form.
4. W. Broonzy and Y. Bruynoghe, *Big Bill Blues* (London 1955).
5. Alan Lomax, *Blues in the Mississippi Night* (Pye-Nixa NJL 8).
6. The best collections of blues verses so far available are the files of the New York *Jazz Review,* which prints a selection in each issue, Paul Oliver's *Blues Fell This Morning,* and Iain Lang's pioneer *Background to the Blues.*

The Jazz Business

1. Blesh and Janis, 60–3; Handy, 91; *Hear Me Talkin'* . . . , 261, 301–2.
2. Taken from A. J. McCarthy, *Jazz Discography,* 1958. Strictly speaking the figures we refer to records released during the year.
3. The High Finance of Jazz, in *Rhythm,* January 1939.
4. W. C. Allen and B. Rust, *Joe King Oliver* (London 1958).
5. R. Gleason in *San Francisco Chronicle,* 6 November 1960, *New York Post,* 18 November 1960, p. 56.
6. Feather, *Encyclopedia.*
7. *Early Armstrong from Jazz Magazine* III, 3 (1947), 1955 records from Jazz Discography 1956 in *Just Jazz* I (1957).

The Musicians

1. *Hear Me Talkin'* . . . , 28–9. A very full treatment in Lomax *Mr Jelly-Roll,* 67–111.

2. *Hear Me Talkin'* . . . , 31.
3. *Ibid.,* 46.
4. *Ibid.,* 232.
5. *Ibid.,* 231, 238, 240.
6. Handy, 273.
7. Berendt, 93–5.
8. Condon and Gehman, 214, 224–5.
9. *Ibid.,* 228.
10. *Ibid.,* 230.
11. Mezzrow and Wolfe, Chapter 12, is one of the earliest and most useful accounts. A. Broyard, A Portrait of the Hipster (*Partisan Review* 1948), and Norman Mailer, The White Negro—Superficial Reflection on the Hipster (*Dissent,* Summer 1957), are fair specimens.
12. Mezzrow and Wolfe, 223–4.
13. *Ibid.,* 225.
14. Howard Becker, The Professional Dance Musician and His Audience (*American Journal of Sociology,* September 1951).
15. J. F. Russell and J. H. Elliott, *The Brass Band Movement* (London 1936).
16. I take these data from the valuable, but fragmentary biographical articles about members of British dance bands in the early thirties, as given in the *Melody Maker* for that period.

The Public

1. Blesh and Janis, 188.
2. Stearns, 211.
3. T. and M. Arnold, Jazz and the Collector (*Jazz Review,* London 1945), 18.
4. Elliott Paul, *That Crazy Music* (London 1957), 228.
5. *Le Jazz Hot,* December 1948.
6. Circulation figures from *World's Press News,* 17 October 1958.
7. This estimate is based on the capacity of the halls booked by such a band, and on some expert information.
8. The material on which these notes are based is sketchy, except for Britain, where I know the scene and the publications best, and have had access to the files of the *National Jazz Federation* (see Appendix One). For France I have had the advantage of conversations with MM. Charles Delaunay, André Hodeir, and J-B. Hess.
9. Quoted in Berendt, 12.
10. Oxtot, The Yerba Buena Band (*Jazz Review,* London 1945), 12.
11. Mezzrow and Wolfe, 5.
12. *Ibid.,* 109–10.

13. Stearns, 186.

14. T. and M. Arnold, *loc. cit.*: an analysis of the readers of *The Record Changer,* the leading collectors' magazine.

15. A survey conducted for KHIP station, San Francisco, by Contemporary Research, 1960.

16. *Billboard,* 15 August 1960.

17. Spike Hughes, *Second Movement.*

18. *Melody Maker,* January 1926, 6–7.

19. *Rhythm,* April 1939.

20. *Western Mail,* 29 March 1958.

21. It is certainly true to some extent of France and Germany.

Jazz as a Protest

1. R. W. S. Mendl, *The Appeal of Jazz* (London 1927), 25.

2. Reported in *Jazz Music,* December 1943.

3. *Melody Maker,* December 1926.

4. Finkelstein is the most elaborate version of the Marxist thesis, also in Iain Lang, which led to some entertaining controversies. Cf. *Jazz Music* III, 2, 1946.

5. *Jazz Music* III, 2, p. 9.

6. Mendl, 71–2.

7. Stearns, 316.

8. The best introduction to the subject is Niebuhr, *The Social Sources of Denominationalism* (Living Age Books, New York 1957).

9. Cf. Ethel Waters, *His Eyes Is on the Sparrow,* Billie Holiday and W. Dufty, *Lady Sings the Blues.*

From The New York Review of Books, *1986–1989*

'Playing for Ourselves'

1. He's been a hell of a man," writes Basie of his discoverer John Hammond. "And he has never asked for a nickel from me or any of those other people he's done so much for. And there have been quite a few of them. All he wanted to see was the results of what was supposed to be happening."

2. Albert Murray, *Stomping the Blues* (Vintage, 1982), p. 166.

The Jazz Comeback

1. Francis Davis, *In the Moment,* p. ix.

2. Hayden Carruth, *Sitting In,* p. 176.

3. S. Frederick Starr, *Red and Hot: The Fate of Jazz in the Soviet Union 1917–1980* (Oxford University Press, 1983).

4. Whitney Balliett, *American Musicians,* p. 3.

5. Davis, *In the Moment,* pp. 206–213.

6. Mike Zwerin, *La tristesse de Saint Louis,* p. 3.

7. *La tristesse de Saint Louis,* p. 1. For the metaphor, see e.g. pp. 19, 46, 61.

8. Carruth, *Sitting In,* p. 52.

9. The book has been put together by an English admirer. However, several of its most touching and instructive passages have long been available in that marvelous collage of the spoken jazz-word, Nat Hentoff and Nat Shapiro's *Hear me Talkin' to Ya* (1955).

10. *Up from the Cradle of Jazz* is most instructive on this collapse of the market for jazz in New Orleans.

11. Whitney Balliett, *New York Notes: A Journal of Jazz in the Seventies* (Da Capo Press, 1977), p. 3.

12. *Jazz Times* (November 1986), p. 18.

13. *Jazz Times,* interview with Benny Golson (November 1986), p. 19.

14. *Jazz Times* (November 1986), p. 29.

15. It is unthinkable that black intellectuals could today write a book like the late Franklin Frazier's *The Negro in the United States,* which, even in the revised edition of 1957, contained no reference to music, though sufficiently hip to include references to the novels of Chester Himes.

16. Carruth, *Sitting In,* p. 173.

17. *Up from the Cradle of Jazz,* pp. 10–16. Danny Barker, a member of one such family of mini-Bachs, throws much light on such kin groups as his *A Life in Jazz.*

Slyest of the Foxes

1. Doubleday, 1973.

2. Mercer Ellington with Stanley Dance, *Duke Ellington in Person* (Houghton Mifflin, 1978). In Mercer's account Duke Ellington was kind to him so long as he was willing to do his bidding and help him with the band. When the son tried to strike out on his own as a musician, the Duke, he writes, did everything he could to discourage him.

3. Martin Williams, *The Jazz Tradition,* new and revised edition (Oxford University Press, 1983), p. 102.

4. Max Harrison, *A Jazz Retrospect* (Taplinger, 1976), p. 128.

5. Alexander Coleman, "The Duke and His Only Son" (*New Boston Review,* December 1978).

6. *Music Is My Mistress,* p. x.

7. Surprisingly, Collier does not quite avoid the same pitfall in his praise of Ellington's three-minute pieces. The 78-rpm record, which provides us with so many of his surviving masterpieces, did not determine the structure of

Ellington's compositions, but only that of the music produced for the recording studio, as the informal recording of his work in ballrooms demonstrates.

The Caruso of Jazz

1. Sidney Bechet, *Treat It Gentle: An Autobiography* (London: Cassell and Co., 1960). It was published after a bumpy ride through publishers, lawyers, and collaborators such as John Ciardi.

2. Paul Oliver, Max Harrison, and William Bolcom, *The New Grove: Gospel, Blues and Jazz* (Norton, 1987), p. 292.

3. However, Ansermet's negative judgment thirty years later ("The days of jazz are over. It has made its contribution to music. Now in itself it is merely monotonous") has not been propagated by jazz-lovers or Bechet fans, though Chilton records it (p. 207).

Hitler, Adolf, xiii, xiv, 10–11, 217
HMV, 143
Hobson, Wilder, 9, 73
Hodeir, André, 57, 78, 81, 86,
   113, 114, 117, 120, 206, 213,
   255, 256, 260
Hodges, Johnny, xvi, xxiii, lxii,
   78, 95, 96, 278, 284
Hold On, 10
Holiday, Billie, xxii, xxiii, xxxiii,
   47, 67, 106, 168, 218, 219,
   261–63
Holy City, The, 26
Home Cookin', 73
honky-tonks, 9, 16, 194–95
Honky Tonk Train Blues, xlvii
Hopkins, Claude, 76, 158
Hopkins, Sam "Lightning," 44,
   66, 132*n*, 222, 273–74
Horseless Carriage Club, 54
Hot Clubs, 210
Hot Discography (Delaunay), 213
Hot Five, xv, 72, 73, 92, 156, 161
Hot House, xix–xx
Hot Seven, xv, 92, 156, 161
House of David Blues, xv
Howard, Paul, 19
How High the Moon, xlii, lxi, 46,
   112, 160
Howlin' Wolf, xxviii, 66
How Long, 10, 63, 64, 116–17
Hughes, Langston, 121
Hughes, Patrick "Spike," xiv, 31,
   156, 214
Hugo, Victor, 327
Hylton, Jack, 28, 142–43, 190
hymns, 7

*I Can't Give You Anything but
   Love*, 47, 112

I Found the Answer, 276
Immortal Charlie Parker, The, lxvii
improvisation, 1, lxii–lxiii, 4, 15,
   41, 47, 54, 65, 69, 76, 77,
   79, 83, 117, 160
In a Mellotone, lxvi
Indiana, xlii, 27
International Youth Festivals,
   222
In the Evening, 64
In the Moment (Davis), 309
Irving, Henry, 109
Irvis, Charley, 113
I've Found a New Baby, 27, 73
Ives, Burl, 222
Ives, Charles, 313
I Want to Live, 264

Jackson, Bessie, 68, 222
Jackson, Mahalia, xxiii, 62, 69–
   70, 166, 276–77
Jackson, Milt, 55, 105, 156, 178
Jackson, Rudy, 30
Jackson, Tony, 205*n*
Jacob, Max, 212, 254–55
Jacquet, Illinois, 95
James, Harry, 167, 212*n*, 303
*James Rushing, If This Ain't the
   Blues*, lxvii
Jammin' the Blues, 123
jam sessions, 48, 49–52, 83, 110,
   188
jazz:
   academic underground of,
      xviii, xxxvii–xxxviii
   accidental factors and change
      in, lviii, 112–13
   African elements of, lix, 3–7,
      10, 12, 57, 63, 68, 76, 101,
      102, 104

108

a priori - ah - pri Oh re
(in logic) deductive reasoning
- reasoning from causes to effects -
ie - without reference to experience -

Marsalis p 310 - 311